The Little Book of Meditation

The Way to Lifelong Vibrant Health,
Peace of Mind, Spiritual Growth and Wellbeing

By
William Bodri

Copyright

First Edition, 2011
Second Edition, 2012

ISBN-13: 978-0-9721907-8-7
ISBN-10: 0972190783
Library of Congress Number: 2011943857

Top Shape Publishing, LLC
1135 Terminal Way Suite 209
Reno, Nevada 89502

For more titles like this, please see www.MeditationExpert.com: *The Little Book of Hercules*, which explains the sequential gong-fu of the path that you experience as you open up your internal chi channels; *Spiritual Paths and Their Meditation Techniques*, which explains the do's and don'ts of meditation and spiritual cultivation; *Twenty-Five Doors to Meditation*, which introduces twenty five different meditation techniques along with how and why they work; *Internal Martial Arts Nei-gong*, which provides practitioners with an understanding of what it takes to cultivate inner gong-fu and energy work; *How to Measure and Deepen Your Spiritual Realization* ("*Measuring Meditation*"), which contains case studies of advanced cultivation practitioners; and *Your Destiny is in Your Own Hands*, which explains about the existence of karma and how to truly change your personal karma, fortune and destiny to transform your life.

DEDICATION

To all those who wish to learn meditation in order to cultivate mental peace, freedom from stress and anxiety, greater clarity, more energy, better health, positive behavioral change, longevity, and spiritual growth.

PREFACE

In the spirit of helpfulness, I hope this book of basic instructions will help others to learn how to start meditating effectively and avoid the many errors I definitely made in my own practice. I have tried to provide some stories to lighten the load of so many new materials that might be unfamiliar to many readers. I have also tried to provide multiple examples as to how ordinary people, great scientists, religious practitioners, politicians, and great masters have benefited from meditation and worked it into their lives. These examples show that it is not only the spiritually inclined who have used meditation, but the practical and pragmatic who have gone on to accomplish great things in life in multiple areas because of the results they achieved through various meditation practices. To help readers, I have also often simplified difficult topics of ontology and soteriology to make them more palatable with the hopes to thereby help lead people forward in making more progress. One will have to proceed to original sources from enlightened masters, such as from within Buddhism and Vedanta, to correct some of the simplifications made in light of skillful means.

My understanding of meditation matters is far from perfect or complete; nevertheless I believe you have in your hands a valuable reference guide to not only help teach you how to meditate, but to also lead you through some of the more advanced phenomena you are likely to encounter on the meditation path. With practice your experience will grow, and from your experience you will be able to make alterations in your practice methodology that will help you naturally make further progress in mental calming. That calming will produce benefits within multiple areas of your life. I am deeply hopeful that your wisdom grows from this book so that you not only gain some understanding of the nature of your mind, but the nature of the world in terms of the various effects meditation can have on your body, health, longevity, mental health and behavior.

William Bodri

CONTENTS

ACKNOWLEDGMENTS

This small book on meditation could not have been written without the many teachings I received from my teacher over the years, and I am extremely grateful for the personal help and concern he has always bestowed upon me in hopes of helping me make progress. I cannot say I have correctly understood what he taught me because there has always been the problem of translating his language into my own, and the fact that I may not have understood what he said even when correctly translated. Nevertheless, I have tried to put my own understanding and experience into this book, and any errors that appear within are mine, not his, since he had nothing to do with it.

I wish to extend my special thanks to the many individuals who have helped to produce this small "how to book" on meditation, and who donated their valuable time to its production. I am especially grateful for their tireless work in reading various drafts and painstakingly editing corrections.

Clairemarie Levine has outdone herself in this regard, and her wonderful editing efforts gave me the confidence to turn an originally tiny book into the larger edition you now have. As I started writing this book I let it slowly expand in size past its original fifty pages only because I knew that she would catch many of my grammatical errors, and thus I felt confident that any mistakes would be caught despite an increasing volume of content. The warmest of thanks also go out to Jeremy Antbacke, Mitchell Houston, and John Newtson who all shared in contributing their efforts to making this the best book possible. They always cheerfully put up with my initial drafts, despite their wandering nature, and made useful comments that helped to shape the course of the book. I hope that any merit that derives from this work goes to all of these individuals for their contributions.

1
INTRODUCTION

The word "meditation" conjures up all kinds of images in Western people. Those associations run the gamut of ideas from stress release and relaxation to crystals, strange Eastern religions, bald headed monks, and hippie dropouts smoking dope.

The truth is that meditation is a disciplined practice that has evolved over thousands of years in both the East and the West, and follows a strict methodological procedure to induce remarkable states of mental peace and changes in the human organism.

To date, meditation is the only proven activity to lower stress hormones. Moreover, modern science has shown meditation can increase neuron density in the brain, increase the size of certain sections of the brain, and will raise the baseline happiness of practitioners. Studies have also shown that it decreases the symptoms of premenstrual syndrome, the occurrence of migraine headaches, instances of insomnia, chronic pain, and it also reduces anxiety and depression. Without a doubt, meditation leads to mental peace and relaxation and can effect major changes in the human body.

Studies in Australia have found that deep meditation sometimes led to the "spontaneous remission" of severe cases of cancer. Western scientists have seen meditation yogis demonstrate remarkable conscious control over their heart rate and other body functions. Tibetan monks who meditate have demonstrated the ability to survive severe cold temperatures because of the mastery over the body's heat function. Various monks have also demonstrated that through meditation they could subjugate physical and mental pain. Martial artists have used meditation to reach much higher levels of superhuman physical mastery. Meditation even gives the ability, at proficient stages, to fasten the mind with stability on whatever you wish, without faltering in concentration, for several days, as famous contemplators have demonstrated.

There are a lot of phenomena that advanced meditation practice can enable you to produce, and thus we could make this short list a lot longer. It is fortunate that eminent minds in the West are slowly becoming more interested in doing research in this field, but ultimately, to get the real proofs and benefits of meditation, reading is not enough. You have to take the first step and start meditating yourself to receive its beneficial effects. The proof, verification, and authentication of the benefits claimed for meditation lie in practicing meditation yourself. The proof is in the doing, not in the reading!

Over the years, many people have told me they wanted a very simple primer on "how to meditate." They wanted some simple meditation methods that would not bore them, a practice schedule, a little bit of instruction, and some interesting stories. They wanted this in a small book which they could give to friends who also wanted to learn meditation and experience some of the benefits we have discussed.

"Don't talk about anything complicated," they would tell me, "I just want basic stuff on what to do, how long to practice, and throw in some interesting stories if you have any to keep me motivated."

I had already previously written a book, *Twenty-Five Doors to Meditation*, which provides detailed explanations on twenty five different meditation techniques, including why they work and how to practice them, but many people told me they wanted even simpler information. Basically, people wanted to add meditation to their daily life, but wanted an even simpler, "no brainer" way to get started. Since you have to serve all the different mentalities of the world, and help people at all stages of accomplishment, that objective became the reason for this book. It is not an all-inclusive definitive guide on meditation. With its simplified explanations, it is just a small guide meant to be helpful. Yet for all its simplicity, it will still deliver to you more information than what was generally available to many spiritual greats who achieved wonderful things through their meditation practice. What you eventually accomplish with the information will be a function of your own efforts.

Before we get started, we should first review some of the most common reasons why people want to practice meditation in the first place.

Perhaps the reason which inspires the most individuals, which we did not yet mention, is the objective of better health and increased longevity.

In most Eastern cultures many people already know that meditation will help to improve your health and heal disease. There are very profound, scientific reasons for this which Western researchers are only now discovering, but Eastern spiritual schools already know this result from hundreds of years of continuous case studies and practical experience. In the East, various esoteric theories have developed to explain this result, but the bottom line is that meditation does lead to better health and longer life spans when practiced correctly.

According to various Asian medical schools and spiritual traditions, the human physical body is crisscrossed by an inner subtle body that carries your life-force energies to all the different body parts, including the internal organs. This life-force or chi (qi) – called "prana" in India — travels through special energy meridians within the body called "chi channels," which are the same thing as your acupuncture meridians. In India these special energy channels are known as "*nadis*." When you meditate, you begin to fill these channels with life-force, and this leads to the beneficial results of energy, health and longevity (delayed aging), as well as mental peace, calmness and relaxation.

Unless you meditate to keep these energy channels open, these chi energy meridians tend to become obstructed over time, especially as we age, just as arteries and veins tend to become clogged with blood clots and cholesterol. When you become sick, those pathways to your organ systems also tend to become obstructed as well. Meditation enables your chi to freely run throughout your body, thus clearing your internal energy channels of blockages and obstructions. The more you meditate, the more these internal obstructions dissolve due to the flow of chi through them and similarly, as these obstructions dissolve, the life-force of your body starts to circulate much easier without friction.

When there's no friction to obstruct the flow of chi within the energy channels, the body tends to last longer and thus we have the result of longevity but with high quality living. Because meditation increases the chi flow of your body, and that chi flow opens up clogged energy channels running to organs and parts of the body that are diseased, latent sicknesses in the body are often revealed and then tend to go away as the arising chi brings pure life force to those diseased regions. *Thus meditation helps banish illness, and many stories throughout history prove this.* Because meditation allows this chi energy to run throughout your whole body, you also typically experience more energy due to this refreshment, which also ends up rejuvenating you.

In other words, meditation increases the free chi flow within your body and opens up any obstructed chi channels, and this in turn produces physical results for the real world. As chi circulation is restored to certain regions of your body, this often leads to a "spontaneous remission" of various health problems. Due to meditation, your chi can reach diseased organ systems within your body characterized by channel blockages, obstructions and deterioration, and that life giving chi helps heal the situation. After your body's chi channels open, this leads to longevity as well since the life force can flow smoothly to all places. Thus meditation leads to health and healing. There are many details to the process, but the basic explanation is as simple as that.

Another reason that people practice meditation is because they have far too much anxiety and stress in their life and want to find some way to relax and find internal peace. Meditation calms the mind, freeing it of wandering thoughts that tend to vex and worry us, and thus is a perfect way to get rid of stress and relax the mind. If you are seeking a way to reduce stresses, anxieties and worries in order to experience mental peace, meditation is the daily practice you should be doing.

Naturally, meditation is not something that you can master after a single practice session, which is why you have to practice meditation to learn how to relax and let go. It's not that you have to learn a new skill, but instead must break an invisible bad habit of clinging to states of consciousness. This habit of mental holding is so ingrained that you don't even know you are doing it. Over time, as people learn to let go of their thoughts due to the efforts of meditation practice, most realize that their mind is naturally empty and free. We busy it with thoughts, but it is naturally empty and we can regain the peace of that natural emptiness through meditation. Due to meditation practice, the negative internal mental dialogue that usually bothers people — including wandering criticisms, anxieties and worries — will eventually die down. Because bothersome thoughts will indeed depart, consistent meditation practice eventually leads to mental peace and relaxation. As the busyness of mentation dies down, meditation reveals an underlying clarity of the mind that seems open, empty and free after all sorts of wandering thoughts have departed. This is not the true nature of your mind, but an experience similar to the true empty nature of your mind.

If one maintains this internal peace and tranquility, which is essentially the fact that the volume of your thoughts has died down, it means that the chi of your body is becoming purified because there's a linkage between consciousness and chi in the body. That is the scientific basis of the mind-body phenomena we constantly hear about today. Your mind (consciousness or thoughts) is connected to the chi of the body, i.e. your consciousness and your chi are linked like the two sides of a coin. On the one side you have chi, and on the other side you have consciousness, and they perfectly match with one another seamlessly. The suspension of one causes the suspension of the other. Therefore, if you can calm your consciousness, then your chi will also become calm; it will flow smoothly and purify.

Conversely, if you calm the chi of your body (by harmonizing its circulation) then your consciousness will tend to calm and purify, so we say consciousness quiets down or "empties out." When your mind becomes empty we also say that your chi becomes full, and that fullness produces a quiet state of mind. This is the basis of the physical results that people usually experience through meditation practice, though in Western science we simply call this the "mind-body" phenomena or mind-body connection. Basically, your chi and consciousness are linked and you can discover this through meditation practice.

Another reason people meditate is that they want to find happiness in life. Many people have enjoyed incredible amounts of money and everything it buys in life and still have not found peace and happiness. I'm talking about lots of sex, eating the finest foods, traveling to the best exotic locations for fun, wearing beautiful clothes, getting great publicity, having power to be able to order people to do whatever they want — you name it. They experience all these luxuries and yet, while at the apex of wealth, power, status, fame, fortune, and popularity they still cannot find peace or happiness.

Many unfortunate ones turn to drugs or alcohol to find this internal peace, but it doesn't come from drugs or alcohol either. The smart ones finally turn to meditation practice, as many powerful kings and emperors of the past have done when they, too, could not find peace and contentment in the midst of their plenty. As people practice meditation and thoughts drop away, they get closer to discovering something that is always there—who and what they are—and resting in that they find peace. Meditation leads people into finding the absolute foundational source of their mind and being. That ultimate source of the mind is empty of thoughts and thus absent of suffering, so the more you meditate, the closer you come to experiencing this always available, ever present bliss of peacefulness, equanimity, tranquility, equipoise and non-suffering.

This leads to the last major reason people choose to meditate, which is perhaps the most important. Without a doubt, meditation is recognized as a powerful form of spiritual practice. It is the premier form of spiritual practice in the world, and is far superior to religious ceremonies, following religious rules of discipline, holy pilgrimage travel, making sacrifices and so forth because it actually produces mental change, behavioral change and spiritual progress. It is the single most powerful spiritual practice possible. Furthermore, the true basis of the most effective spiritual practices within religions is usually disguised meditation practice in some form or another because the ultimate objective of spiritual practice is cultivating an empty mind absent of the ego that can "realize a union with God" as the ultimate ground. That spiritual objective is called different things in different religions but it is the same objective nonetheless.

The inherent reason behind meditation as a spiritual practice lies in the two principles of cessation and observation, or cessation and witnessing. These are the two principles within all meditation (and other genuine spiritual) practices that make them effective. Thoughts die down from meditation, which is the principle of *cessation* since thoughts "cease" or quiet down, but the mind stays awake and aware when this happens, which is the principle of *witnessing.* Therefore you have cessation-witnessing, or "beholding."

Witnessing is being aware of consciousness and its movements. Witnessing awareness is why you can discover the root source of your mind – because the faculty of knowing awareness always still operates and through insight, wisdom, understanding, discrimination or however you wish to word it, you can awaken to a realization of what your true nature is. This is an experiential awakening, accompanied by insight or understanding, and not simply an intellectual understanding that you might pick up from reading a book. You *become the experience*, and with reflection know it is so. You know it is true because you experienced it for yourself.

As you meditate your mind will tend to calm down, thoughts will tend to dissipate and you will reach a state of mental quietness and tranquility. Try it and you will see this naturally happens because you simply let go of thoughts and refuse to follow them to become entangled. This quieting result comes from abandoning our unnatural attachment to thoughts, so thoughts die down. Meditation practice is learning how to "let go" of thoughts –

whatever you personally discover that means – so that by not feeding them undue energy or attention they dissipate and die away. The fact that the mind becomes quiet is just a natural result of this process that you can prove for yourself, so there's really no need for a theory to insure you that it happens. There is just the proof of direct experience that it happens, which is what it's all about.

That quiet state of tranquility that is reached, which is an emptying or disappearance of miscellaneous wandering thoughts that usually occupy the mind, is called a state of cessation, stopping or halting. It's so named because you're not experiencing the busy monkey mind of wild thoughts anymore. They have died down in volume. They are gone, they have stopped, they have disappeared, they have ceased, and so the mental state is tranquil, peaceful, calm and quiet. Therefore you are experiencing quiet, purity, equipoise, stillness or peacefulness in the mind. That's a state of *cessation or tranquility that is also called stopping or halting.*

While you are in that state of quiet, purity, emptiness or cessation you are not asleep; neither are you in a coma or a state of stupor or oblivion unaware of your environment. Rather you are still aware, you are perfectly awake, you are still attentive to the contents that arise within your mind. You are still aware of your consciousness. You can still think and give birth to thoughts, but you just don't attach to them because the habit of clinging is gone, and so they will arise whenever they must, and then they will naturally depart without undue lingering. That is, if you refrain from attaching to them. So, you can still ponder, think, reason, and have wisdom, insight or realizations because you are not suppressing thoughts. You are not suppressing thoughts or your mind in any way. What is unnecessary in the mind stream simply goes away over time after you get into the habit of practicing meditation.

Once again, you are always still witnessing consciousness in advanced meditation states. You are always aware of the mind but you are just not attaching to the thoughts that flit through the mind. You are now letting them flow without clinging to anything. You are always still aware of your consciousness and can observe what's happening in your mental continuum.

This is the second principle within all meditation practices, and it's called *observation, witnessing or watching.* There is never any problem with this witnessing, for it is natural and inherent. You always have awareness naturally there, so there is always witnessing. You don't have to do anything to have awareness, for it always exists. The problem is that you obscure it through thought-attachments, and then *witnessing consciousness becomes enmeshed with the flow of thoughts and you lose the sense of presence.* The problem is that excessive interest leads to getting entangled up with thoughts. You start self-identifying with thoughts, such as the constant sensations of the body, when you are actually formless and have nothing with which you should identify. You get entangled in thoughts when you don't have to get tied up with their flow, and then you lose the experience of the clear basis of your mind.

Because it is effortless and doesn't involve mental effort other than watching, meditation is thus a practice of bringing the mind naturally to a state of stillness or cessation where all sorts of busy thoughts die down but you still maintain full awareness without mental clingings. This means that you're still wide awake and aware, and you still know what's going on even though your mind is quieter. You can still fully function in the world, but in a constant state of independent peace with a mental presence that does not fall into erratic emotional states or get trapped by whatever else arises. You are always clean and pure in the midst of disturbance. To attain this, you do not try to push thoughts away during meditation practice, but let them naturally die down and leave on their own so that you can experience a mental scenario that seems internally quiet or empty. Next you learn how to carry this state with you into the regular world, and which then allows you to do all the things you always could do but without getting disturbed.

As you practice meditation, there are also physiological changes that will occur in your body if you practice well enough. Many people start to feel energies here and there because their internal chi channels start to open. Science doesn't yet recognize this result, even though you cannot deny its truth when it happens to you, but science does recognize the fact that your hormone levels change, blood markers change, and even the structure of your brain changes, too, from consistent meditation practice.

All these changes have been measured, and all have been found to be positive transformations. You will never find a single negative or detrimental thing that happens because of meditation. If you think something detrimental occurs to you or others because of meditation practice, you are imaging things. Your physical body changes due to meditation practice because your consciousness and your life-force are interlinked, and your life force is connected to your body in general, so of course there will be bodily changes due to the purifying changes in consciousness. When one changes, the other changes; when one transforms, the other transforms in response; when one purifies, the other purifies as well. This is why meditation tends, through the "opening of the chi channels" or "purification of the chi," to lead to better health and longevity. You can find a detailed description of this in *Tao and Longevity,* by Nan Huai-chin, which I always recommend to those who truly want to learn meditation and all its details.

There are many types of meditation used in spiritual practice, but they each have the same major objective of helping you to calm your wandering monkey mind. When your mind becomes emptier and clearer because of meditation, you can eventually see through to the very foundational basis of the mind and find that the ultimate origin of thoughts is "emptiness" or empty mind. The real mind, *the real you of pure homogenous being,* transcends the comings and goings of thoughts and you can progressively reach this nirvana through the path of meditation.

If you keep tracing thoughts back to their ultimate source by quietly observing the contents of your mind as they flit past, you'll find that the human being is actually akin to a substrate of bodiless awareness, or pure consciousness, which has no fixed body or substance that is phenomenal. Pure consciousness is just that – it is not anything we can identify as anything that's a phenomenon or thing. You can therefore say that the fundamental essence of the human being (or any living being) is "empty" to denote this lack of a substance, and yet there is still awareness or consciousness that is there. The nature of your truest most fundamental being is therefore often described as co-joint emptiness and awareness; your true self is not any substance or any-thing caused and conditioned, so it is "empty," and yet has awareness as its nature. Some therefore call it empty or pristine awareness, or pure consciousness. Others call it "emptiness that has the nature of awareness." There is an underlying unity of emptiness (the non-existence of anything phenomenal) and existence (awareness) that is the real you, and you cannot say you are absolutely one or the other.

If you say you are emptiness then the problem is that there is awareness that's there that knows all sorts of consciousness appearances; if you say you are awareness then the problem is that its fundamental nature is emptiness, meaning a lack of fundamental substance or essence and a lack of content, too. The funny thing is, these two sides match up! In terms of the awareness aspect, the world you see as an appearance within the awareness aspect never stays but moment-to-moment continuously transforms; like a dream nothing can therefore be grasped as substantial within awareness, and since nothing has its own self-so nature of solid unchanging existence down to the tiniest moment, that non-existence of permanence doesn't conflict with a stationary true reality. You cannot say nothing is there; you cannot say appearances are not existent. Yet you cannot say anything is there that is REAL since the appearances are always changing and different from what they were a moment ago. Nothing remains with a fixed identity of its own and nothing exists just from itself, so nothing is real in a self-so sense that is self-produced, self-born, self-sustained, self-reliant and un-caused. Since nothing is permanent or unchanging or uncaused, nothing has a substance that represents a lasting nature with a fixed character and thus every phenomenal thing we can identify lacks a fundamental substance, essence or self.

All living beings are actually manifestations of the same ultimate substrate, or original nature, but this is something you can only prove after much meditation work. You can actually realize that there is one base state which gives rise to ALL awareness, or consciousness, and you are *This.* Everything is the one base fundamental essence; everything is this all-base, or fundamental nature. All is one, and you are that All (that has reached self-awareness by poking through this non-separate mind and body), but you think you are an independent self. That realization, which is maintained by countless saints from different religions who have done the appropriate meditation work, is one of the primary goals of meditation as a spiritual practice. If you can actually experience this realization for yourself, it is said you have *won spiritual liberation or salvation and become a saint, sage, a prophet, a master, a real man, an enlightened being, a jnani, a Buddha, a self-realized one.*

In any case, it's up to the practitioner to decide why they want to meditate and how much they want to meditate. Your ultimate goals for meditation practice are totally up to you. Nevertheless, for all people who meditate correctly, they will always have phenomena that appear in the fields of mind and body. The mind will calm down (or we say "empty out"), and your chi will arise and start to open up your body's chi channels, which produces all sorts of physical reactions that people always feel. Those responses are the personal proof of the existence of chi and the effectiveness of meditation. If you practice, those results will appear for you. If you don't practice, you can only read about them. If you practice and they don't appear, it is because your practice is as yet insufficient.

All the spiritual schools of the world that encourage meditation also tell them that you should study the theory of spiritual practice to get the most out of your efforts, whether your objective is for better health, relaxation, longevity, or spiritual progress. If you shoot for the highest target then you will achieve all these lower objectives, but you have to understand what you're doing, why you're doing it, and what are the correct principles of meditation practice. Study and practice are like mixing flour with water to make dough. You have to take your intellectual study and mix it with your actual practice and then bake them so that in time you produce bread. If you practice meditation, many effects will arise, and many questions, too. If you really want to understand these results, you have to understand many connections between various topics and this requires diligent study.

To understand the highest possible attainment from cultivation – which we call "self-realization" or realization of the self's base of pure consciousness – we must discover that the human being in its essence is really pure consciousness or pure awareness. The traditions that best describe this are the schools of Vedanta and Buddhism, especially the Buddhist school of Yogacara. One such text which I highly recommend for understanding consciousness is *Everyday Consciousness and Primordial Awareness*. You can also read what I consider non-denominational books by Ramana Maharshi and Sri Nisargadatta (and Sri H. W. L. Poonja, David Godman and others), which don't rely on religion at all, to understand Advaita Vedanta. Buddhism has many English translations, but by first reading Vedanta you can better understand the meaning of Buddhist texts which often seem a bit off in their translations.

If you want to understand the many details, facets and techniques of meditation practice, the school of Buddhism has the finest repertoire of methods and explanations available in the world, especially the Buddhist wisdom sutras. "Wisdom" means understanding, so the Buddhist wisdom or "understanding" sutras provide you with an understanding of your mind and the cultivation path that is helpful for your meditation work regardless of your school or tradition. And if you want to understand how the body's chi channels open up and change over the course of meditation practice you can also turn to the school of Chinese Taoism, the Yoga schools from India, or even Tibetan Esoteric Buddhism since it slowly developed as a combination of these other traditions. I have put the details of these transformations in *The Little Book of Hercules* for those who are interested.

In general, people have all sorts of different reasons for wanting to learn how to meditate, and there are all sorts of schools and traditions they can turn to for meditation instructions. Based on their objectives, the most common question people typically ask is, "What type of meditation should I personally practice?"

There are an incredible variety of meditation practices possible. In fact, one of the popular pictures of the Buddha Kuan Yin (Avalokitesvara) shows him possessing ten thousand arms, each arm representing a different meditation or enlightening technique one can practice. The Buddha Manjushri just holds a single sword to represent all the methods used for cutting off thoughts to cultivate a quiet mind. The basis of the Zen school, which practices *dhyana* meditation, is that anything can bring an enlightened awakening after you practice meditation and lay a sufficient foundation that prepares you for awakening. Nevertheless, to simplify matters I always tell people there are four or five general methods that they should practice and turn into a daily practice schedule if they possibly can. Each of these methods works to calm the mind *based on an entirely different princip*le, and so by using several methods together one maximizes their chances for success. You never know which principle will best work to calm the mind for you.

The first of these methods is **mantra practice**, which is very easy to do. It doesn't require you to set up a special time period; you can practice reciting mantras at any time and anywhere. **Prayer recitation** is very similar to mantra practice, so most of the principles that apply to mantra recitation apply to prayer recitation, too.

The second meditation practice I recommend is the method of watching the mind called **vipassana** or **mindfulness practice**. It goes by many other names, too, such as introspection, cessation-observation practice or witnessing, but this is essentially the basic practice people think of when they hear the word "meditation." You basically sit down and start watching your thoughts without adding any extra energy to the process, and in time they die down because you just watch them without giving them any extra energy. You stay mindful of the watching, so it is also called mindfulness practice in that you are always watching and knowing your mind, which is being mindful of it.

If somebody wants to do even more meditation practice other than that, I advise them to practice a **visualization** technique such as the white skeleton visualization method, as well as **pranayama** and **anapana** breathing practices. Visualization practices, of any type, help you learn stable concentration, which means how to develop a "one-pointed mind." You learn how to keep your mind on a topic for an extended period of time, and this helps to banish (and keep away) other wandering thoughts that might distract you.

A "state of concentration" is just a stable, steady mind that is absent of wandering thoughts, so it is involved with one primary topic and ignores all the other miscellaneous thoughts that always arise. Hence it is sometimes called single-minded thought. "Concentration" does not necessarily mean holding to just one thought, for if you are trying to solve a math problem, for instance, then this may require various mathematical thoughts and approaches to come up within your mind. These are all different thoughts, but it doesn't mean you have lost concentration. Concentration means that you are staying with that single topic rather than letting your mind slip and start thinking of something else other than the math problem to be solved.

Another example might mean figuring out how to solve a business problem, or anything else. It doesn't just mean holding on to a single thought, though that is an excellent way of training for concentration and is used in many meditation methods because of the benefits it brings. Most people cannot concentrate very well, so to help people learn concentration a variety of meditation methods have been developed over the ages. These methods teach how to concentrate on a single object that people can hold in their mind, such as a single thought, sound, or image. You can even do this with a single taste, smell (odor) or physical sensation as well. If you can learn how to hold to any single sensory phenomenon, this is learning concentration, and I have explained how to do this with visual objects in my book, *Twenty-Five Doors to Meditation.*

Most people can benefit from learning how to concentrate on something so their mind does not waver, and in visualization practice you use a visual mental image as the focus of concentration to develop this type of stability. In mantra practice you learn how to focus on a sound so that the mind quiets of miscellaneous thoughts (even if the sound has no meaning), while in reciting prayers or affirmations you focus on holding to a single thought. Anapana practices involve watching your breath instead of watching your thoughts, and both these forms of watching, or mental witnessing, teach you how to stay aware and detached while focusing on moving processes rather than stationary items like an internal visual image. In other words, with anapana practice you concentrate on following your breathing.

Pranayama breathing practices are a bit forceful because they involve learning how to hold (retain) your breath, but this greatly helps to transform your body so that it's easier to make progress with any other meditation technique that you try. When you meditate to a deep level, your breathing tends to slow to a halt, which is another kind of cessation, and pranayama practices help you prepare for that great accomplishment.

If someone is very devoted to meditation practice and wants to get to the highest levels, they can also, after they lay a steady foundation of practice, turn to a variety of Zen techniques or Vedanta techniques. Their ultimate purpose is introspection, which means they guide you to investigating, analyzing, and contemplating the nature of the substance of your mind so that you eventually discover the ultimate source of consciousness, which is the real "you" or self behind what you call the "I." You look within at your own mind and with logical discrimination analyze your consciousness to discover its various parts or functions and their nature, and detach from those functionings during meditation to experientially find their root source.

You are actually looking for your true fundamental self beneath all the thoughts and emotions which come and go, and which transcends the entire body of consciousness that appears as your mind. You are looking for the everlasting original foundational substrate of what you truly are because that ultimate source or substrate is actually the real "you." This real you, or true self, has the capability of knowing, awareness, or consciousness – however you wish to word it – and you have to find that ultimate origin to attain freedom and spiritual liberation. Once you have found it you are out of the realm of consciousness, and suffering. Consciousness still goes on – the world is the same as before – but you are no longer trapped within the entanglements of consciousness itself, but remain independent and clean as the witness, pure and free of pain and suffering. In fact, the extent of consciousness that you can then know expands to include the entire universe because *it is you.* It all originates from that primordial mind of purest consciousness which you are.

You are always attached to the doings of consciousness, and when you detach from clinging to consciousness objects and appearances, so that awareness or knowing just functions without friction or restriction, you can turn around to find your True Self that has always been there and always will be, regardless of what appears and disappears across its face. Since it is always there and is what prepositionally stands behind, animates, or powers what we call the soul or self, it is the true self. It is what you really are. In fact, when you cultivate meditation to a high enough state of perfection you will experientially discover your original nature and directly, nakedly realize that you never were the small self you imagined yourself to be, so this is not just a logical argument.

The ultimate purpose of spiritual practice, and highest possible objective of meditation practice, is to find the *real you* enjoying all these experiences we call life. You must strive, during this short human life, to discover what you ultimately are. That real you, whether you call it "God" or some other term, is what you are actually hoping to find through religious and spiritual practice, but you can only find it by discovering the ultimate source of the mind that transcends consciousness. We suppose there is a disunity or separateness between ourselves and our true nature (as if we were independent beings) but there is none, and this fact also has to be discovered.

Meditation practice is the only method that helps you to directly discover your true self, true fundamental nature, true essence of being, or however you wish to word it. That discovery will bring you peace and freedom. If is the apex of all spiritual practice and spiritual perfection.

Along this path there are a variety of other practices that you can use to help you make progress, such as **detoxifying the body**, **stretching exercises**, **sexual discipline** and **merit accumulation**, and we'll touch upon those as well. But the gist of a very tightly focused meditation schedule is to be practicing mantra with vipassana, emptiness meditation, the skeleton visualization, and pranayama and anapana practice. And that's how you make progress, which is by sticking to a core set of basic meditation techniques. You should simultaneously practice a variety of techniques that work through different principles towards the goal of calming your mind.

2

MANTRA PRACTICE AND PRAYER RECITATION

The easiest meditation method you can possibly practice is mantra recitation. People always complain they have no time to meditate, but you can silently be reciting mantras at any time and in any location. Therefore mantra recitation, as a meditation practice, readily fits into any person's busy schedule, and we can therefore say it takes no time at all. There is never a moment when you cannot be doing mantra practice, and therefore this is a cultivation method that makes use of all wasted moments during the day. It offers no interference to whatever else we are doing.

If we substitute the word "prayer" for "mantra," everything you just read still holds true. We can be silently reciting prayers, just as we recite mantras, anytime and anyplace. We can certainly benefit from this if, when reciting prayers, we follow the correct principles of cultivation practice to use this to develop concentration and prevent this from just becoming a method of talking to oneself. If done properly according to the correct principles, prayer recitation can become truly effective as a form of spiritual practice that actually leads to something significant in spiritual progress rather than just a simple reciting of some words held with intent.

If you were thrown in jail or were captured as a prisoner of war, you could still make incredibly positive use of your time by engaging in silent mantra practice or prayer recitation that is unnoticed by everyone else. If you were feeling alienated, lonely or depressed, reciting mantras or prayers can help you change your mental state for the better. When sitting idle on a bus or in a plane, working on a manufacturing line, or doing any type of activity that does not require concentration, you can simultaneously be engaged in mantra or prayer recitation to quiet and purify your mind. Every idle moment can be used for this type of meditation practice.

Even when you are experiencing some type of terribly bad fortune, you can always make some positive use of your time by engaging in either of these two types of cultivation practice. After you get into the habit of continuous prayer or mantra recitation, you can be involved with all sorts of activities at the same time and this method of mental cultivation will not interfere with them one tiny bit.

This is why I always tell people that they should be doing some form of mantra or prayer practice as part of their cultivation effort. As the years go by, you always accumulate the results of your practice and by practicing mantra or prayer recitation at idle moments, it will seem as if you did nothing at all to attain your results because you practiced during "down time."

Mantra recitation, also known as *japa* practice in India, is simple to explain. It is the repetition of a particular phrase over and over again in a continuous manner, and while reciting the mantra you listen to the sound rather than pay attention to all the other thoughts running around in your head. Because you place your concentration on listening to just the sound, that attention ignores the other random thoughts that usually wander around in your mind, and they quiet down when you ignore them. The internal chatter of your mind quiets, and you end up eventually experiencing a mental realm of peaceful quiet and tranquility as happens with all meditation practices. This is therefore a method of concentrating on (listening to a) sound so that your mind quiets of wandering thoughts.

This same result occurs for prayer recitation when you go about reciting prayers correctly. The important principle is to let go of wandering thoughts except the one thought of the prayer. You concentrate on listening to the prayer, or concentrate on holding to the meaning (thought) of the prayer, and ignore everything else that arises within your mind. If you do this, then wandering thoughts will also calm down, and you will develop an empty, quiet mind of peace.

With mantra recitation you listen to the sound of the mantra and ignore wandering thoughts that arise as you recite, and with prayer recitation you concentrate on the thought encapsulated by the prayer, and ignore other wandering thoughts that arise. You can also just concentrate on listening to the sound of the prayer as done in mantra practice, but then it effectively becomes mantra practice. If a mantra has a meaning and you hold to the meaning during recitation, you can also say this is prayer practice although the normal nomenclature is to continue calling this mantra practice since a mantra is being used. This type of concentration naturally quiets the mind after you do it for awhile, which is the result you are after. Hence, in reciting prayers or mantras, you have a very simple meditation technique.

Typically the mantra sounds or phrases you recite are considered special in some way. There might not be any meaning to the mantra because what is important is to develop your mental concentration (which means a quiet mind) by listening to the sound. However, individuals in the past have found that some special sounds are more effective in calming the mind than others. Therefore, you can achieve a greater calming effect on the mind, and opening of chi channels within your body, from reciting the special sounds encapsulated within mantras rather than random words like "Coca Cola," "Klatu barada nikto," or some other nonsensical verbiage. There is actually a deep science behind the creation and usage of sounds within mantras.

Sometimes a mantra has a meaning, and sometimes it does not. Sometimes it originates from a religious text, and sometimes it was given to us by an enlightened individual because of what they found worked for them. In all cases, in reciting and listening to a mantra your objective is to use it to quiet your mind. In some cases the mantra recitation can help transform the inner chi of your body because of a relationship between particular sounds and the rhythm of inner chi flows, or because the mental calming you achieve from mantra recitation awakens the chi within your body that in turn leads to subsequent stags of chi purification. That's actually the main principle upon which it works.

Because of their similarities in possible usage, continuous prayer recitation can be favorably compared to mantra practice despite people's objections to the contrary. Since some mantras can be recited with a specific objective in mind, just as a specific intent is usually encapsulated in the words of some prayers, the two are sometimes interchangeable, but not always.

Various Christian sects emphasize ceaseless prayer for the spiritual life, and this is often the same as ceaseless mantra practice when similar principles of practice are followed. The two methods can produce roughly the same beneficial results. When Christians, or other groups, say they feel the grace or power of God from their efforts at ceaseless prayer recitation, this is the same as others saying they feel all their chi coming up from their mantra cultivation practice, which as a result fills the body with a sense of energy, power and fullness. This is what you normally feel when your chi, or life force, arises in volume, though people usually subsequently lose those energies through engagement in sexual activities. If retained, those energies will produce transformations in your body due to the opening of the chi channels and chakras they engender. One group simply wraps religious notions around this natural, non-denominational result while the other holds to a more rational, scientific explanation.

Sometimes the mantra is a special set of sounds, without any particular meaning, that has been given to us by a great enlightened sage of the past. Often those mantras are filled with special sounds such as "Om," "Ah," or "Hung" because of their particular helpful effects on the body and mind when recited in the proper way. **"Om Ah Hung,"** for instance, happens to be the main mantra used in Tibet for opening up the body's central chi channel pathway. Its three syllables are often recited at different chakra locations along the central channel, and the final "hung" sound is recited with a strong exhalation force.

You will find most of the mantras in the world characterized by a set of special sounds, and how to link these sounds together for special mental and physical results is actually a forgotten science. Regardless of the origin of the mantra, you should be reciting the sounds, listening within to those sounds (concentrating on them), and letting go of all other thoughts while so doing so that they depart naturally and your mind gently reaches a state of internal peace and quiet.

As you listen to the same mantra (or prayer) sounds repeatedly, your wandering thoughts will tend to disappear, your mind will calm, and you will eventually reach a state of internal peace or quiescence because extraneous thoughts have been driven away. The mantra recitation itself, after some time, can even become quite automatic and take on a life of its own so that you are always continually doing it without any effort. Always let that happen should such self-activation ever occur. This is a great result. Like all things in life, this result does not happen instantly but only happens after devoted practice, and is a sign of excellent progress. You might even find yourself reciting mantras in your dreams, which is another sign of progress.

An even more advanced technique than recitation alone is to recite mantras at certain chakra points in the body, and to combine mantras with visualizations you try to hold with stability (so that you are jointly cultivating sound and light), but beginners rarely do this because they never receive the proper instructions on how to do it correctly. If you concentrate on bringing both sound and light to a certain region in the body where you hold them with stability, it will bring your chi to that region and you will quickly feel the subsequent opening of the chi channels in that area. This usually produces discomfort, for you will typically feel a warmth and frictional response when the chi channels start opening. Some people might even see internal visions at those regions if they cultivate with enough effort to maintain a consistently stable but non-forceful focus in those regions.

The big principle of mantra practice is that you must listen to the sound rather than follow any other internal thought dialogue going on in your head, and this listening will eventually result in the calming of your mind. The same goes for prayer recitation; hold to the meaning of the prayer, and in holding to that one thought you will banish other thoughts from your mind. When thoughts leave and your mind empties, you will then be in a constant state of presence, which is a theme that permeates most religious exercises.

You can verbally recite a prayer or mantra out loud, you can semi-voice it with your mouth closed, or you can recite it internally in your mind, which is the highest technique one can practice. Once again, you can recite a prayer or mantra as you go about your daily activities, or you can set aside a few minutes each day devoted exclusively to reciting the prayer or mantra. This last type of practice tends to bring the best results because it allows you to focus your concentration without interruption. However, this is not the only time you can be reciting prayers or mantras because an excellent form of meditation practice is to be reciting the prayer or mantra all the time, continuously. When you keep something in your mind all the time it is a practice called "mindfulness." Mindfulness means that not only are you always constantly doing it (continually practicing it), but your mind is always focused on it with a gentle form of following, or concentration. You are always remembering to do it, so this is also often called a type of "remembrance" practice. For instance you should always be listening to a mantra which you are constantly reciting, or as Saint Paul and other spiritual greats have recommended, you should be reciting a prayer without ceasing day and night while keeping your mind focused on its meaning. This is known as mindfulness without distraction. The idea is to tie up consciousness on one thing and abandon (or drive away) everything else so that only the one thing is left, and then to eventually abandon it when you get to a quiet state where you can gain an experience of your naturally empty mind.

Mantra practice is so simple that anyone can do it—you simply recite the mantra and listen to your recitation. You continue listening to it as you recite it, being mindful of the mantra, until your mind quiets. When your mind quiets you don't have to recite it anymore, but should simply remain in that state of quietness and abide there. You mantra to attain mental silence or stillness, or you can try to cultivate the mental quiet directly through other meditation methods such as by just letting go of thoughts directly because you refuse to attach to them.

Whenever you reach a state of quietness from practicing some meditation technique, you should simply remain in that quietness and witness the workings of your mind. Awareness is still there when your thoughts have quieted, and thoughts will indeed still arise so that you still "know," but the mind actually seems quiet or empty of thoughts. At that point you should ask yourself a variety of questions to contemplate your state of mind and look for the answer in your consciousness itself, such as, "Where do my thoughts come from? Who is the one experiencing this quiet? Is this quiet itself a thought? If this is mental quiet that represents an absence of thoughts, how come I can know this quiet?" This is called mental investigation, or wisdom analysis.

The purpose of mantra practice is to help you initially reach a state of inner peace and silence when you don't have too many thoughts. Usually your mind is like a bustling marketplace of thoughts, and by concentrating on just the mantra alone you can bundle up all these wandering thoughts and throw them all away to experience an inner silence. After you attain that state of peace, you simply abide in that silence without clinging to it, and practice introspection to investigate that mental state to realize the nature of your ordinary mind. To know the nature of your mind is the beginning of spiritual practice, and so you use meditation practices to first calm your mind, emptying it of thought, so you can then investigate that state of empty consciousness and fathom everything about it. Your mind quiets and then you rest in clear awareness, contemplating the nature of the empty mind/consciousness you are experiencing.

The funny thing is, you'll eventually find that your mind – which you think is essentially the "you" – is really pure consciousness, or pure awareness empty of any content, and the thoughts that run through your mind are not you but just things that arise on the empty screen of your mind and then pass away. They are not something you can depend upon. They are constantly coming and going, and you cannot shut them off. The thoughts that arise come about because of the entire field of interdependent origination, an endless interlocking web of cause and effect that links all things in existence, and this flow cannot be shut off. You can detach from it to transcend it, but you cannot stop it. To realize that, to actually see that from personal experience and know it for a fact is the beginning step of any stage of true spiritual realization.

Mantra practice is so easy that you can do it any time of the day, anywhere, and in any situation, and no one has to know that you are doing it. You can quietly recite mantras on your way to work, you can recite them internally while you're working, and you can even do mantra practice while you are mindlessly watching television. There is never a moment when you cannot be doing mantra practice, or prayer practice, and thus, this is a meditation method that makes use of all the wasted moments during the day. It offers no interference to whatever else we are doing. We call it a meditation method, or cultivation method, because its purpose is not to ask for anything but to help your quiet your mind and awaken to its true nature.

The highest form of mantra practice is to recite the mantra internally, rather than out loud, and to concentrate on internally listening to that sound until thoughts still. Initially, when learning a mantra, many people first practice reciting the phrase out loud, which helps in learning the pronunciation, but it is not necessary to continue doing this. Nevertheless, it is often beneficial to mantra out loud, and even join mantra recitation groups to learn how to do this, because the external recitation of mantras often helps to cultivate the chi of your inner subtle body, and in this way helps you transform your body by opening up your chi channels so that you can reach an inner state of quiet much quicker.

Some people find the idea of mantra recitation alien, but as stated, you can alternatively recite religious prayers over and over again. For instance, the Christian Eastern Orthodox Church recommends a ceaseless recitation of the **Prayer of the Heart**. It even says its recitation will ignite a type of spiritual energy (your chi will arise) that will "crack open your heart and lead to the resurrection of dormant powers." This is just the Christian way of saying that your chi will arise, your body will fill with its energy, that chi energy (*kundalini*) will open up your chi channels, and this will lead to all sorts of other special physical and mental phenomena.

Everyone experiences the same process, but each spiritual school and religion tries to claim these results as their own and uses their own peculiar descriptions to do so. Consequently, people get confused and run from here to there looking for the truth but no one tells them about the non-denominational processes and procedures used to attain real mental calming, internal peace and spiritual gong-fu.

You must be careful as to the prayer you choose for recitation practice because reciting a sentence with a particular meaning, over and over again, will have definite psychological ramifications. It is like reciting an affirmation that tends to bend one's thoughts in a certain direction. Mantra recitation, because there is often no meaning to the sounds, usually avoids this potential problem. On the other hand, in most types of prayer recitation you should concentrate on holding the meaning of the prayer with one-pointed concentration, *so you should select a prayer carefully in light of its specific meaning.* Drumming a particular view into the subconscious over and over again can produce a certain type of negative personality response that must be abandoned and certainly unwound to get the Tao, so select your prayers and affirmations wisely. In Tibet, for instance, meditation practitioners pray very wisely. They typically pray for four things to happen: that their bodies become softer and healthier, that their chi channels all open, that they transform their behavior to become better and abandon evil tendencies, and that their real chi arises so that they can reach a state of mental calm and physical bliss. This is a positive form of prayer, and yet there are even higher objectives beyond this.

The best type of prayer practice is to keep reciting a prayer with the focus on becoming one with God through selflessness, through giving everything away including your thoughts and ideas of being a small self so that you can become God's infinite self. This type of objective helps move you closer to self-realization, which is the highest result you can go after through prayer practice.

One can perform a variant of this type of practice by reciting the words of a prayer while recognizing that God is like the invisible light within space since light illumination is omnipresent, everywhere, and perfectly clear in space. One therefore strives to "become one with God," or like God, by trying to become like this omnipresent clearness while praying, and tries to develop a similar mind by letting go of all thoughts when reciting. If you try to become like the infinite illumination of awareness in infinite space while reciting, this will help you let go of all mental holdings so that you can experience the natural formlessness of your true mind.

Try to let go of holding onto thoughts so that you become boundless and transparent like light; light does not get dirty in dirty water, but always illuminates everything while retaining its purity. It is formless and invisible but everywhere. Try to be like that, which is a meditation method in itself that teaches you to forgo mental holding and just let your awareness become vast like the boundless emptiness of space. In Taoism this is equivalent to the cultivation of *shen*. Just let go of your thoughts, give them away, and rest in the inherent emptiness of the purity of your mind which doesn't have thoughts or content, but is always clear and clean like light that is ready to illuminate whatever comes in front of it. That is the natural base of the mind, but it's hard to discover it until you let go of wandering thoughts that obscure it and realize this ever present base of pristine empty awareness.

One of the highest results of prayer practice recognized by the Eastern Orthodox Church of Christianity is "entering the Kingdom of Heaven." This is called *kenosis*, which is translated as "emptiness." Thus, even the Eastern Orthodox Church of Christianity recognizes that the purpose of prayer practice is to leave us with a quiet mind that is an experience of emptiness. The mind should become empty, but remain clear and aware and awake (rather than suppressed) so that it can know all things.

This is a description of the empty clarity nature of the mind, which is like the illumination of light in space; you don't actually see light itself in space, but you see the illumination of objects through its presence. That's how awareness functions; it's always clear, always present, always operating but is always unseen and yet it is because of its presence that we can know the objects of consciousness. Hence all in all, while mantra and prayer recitation are not exactly the same, the principles of practice, the proper practice methods, and the end results of successful practice have an extremely high similarity.

VARIOUS MANTRAS

In India, people use an incredibly large variety of different mantras in their meditations and spiritual practices, and especially the Gayatri mantra which runs as follows: "**Aum Bhur Bhuva Svah, Tat Savitur Varenyam, Bhargo Devasya Dhimahi, Dhiyo Yo Nah Prachodayat**." In fact, the mantras used in Hinduism, such as the popular Shanti mantra and "Ohm Namah Shivaya," are almost too numerous to count. Jainism and Sikhism both use mantras as well.

In Judaism, people often recite the prayer, "**Ani Yod Heh Vav Heh**." Rabbis often tell people to recite this in rhythm with the breath, which means reciting the words rhythmically until your breathing and the mind both calm down. This type of practice is therefore equivalent to mantra recitation and is not different at all regardless as to what one says. When you start to practice meditation, you must come to understand that all across the world, religions borrow the same meditation principles and practices and then re-label those techniques, sometimes adding just a tiny twist her or there, so they can call them their own. It has to be this way because everyone is depending on the same non-denominational principles, and yet every school wants to call itself unique, independent, separate from others and supreme.

Muslims on a daily basis recite the famous, "**La Illaha Il Allah Hu**." You can easily notice the prevalence of the "Ah" sound in this prayer, which accounts for part of its effectiveness. When Muslims recite it in tune with the breath, the practice is called *dikhr*, and once again this prayer practice is essentially the same as mantra recitation when the correct principles are followed.

You should constantly recite a mantra or prayer in tune with your breathing, and in turn your mind will eventually quiet down (wandering thoughts will depart) and your breathing will calm down, too. Next, you should stay in that quietness you reach, and then observe your consciousness whilst in that state of peace. You should not fall asleep once you reach a state of internal quiet, but practice maintaining full awareness because you want to eventually learn how to bring this quiet presence of awareness into your non-meditative states. This can only happen if you learn how to cultivate wakeful awareness that does not hold onto mental states rather than an awareness that is bogged down by states of sleepiness, dullness, suppression and torpor.

Most religions emphasize prayer recitation, claiming that the specific prayers one should use were written by God-conscious holy elders inspired by the grace of God. Well, you can say that about mantras as well. You can recite prayers if you like, but I prefer the practice of mantra recitation for numerous reasons, and the mantras that I like most have been left to us by enlightened individuals who have promised to offer various types of assistance to people who recite their mantra. Because more individuals have seemed to achieve enlightenment via this route, it is another reason I personally prefer it over prayer recitation.

Rather than reciting a prayer over and over again, which definitely tends to quiet the mind because of the principle of repetition, not only are you reciting a sound that will quiet the mind with these special mantras but you are tapping into the power of an already enlightened being who has vowed to help you with their spiritual power. This is like getting extra power for your efforts in cultivation practice.

As my teacher often said, in such cases the mantra is like a computer password that connects you with the account of that enlightened being. All consciousness is essentially one, so it is like plugging into their power, and the mantra thereby works in a mysterious way that only sages understand. By using their mantras, you are tapping into their powers to help you calm your mind, transform your body, and awaken or accomplish whatever is the purpose of the mantra, which you can hold with one-pointed thought.

Enlightened beings have no religious denomination because they have achieved self-realization, meaning they have merged with the source of all, and since we share that same common self-nature, it is foolishness to overlook such offers of help and assistance because "the mantra is not part of my tradition." When someone reaches the root source of the mind, they arrive at the source of all traditions and can say "I am the One." They can say, "I will always be with you" because the original nature is always with you since you are the original nature, too. Thus it behooves you to make use of their teachings and offers of assistance.

The mantra I most often recommend is Buddhism's Zhunti mantra because this mantra, as related in the Buddhist sutras, has been used by billions and billions of beings in countless worlds to help them achieve enlightenment. That's how long this particular Buddha has been teaching. Because it is something that you can continuously recite to not only quiet your mind but also help you change your worldly fortune, it can be used for multiple purposes.

As is often taught about Christian prayer, one way to practice the mantra is to simply recite the mantra, listen with your mind to the sound, and surrender all your cares and concerns over to the Buddha. Just let go of your thoughts and listen to the sounds until they quiet. As the mind quiets and your breathing quiets, you remain detached from those states, and simply continue to shine awareness on consciousness throughout whatever arises. This idea of surrendering, or letting go, can be applied to most mantra and prayer techniques. You forget about everything and just mantra, and in turn your mind quiets. In fact, in Christianity you are supposed to "give everything over to God," let go, and mantra with that type of mind.

The Zhunti mantra runs: "**Namo Saptanam Samyaksambuddha Kotinam Tadyatha Om Cale Cule Cundhi Svaha**." After about one million repetitions you can shorten its recitation to "Om Cale Cule Cundhi Svaha" which phonetically sounds like "Om Zhuli, Zholi, Zhunti, Soha." You can easily find recordings of its pronunciation on the internet.

When asked, I typically recommend that people recite the Zhunti mantra as the basis of their daily mantra practice. Of course, you can also use whatever mantra, or prayer, you prefer from whatever spiritual tradition you come from. The point is that you should be doing mantra or prayer recitation all the time, incessantly, and in that way you'll make progress. You just do the practice without expecting any returns, and let the results take care of themselves.

Mantra practice is like the Christian practice of saying a prayer and then thinking, "Let me give all my cares and concerns over to God," and just reciting the prayer without holding on to a specific meaning or wish. You should practice constantly, and that is called mindfulness practice because you never let go of the prayer or mantra, but are always mindful to be reciting it. You are reciting it to quiet your mind, so if you add on the extra thought of surrendering your concerns, that is a way of abandoning troublesome thoughts, too.

If you want an even easier Buddhist mantra there is the recitation of "**Namo Amitofo**" which is extremely popular in Asia and has its own unique benefits. Tibetan Buddhists often recite "Ohm Ah Hung" on three chakras points within the body (in conjunction with special breathing techniques) to help open up the internal channels, and many other mantras from enlightened Buddhas are available for practice as well such as Avalokitsevara's six syllable mantra, "**Om Mani Padme Hung**."

People always think that the exact pronunciation of a mantra is the important thing, and while important that's not as crucial as how to utilize the mantra to calm your mind. For instance, the Zhunti mantra, when translated into Chinese, sounds very different from its original Sanskrit pronunciation and if you have an accent, any mantra you recite will sound different from what others might consider the "proper" pronunciation, too. Many mantras are translated from one culture to another, syllables get lost through those translations, and people have different accents even when they are pronouncing it correctly. So *pronunciation differences are to be expected and not to become the stumbling block to mantra practice.* Mantras work not so much because of the sound frequencies or vibrations they entail, but because they somehow also tap into an established enlightening power. They are like a call for help asking higher spiritual powers to assist you with your meditation efforts.

You will find countless stories of spiritual masters who, in their autobiographies, stated that they recited mantras millions of times, which helped them succeed. You will find stories of countless religious people who succeeded through constant prayer recitation as well. There is no other active practice which is simpler than this. And when you employ the mantra of an enlightened being, rather than simply recite a prayer, you have the extra "Umph!" of connecting with their enlightening power and their vow to help with your practice. This is therefore the first meditation method that I always recommend people practice.

I greatly respect those who strive to discover the original form and pronunciation of various mantras, and whole-heartedly applaud their efforts and the great merit they earn by disseminating this information. Nevertheless, the important point is to get started with the pronunciation that reaches you rather than wait for the perfect information to arrive. Don't put off starting mantra practice because you don't know the perfect pronunciation of the phrases, because once that new information somehow reaches you, it only takes a little while to learn how to change your pronunciation. Once you read a mantra in some book, immediately pronounce it out loud and you have begun. It is that simple. That's what I do all the time, especially to see the effect of the mantra on my chi and channels, and I don't care about the tradition it comes from at all. The internet even makes it easy to learn how to pronounce all these mantras correctly.

Once again, the effectiveness of mantras doesn't necessarily lie in the exactly correct pronunciation or the "secret syllables" of the mantra. If you hear something that quiets your mind, that in effect is a mantra because it has quieted your thoughts. The fact that you reach a quiet state of mind from reciting the mantra, even if mispronounced or "slightly off," is what is important. An incorrect pronunciation does not render a mantra ineffective in this regard.

If the mantra works in quieting your mind, who cares about having perfect pronunciation anyway? Who cares how it works? Who cares how many you had to recite if you got that quiet end result? It's working! The only thing that's important is that you reached a state of mental quiet from its usage. When you finally reach that quiet state then let go of the mantra and remain in that mental quiet, abiding in the silence and stillness but staying alert, watching your mind, without falling asleep. In the next chapter we'll get to what "watching the mind with awareness" means.

Unlike prayers, mantras are usually designed in such a way that their repetition stabilizes your breathing so that both your chi can change and your mind can also calm down, which is the result you are after. When you are trying to spiritually cultivate, you must focus on the important things like this which are the principles of the practice and end objectives you desire, and not get lost on trivial matters or unimportant targets such as an ultra perfect pronunciation.

MANTRA STORIES

There is a famous story illustrating the futility of running after the perfect mantra pronunciation. It involves an accomplished monk who was traveling on foot across the country, and in the distance he saw a house that was surrounded by a spiritual aura of light. He knew it must belong to an advanced spiritual practitioner, so he went to investigate and found an old uneducated woman who was reciting the famous mantra, "Om Mani Buy-me Hum" as her spiritual practice.

The old woman was extremely happy to see a distinguished holy visitor. She happily fed the monk and gave him a place to stay for the night. As he was leaving the next day, she asked him if there was something she should do to improve her spiritual practice.

The monk said, "Ah, yes, there is one thing. The correct pronunciation of the mantra you are reciting is not "Om Mani Buy-me Hum," but "Om Mani Pay-me Hum."

The woman thanked him profusely, and then he went on his way. As he looked back at her house from a distance, however, he no longer could see a spiritual light shining around it anymore. He then suddenly realized he had made a mistake in telling her that her practice had been wrong. With compassion but without wisdom, he had disturbed the woman's mind by teaching her to discard something that was already effectively working. Previously her mantra practice had helped her to calm her wandering thoughts, but now she was so worried about the correct pronunciation of the mantra that she could no longer quiet her mind. The monk had forgotten the principle that it is the result that matters rather than the fact of strictly following the external form of practice correctly.

Tolstoy relates a similar story about a Russian bishop who happened to meet three hermits accomplished due to their spiritual practice. The bishop was traveling on a ship, and it stopped at an island so that he could meet three illiterate hermits. When asked about their practice for serving God, the hermits said they had no idea how to serve God, but only served and supported each other. The bishop therefore thought it his duty to teach them how them how to pray unceasingly, and did so, returning to the ship thinking he had done a great good deed.

As the boat was leaving the island, however, the bishop and other passengers were dumbstruck when they saw three men from the island running on top of the water towards the ship. When they came close, they implored the bishop to teach them the Lord's Prayer again as, being simple, they had already forgotten it. The bishop then realized that whatever they were doing as their spiritual practice was already more effective than his suggested prayer recitation, and asked the three to continue their own method of spiritual practice, saying they did not need his instruction. As in the case of the old lady who did mantra practice, as the ship departed the travelers aboard could all see a light on the island as it slowly disappeared in the distance.

The point, as has been already made, is that the effectiveness of prayers or mantras doesn't necessarily lie in the words or the meaning or the pronunciation, but in the correct application of the practice principles which can override any minor mistakes being made by practitioners. If you hear something that quiets your mind, which cuts off thoughts to produce inner silence, that is a spiritual technique! You need not resort to anything else that's artificially constructed. It's the result that is important.

Let me relate yet another mantra story which also shows how reciting a few words, even just once, can quiet the mind. One time my teacher, after his enlightenment, left for Mount Omei in China where he had decided he was going to spend three years in solitary retreat. The retreat would give him undisturbed practice time to deepen and stabilize his progress without having to attend to the worries of the world.

At the foot of the mountain there was a shrine to a holy fox spirit. It was said that she had been cultivating on Omei Mountain since Bodhidharma's time ($5^{th}/6^{th}$ century AD) and had achieved such spiritual gong-fu from her practice that she was still living after several hundred years' time. She had not yet achieved enlightenment, but had cultivated *samadhi* to some extent and thus had attained some strong spiritual powers that had given her some miraculous abilities.

This female fox spirit was known to use her formidable spiritual powers to play all sorts of tricks on the monks in the mountain's temples. If a monk was not meditating well, she could appear out of nowhere and blow upon him with her breath, and he would fall asleep. She could cause young monks to see visions of beautiful women in order to tempt them into sexual fantasies. If she met a monk walking on the narrow mountain trail, she might slap him in the face and cause him to tumble off the mountain path. Out of nowhere her footprints used to appear at places in the mountain snow, and then they would suddenly disappear without any exit trail. She had all sorts of special abilities because she had been cultivating for many centuries.

My teacher knew this fox spirit lived on the mountain, and announced himself at the little shrine at its base before he went up, saying, "I'm going to be here for the next three years in retreat, and I'm here to let you know that I'm not like these clean-shaven, bald headed monks who are trying to be good all the time. I'm a quite different sort of character. Now if you leave me alone during this time, I'll be able to succeed and in turn will help you succeed in the Tao; but if you bother me and cause trouble, I'm warning you that I'm not a nice guy and will come down to destroy your little temple here. I'm just putting you on notice and letting you know I'm not like these goody-goody guys. You just be careful and leave me alone and then things will go well for both of us."

During his three-year stay on the mountain in his secluded room, the fox spirit still acted up playing her normal shenanigans on the monks, but always respectfully stayed away from bothering him. That is, until one day my teacher was talking through the wall to the head monk of the temple, who was doing a temporary secluded retreat in an adjacent room.

As they were discussing matters of cultivation, all of a sudden, there was a loud banging on the door. "Bam, bam, bam, bam! Bam, bam, bam, bam, bam!"

My teacher, who already knew what was going on, asked the head monk, "Who is it? Don't they know we're not to be disturbed?" The head monk replied, "It's that fox spirit, and she's come to create trouble."

The fox spirit wouldn't stop banging on the door despite the head monk yelling at her to leave, so my teacher asked the head monk, "Do you know any mantras for destroying evil?"

The head monk replied, "Yes, I do."

My teacher, whom everyone on the mountain knew was already enlightened, ordered him to recite them.

The head monk replied, "I dare not do it because of the bad karma." My teacher replied, "Recite them! I'll assume the consequences."

So the monk started reciting this special mantra, but the knocking got louder … "Bam, Bam, BAM, BAM!" The monk in turn recited his mantras even louder, and the knocking increased in severity as well. Back and forth the sounds increased between the two, as if a titanic battle was going on. The monk had started sweating profusely from his exertions, and his voice was starting to waiver from the efforts when finally my teacher yelled out, "Stop! You've tried your special mantras. Useless! Now, listen to my mantra."

My teacher paused … and then in an extremely angry voice shouted at the top of his lungs, "Fuck you! Fuck your mother! I'm going to come out there and destroy your temple!"

And with that … the knocking immediately ceased and the holy fox spirit ran away at full speed, never to bother him again.

That's an example of real mantra practice—just a few words that cut off troublesome mental noise in one stroke. When your mind thereafter becomes quiet, just rest in the resulting emptiness.

If you can say something that quiets your mind instantly, that's like experiencing the effect of mantra practice! Sometimes it's a realization that quiets the thoughts of the mind, sometimes breathing methods, sometimes tying the mind up in a complicated activity until it just gives up and lets go, sometimes just the fact of witnessing thoughts without getting involved. Anything that instantly cuts off thoughts and quiets the mind can be compared to the sword of the Buddha Manjushri who, with one swish, can instantly cut through the stream of endless thoughts to produce peace and end ignorance. Thus we have our first meditation technique of mantra practice which can help us cut off our thought chatter.

As to the fate of the fox spirit, as promised, after my master left his retreat he encountered her once again, and entered into a conversation about her practice. He asked her what she had been practicing, and then told her that the method that she had been using since Bodhidharma's time was wrong, for she had been incorrectly trying to steal energy from people to try to supplement her own, and he then taught her the correct way to practice. She then left the mountain for somewhere else to continue her cultivation correctly, and hasn't been seen there since.

No matter how evil, the Buddhas and Bodhisattvas always have mercy on those who want to cultivate for realization or who want to sincerely change their behavior. Whether a human being, animal, ghost or other, one should always help others who wish to change themselves for the better, purify their personal behavior, and cultivate to awaken.

3

WITNESSING PRACTICE, OR WATCHING THE MIND

The basic practice of meditation is often called "watching the mind." There are also meditation practices where you watch your breathing or the sensations within your body, but all these various types of meditation practice are basically watching practices. You sit and become aware of the contents of your mind, and don't attach to them or become entangled with them but just observe them as they come and go. This is also called "observation" or "witnessing" practice as well because that's all you do – you stay aware and witness what goes on within your mind without becoming enmeshed with the stream of consciousness. You become mindful of the contents of your mind, and continually watch those contents without clinging to them. Try it!

Of all the spiritual teachers, it is probably Confucius who described this type of meditation practice most clearly. He basically said, "No matter where you are or what you're doing, you should always watch the thoughts that arise in your mind. You should always inspect yourself, watching your behavior in this way, too. Because of always mindfully watching, which is cultivating awareness, you can also then correct your thoughts and behavior when you see them going astray. By constantly observing your thoughts and motivations as to whether they are good or bad, right or wrong, you will also eventually arrive at the stage where there are no thoughts of good or bad and right or wrong anymore because thoughts have died down and the mind has become very empty and pure."

This is perfectly true, and matches the practice of meditation with the objective of how to improve our behavior and become better people in the world. In life you should always strive to be aware of your thoughts and behavior – you should be "mindful" of them — and that is basically true meditation practice integrated with the real world. When you see an errant thought in your mind, you should learn how to cut it off or just ignore it by letting it go rather than holding on to it, following its call and feeding it more energy. In not acting on it and not clinging to it, it will simply go away. In not following it, you will refrain from feeding it energy and subsequently that impulse or thought stream will eventually die down.

If a particular thought is bothersome or troubling, you can use various expedients to try to cut it off, which is what the sword in the hand of the Buddha Manjushri stands for. He just swings his sword and, "swoosh!" he cuts off that particular thought stream right at that moment so that it no longer causes trouble. The actual practice principle of watching thoughts, however, is that just by shining awareness on thoughts, without attaching or clinging to them, they will eventually depart even if they try to stubbornly remain to bother you. In time, just from watching or witnessing your thoughts without getting involved in the mental continuum – just by acting as a third party observer who is attentive to what's going on because he is witnessing it while remaining independent – the mind will naturally quiet down because thoughts will leave when you stay detached and pay them no heed.

Therefore when you sit in meditation practice, you should relax your body, close your eyes and just start watching your thoughts. You just sit there and start witnessing your mental scenario without becoming attached to anything or expecting anything. You do nothing but witness. You do nothing but observe the arrival and departure of thoughts in your mind. Yu don't try to change anything or hold any expectations. If you don't attach to thoughts, then in time they will die down and dissipate, and your breathing will calm down as well.

This simultaneous calming of your respiration as your thoughts die down is an important meditation principle to recognize. It occurs because your mind (consciousness or thoughts) and your breathing are linked. As your mind calms down your breathing will also calm down, and if your mind gets excited, your breathing will also quicken. For instance, if you become mentally frightened then your breathing will speed up; if you are relaxed (after making love, for instance) then your breathing will calm down. There is always an interrelationship between your mental states and your breathing, a mind-body connection. *The chi within your body is also linked to your breathing, so as your breathing calms or quickens then your chi will also calm or quicken.* This essentially explains why people can use breathing exercises as a form of meditation to affect their mental state. They can use breathing practices to effect their chi, and their chi will affect their mental states.

This idea of mental and physical calming is known by another common name – relaxation. Relaxation is something that accompanies all meditation methods you might practice when you practice properly. If you are accumulating tension while meditating – whether in the body, in your emotions, or mentally – then you are practicing meditation in the wrong way. Your relaxation should deepen the more you practice meditation, and in time your body should warm and soften as your internal chi starts to circulate due to that relaxation.

A portion of these results should come from the fact that you are mentally letting go of your body and your mental concerns. Another portion of your progress should come from the fact that meditation is opening the chi channels of your body, and when that happens, your body always tends to get warmer and soften because its internal energies flow much better. This, of course, makes it easier to relax because your body becomes warmer, softer and more flexible.

The same principle of improvement is expected for your mental clarity when you meditate. To meditate is not to create a muddled, sleepy or drunken mind where thoughts are hazy or unclear because that is not the meaning of an empty mind. You are not trying to repress or suppress thoughts to create an inner silence either. It is not a psychedelic or trance state you are after but a vivid mind that is fully awake and knows all the thoughts that arise. That's *clarity*. As you properly meditate, the volume of your wandering thoughts will decline over time, and you should start to experience tranquility and peace from their absence while simultaneously enjoying incredible mental clarity. That empty state of mind you reach, wherein your awareness is still active and able to know thoughts, becomes a mental clarity as crystal clear and large as space itself.

A third point is that you should become happier, more peaceful and content because of these advances. If this isn't happening you are either suppressing the energy streams which start to arise within the body, or still tightly holding on to thoughts and negative emotions, including negative self-talk and self-criticism, which suppresses that buoyant energy. Most of what runs through our minds all the time is negative self-talk, but this tends to eventually drop away due to meditation. We tend to mentally rehash things in our head, and engage in elaborate orchestras of self-talk that give us no peace. Meditation practice is the solution.

Clinging to thoughts and running mental scenarios over and over again is therefore incorrect meditation practice because it means you are following thoughts. If you want to progress, you must learn how to stop the useless practice of feeding and holding on to negative feelings, which gains you nothing. Letting go means just that—letting go. There is no way to do it; you just do it. Just act as you should in any situation, and then don't hold on to the situation any longer after it is over. Forget about it and stop rehearsing it in your head. That's letting go.

These three – relaxation, clarity and happiness – should slowly increase in your life because of your meditation practice. If they do not, you must reevaluate if you are practicing properly. The primary obstacle is that most people continue to hold on to thoughts when practicing meditation so they aren't following the basic instructions of just watching your mental scenario without getting attached to the thought streams of consciousness which arise. If they cling to states or streams of consciousness, this prevents their chi from flowing freely within them, and that state of inertia inhibits happiness, physical bliss and relaxation.

When you are going to sit down for a meditation practice session, it helps tremendously to first cultivate a feeling of satisfaction and contentment without any worries or concerns. You don't want to start meditating with worries on your mind. You might first say to yourself, "I have nothing I need to do right now, so I'll just take this free time to experience some peace. I don't have any expectations, there's no need to rush or hurry, and there is nothing to fear. Let me give away all my worries and concerns at this moment. I can pick them up later, but right now the world is alright and so am I. I am free to just sit down and relax, throw all my concerns away, and just experience perfect freedom and peace."

With no concerns to push you here or there, and no worries or anxieties to consider, you can then sit down to meditate and relax. It's like the Christian practice of sitting down for a moment and saying to oneself, "I'm going to give all my worries and concerns over to God," and then letting go to find mental peace for a short while. Thoughts will always arise, so you can just sit in a relaxed state and begin to watch those thoughts without involvement. The more you can cultivate the ability to enjoy doing nothing without any stresses or worries, and just watch with detachment, the easier it will be for you to practice meditation.

Essentially, watching your thoughts without getting involved with them so that your mind-stream calms down is basic meditation practice, or "**Meditation 101**." You don't have to pay money for any special course to learn this because you just learned how to do it. You sit down, close your eyes, witness the thoughts in your mind without becoming attached to them, and relax while observing the contents of your mind. Basically you are doing nothing at all except observing the contents of your mind.

There are two major principles involved with this practice – witnessing or observing the mind, called *vipassana*, and the quiet mental state that is eventually produced from doing this, called *shamatha*. You can call this practice of mental watching and calming by many names usually by citing one or both of these factors. We therefore have various descriptions found in many spiritual traditions such as:

- "*Vipassana*" or "witnessing" practice because you simply watch your mind, like a third person observer, when practicing

- "*Shamatha*" or "calm abiding" because you eventually arrive at a mental experience of silence, peace or calm and abide there

- "Cessation," "stopping," "halting" practice because thoughts die down due to the practice and therefore cease, halt, stop or disappear

- "Emptiness" meditation because thoughts depart and the mind becomes empty of thoughts

- "Observation" or "watching" practice because you observe the mind's contents just by watching or witnessing them without involvement or entanglement of any sort

- "Mindfulness" practice because you are continually mindful of watching your thoughts and never cease doing this even for a moment

- "Remembrance" practice because you're always trying to remember to watch your thoughts without getting lost/entangled in those thoughts

- “Cultivation of silence” or “cultivation of inner peace” because after thoughts die down your mental state becomes relatively quiet, absent of most wandering thoughts

- “Detachment” because you're not attaching or clinging to your thoughts but letting go of them, hence detaching from them

- “Surrendering” because you give up the activity of mental clinging and let everything go

- “Calm abiding” because you let the mind rest until it calms, and then you look at it with precision, meaning with analysis or discrimination

- “Naturalness” or “effortlessness” practice because no effort is involved with watching thoughts and no effort or clinging is entangled with mental realms, you just naturally abide without effort

- “Introspection” because you are looking within, inwards, paying attention to the contents of your mind rather than focusing on the external world

- “Knowing your mind” because in watching or observing your thoughts you are simply knowing the thoughts of your mind

- “Letting go” because you are just freely watching thoughts while abandoning all clinging attachments to them

- “Renunciation” because you are renouncing attachment to your thoughts by just letting them come and go without clinging, and when they die down it’s called a state of “mental poverty” since thoughts are absent (the mind is *poor* because it has few thoughts). Renunciation is not grasping or holding onto anything including thoughts or one’s life

• "Awareness" practice because you are watching your thoughts by practicing pure awareness

• "Presence" practice because in not attaching to anything and by not getting enmeshed, you are simply practicing the presence of awareness.

There are lots of ways to describe this basic meditation practice, but you're essentially just watching your mind without becoming excessively involved in your thoughts. That involvement typically gives thoughts more energy, and then you get lost in your thoughts, they start proliferating and you never find mental peace. As a result of training to become independent of your mind stream so that you just watch/know your thoughts without adding any extra energy or clinging attention to the knowing, what happens is that your wandering thoughts will always eventually calm down and disappear. This just happens. In fact, it is like a principle of science in that it *always happens.*

Now of course you must always be aware of your mind, rather than suppress it, and act as necessary when thoughts arise concerning something you must act upon. But when those thoughts depart, you don't have to hold on to them any longer. If the doorbell rings, you answer the door, but you don't keep thinking about answering the door an hour later. When you get hungry, you eat, and then you forget about it and move on.

You cannot hold your thoughts and prevent them from leaving anyway, and so the reality is that the mind you experience is always ever fresh and vibrant because thoughts never stay in your mind. They cannot stay. The actual nature of your mind is always clear and lucid but you don't know this right now because your mind is busied by thoughts. However, thoughts cannot last but must depart, and if a lot of them depart you will end up experiencing natural mental quiet and become able to see the empty quiet nature of your mind that is always there.

In truth, the real you is the root of the mind, and is basically just a functioning of bodiless awareness that sees those thoughts always going by. In this meditation practice of watching or observing thoughts, you try to be just that functioning awareness that doesn't attach to these thought streams. You try to become the pure awareness that knows thoughts by viewing your consciousness, as you always do, but without clinging to your mental mind stream (which is a bad habit you've picked up). Clinging to thoughts disturbs your mental peace, and is a wrong habit you have developed over time. You cannot hold your thoughts anyway even though you try, but you've picked up this invisible habit and it has muddied all your mental states.

HOW TO PRACTICE

The correct meditation practice of watching thoughts, called witnessing or mental observation, is like a hotel manager who just stands there watching all the guests come and go through the hotel lobby. He simply stands and watches without moving or lifting a finger. It's like a mom who sits there motionless while observing all her children run around on the playground until they become tired and come back to fall asleep on her lap. It's like standing in front of a two-lane highway, watching all the cars go by without paying particular attention to any one vehicle. For most people, however, when a car comes by with your friends inside, you will start following that particular car down the road because of interest. That's attachment or entanglement! That type of following is the wrong way to practice meditation because it represents distraction, and in becoming distracted you lose your independent sense of presence that is simply a witness. Your attention becomes fragmented because you lose sight of everything else. However, when you are engaged in any sort of meditation practice and find that you have become distracted and lost your attention, you simply accept that it happened, and then return to remaining mindful with your practice once again.

When thoughts pop up, you should never get lost in any story line that arises. You do what you have to do, but without attachment, seeing what each moment calls for. "Without attachment" means detachment, but when people hear this word they think it means that you lack normal human emotions. You always let emotions arise, such as joy or sorrow, but you just experience all things without holding. The holding cannot make them stay anyway, but people always get confused on this point.

The right way to practice vipassana meditation is just by watching your thoughts without getting involved with them. Nothing is to be done other than witness consciousness. You just observe your consciousness as if you are standing apart, like an independent third party observer. During meditation practice things will appear within your consciousness, but you remain unconcerned about them and just know them without doing anything. You refrain from grasping at them and do nothing but just watch. You just know the thoughts that appear as they appear, and of course they always depart to be replaced by new ones that you also know, witness, watch or observe without doing anything other than see them. Because you can see them, you can realize that you transcend them. You must stand or exist beyond them in order to know them. Think about this. Is this not true?

You are in a position to watch consciousness, so you cannot be consciousness. *You must be outside of consciousness to be able to know consciousness.* What is outside of consciousness, able to know thoughts, must be the real you, and you practice being just that real you during your meditation practice. The rest of the day you are always enmeshed with thoughts, and lose that sense of independence, but during meditation time you practice just being that independent awareness. Later you'll learn how to bring this capability into the real world. So like a third-person observer, you should just sit there during meditation practice and watch your thoughts or mental phenomena as they come and go, which is vipassana practice.

Thoughts will appear and depart, but you should not pay them any excessive attention as they are born and then die away in an endless stream. You are outside them, so just watch them. Stay in the stationary aloof awareness that knows them. You are separate from them so stay detached from them. The knowing of thoughts is enough. That's the correct meditation practice. Just remain in the independent awareness that transcends thoughts. You don't have to self-identify with them and somehow get entangled with mental states. Stand beyond them by just witnessing them.

What needs to arise as a thought will always arise, which is "birth," and it will depart when necessary, which is "death," so there's no reason to try to hold on to anything. For instance, you might hear a sound from outside your window and immediately know it's a bird. That thought then immediately departs, and you don't need to hold on to the concept of "bird" anymore. You know it is a bird – done! If you need to think of what you just knew, the concept of bird will arise again from your memory, so once again there is no reason to cling to anything. The right thought will arise when you need it. You just observe what you know as it arises because knowingness or recognition just naturally functions without extra work on your part, and you don't cling to any of this knowing. If you need a new thought or something from your memory, it will arise, too, and hence there is no reason to cling or attach to consciousness. You just practice being aware without any stain of mental clinging to your knowing.

You don't need energy for this type of awareness practice because awareness always is. Awareness always independently shines. Awareness is effortless, natural and inherent. It is always perfectly clear and pure and never becomes clearer or purer; purity is its nature. You don't need to do anything for awareness to exist either because you are always aware, but thoughts may or may not be present for awareness. In short, awareness is always there functioning. Primordially, fundamentally, you are essentially pure awareness that is always there, but that discussion is something we'll have to enter into later. The existence of awareness is not the issue—what you must do is stop clinging to the thoughts seen through awareness. Abide in the awareness that observes; stand apart and don't get caught up in the thoughts but preserve your independence and just know them. You always get mixed up with them and then lose the state of clear presence, which is the shining of awareness without entanglements. You want to cultivate the overriding awareness that knows all states without clinging.

During meditation you get a chance to practice this non-clinging. You want to cultivate being the ongoing clear awareness which doesn't cling to thoughts rather than spacing out and slipping into a trance, or getting lost in thoughts. People have all sorts of strange notions that they should be cultivating unusual mental states during meditation, but you are only *cultivating your ordinary mind.* Your ordinary mind of awareness is always there, but we are always engaged in clinging to thoughts, and that tends to obscure the abiding awareness which is always clear. As we let go of clinging to thoughts, our mental realm will become less sticky and more vivid, empty, lucid, and clear. The empty clarity of awareness never changes due to meditation, but the size of the mental realm seems as if it gets larger.

The cultivation path of meditation practice is therefore very ordinary, practical, natural and humanistic. You just remain in your clear awareness and witness the workings of your mind without becoming attached or entangled with those streams of consciousness and mental functions. It is really simple to do, and so simple that you will wonder why there can be courses on meditation if the instructions are so simple.

There is no religion or theology to this. There is just the fact that in witnessing without attachment, attachments to thoughts will melt away, thoughts will slowly clear out, and your mind will gradually empty out its busyness to become clear. You are not creating a new mind, but just uncovering the ordinary mind which is already there, perfectly pure and clear underneath all the wandering mental noise. Hence, you are not creating anything new in the process of meditation but just observing your mind, and by so doing you will eventually discover what's already there as your underlying base of consciousness when enough thought volume departs. That base of consciousness, beneath thoughts, is always peaceful, empty and pure, and free of sorrows and concerns.

Let me describe this process of meditation in another way. There is nothing strange going on during meditation except you are learning to relax your habitual tendency to cling to mental states, and from doing this your mental realm will gradually empty out of all sorts of random thoughts running about. You don't even know that you are always clinging to (getting lost in or following) mental states because the habit has become so ingrained that's its nearly unnoticeable, but you discover it is there after you do a lot of meditation. Once you truly practice letting go of thoughts because you just witness them without interfering with them, then you can slowly dissolve this incorrect habit of clinging. That's what brings all the positive changes reported of meditation. Our tendency to hold on to thoughts binds up the chi flow throughout our body, and this also affects our mental business and mental purity.

You may not realize it, but you are always becoming lost in mental engagements and trapped within your own thought streams. When you learn how to free yourself from this entanglement of your own creation, not only will your chi change and body transform, but you can eventually realize a substrate of clear awareness that is beneath all that activity.

What underlies the mind of mentation as a final substrate is pure awareness, witnessing, or pure consciousness. There is an underlying (or we could say "transcendental" since it transcends or is beyond thoughts) capability of knowing that is absent of thought appearances. This capacity for knowing doesn't have any phenomenal substance for its body, essence or nature. It is not energy, because that is something phenomenal, but is more akin to an unborn potential that transcends the entire realm of the phenomenal which can appear within it. It is just an insubstantial clear functioning – that is essentially what pure consciousness or pure awareness is – that within its nature reflects things that themselves lack any true substantial existence. Awareness is the purest consciousness that is empty of all content, but pure consciousness can know thought-consciousness as a transient reflection, manifestation, or appearance within itself. The appearances of consciousness arise within it, and this is what it can know. That knowing is happening to consciousness itself, which is the subject, object and perceiving, so the ultimate underlying substrate is, in a way, just talking to itself. In another sense we can say that nothing is really happening at all. Nothing true is really arising or vanishing.

Awareness always remains pure and clean, and can never be made more pure. It is pure by nature, and this purity can never be changed. Upon its empty screen, or empty nature, thought appearances come and go. That empty pure awareness never changes, however, but always remains unmoving, pure and clear. Nothing ever truly happens to the absolute nature of knowing, which remains pure and free and undisturbed throughout all this. The best simile is that it's like a mirror in that it always remains clean and unaffected by the images which appear within it. Just as a mirror reflects images, pure awareness allows thoughts to arise within it and generate knowing. When the moon becomes reflected in water the moon does not get wet and the water doesn't break or get disturbed in any way. This is how pristine awareness functions as regards its ability to host mental appearances.

It is hard to explain this, but the inherent emptiness of awareness and its non-difference from the realm of interdependent origination is a fact that you discover through advanced spiritual practice. To get to the stage where you can realize this you must practice witnessing meditation, which means watching your mind during meditation practice as if you were an aloof independent observer. You rest or abide in the awareness that transcends thoughts and just watch them pass by. In other words, you abide in your (empty) knowingness nature itself, which is not any type of substance, and observe the thoughts arising in your mind. You don't try to be a separate entity that watches, but just let go of thoughts as they arise while still knowing them.

This underlying knowingness capability of life is sometimes described as natural, fundamental, original or primordial clarity, vividness, awareness or illumination and this is what allows you to actually experience all the appearances in your mind. This is why there is this thing called life rather than an inert existence or primal nothingness. We have sentient life in the universe because there is this illuminating power of the original nature that produces consciousness, and within the realm of consciousness appears personal consciousness. This natural illumination or pristine fundamental awareness underlying consciousness is what life, in the ultimate sense, is. The original nature of ours is pure consciousness – what we call pristine awareness—and all of Creation, manifestation or reality is also only That. The universe of matter is also nothing else other than what it is made of – this pure consciousness that is not a substance or anything phenomenal. The essence of the universe is insubstantial, empty pure awareness. The appearances that arise within your consciousness are also, in essence, that awareness. This fundamental awareness, in turn, is a function or characteristic of the absolute nature or fundamental essence of the universe.

The appearances within your mind are actually of the same substance as the mind itself — consciousness-stuff — and you can actually realize this underlying empty substrate nature of the mind when mental clinging becomes absolutely and perfectly zero so that random wandering thoughts die down. Thoughts still arise, but the volume of wandering random thoughts decreases. If you learn how to just observe thoughts with the always independent awareness, and without having your attention getting sucked into and then entangled with the thought stream, that is proper meditation practice. That is what you try to practice with vipassana. Eventually, by practicing awareness on this present moment only through the initial vehicle of watching thoughts without getting lost in them, the rushing stream of thoughts eventually stops and you find true peace by always being in the moment.

Hence, like a dispassionate hotel manager who is constantly watching the scenery of his hotel lobby, meditation trains you to attain a proficiency in maintaining clear ordinary awareness. The proficiency is that you don't become attached to the things appearing in your mind. They appear, and you act on them as when required, but you sever a long ingrained habitual attachment of clinging to the thought streams of consciousness (by getting entangled with them) and losing your state of clear presence. You do not dwell on anything because all thoughts are gone forever. You are always mindful of the present moment. There is nothing to control because thoughts and feelings leave anyway. Hence, in not dwelling you become more vibrant and alive. Nothing actually changes from meditation practice except that a tendency for sticky mental holding departs, and your mind becomes more open, empty and free. Your mental realm becomes more vivid, clear and seemingly larger. You learn how to be *in this moment only, which is the only moment that exists.* These are the benefits of practice.

You can always, of course, hold a thought in your mind when you want to, such as holding an image of your mother if you want to think of her picture in your mind. This is called concentration. The act of concentration, or holding the mind on one point/topic, is exercising a function of the mind and you never try to destroy the mind's functioning capabilities. You just try to destroy the tendency of getting blindly sucked into wandering thought streams and mental states through clinging attachments, but that doesn't mean to give up the functioning capabilities of the mind such as being able to abide in some topic when you need to concentrate. You are basically, with meditation practice, learning how to properly use this functional equipment called consciousness or the mind. You've grown up with a mind, but no one has ever bothered to teach you how to properly use its functions, and now you are starting to learn how to fully, effectively, skillfully and properly use this thing called consciousness that you have. This is what you learn though meditation practice. You can start clearing out some cobwebs so that you use the mind properly.

Therefore, you always let thoughts arise, you always let the mind give birth to thoughts, but you should rest in the transcending awareness that knows the thoughts rather than get tied up and enmeshed with the thoughts themselves. In that way, by staying detached as the witness, you will never lose your independent bearing.

As previously explained, to "be detached" doesn't mean you won't ever get angry, sad, elated or delighted in response to situations. It doesn't mean you won't ever yell at people or feel sorry or regret. It doesn't mean emotions disappear or should be suppressed. All the natural emotions that arise will and should arise, for that's natural. Bad emotional reactions might not arise if those habits become purified, but the purification of emotions is a different issue entirely. This is an issue of not mentally clinging to the contents of consciousness or trying to suppress them, which you must not do. That clinging does not add anything positive to the situation, but actually produces suffering.

Sometimes it's the feelings generated by the body that you become attached to during meditation such as internal energies and the pressures and sensations involved with them. You get focused on them, and then start playing with them and push them here or there, forgetting the fact that you should just know they are there and leave them alone. That's watching them instead of following them or getting entangled with them. We especially feel the borders of the physical body all the time, and tend to feel the energies inside the skull when we are thinking. Because we feel those energies when thinking, and because they move with our thoughts, we start to identify with the body as our self. You will eventually stop feeling these kinds of inner tensions as your chi channels all open, but the initial enemy is the habit of "dropping into the body" and clinging to its various states of transformation, playing with them and taking them as your self.

Usually the body is feeding your mind with so much sensory input, such as physical sensations, that this input simply monopolizes consciousness. With so much of this input always there, you tend to lose your bearings and mistakenly take the body as your self. You overly identify with the body and take it as "you." The body becomes the "I" and the "I" is then only the size of the body. You become blinded to the fact that your true self is awareness which is actually non-local, everywhere, formless and boundless. Awareness is actually possible for everywhere and everything, but that capability has become screened by the habit of attaching to the body and clinging to its small related consciousness as the self.

Everything you see, feel, smell, hear, and taste appear as experiences within your personal consciousness. They are appearances within consciousness, or consciousness appearances. Call them thoughts, call them appearances, call them consciousness or states – it's all the same thing. They are the objects, thoughts, marks, signs, appearances or phenomena of consciousness. They are consciousness-stuff.

Now to know consciousness, you must already be beyond it. Since the world you see is just your consciousness – which means it is mind-only – the real you must be transcending the world and your limited mind. Since your consciousness can encompass the whole world, so the real you must also transcend this world. This is what the sages tell us, but it is something we must prove through the results of meditation practice rather than just accept because of the logic or because of blind faith.

For us, however, the conventional world is here right in front of us. How do we handle the daily challenges of the mind and body? You basically maintain detachment from thoughts and sensations and just let them come and go, and then because of that non-clinging, they will eventually die down. Your random wandering thoughts that busy your mind will go away and your body sensations will decline as the chi in your body changes, *if you let this all happen*. You can put an instant stop to this process of purification if you simply start attaching to thoughts again. Attachment, or mental clinging, is the enemy.

When you start to let go of thoughts, at first internal body sensations may increase as various energies start to arise within your body and try to open your energy channels. After they open, the sensations will die down again and the body, which will now be in better shape since its internal energy channels will have opened, won't be as much of a distracting obstacle to your mental objective of becoming clear and peaceful. So don't thwart the process because you think those internal energy sensations are a disturbance. You need those processes to continue to open your chi channels, and transform your physical body, so that it no longer represents an obstacle or burden on the path.

When you meditate, the chi of your body will start to transform as your channels open and your consciousness purifies (empties out). In short, your chi will purify as your mind becomes quieter. Your internal chi flow, which is linked to your consciousness, will eventually stop being jumpy and irregular. Meditation will help you achieve a smoother circulation of chi that leads to deep relaxation, physical softness and health, mental calmness and quiet. As mentioned, due to meditation your chi channels will start to open because when you stop holding on to thoughts, the chi that runs through your energy channels can then start to reassert its natural circulation, and the lack of circulatory diversion due to thoughts will allow many shunted channels to finally open.

This explains part of the process and why it happens, although the full explanation of the process is much more complicated. Actually, all you need to know is that when you let go of thoughts, your mind will calm. When your mind calms, or quiets, the real chi of your body will arise. That rising chi will then open up your internal energy channels. When your channels open, your chi flow will then become smoother. As your chi flow becomes smoother, your mind will become more peaceful, empty or even and you will find mental peace. Why this all happens because you start to let go of thoughts is something science may one day discover, but for now you only need to know the result and try to attain it through meditation practice.

It takes a certain devotion to practice effort to get good at meditation and start achieving these results, but the better that you learn how to just watch your mind with detachment, the quicker you can learn how to relax and reach a new level of clarity and mental freedom that is 100% perfectly natural, effortless and uncontrived. Why does it become effortless and natural? Because your chi channels eventually open so your chi flow becomes more natural and harmonious. The scattered mind of wandering thoughts will also die down through meditation practice so in time you will also attain a peaceful empty mind that is free of stress, anxieties and worries. All you need to do is simply start watching your mental processes – consciousness or thoughts – without becoming entangled with them. View them as if you are a detached, third person observer. That is the meditation practice of watching your mind, or Meditation 101.

When people ask how they should meditate, that's the basic practice you need to teach them. People think meditation is some mysterious process, but you can teach anybody how to meditate in just one or two minutes by telling them how to watch thoughts without holding onto them. You're just watching your thoughts instead of playing with them, getting caught up with them, or deliberately using them to create something or arrive at a decision.

All those things are the activities, functions or capabilities of the mind, but during meditation practice you just watch your thoughts and remain in the clear awareness that lets you know them. You just know them or witness them without holding. Period. In time, meditation brings internal peace if you learn how to do this correctly. Meditation doesn't cost any money, and it doesn't take a lot of time to learn. It just takes the time of practicing inner witnessing once you've gotten the instructions. However, few people want to practice meditation. That's the problem! They want the results, but they want them instantly and so they don't want to practice. The problem is, meditation involves breaking a habit, and that takes time and the effort of practice. Meditation can bring countless benefits to your life, but like anything else beneficial that you want in life, the hurdle is to make its practice into a daily habit so you can eventually gain those results.

THE BENEFITS OF MEDITATION

Because of your habit of mentally clinging to thoughts and getting overly entangled with them, it's very hard to reach a mental state of peace and tranquility where your thought flow has diminished. This tendency to cling has developed over time and is nothing more than the wrong use of the mind. The true origins of the problem, it is said, come from the accumulated bad habits of countless past lives. Dissolving this long term habit brings peace, physical comfort and other countless benefits, but you cannot reach a state of internal peace, quiet, tranquility, calmness, emptiness, halting, cessation, or quiescence until you actually start letting go of thoughts.

Meditation allows you to break the habit of mentally clinging because you observe your thoughts without attaching to them, and you thereby always just live in the genuine present moment. A thought is there – it's gone. Another thought is there – it's gone. If you never cling to a single thought in this flow, or the flow itself, you are always in the present moment living fully and freely. You are always in the state of present mind rather than getting lost in thought. And because you know the thoughts that appear and depart, you are always in a state of clarity. This is pure meditation practice, and also the right way to live. That's why we practice meditation, and why it is a spiritual practice, too.

The added benefit of doing this (watching without attachments) is that wandering thoughts which busy the mind eventually stop appearing over time, and your mind becomes continually clear and stable without random clutter. Your true mind is always clear but you don't know this yet because the volume of wandering thoughts screens this realization, and you get confused by that volume or by the type of thoughts that arise. You always are entangled with following thoughts, so you never become able to recognize the true clarity nature of your mind even though it is this underlying pure clarity of the mind that always lets you know thoughts in the first place. That clarity never disappears, but we say it becomes "dimmed," polluted or obscured by thought attachments, which is just a colloquial way of speaking.

Once you start learning how to let go of your thoughts that arise in your mind (and thoughts includes emotions, passions and desires, etc.), then your consciousness will start to pacify and become calm. We say it empties out, which just means it calms down because the volume of wandering thoughts decreases. When your consciousness quiets down because the volume of these thoughts dies down, your chi will start to arise within your body. It's just a natural process that always happens, and we need not know why. We only need to know that it always happens and recognize when it does because that event proves our progress.

When your chi arises, it will start clearing out your chi channels, and this often produces various physical phenomena and sensations that I have summarized in many other books. Because of this chi and channel purification, your mind will in turn get clearer. This is because your consciousness is connected with your chi flow, and that chi flow is now more smooth and clear. Accordingly, your consciousness will become more equanimous, or quieter, since (for the non-enlightened or ordinary person) your mental state is always connected with the state of your chi. This process of progressive purification, of both your chi and mind, will always improve in gradual stages as you make further progress with your meditation practice.

The more you let go, the more you will feel the energy arise in your body and start to open up your inner chi channels, and the more progress you will make. Everyone gets startled when they first start feeling this energy, which is the real chi of your body. Specifically, it is the yang chi of your body which the Hindus call *prana* or *kundalini* energy. Other religions call it by different names, but these are the most well-known terms. The arousal of this inner energy, which is your life force, is a natural process that will only commence when you stop holding on to thoughts and reach a state of mental quiet. Mental busyness and mental clinging interferes with the body's natural chi flows and prevents the real energies of health and transformation from arising.

This chi of yours which arises due to meditation is your *true life force*. This is the real spiritual force of transformation which is inside all sentient beings. When you let the body's natural chi flow start to reassert itself once again due to the practice of non-clinging, that natural chi flow will not only end up quieting your mind, but open up your chi channels and transform your physical body. That's why you get healthier and begin to feel states of mental and physical bliss. It all comes from this life force flowing through your chi channel circulations.

Confucius explained that if you shine awareness on your mind, your thoughts will eventually stop. Hence his method of spiritual practice, or meditation, is sometimes called introspection practice (since you are always inspecting or watching the mind) and is just like Buddhist mindfulness practice or cessation-witnessing practice. Confucius taught that you should always remain mindful of your thoughts, meaning that you should always keep awareness on your thinking process. By watching your thinking process as a third person observer who can dispassionately evaluate it, you will know what is good or bad to do, and wandering thoughts will calm down.

Because of that calming, stillness or quiet, Confucius also said that you will eventually experience physical bliss and mental tranquility, and your wisdom and clear knowing will eventually arise if you continue to cultivate and maintain these states. This is the same sequence of meditation progress as described by everyone else and occurs because your chi starts to arise.

Basically, if you just purify mental afflictions and negative tendencies of the mind, the resultant purity you achieve by watching your mind and behavior will eventually produce profound meditation experiences. First thoughts will calm down. After they sufficiently calm down, you will eventually be able to realize the transcending clear awareness that is always there behind your mind – which is not a thought itself – that knows thoughts. If one can "stop at" or center oneself in that clear purity, and abide in that clear purity of awareness without falling into thoughts, then after a while thoughts will calm down and you can reach a very high meditation state called "*samadhi*."

When you try to remain as the pure witnessing which stands behind the mind, allowing you to know thoughts/consciousness, you will eventually attain calmness and detachment. If you "abide" as the transcending awareness rather than get entangled in the thought streams of consciousness, you will eventually become totally free of thoughts and will then never be tempted by them. In other words, you will become able to see everything that appears in your mind but never fall into those thoughts, and thus you will always remain independent, calm, serene, peaceful and content. This is how one finds the truest, highest, purest peace and contentment promised by meditation.

Confucius, of course, is not the only one who taught people how to meditate by watching their mind. Watching your thoughts is a standard practice in Buddhism called mindfulness practice, and the Tientai school specializes in emphasizing cessation-observation practice, which is similar to this technique. The "cessation" means that thoughts will stop simply from watching them (without getting involved with them). "Observation" refers to the act of witnessing your mind/thoughts, which is maintaining an independent awareness of them without getting sucked in. The calming or quieting of thoughts that results from mindfully watching consciousness is due to the basic principles we have just gone over.

SEVERAL WESTERN APPROACHES

This basic practice of watching your thoughts was also something that many Jesuits would practice as part of their religious efforts, and it is the basis of much of Eastern Orthodox Christian spiritual practice as well. All the world's various religions want to teach people how to calm their minds and reduce their errant behaviors, so they typically teach this type of cessation-observation practice in one form or another. You simply watch, witness or observe your thoughts and then they eventually die down, or cease. When the mind becomes quiet then your chi energies will arise, and then your spiritual progress is on its way! This type of meditation practice is available everywhere, but whether or not people use these practices is another issue entirely.

Religions also commonly offer other ways for people to cultivate peaceful minds, wherein there is a reduction in wandering thoughts, using various means such as reciting prayers when done in the right way. Yet, most people don't understand the proper principles of practice, or the fact that the final objective is that of mental calming, and thus they rarely achieve the benefits that are intended. Only the saints, who were cultivating all the time, seemed to secure the benefits but most of them were never instructed in these basic principles of practice. If many saints had these instructions available, they could have achieved the same results, and in far less time, even if they were lay practitioners like you and me.

Christian Eastern Orthodox teachings along these lines are especially instructive because they maintain that it is common for negative thought forms to assault the human mind, and if you enter into an interaction with them (for example, an inner dialogue such as "nothing will happen if I do this just once to try it"), they can take hold of you. When you give in to such temptations, this is called a *stage of consent* which leads to an addiction to certain types of troublesome thought forms. If you cannot free yourself from such urges, they can become a habit and then you can become the captive of the habit, repeating it over and over again. This is how addictions start, and how you become captive of certain types of wrong thinking that can control you. If you are not careful, as Confucius warned us to be with mindfulness, a thought form can become a passion or obsession that is destructive to you and others.

This warning not only applies to such habits as drinking, gambling, watching internet pornography, smoking, overeating, drugs, shoplifting and so forth, but to personality characteristics and errant misbehaviors such as anger, envy, pride, laziness and so on. Meditation is one of the absolute best ways, but not the only way, to therefore help decrease these bad behaviors because we are always policing our mind through watchfulness, and can therefore cut some of these errors off before they go too far.

The Eastern Orthodox Church also teaches us how to cut off *logismos* (negative thought forms) once they've taken hold of an individual, and calls this the *spiritual practice of purification*. In other spiritual schools or traditions, it is also explained that you are purifying your consciousness, thoughts, or mind. Hence, everywhere we find teachings for the common objective of mental pacification/purification so that we can be free of bothersome thoughts, wandering thoughts, the busy mind, monkey mentation or however you wish to word it. You want to cut off bothersome or troublesome thoughts to be able to find peace, and so as Confucius explained, you start by practicing internal witnessing which will eventually loosen their hold on you.

In the Eastern Orthodox Church, spiritual elders explain that you should always protect yourself from negative thought forms, or *logismos,* that want to enter your mind and take root, just as Confucius explained. You watch your mind, or monitor your mind, so that they don't take root. This, then, is not just meditation but a type of spiritual practice. You must police your mind with awareness to prevent this danger, and those instructions overlap with the methodology of Confucian meditation practice as well as the mindfulness and cessation-observation methods espoused within Buddhism for cutting off negative thoughts, desires and emotions. Once again, people are basically employing the same practices the world over with tiny differences here and there.

These Western methods for mental purification, or *catharsis*, therefore mirror those used in the East, and they start with the process of awareness. The basic method of practice is to watch your mind and ignore a *logismos* that might arise, such as a desire to do something foolish or errant, by treating it with indifference. You simply disregard it when it enters the mind, and then it will quickly depart because that's what happens with all thoughts that you ignore. Colloquially speaking, we say you "pay it no mind" or "pay it no special attention" and thus it departs. That's basically what you do during witnessing meditation by refusing to become attached; by just watching, in time the stream of thoughts within the mind transforms to leave an empty scenario that's peaceful and pure.

Another method is to use logic or wisdom analysis to defeat an arising *logismos*. With this technique you apply reasoning to the thought form so that you can dissociate from its attractive pull. Buddhism suggests this method, too, such as by remembering the consequences that will happen if you give in to what seems an attractive idea. You look at the *logismos*, consider it with wisdom, and in that way you can free yourself of its influence so that it departs.

You can use other methods to cut off bothersome thoughts, too, when these other methods don't work. You already know of one technique, which is to redirect or occupy the mind by reciting mantras. With witnessing meditation practice you simply watch them and observe them carefully without attaching to them, and in time even the most troublesome will depart. You don't have to act on a thought, but just know a thought is there because of your awareness, cognizance or attention. That's enough, and it will eventually leave unless you hold on to it or start following it.

Another method of *catharsis* is to switch the focus of your attention to something more interesting, challenging, compelling, or distracting when a thought bothers you. You try to busy your mind with something else other than that thought. You counter the attraction of the thought by shifting the focus of attention to something different, substituting it as the new object of attention. That new focus might be something that requires one-pointed absorption such as prayer, or even physical work, or sport. It doesn't matter what you shift the focus of attention to as long as you move your mind's attention from being centered on the bothersome thought. In essence, you cut off the process of clinging to that thought by shifting the focus of attention to something different.

Some Western psychologists have even come up with a psychological model of behavioral change, called the "transtheoretical model of behavior change," which can also help us understand how to detach from addictive thoughts and habits via a "scientific process." You can find it in the popular book, *Changing for Good.*

According to this model, if you finally want to change behavior that comes from errant thought habits that continually arise, that desire initiates a stage called "Contemplation" where you finally recognize the problematic nature of your behavior, as well as its pros and cons. Prior to this you don't even know there is a need for change, so the recognition of the need for change requires awareness. Everything starts with awareness, and without cultivating awareness it is impossible to change your mind and behavior. You must always be cultivating awareness in some form or another.

After acknowledging your problem and the desire to change, next the process of "Preparation" can begin where you start to take small steps toward transforming your behavior. The following stage, called "Action," is where you start working on actually transforming your behavior in a substantial way, and change starts to be noticed. You must then work on "Maintenance" to prevent relapse, and in the stage of "Termination" the problem does not arise anymore. If you succeed in cutting off the errant thought habits that create improper behaviors, success means there is eventually zero temptation to indulge in the old thought habits. The thoughts are gone, never arise, or present no attractiveness, and that is the stage of Termination.

The whole idea of this process, as well as its policing and maintenance, revolves around the idea that *you need to become aware of your problem and monitor/watch your mind to effect change in your life.* In coming up with this procedural scheme the modern scientists didn't use the same terms employed by Confucius, Buddhism, or the Eastern Orthodox Church, but the entire solution they discovered revolves around awareness and mindfulness practice once again. Basically, even Western science has discovered that focused awareness inhibits automatic thoughts through subcortical circuits underlying attention, and hence mindfulness practice helps you change your behavior.

Whether we are talking about Eastern or Western methods, awareness, which comes from watching your mind and its contents, is the key to changing your behavior and transforming your life. The process of behavioral change requires the mindful introspection, policing or watching of your mind. Whether you talk of Buddhist cessation-witnessing practice, Eastern Orthodox practice for freeing yourself from *logismos,* Confucian introspection or mindfulness practice, Christian contemplation practice, or any other technique, they all involve monitoring your thoughts with what you and I are now calling meditative awareness.

Sages have even taught us that this very basic practice of always introspectively watching our minds can actually help us change our karmic fortune. For instance, this teaching is found in the famous Chinese story of Liao Fan which has spawned dozens of copycat versions throughout the centuries because of its uplifting message. Liao Fan was a Chinese man who lamented his poor fortune in life, but admitted that part of his problem was due to the fact that he had a quick temper, talked too much, stayed out too late, and drank too heavily. However, by using mantra practice to calm his mind in conjunction with mental mindfulness practice of the sort just mentioned, he was able to change his fortune for the better.

Meditation practice can definitely produce the ability to change our lives and fortunes, but we normally do not notice this since we do not know what would have happened had our thoughts and behaviors not changed. We usually have no way to directly connect the results of our meditation practice to our karma, life or fortune (however you want to word it), but meditation does have a positive effect in these arenas if it helps us change our behavior. It is just that this effect is hard to measure since we have no comparison stick. However, just as we know that "character is destiny," we can definitely know that meditation and other cultivation efforts that allow us to become healthier, police our thoughts, and abide in peaceful mental states will have a positive effect on our life. Those results would not happen otherwise and those benefits would work their way into our behavior thus certainly affecting the results we reap.

The Autobiography of Benjamin Franklin also relates how this great American, perhaps the greatest of Americans, would watch his thoughts and behavior every day in order to try to cut off behavioral errors and become a better human being. Franklin's set of incredible life achievements are partially due to his mindfulness approach to self-perfection which was based on these very same principles of meditation.

As a businessman, Franklin set up the first media conglomerate of printing and newspaper franchises across the United States; as a scientist he discovered electricity, charted the Gulf stream and conceived of Daylight savings time; as an inventor he developed bifocals and the Franklin stove; as an author he wrote the bestselling *Poor Richard's Almanac* which is still selling today; as a citizen he participated in many acts of merit such as founding the first American public library, the first fire department, and the first nonsectarian university; as a civil servant serving as Postmaster General, he revolutionized the delivery of US mail; as a diplomat he secured the American treaty with France which helped secure the success of the American Revolutionary War; and as a politician he became the only Founding Father to sign all four major documents of America's founding (the Declaration of Independence, the Constitution, the alliance with France and the peace treaty with Britain). All these accomplishments, and more, were due in part to his famous mindfulness or awareness practice of watching his thoughts and behavior that he wrote about in his autobiography. He used a special version of mindfulness practice to transform his behavior from bad to good, just as Confucius had recommended, and reaped countless rewards in the process. He left us this motivational story in his autobiography, and encouraged us to duplicate his technique.

The mindfulness practice he employed of monitoring his mind and behavior – as Confucius and Liao Fan and others have all recommended – can help you become a great man or woman in life because the technique is the basis of all self-improvement, self-perfection, self-actualization, and self-achievement techniques. Benjamin Franklin's example clearly shows that a life of great accomplishment results from the incorporation of mindfulness (mental watching or awareness) practice into your daily habits. It is something you need to schedule into your life every day, like bathing, and then slowly make into a constant habitual behavior as your mind becomes progressively more pure. You simply constantly watch your mind (known as "shining attention" on your mind) and know clearly what you are doing rather than become lost in thought and lose yourself.

As a third person observer who always watches what he is doing, you prevent great errors this way. Franklin did this while going about his daily activities, but in meditation practice you first learn how to do this by sitting down in a cross-legged posture to watch your mind, and later you learn how to bring that clear awareness into the regular world and integrate it with your daily activities.

THE NECESSITY OF PRACTICAL WISDOM AND KNOWING WHEN TO STOP

Because most people are familiar with the religions of the East, they usually correctly assume that the ultimate or highest possible goal of meditation practice is to become spiritually enlightened, which is to become a Buddha, sage, *jnani*, master, or self-realized one. However, they have strange notions as to what to expect as the characteristics of a Buddha, or enlightened one. They always imagine a person along the lines of a marbled Greek statue of perfect form, without flaws, who does not fart or shit, enjoy a dirty joke, forget names, eat meat, smoke cigarettes, drink alcohol, get angry, enjoy sex or need money to survive.

People usually hold strange, idealistic religious notions of what it means to be awakened, as if the laws of physics and the necessities of human living suddenly ceased functioning for such people. As my teacher explained, these are mistaken notions held by people of little wisdom and experience. The ignorant commonly hold naïve and impractical notions that do not reflect the real nature of things in many areas of life. If you pursue the path of meditation, you must learn to ground your thinking in solid realities. You don't want to champion fantastic flights of the imagination, but simply need to learn how to quiet your mind and function more effectively in the everyday world that will always exist around you. In mastering meditation you can indeed develop more mental powers, but in effect you are learning how to purify and then better use that consciousness we call your mind.

To be clear, an enlightened individual is just like you or me in everyday behavior, but is usually more wise and compassionate in what they do and how they respond. Most of all, they have penetrated through to the root source of body and mind, and know that he/she is actually the original nature rather than the false self veneer of the personality or body. They may have more mental capabilities than you or I because of that, but this is no reason to expect miraculous interventions from their presence. How would you ever know anyway? All you can say is that their words, thoughts and deeds then flow out of that unity (or "recognition") that they are the original Self of us all, and their actions and teachings try to help us also attain enlightenment and alleviate us of our sufferings.

An enlightened individual can be poor or rich. He or she can be a king or queen, general, politician, merchant, artist, athlete, banker, scholar, plumber, policeman, singer or even a prostitute. Anything is possible because no occupation conflicts with reality; occupations just have different consequences or outcomes, that's all. My teacher often said that a Buddha is most definitely like a prostitute because he or she has to hear things they don't want to hear, say things they don't want to say, and do things they don't want to do. They are like a medical doctor who takes on all the problems of others, so he or she gets sick all the time while in the activity of exercising boundless wisdom and compassion to help others. Just because someone attains enlightenment doesn't mean they don't get sick or don't have feelings because "they are empty."

Those individuals with immature ideas who expect the spiritually accomplished to behaviorally conform to their own limited notions cannot possibly understand all of this, or what the enlightened want to accomplish in the world, or the techniques they use to do so. What an enlightened person is, and the way they act, will almost certainly go against the expectations of the crowd. They do what they must to get things done even when that behavior goes against the expectations of the overly religious.

My teacher often explained that a Buddha should actually be compared to a unified combination of a hero, saint, mafioso and robber. Yes, the characteristics of a real enlightened individual in the world can be compared to a mafia don and thief because of what they must sometimes do to help cut off evil and encourage the good to prosper!

Selfless in their mind they are, but that does not mean that their actions on the surface might not seem absent of self-interest, calculation or contradictions. They are what they are and do what they must do as required by the situation, and have a compassionate vision they wish to accomplish which they achieve through endless varieties of skillful means. They have boundless wisdom and compassion in their mind, and always act with virtue as their intent because they know that there are karmic consequences to all actions. Nevertheless, with great vision they act as they must to do whatever needs to be accomplished for the greater good. At times, that may even mean that hurt and harm comes to some individuals, such as when the government raises taxes, for there is rarely such a thing as an action that does not harm someone or something in some way. Every action has consequences, and there is no such thing in worldly affairs as purely good behavior. Even the sun has sunspots, so it is almost impossible to find a perfectly pure action, circumstance or situation that does not hurt someone.

The key is that they skillfully and compassionately play the part of the role they assume, and know all of their own thoughts and intentions clearly so as to act on those which are best for the situation. If a Buddha becomes a king, his responsibilities to his country might result in a declaration of war, or all sorts of other things that people would not expect because they are ruled by religious notions rather than a correct appraisal of reality. In fact, if most people were to peek behind the screens as to what goes on at the very top of orthodox religious structures, they would be shocked at the inordinate concerns over politics, power and money flows they would discover. It's never as pure as people imagine it to be.

Even if you do not achieve the ultimate goal of spiritual enlightenment from the mindfulness meditation practice of watching your thoughts — which you can also call the practice of awareness, witnessing or presence — you can certainly use it to positively change your behavior and become a better human being. This is what everyone wants to do, isn't it?

As Aristotle might argue, you can use this type of practice to become more virtuous. As Benjamin Franklin said when he wrote about this practice, he had the satisfaction of seeing small errors in his behavior disappear, big ones reduced, and seeing virtuous ways become second nature from this technique. He said that he was a happier and better man than he otherwise would have been for having used it to improve his life.

This type of inner watching is the basis of Meditation 101, which is to sit quietly and watch your thoughts during meditation practice, and then to eventually bring the practice of introspection or mindfulness in daily life. This is something we need to teach to our children and society as a whole to prevent large mistakes in individual behavior all the way up to errors in grand policy and grand strategy. Yes, we must teach this because when we are planning for posterity, we must remember that virtue is not hereditary. By practicing introspection and awareness, we help avoid the tragedy of self-deception that in aggregate can topple nations. A society that is centered on the idea of self-improvement, advancement and avoiding errors is a society that will blossom within a generation, but it needs the individuals within it to know how to inspect their minds and fathom the results of their actions and behavior.

The way to generate merit for the meditation path is the following. If you see that some good actions should be performed that are not being done, then do them. Always do what is undone that you know should be done, and always support the ongoing efforts of virtuous deeds that are currently being carried out. Rather than thwart them or ignore them, give them aid rather than throw up obstructions or indifference. Most people are passive rather than vigorous in the support of goodness and virtue, but this is what you should be if you want goodness and virtue to grow within society.

On the other hand, if you see evil or error being done by yourself or by those under your influence, you must immediately try to cut it off. If you see it being done by an overarching power over which you have some authority, act to cut it off before it becomes a problem too big to handle. The problem of going too far, of extending oneself past what is reasonable, is the problem of greediness, arrogance, over-extension, inappropriateness or hubris that commonly topples both individuals and nations. To prevent the tendency of going too far we must certainly practice mental introspection. It is like learning meditation to cut off thoughts. We must learn to watch our thoughts to know when to stop and then stop afflictive activities from continuing and growing stronger.

Our typical failing is that we never try to prevent evil or error from arising in the first place. We must try to arrange circumstances so that errant ways are never born, for the best solution is always prevention rather than cure. That is why governments create systems of checks and balances. One must institute safeguards to prevent extremes, checks and balances to prevent flights of fancy, and we must always fight for what is right by immediately opposing injustice before it takes hold, grows and becomes too strong. Otherwise, having done nothing to object to what is wrong, you will live in shame for not having opposed the errant that will eventually grow to become a situation usurping all.

To oppose evil, one must act with wisdom and adjust oneself to the time and circumstances. If change is possible, you must act in the face of potential failure while ignoring the possibility of failure. This is the necessary discipline of right living. You must never think the opposing force is too big ("so why bother?"), but act to cut something off as soon as you see what is errant, and act to curb what you can after it has already arisen. If you do not, the circumstances in which you live will never be conducive to justice and good living. Just as evil starts small before it grows larger, opposition that is truly just starts small and collects adherents as it grows, and when righteous it often blazes. The failure to act to cut off evil or errors you see being done around you actually means acceptance and complicity.

The world has seen so much evil because good men failed to act. Good men that were clean themselves wished to remain clean, and therefore stayed away from the actions and efforts necessary to stop the advancement of the wrongs they saw growing. They did not generate the resolve and energy to do what was right, which was to correct the wrong and prevent evil from growing. It is a general principle that "evil prevails when good men fail to act," and this is because virtuous men, desiring to maintain their personal purity and peace, stay removed and failed to forgo their selfishness for the common good. They wished to be left alone, and evil thereby grew to encompass all because of inaction.

It is a human responsibility to sacrifice one's peace, purity and complacency to prevent evil from gaining sway in societies, otherwise evil will indeed grow and sacrifice you after its ascendancy. When good men fail to prevent evil from arising in the first place, especially within government systems, it is usually not because they were blind to the danger, but because they did not raise their voices in unison to object to it during its infancy. They did not immediately nip it in the bud and stop it from growing further, and that complacency allowed evil powers to expand until they detrimentally dominated the lives of men. The failure to oppose evil is actually due to selfishness, namely the idea that "I don't want to be bothered to exercise my civic duty. Please give this problem to someone else to handle."

In this light, within our modern age of democratic republics it is our duty and obligation to keep bad government from growing and gaining control. We must employ independent thinking away from groupthink to consider what is right, and then remain vigilant to prevent actions from overreaching and going too far. Those actions, if left unchecked, tend to accumulate and in time topple the entire system. Governments always seek unnecessary control over their citizens, and are easily corrupted by moneyed interests who try to bend them to their will against the general welfare of the people. This type of corrupting influence usually gives rise to incredibly bad policies, and then those policies end up corrupting the entire system, sometimes bringing it to its end.

When a citizen sees this and raises his or her voice, this is an example of the Confucian principle of *knowing when to stop* to prevent things from going too far, and acting to stop them. It is the principle of cessation within cessation-observation practice so that a society is left with peace rather than disturbance. Do not make the mistake of thinking that meditation teaches you to stay apart and observe, but not to act. When you see something wrong

That is the wrong meaning of meditative dispassion or detachment. One must act to cut off errant, mistaken, incorrect or evil ways once found. A clear mind, achieved by cultivating introspection, helps you see the errant. What is especially important is to cut off evil as soon as it is spotted, just as one tries to cut off a *logismos* before it takes hold. Remember, one does not do bad actions and sincerely tries to do what is good. This is the right way to live and as Confucianism, Christianity and Buddhism teach, it also naturally clarifies the mind as well.

Societies often fall by allowing the evil of hubris to grow supreme, and so to prevent error for the benefit of all, we must stress the ideals of self-improvement and introspection to correct our personal faults just as we must also police larger societal and political actions and strive to change them when they are found to be errant. We must work to prevent or restrain errors that might grow to affect us all in detrimental ways. The failure of good men to act within democracies, until it is too late, has been the general history of doomed societies and nations. A saying runs that virtuous men are very good, but in their goodness they lack the nerve to do great things. You now have a larger picture of this, which is how it connects with meditation practice.

Along the same lines of discussion, we could also make an argument that we should actively and energetically step up and assume the responsibility of doing good works in society and supporting virtuous actions that are not being sufficiently supported, such as founding or funding philanthropic efforts. Some of the greatest individuals have chosen to devote their lives to such noble efforts, and we all should applaud and emulate their behavior to the best of our abilities. They have chosen the path of performing evermore good, and their karmic returns will be tremendous. One should not just oppose evil things that have appeared in the world, or strive to prevent them from arising in the first place, but we should also support good things that we see being done, or help them arise in the first place when they are non-existent. This is so obvious, however, that I must emphasize the cutting off of errant ways because this ties in most clearly with meditation practice. If you weed a garden, what is left will grow unencumbered even without the fertilizer, and that is the lesson to remember.

People often wonder how the principles of meditation connect with the world at large, and this short discussion on opposing what is wrong illustrates just one example that can even be expanded to the business or economic sphere as well. As Socrates hinted in his discussion of his inner *daimon*, we should know what not to do, and thereby be deterred from doing wrong. The Confucian ideal is that in all your behavior you must always know what you are doing, and must know what is right or wrong so that you know how to properly act with an emphasis, once again, on cutting off errors. You must know your present actions, your motivation, and the consequences of those actions. *You must know when to stop*, and when to avoid going too far.

You must look at things realistically, and this clarity of consideration, or rational analysis, is something you should never abandon. As we'll later see, we can and should even apply a discriminating analysis to investigate the nature of our minds, too. You should never try to destroy the various capabilities of your mind by blunting them out, or try to get rid of reason, logic, and analysis. You should always use discriminating analysis to try to create better policies for yourself and the world, and use them to help awaken.

Everyone is responsible for their own behavior in life, and the aggregate of that behavior, in total, determines the fates of individuals, cultures, nations, states and societies. The striving to become a better person is good for us both individually and collectively. No one can be truly happy as an individual if they are surrounded by suffering in society. By cultivating your own body, mind and behavior – by watching them with mindfulness—you can prevent great errors and can start cultivating a path of self-improvement. With your own improvement, you can then help your family attain peace and order. If a family cultivates in this way, then a family, as a unit, can learn to conduct itself properly. If all families cultivate in this way, then the state will eventually find itself in harmonious order. If a nation of states cultivates introspective analysis, and everyone is policing their behavior and considering what they are doing in aggregate, then the state can cultivate peace and prosperity, and avoid the large errors that might result in its downfall. However, without a firm stand on moral conduct and proper wholesome behavior, morality and virtue and society decline.

The peace and prosperity of a nation always starts with the wholesome actions of the individuals within it, and when an individual improves their actions and behaviors through mindfulness, the ripple effects can extend to the state and nation as a whole. Such was the example of Benjamin Franklin, or of Liao Fan whose model life story still provides inspiration for many people today. Their stories show us how to become better people through the simple practical practice of watching our thoughts to improve our behavior and change our own lives. *When we each are better people, we all are better people. All being better people enables us to live in a society, state and then country that allows greater happiness.*

On the personal level, you simply cannot change your behavior *unless you first see it* because of mindful awareness. In life, for life, you must therefore learn how to watch your mind. You must learn how to watch your thoughts and become ever mindful of this practice. Hence, this particular idea of watching your thoughts is the basis of not just changing your behavior for the better, but of changing your life for the better in total. It allows you to eliminate bad habits and make better decisions in life with far better consequences than simply acting without knowing your mind. It allows you to purify consciousness. That is what changes your karma, or fortune, for the better. Such grand objectives, such powerful results can all start to occur through the simple vehicle of daily meditation practice.

Watching your thoughts, without attaching to them, is taught as a way to attain a state of internal peace and mental calming, but now you know that this practice can offer so much more. Nevertheless, the main task for meditation is how to quiet the mind. All of us experience too many wild, crazy, random and troubling thoughts that we want to get rid of, and that's why we are seeking peace. Because of these disturbances, our minds cannot rest. They cannot relax and we cannot find tranquility or freedom from stress and anxieties.

All day long in this busy world we are buffeted by new cares and concerns, stresses, worries and anxieties. Meditation, rather than a drug prescribed by a doctor or psychiatrist, offers a solution. The solution is not instant, but it is a definite solution with far better results than a pill. If you learn to meditate, in time your thoughts will calm down and eventually, you will become able to carry that state of inner peace into the everyday world always and everywhere. It is through meditation that you can untie both psychological and physical knots, including some of the physical knots supporting psychological aberrations. The internal peace you cultivate through meditation will not be something you just experience during meditation practice, but because meditation has transformed the currents of your body and mind, peace and contentment will become a permanent feature of your personality that allows you to laugh more, relax more, and enjoy more of life.

When you start to reach that mental state of peace, quiet or calm produced by meditation, the next higher stage of progress is to try to fathom who is actually experiencing this mental state. You do not have to do this at first, but this is an avenue of exploration that many choose to take. This is the pathway of inquiry or discriminative wisdom analysis that inspects the mind in order to lead to much higher spiritual attainments. With a quiet and clear mind, you can start to analyze your consciousness. You can inspect the workings of consciousness and the actual substance of consciousness itself which I like to call "consciousness-stuff" or "mind-stuff." With a clear mind along with logic and reasoning, you can eventually probe the very nature of the substance of consciousness, and that is an extremely profound level of meditation practice. However, you need pure concentration, wherein the mind is not cluttered with thoughts or sunk in oblivion, to be able to recognize the pure mind.

This all starts with the simple meditation practice of mental watching or inner witnessing. From mental watching you can develop a calm mind, which means you reach a state of cessation or mental quiet. Because of mental watching, you can also start to become a better person, and at its ultimate, you can even turn this ethical, moral, virtuous practice into a practice of spiritual development.

My recommendation is that every day you should do mantra practice, and every day you should practice sitting meditation to watch your thoughts like a third person observer would, which is the standard description of "meditation" you usually find everywhere. You just watch your thoughts come and go without attaching to them. There are several other meditation techniques you can also work into a daily practice schedule, but the basic technique of nearly all meditation practices is reaching a quiet mind by dispassionately observing your mental state without attachment. This is a state of quiet emptiness or cessation.

As you sit in meditation and your mind slowly quiets, miscellaneous wandering thoughts will slowly start to leave just as dirty water eventually drains out of a bathtub. Then you can take that clean mental state into the world wherever you go, and with everyday mindfulness you can learn to maintain it and use it to transform your behavior for the better.

Confucius therefore recommended this technique, Saint Augustine and the Jesuits recommended it, Benjamin Franklin and Liao Fan used it, and the practitioners of many other religions have also heavily relied on this technique as a basic cultivation practice. So many people have used this basic technique of effortless mental witnessing because the cultivation practices employed in the world are truly shared, non-denominational practices. This basic inner-witnessing method not only calms your mind of random thoughts but helps you monitor and police your behavior in order that you can transform your behavior to become better. If people recommended and relied upon this meditation method in olden days, when life was simpler and much slower, imagine how much more so we need to be applying to our lives today!

In short, the two principles of cessation and observation – that your mind will quiet (cessation) when you watch it with dispassion (observation) — are inherent in all meditation techniques, and this becomes particularly obvious in this mindfulness practice of mental observation. Once again, *the principles of cessation and observation are inherent in all meditation techniques.* If you sit in meditation practice and just watch your thoughts like a detached independent observer, your random wandering thoughts will definitely eventually calm down, and you will start to experience mental quiet. You can thereby establish a basis for more advanced meditation practices after you learn what "quiet" means in terms of some experience of mental emptiness, but all these practices depend on the principle that your wandering thoughts will start subsiding when you practice witnessing them without involvement. You just know them without attachment.

If you can spend forty-five or fifty minutes per day meditating, that's fantastic. If you cannot do it all at once, then try putting in that much time by breaking up your sitting throughout the day, perhaps right before bedtime, or right when you wake up.

Some people find it's best to meditate at night, and some in the morning. You have to determine what's best for you, but it's a general rule not to meditate on a full stomach or you are likely to stop watching your mind and just fall asleep. Some people, however, meditate quite well on a full stomach, so you have to adjust your practice time to your capabilities, opportunities and potential.

If you space out constantly in your meditation, lingering in drowsiness and muddiness or dreaminess, this is also incorrect. Your mind should get clear rather than busier or confused. If you always become sleepy during meditation practice, you should also consider taking a nap before you meditate otherwise you won't be able to practice correctly but will always be falling asleep. You're the one who has to arrange mundane scheduling factors such as this.

The more you meditate, the easier it will eventually become to relax and enter into a calm mental zone after awhile. Initially, it's not that easy to experience these fruits of practice, but just as with all other things, with practice these results start to come naturally, and therefore you will improve with time and start to experience all the benefits people talk about that are attributed to meditation.

Meditation is easy to do because you just sit there and watch your thoughts, and this really doesn't require any effort at all. However, to claim the benefits you must practice this regularly until your mental realm starts to empty out and you begin to integrate this clarity with your daily life. Other than mantra practice, which you can do any time or any place, the simplicity of witnessing practice, or mental mindfulness, is the reason I most often recommend this meditation technique for people who want to learn meditation and start reaping its benefits.

Hence, you don't really need to spend money to learn meditation. I have just taught you the key instructions for most meditation techniques. You sit comfortably, let go of thoughts, and just watch your mental state without gluing yourself to the thought stream. You remain aware of the coming and goings of thoughts and let them flow without clinging to them or trying to hold them, feed them energy, or transform them. You just know them without clinging. In time your mental realm will quiet from applying this type of practice and you will eventually experience a minor taste of "empty mind."

That's it. That's all you need to know. The hard part is not the instructions on how to meditate. The hard part is setting up a practice schedule to actually do it, and then consistently following that practice schedule. Since you know all the possible benefits, if you don't practice meditation then you must search your mind to find out why you are not sufficiently motivated. Your progress will not come from reading more books to gain more understanding, but simply from doing the actual sitting practice without holding onto expectations. Holding onto expectations is a type of mental clinging, so you "sit just to sit" and watch your mind.

4

VISUALIZATION PRACTICE

A third method of meditation is visualization practice. In visualization practice you create an image in your mind and practice holding that image with unwavering stability. That is, you learn how to hold an imagined picture in your mind with stability so it doesn't waver. It takes concentration to be able to hold anything in the mind firmly with stability and without distraction. With visualization efforts, you don't lose your concentration by flitting to a different thought but just stay with holding that one mental image in the mind. No one can actually *teach you* how to do this, for you just have to learn how to do it by practicing yourself.

How do you hold an image in your mind for a few minutes without wavering? This is what you set out to learn through daily visualization practice, which only requires just a few minutes per day. It is just another technique for quieting the mind because while you are concentrating on holding a visual image, you are banishing all sorts of wandering thoughts that would normally distract you. You replace many countless wandering thoughts with one mental objective, which is holding the image in your mind.

The mental stability involved with successfully holding a steady visualization comes from learning how to concentrate. In other words, holding a stable, unwavering image in the mind requires the gradual development of one-pointed concentration. You cannot learn how to do this in one day, but you must gradually practice over time to finally become able to hold unwavering attention on a mental image so that it doesn't go away. Mastering this practice will eventually bring you great dividends in terms of life skills.

You must practice provisionally creating a mental image (picture) and then you must gradually learn how to hold onto that image so that it doesn't fluctuate or disappear. During that state of mental stability (wherein you do not lose your image because you end up focusing on something else), you are effectively banishing other thoughts that usually run around in your head because you're replacing them with that mental construct, the image.

When an image becomes stable in the mind, this success means that miscellaneous wandering thoughts have died away otherwise you could not have reached this state of concentration. You have essentially learned how to calm your mind by focusing on one thing, and that one thing is an internal visual image you created. When you reach that point where the mind becomes calm and stable from this type of concentration, you should then release your hold on the image in order to experience an empty, peaceful mind. The point is not the stable image itself but using its creation to afterwards experience a quiet, empty mind that is "empty" because you've already abolished the wandering thoughts that normally disturb it.

Once again, you practice creating and then holding an internal visualized image in order to learn how to ignore most other thoughts running around in your mind. You are learning how to get rid of them by mastering concentration on something else. That something else is a picture in the imagination. You are using an image as a focus of concentration, but rather than staring at something in front of you to serve as that image, you create a totally internal provisional image to serve as the focus of concentration. When you can finally steadily visualize something, then you afterwards release that image. Why? Because you want to experience the mental quiet that then exists when random thoughts have departed due to your concentration.

In this way, you become able to cultivate a bit of mental emptiness, tranquility, stillness, quiet, equipoise or quiescence (however you want to word it) in a different way than by listening to a mantra or watching thoughts and seeing them depart. You can attain a peaceful, calm, empty and quiet mental state by mastering one-pointed concentration, which essentially ignores them so that they leave. This is just another technique for becoming free of wandering thoughts – you concentrate on an internal image, and thus ignore them and they die down. The thoughts that normally run around in your mind depart because you've been concentrating, or putting your full attention, on something else and ignoring them. After you reach this experience of relative mental quiet, you then apply the normal rules of contemplation to just stay in that empty quiet and inspect the mind.

That, in short, is visualization practice. We can call these instructions "**Visualization Practice 101.**" Visualization is just another method for learning concentration so that you can ignore, and thus abandon wandering thoughts.

HOW TO PRACTICE VISUALIZATIONS

Once again, you start by provisionally creating an independent image in your mind. People are usually told to choose an auspicious image such as the figure of a holy individual, or a complicated image such as a mandala, or something simple like a shining letter, moon, diamond or triangle. The choices are endless but it should be something happy and auspicious that promotes yang chi arising rather than something dark and gloomy or sad.

For the actual meditation practice, you just hold that image steady in your mind and ignore all the other thoughts that come and go while you are practicing. You don't push your chi around when trying to form that image either, but just mentally visualize the image and try to maintain it. If you lose it or you get distracted, you simply start visualizing it again. Concentration simply means to focus on the image and ignore other thoughts, so you don't have to apply force in any way, such as in moving your chi around to form the image or even to wrinkle your forehead as a sign of concentration. This practice is totally detached from the body. You are trying to learn how to develop a stable mind wherein you ignore everything else except the image.

While holding the visualization, never tense your muscles, such as to tighten your muscles or furrow your brow, but just stay totally relaxed and focused on the mental picture. You should also ignore your body sensations during this time because those sensations are also considered wandering thoughts that arise in the mind. This is a mental exercise, so you detach from the body and ignore it while practicing because it is entirely done within consciousness and has nothing to do with the body or its internal movements of chi. Therefore, relax and ignore the body while practicing visualizations.

With mantra practice, you abandon your wandering thoughts by listening to the recitation of the mantra. Listening to the mantra as the focus of attention helps you ignore all the other wandering thoughts running around in your head. Just repeating the mantra itself gives little room for other thoughts to proliferate as well because you are already spending your mental energy on reciting the mantra. Because of the constant repetition of the mantra, it predominates in your mind, so some people even say it drowns out their wandering thoughts, pushing them all aside.

Whether you ignore those wandering thoughts or push them aside, thus they die down. Hence, with mantra practice you will eventually experience an empty mind. By listening to the mantra, you are switching the focus of attention from wandering thoughts to the mantra alone and giving everything else other than the mantra less sway. Therefore the other thoughts in the mind, not given energy or attention, slowly but surely fade away. As a result, mantra recitation always ends up producing states of internal mental peace and quiet.

In vipassana practice you're letting go of everything—all the thoughts that arise in your mind—and just directly detach from all the mental activity that comes and goes while continuing to observe it. You're just like a detached observer who watches thoughts but who refuses to get sucked in by them, and so thought streams naturally dissipate. You are fully aware and simply witness, but do not become attached; you stand apart. You don't negate the world, because you still have to deal with it, but just refuse to grasp and cling to the mental phenomena which come and go. You simply function as you always do but without extraneous clinging.

When your mind gets quiet from letting go of mentally clinging to thoughts, you should always inspect that mental state of quiet. You should contemplate it by asking questions that might spark a realization such as, "Who is the one experiencing this mind?", "Who am I?", "What is this consciousness-stuff that I am experiencing?" or "Where does the I-notion or I-sense arise from?" and so forth. You should ask questions that help you investigate and ponder your mind, namely, what is the nature of your consciousness? This is the path of wisdom inquiry and discriminative analysis. Once you have established a strong foundational basis in meditation, this type of active questioning and looking at your mind, to inquire about its nature, is one of the quickest ways to help you penetrate through the veil of thoughts to apprehend your formless nature, which is your true self.

You have to seek with a mind turned inwards, by actually examining the very consciousness-stuff that you are using this very moment, to try to discover the answer to these questions. You are not looking for an answer from a book but have to actually look directly at your own mind to try to find answers to these types of questions. This is why many meditative instructions say to "turn within." This means to stop fixating on the thoughts and appearances which arise within consciousness, and to concentrate on the object of consciousness itself, which includes the awareness which knows these forms of consciousness.

Zen and Vedanta offer all sorts of such questions you might use for this type of practice of directly examining consciousness itself. You can engage in all sorts of enquiries that help you determine what is the nature of your mind. You want to penetrate through the fog of mental phenomena that are always changing until you can find the true you that is always aware, always pure, and which never moves and never leaves.

To analyze your mind and ascertain about its nature, you can also analyze the various types of mental experiences that come up in the mind as thoughts, appearances, emotions, sensations and so forth, and continually ask how you might further let go of them to break the habit of clinging to your mental contents. When thoughts die down, you can engage in contemplation of the mental state of quiet within your mind, which is why cessation-witnessing meditation or cessation-observation is often called cessation-*contemplation* practice, to discover the underlying awareness that has the nature of emptiness.

Buddhism catalogues all sorts of wisdom analysis techniques that you might employ for looking at consciousness, such as discrimination, insight analysis, inquiry or contemplation. All these mental analysis techniques were created with the objective to help you ascertain that the mind's natural nature is empty, but to realize this fact you must first get rid of a lot of thoughts flitting back and forth that might screen this basic observation. That requires abandoning extremely deep habits of mental clinging. If you can let go of attaching to thoughts to the extent that there is nothing left to cling to, you can eventually reach a realization of the ground state of the mind which is just an empty, bodiless awareness without content. It is empty but it can always give birth to consciousness when circumstances warrant.

That empty, never moving, pure, peaceful, equanimous, and beginningless state is your true self. It is naturally empty but aware. There is nothing there at all except an insubstantial pristine awareness, knowingness or natural lucidity that is empty of content. If it wasn't there with the characteristic of pure consciousness, we would not exist and the universe would just be an inert existence. The proper way to cultivate meditation once you realize this underlying true nature of pure consciousness is a middle way that is non-dual. It means neither clinging to the fact that your original nature is empty, and not clinging to the transient, interdependent appearances that arise within your awareness either. You never cling to its emptiness aspect or awareness (lucidity) aspect.

The initial purpose of analyzing any "empty" mental states you bump into through meditation practice is to realize the fact that the emptiness or silence you experience is still an image in the mind. The silence you typically experience represents just a lower volume of thoughts, so it is still not a true experience of emptiness where there is absolutely nothing, no content at all. There is still the knowing that you are experiencing an emptiness like space, so that emptiness is still a mental construction of thoughts rather than real, true emptiness. It is still a something, object, form, appearance, thought, or phenomenon.

You want to eventually go past that image so that the mind is truly empty of all thoughts and images, but that means getting to the root of the original nature. To do that you must try to investigate consciousness to fathom who it is that is actually experiencing that image of emptiness in the mind. Where and what is the ultimate "I" behind all perception? It is not the false self of the ego, for the ego is just a bunch of thoughts. If it is your "I," then where was your "I" that you take yourself to be before you were born when you didn't exist at all? At that time you didn't know anything – can you imagine what that state was like? If you can drop all ideas of an assumed self and simply have a direct experience of this state, that experience would be akin to a real emptiness experience that could help your cultivation.

This is difficult to reach and difficult to investigate, and the steps are beyond the introductory level of this text. However, you've been given enough information to get started on this road of investigation. If you reach a profound state of emptiness or mental quiet from your meditation practice, the next step is to elevate your practice further by turning to Vedanta, Jnana Yoga or Zen to see how practitioners break through this experience to find the ultimate absolute root source of the mind. As my teacher often told me, *the key is letting go, or "emptiness cultivation" every step of the way*. Once again, because the discussion on how to actually attain the enlightenment of self-realization is so advanced, it is left outside this introductory text. We are simply introducing the basics of meditation practice, and you can use those basics to attain the objectives of health, longevity, self-improvement, relaxation or spiritual pursuits. If you choose the objective of attaining advanced spiritual realizations, my hat goes off to you. If not, you can still use everything you've been taught to achieve any of these other objectives.

As to visualization practice, you are trying to tie the wandering mind up by using the practice of concentration, and when you reach a calmness of the mind because you've made the image very stable, all the wandering thoughts that usually run around in your mind have accordingly died down. You are basically trying to reach that same state of quiet or emptiness we are always talking about, wherein most discriminating thoughts are absent, but by using a different method than the other meditation techniques that we've already discussed.

No matter what the type of meditation practice you use, it's always the same objective of mental peace, silence or "emptiness of thought" you want to reach. However, there are different ways you can attain this, and so we have all sorts of different methods that approach this one target from different angles. This is why the Buddha Kuan Yin is shown with ten thousand arms, for there are countless techniques that can help you achieve a realm of mental peace that, when pursued far enough, can eventually lead to spiritual enlightenment. The higher the stage of emptiness experience you reach, the more your chakras and channels will open, the more purified that your chi will become, the better your chi circulation will become, the more your consciousness will transform, the more your body will transform, the less stress you will have, the more energy you will have, the more wisdom you will have, and the healthier your body will become because of your efforts.

Everything links together in one whole. If you untie physical and psychological knots, and free up your internal energy channels, of course you will feel more energy and become healthier in many ways. These are not baloney results, but few people cultivate hard enough to attain them to the fullest extent possible.

POSSIBLE IMAGES TO MENTALLY VISUALIZE

What mental image might you try to envision if you choose to practice visualization methods? In Tibetan Buddhism, you are taught to concentrate on forming complicated mandalas or colorful figures of deities. In Roman Catholicism, you are taught to concentrate on creating within your mind Biblical images such as the figure of Jesus on the Cross or the Kingdom of God. You are supposed to visualize these images and then hold them with stability until your mind stabilizes. In Taoism, you might visualize the Big Dipper or various deities. In Hinduism and Kashmir Shaivism, you might visualize special images, called *yantras*, which represent the chakras of the body stacked on top of one another. In Buddhism, you might be taught to visualize the body of the Buddha or the picture of a Buddha land such as Amitofo's paradise.

There are countless images that have served as objects of concentration in various traditions, but the visualization method that I most highly recommend is called the body impurity visualization or white skeleton visualization technique. There are several dozen different versions of this practice and I'm only going to introduce the one I favor most. In this practice, you progressively visualize that you strip off and give away all the flesh of your body, so that there is no mental holding to the body anymore, until you arrive at the point where the only thing left is your bright white skeleton emitting light.

After the skeleton image becomes stable, you then release that image by imagining that it becomes dust which blows away and becomes empty space. Your whole body becomes dust, blows away, and then nothing is left there except empty space. Your mind should then rest like space at the end of the visualization; you don't imagine space but just let everything go so that your mind becomes boundless, like space, without any content. There is no "me" anymore but just space. In other words, just release the visualization and try to experience *what it is like to have an empty mind without thoughts at the finish.* That is the ultimate target of practice. Just forget your body and mind and rest in mental emptiness as if nothing is there anymore. There is no remaining body-self.

Some people, who have cancer, may benefit by visualizing that their bones burn with fire and then become dust, which blows away to leave this empty state of mind. Practice should always be like space at the end, which means free of images and wandering thoughts. The only way to explain that is to say that the "mind becomes like space," which just means thought-less empty mind. This empty mind, or thoughtlessness, is the same thing we have been trying to reach through other meditation methods as well, and we're just using a different terminology to describe the same desired end state once again. It just means the same old state of silence, peace, tranquility, cessation, emptiness or no-thought we have always been talking about. In this case you reach that tranquility by holding tightly to a visual image, and then eventually letting go after the image becomes stable or after you simply give up the attempt.

Individuals with high blood pressure can benefit by practicing certain visualizations such as imagining that their toe bones become like burning candle flames, and this little trick, afterwards released after a few minutes of concentration, tends to lower blood pressure. It sends the body's chi down to the toes, and this is what reduces hypertension. The final mental scenario you want to experience is always just an empty mind, which means thoughts have become relatively quiet or absent. Hence, the skeleton visualization is just the means to arrive at that same desired experience of emptiness we always target.

Once again, this is the same final objective as in every other meditation technique, yet people never seem to realize this fact. They always seem to think that different forms of spiritual practice have a different end target or objective, but in the ultimate analysis they are all designed to simply help you experience a quiet, tranquil, peaceful empty state of mind that doesn't have so many thoughts. We call this emptiness, empty mind, no-thought, stillness, cessation, quiet, peacefulness or quiescence. You can use all sorts of different names, but they all mean the same thing. Some methods approach this quieting by having you focus on your chi or breathing. Other methods work by tying up wandering thoughts, or by having you ignore wandering thoughts, or by drowning out wandering thoughts. Many approaches can be used. No one can predict which method will work for you, which is why I am introducing several core meditation practices that are each based on different quieting principles.

There are many ways to approach the final objective, and since you never know which method will work for you, this is also why I always recommend that people practice multiple meditation techniques if they really want to achieve results. This is a book on effective meditation, and to have your meditation practice become effective you must understand the principles of practice. If you understand the principles of practice, as I have been explaining, then you can quickly obtain the objective of a peaceful mind from almost any technique because you'll know how to properly practice. However, to maximize the chances for this, I always encourage that people set up a practice schedule that employs several different methods.

THE WHITE SKELETON VISUALIZATION PRACTICE

To practice the white skeleton visualization, you always start by imagining the bones of the left foot first. Shakyamuni Buddha taught that you always start the visualization from your left big toe and you progressively visualize all the bones in your left foot, and then all the bones in your right foot, and then all the bones in your left leg going up and then your right leg going up; then your hips and then your spine going up and then your ribs and then your arms and then your head. The visualization practice *always starts by visualizing your left big toe first.* Perhaps someday someone will make this into an iPhone or iPad app to illustrate the visualization.

You basically strip away all the flesh from your body in a progressive fashion, working upwards, and you end up visualizing that you're just a shining, bright white skeleton of bones. Once you've got that picture in your mind, you hold that visualization. If you lose it, you try to create it again because the point of concentration is to stay with the selected focus or topic. When the visualization becomes stable, then you can finally let go of holding on to it, and you should then rest in the peace of a quiet mind and ignore any thoughts or body sensations that come up such as the energies that start arising when you cultivate an empty state. "Stable" means that you have an even, unmovable image that does not flicker.

When you cannot hold the visualization any longer, or have to stop your practice for any reason (no matter how far you got), you always end by letting go of your thoughts and resting in emptiness. This mental state absent of thoughts which you reach, together with the fact you are not attaching to your body or its sensations (and just letting them do their thing), is the important target of the practice. *The point is not whether you can actually visualize all the individual bones within the skeleton with accuracy* (although of course this shows a very high stage of mental attainment). Who cares if you miss a bone or two, or even visualize incorrectly? The point is that you can cultivate a mental state of stability from the visualization practice, and *then release it to experience mental emptiness to some degree.*

When your mind is concentrated on an image and thereby becomes stable, it must mean that miscellaneous wandering thoughts have already somewhat died down. Otherwise you could not achieve the stable or non-moving aspect of the visualization. Your mind becomes quiet except for the visualization, so distracting thoughts must have departed. When your mind becomes quiet, your chi will then arise, that ascending chi will start to open up your chi channels, and by resting in mental emptiness you will abandon any interference in its process of opening your chi channels. Presto, you have a wonderful meditation technique!

Visualizing the framework of your internal skeleton, because it mimics the route of chi circulations throughout your body, has the extra bonus over other visualizations in that it gives you a tiny extra boost to opening up the channels within your body and cultivating all your chi as one single unit. There is a scientific principle that wherever you put your mind your chi will go, and hence by performing an internal visualization of your internal skeleton, your chi will run throughout the entire course of your body to help open up all its channels. Of course, when your chi channels start opening and your chi arises, this often gives rise to sexual desire, which is one of the difficulties of this practice. If you succumb to sexual desires and lose your energies, then you accordingly lose at that time all the chi that would normally be used to open up your chi channels.

No matter which mental image you choose to visualize with visualizations, you must learn how to hold the visualization with stability and then you must eventually let it go at the end so that you can experience a mental continuum that's like empty space because it's absent of miscellaneous thoughts running around and like space, holds no attachment to anything. Thus we have yet another technique for helping us to get rid of our wandering monkey mind. Visualization practice is simply another technique for cultivating mental quiet.

The target of the practice is not really the mental generation and holding of the stable visualization. You should not worry that your image of the skeleton is not perfectly correct either. The important objective is practicing mental concentration and using that practice to achieve an absence of discriminative thoughts in the mind which is a resultant state we call emptiness, silence, peacefulness, calming, tranquility or equanimity.

The white skeleton visualization technique, in brief, is as follows:

1. First assume a comfortable meditation posture. For reference purposes, you might place a picture or small model of a human skeleton in front of you which you can easily see when you open your eyes. I always used to practice by studying pictures in books and memorizing the shapes of bones until I purchased a small model of a white skeleton, which is easily found on the internet. My teacher always told us to paint the skeletons white because some people might become sad or depressed looking at a yellowish skeleton model when first learning how to do this visualization. If you tend toward mental problems like this, then don't practice the skeleton visualization but just use some other meditation technique. As a prerequisite for the practice, individuals who practice visualizations should also practice physical exercise so that they can handle the energies released,

and should be securely grounded in the mundane world of human interactions so that they do not become imbalanced.

2. With a picture or model of a white skeleton in front of you, now close your eyes, and begin to practice. Try to visualize your left foot bones first, starting with your left big toe. If you have not memorized the skeleton, whenever you need to see more bones to help complete the visualization, naturally you should open your eyes and take a peek. Arouse the idea that this body of ours is actually quite dirty, a thing of disgust. It is actually a very impure thing, and one of the cures for sexual desire is to keep reminding yourself of physical impurity so that you can detach from the body and the pulls of the physical body. Next, imagine that you joyfully strip away the dirty flesh and organs surrounding your bones as you visualize them. You visualize stripping the flesh off your bones and offering it away to repay any debts you might owe to sentient beings, and the only thing left there is the white bone underneath. This joyous offering of all your flesh should not take minutes, but can be mentally imagined as happening instantly after you have mastered this practice for many months. You can even hold to the emotion of joy as one big super thought to drown out other wandering thoughts as long as you release it at the end to experience empty mind; the basic technique has many possible derivations you might use depending on what works best for you in developing an empty mind. The point is to eventually reach a stage where you imagine that you are just a skeleton of white bones sitting there in your meditation posture after all your flesh is offered away and gone. For instance, when you get to your calf bone you can look at your leg, imagine that all the flesh of the calf is gone and nothing is left but the white bone that's inside it. See the white bone inside the leg, as well as all the other bones visualized up to that point.

3. The visualization of your body as just a set of white bones should always start with your left big toe. You start by imagining that you strip away the flesh and then can see the left big toe bone clearly there in white color. When you do this meditation

practice many times, you might even see lights within your body around the bones because your chi will go to there, and the concentration will cause a chi light to shine. This is not real, but just a false internal vision. In any case, after visualizing that you strip the flesh off your left big toe and a white bone is left, you next imagine the same process for the rest of your toes on your left foot. One by one you imagine the flesh coming off each toe, and discern each bone as shining with white light. After visualizing all your left toes, you can visualize the rest of the bones in your left foot, and then go to the right foot and repeat the process. You eventually finish visualizing the rest of the bones of your left foot (referring to a picture or model when necessary), and then you finish visualizing them in your right foot. Next you visualize the bones of your left leg, then right leg, then left calf and right calf, and slowly proceed upwards visualizing all your clean white bones until you can visualize all the bones in the body clearly up to the top of your skull. You visualize your toe bones, ankle bones, shin bones, kneecap, thigh bones, pelvic bones, spine, ribs and shoulder blades, etc., visualizing the flesh being stripped off from both sides until they are clearly perceived in dazzling white light. The same goes for the shoulder blades to the elbows, wrists and fingers. You imagine the flesh splitting open and falling off, or being peeled away, and what is revealed to remain is a dazzling white bone in its place connected to all the others. You want to see a stable image of the bones in your mind, and you should try to imagine them shining with white light so you look like a snowman. Be sure to focus on the extremities with this meditation practice – such as head, hands and feet — so that the chi channels get some attention in these difficult-to-open regions. This will prepare you for opening a complete channel circuit when your chi is finally ready to punch all the way through the final obstructions within a circulatory pathway.

4. All these bones should be visualized as shining with a bright white light, or just being bright white in color like dazzling snow. You can imagine a bright white-silverish light shining there or can just imagine that the bones are colored bright white

– whichever is best for your concentration practice. Remember that the objective is to master concentration on a visualized form within the body, not a specific practice followed to the letter. You can always change details as long as you understand the principles of practice, and adjust what's best for you accordingly (but of course, don't stray too far). Some people try to feel the shape of the bones by rotating bright lights inside them, or caressing their external shapes with visualized light, but don't concentrate on these tricks too much, as you should not play with your energies while engaged in any form of meditation. The real practice is to just see the image of white bones in your mind, and to stay with it. If the bones always seem brown or darkish in color, search your mind for the wrongs you do in life, repent of those activities vowing not to do them again, and continue trying the practice again; over time that dark color will change as you make progress. You know the white bones are there because of your concentration, and you are practicing stable, one-pointed concentration, which means holding a mental image without wavering and flitting around entertaining all sorts of other random thoughts. Similarly, you can also mentally shine a light on your bones to mentally illuminate them as long as this becomes a stable visualization. While performing such visualization practices, your energies are sure to arise, so you must ignore the energies in the body which arise from this practice. They simply indicate that your chi is stirring and starting to move. You simply want to develop the ability to visualize all the white bones in your body without trying to move energies around or play with your chi; let that happen by itself. You're trying to generate a *stable image* in your mind. Where your mind goes your chi will follow, so this practice will help to even out or "harmonize" the chi flows of your body because your entire body is visualized at the same time. Once you achieve that state of full body harmony, you can also let go of the visualization.

5. Once again, as you start to learn the white skeleton visualization you can open your eyes to glance at the skeleton model (or picture) in front of you every now and then as

necessary until your visualization becomes firm and secure. In time, your body may actually become warm around certain bones that you visualize properly, and this can actually be used for self-healing purposes. Certain areas within the body may seem to glow, and the body will often become warm. When the whole body becomes full of chi because of the efforts of this full body practice for loosening all the internal chi channels along its length, this actually helps all your tissues and organs.

6. When you can visualize your whole body in this way, and your chi has become balanced and harmonized throughout your body, you then imagine the visualized bones turning to dust, and then blowing away, leaving endless open empty space. In other words, you release your visualization and rest in an empty mind. All that's left is emptiness – no body whatsoever to cling to or hold onto, and no wandering thoughts to hold onto. There is just empty awareness. The remaining experience should be like the center of open space, with nothing to cling to or abide in. You are just empty, insubstantial awareness.

Remember, once the visualization stage is over, you should remain in that resulting mental experience of emptiness, and try to forget any sensations or attachments you have of your physical body. They are just experiences that arise in the mind, and are not the real you. Remain with that state for as long as possible — forgetting both your mind and body — and in time you'll enter a deeply profound mental state of meditation, empty of thought, called "*samadhi*." This is a stable mental state wherein the mind is naturally quiet and remains so without effort. The ground of the mind is no longer covered by thoughts and images but just shines solitarily by itself.

The skeleton visualization technique will help you achieve a stable mental state that's empty of thoughts, and will also help your chi start to flow throughout your entire physical frame. That's one of the physical results of the practice. Another common result is that the practice often leads to an increase in sexual desire because of all the rising energy, and you should ignore these energies so that they can work at opening your chi channels. If they are deployed in sexual relations, they'll simply be lost and you'll lose most of the fruits of your practice.

You can call this a meditation method for attaining mental quiet, or a meditation method for cultivating the chi of your body so that it arises and starts opening up your chakras and channels. Those are flip sides of the same coin, and always happen simultaneously.

If practiced correctly, in time it is possible to develop a deep state of mental quiet through this meditation practice, and the transformative results will be reflected in a more healthy body because your chi channels open. That's always one of the objectives of meditation practice, and this particular meditation helps produce that result since it cultivates both your mind and chi channels directly.

Once you attain this state of deep quiet, which means freedom from thoughts because "the mind dissolves away," you must forget that you have any body at all, and let go of any attachments to body or mind to realize an even deeper stage of emptiness. Everything in spiritual practice is always about letting go of attachments to mental phenomena, including the experience of emptiness, until you can finally realize the fundamental base state of the mind which is *truly empty* of even images of emptiness. It just is – open, boundless, empty, pure, insubstantial, liberated and free. It has no appearance, qualification or form and thus is not transitory and impermanent. That non-dual base state is your true self, always there, but is empty of content, which is why you never realize it. The content is the world that arises in its functioning of awareness, and this transient content is not a real, graspable world that stays fixed or solid even for a moment, no matter how small you make that moment. The conventional world we see is more like a dream that flows rather than the more solid world we take it to be.

There is nothing strange or unusual about the white skeleton visualization practice. You are just visualizing your skeleton inside your body, which is a route along which your chi channels run, but most people never think about this fact which accounts for a portion of its great effectiveness. People turn to the esoteric schools because they usually want to be told to perform some elaborate, esoteric visualization when simplest is best, and visualizing your skeleton is a pretty simple objective.

Some spiritual traditions teach you to visualize complicated mandalas in your mind, but because they're so complicated you have to work hard to tie up your concentration to visualize the complicated pictures. Some want you to visualize extremely colorful, complicated pictures of deities in various positions with various accoutrements. Some pose simpler objectives, and ask you to visualize "holy letters" and hold them with stability. Of course by now you should realize there is nothing holy about them; you just need some targeted image for the focus of internal visual imagination and concentration.

The point is to practice reaching a quiet mental state through stable, unwavering concentration practice, rather than actually perfecting the imagined visualization. This is because the objective is that you want to experience an empty mind rather than perfect a visualized image. Then again, if you can perfect a stable visualization, bravo! There are benefits to developing this mental ability, too, as we'll soon learn.

TANTRIC VISUALIZATION PRACTICE

In tantric yoga techniques, which you find in India and in Tibet, you're taught to visualize all the internal chi channels and chakras of your body to a point of stable imagination, meaning an unwavering mental picture. These methods are called tantric visualizations, and this type of complicated body form visualization is equivalent to the skeleton technique wherein you visualize that your whole body becomes the white skeleton (which is its underlying frame) instead. You don't need to visualize chakras and channels – just visualize your skeleton within you.

These sorts of tantric body-based visualization practices, of visualization and concentration on chakra points and internal channels within your body, are like the skeleton technique in that they have a dual objective. The first objective is the normal objective of helping you cultivate a stable mind that is empty of mental fluctuation, and thus which becomes quiet because it is relatively empty. You learn how to develop mental stabilization, and thus mental quiet, through concentration practice on holding a steady visual image. After reaching that state of mental unwaveringness, the constructed mental image must be released so that you can then experience an empty mental state just by itself – the shining of awareness without thought contents.

A very wise visualization practitioner also eventually realizes that the stable image they create within their mind is made of the same mind-stuff as the appearance of the room they are presently seeing within their mind, and from understanding this basic equality of mind-stuff, they learn that they are only ever experiencing consciousness. You are the very manifestation you are seeing right now because it is consciousness, and that consciousness is you/yours. You are seeing a mental image of the room, and that mental image is your consciousness or mind. You are just experiencing your own consciousness rather than a room, and that consciousness, being you, is what you are experiencing. Hence a saying runs, "Before your eyes there are no phenomena; There is consciousness before your eyes. It is not phenomena before you there; What it is cannot be reached by eyes and ears."

Consciousness can take many forms, but you are only ever experiencing your own consciousness and nothing else. What you see, hear, etc. is your mind, not a true, independent object. The contents of your consciousness can be a totally imaginary image which you provisionally create in your own mind, or the contents can be the images you now see in front of you of this book. In fact, another form of visualization practice is to select an image of something in front of you (such as an apple) and learn how to hold to that image with stability. However, we will not go into this type of visualization effort. Countless different visualization practices, like this, are possible.

There is another issue that differentiates the white skeleton visualization and tantric visualizations (of chakra points and chi channels) from other visualization techniques, and this is the second objective. Wherever you put your consciousness (send your mind) in your body, your chi will go there. If you therefore visualize all the bones of your body, your chi will go to your bones throughout the length of your body. That influx of chi will tend to loosen up your body's chi channels since those chi channels run throughout your body wherever your bones are.

With tantric visualizations, such as the Six Yogas of Naropa, you try to visualize all the chakras and channels of your body directly to help pry open those structures, and in the skeleton method you accomplish this by just visualizing the bones inside your body *without having to know anything at all about the existence of channels and chakras.* You know what the shape of the bones should be; you visualize them inside you, and hold to that picture with stability. Just visualize the mental images of the white bones inside you.

You are not doing this when you are independently visualizing a "holy" Hebrew, Greek or Sanskrit letter in your mind, or even a mandala or some other image. Those are images you create in your mind that are not internal to your body. You are just trying to generate an independent mental image and hold it with stability.

From that mental stability your wandering thoughts will depart; from that quietness reached during this concentration your breathing will calm and your yang chi will arise; and from that yang chi arising your channels will start to open as they are pierced by the rising energy. The tantric visualization speeds this process along, and thus is a superior technique for some individuals. Then again, some people succeed by visualizing a provisionally created object, such as a Sanskrit, Greek, Hebrew letter or other image as discussed, and for them this is a superior technique. There is nothing holy about any of these techniques, or even the images you use. You simply use what vest works for you. *This is about mind training, so there are no religious overtones.* As a human being you need to learn how to use your mind in various ways, so *this is human being training for creating internal visual images and holding them with concentration.* It is quite scientific training. Along those lines, whatever technique works for you is what is best.

The extra hidden benefit of the white skeleton visualization practice is therefore that you tend to end up cultivating your chi channels directly at the same time that you are practicing mental stabilization to cultivate emptiness. Because chi goes to the area of your bones, along side of which channel routes definitely lie, it helps you loosen up all the chi channels of the body more quickly, or more quickly lays the foundation for their opening.

To practice this technique, you don't even have to know that chi channels and chakras exist within you, which is a superior way to practice since you are then not biased by any sorts of expectations that would lead you astray. Truth be told, most people become poisoned by information on the existence and position of chakras and channels, and this can affect their practice in detrimental ways by creating false or biased assumptions. Therefore you need not study them or have any advanced information on their existence at all! I've read dozens of books on chakras and found such information is rather useless anyway, except perhaps that it may prepare you from being startled by various internal pumping sensations or chi flows you feel that may occur when your channels start opening.

Using the white skeleton visualization meditation, you don't need to imagine the chi energy within your body ascending up your spine into your brain or anything else like that either. Because you are imagining all your bones, the chi everywhere within your body can slowly start to break its chains and begin to move as it must, at first sluggishly and sporadically wherever the channels are open and free. Hence, that result will come about naturally. There is simply no need to know about the exact route of chi channels because many follow the route of the skeleton. Taoists who like to visualize their internal chi circulations should take note of this point of excellence.

It's particularly important with the skeleton visualization to make sure that you visualize the feet and also the hands, shoulders and hips, because it's very hard for the chi channels to open up in these regions, and so you should give them some extra attention. One sits cross-legged while performing the visualization practice, which helps to open the leg channels within the body. Practicing the martial arts horse stance helps open up your leg channels, too, and sitting cross-legged in a full lotus position also helps you open up your leg channels as well.

RISING ENERGIES AND SIGNS OF PROGRESS

Now this particular meditation practice of the white skeleton visualization tends to release so much chi within your body that it prompts the arousal of sexual desire. You don't want to lose those energies when they are finally stirred into arising by squandering them through sexual dissipation. If your sexual desires become too strong because of your meditation efforts, simply switch to a different practice, such as breathing techniques (anapana and pranayama). Pranayama *kumbhaka* practices that require breath retention are particularly effective for handling sexual desires because they use up a lot of this excess energy. Some people try to solve this problem of sexual desire by eating less food (decreasing their food intake), or by imagining a Buddha on top of their head (to bring up the energies), but the excess energy and presence of extreme sexual desire is not something that can be cured in one stroke.

The practice of imagining a Buddha on top of the head, or visualizing a Buddha and consort in embrace over the head, or imagining dozens of chakras over the head rising into the sky, are just alternative skillful means to help your chi ascend when the energies become too powerful. They are all ways of basically imagining that your chi comes up and goes out the top of your head when it becomes too much to handle. These are various methods that were invented over time, in various traditions, to help you pull your chi up naturally so that you don't concentrate on all the energies below, engage in sexual activities, and then lose them. A master in the past simply invented such a technique, found it worked for his culture and tradition, and then passed it on, but it has no reality in itself because it is just an expedient skillful method.

If you practice such visualizations to help deal with the problem of sexual desire due to rising energies, you must forget both your body and mind, and let the energies proceed throughout your body without becoming entangled with it or becoming motivated by the thoughts and sensations it produces. It helps if you curl your tongue and swallow the saliva when doing this type of meditation practice to harmonize the energies when they arise.

Once again, you must just remember that this is simply an expedient method invented to help cure an ill, namely, to help you handle internal energy imbalances. If you can find another virtuous, non-harmful method that allows you to smoothen the chi flows within your body so that sexual desires do not bother you, then of course you would use it. People think these methods are all so mysterious, but they are all based on common sense principles as simple as that. Expedient methods such as this commonly assume the unusual forms they do simply because of the cultures they were invented within. They were given forms that would help keep the practices alive and transmitted to subsequent generations.

If you leave these rising yang chi energies alone and do not succumb to sexual temptations and the subsequent loss of energies this entails, that energy will work to open up the obstructions within your chi channels, which is what you are after. When people recite mantras they often feel their belly become warm, which is a similar sign indicating the opening of the internal chi channels. Warmth, movement and even physical discomfort are all signs that your chi is opening up the channels in a body region.

All meditation techniques, correctly performed long enough and with consistency, work to open up the body's chi channels, and when that happens people always encounter various unexpected physical phenomena they cannot explain. These are never anything to worry about when due to meditation, but are simply the sign that your real chi is arising and that you are sure to get the results you are seeking. The benefit of having such experiences is that they prove the truth that chi does indeed exist, and confirm the existence of the cultivation path.

The white skeleton meditation is a particularly useful cultivation technique for people in the health care field because after they can visualize the skeleton, many report that they are able to feel the energies of other people from a distance, and because they can feel other people's energies and obstructions, this often helps with their skills at medical diagnosis. It is therefore a meditation method I always recommend to doctors, massage therapists, martial artists, bodyworkers, dancers, and the like. Some people can even start to feel the outline of the skeleton within other people after they start practicing this meditation method. In practicing this technique, one often becomes able to feel the energies within other people, and various *thangkas* from Tibet show pictures of Buddhas and their consorts standing on skeletons to indicate that people who want to open up their channels should be practicing this technique.

We have mentioned the arousal of sexual desires due to ascending chi, but when people start to practice meditation techniques correctly, the energies that arise do not always result in sexual desire. Meditation naturally tends to increase the chi flow within the body, and for most people this simply gives them extra energy or makes them feel energized. It is only the very best practitioners, who awaken the deepest energies within their body, who *might* feel sexual desires. Most people will just feel extra energy, and so meditation is typically a very powerful way to bring more confidence and energy into your life. Meditation also helps to end cases of depression or sadness because of this increased chi flow. That is, of course, if the practitioner learns how to let go of their thoughts rather than continue clinging to these mental states. You have to want to let go in order to get rid of various emotions that continually arise.

Your internal chi flow is the natural life force of your body, but ignorant people who first feel this chi energy due to spiritual practices often tend to impose mystical or superstitious notions on its appearance. They often attribute these sensations to God or some other mystical religious process when its appearance and movement is simply a scientific physical phenomenon. You cultivate, your chi rises, you feel it. It's as simple as that. When your chi channels start opening, you'll experience all sorts of various phenomena, as explained in *How to Measure and Deepen Your Spiritual Realization, Tao and Longevity*, and *The Little Book of Hercules*. Those experiences and their sequence of occurrence are part of a scientific process, and the happenings are all non-denominational phenomena.

You must learn to ignore and let go of all the sensations that arise in your body as a result of meditation practice. Such feelings of internal energies will definitely arise. Remember that you are not the body, and all of the chi energies that arise are not you either. You can only say they are the process your body uses to purify itself of internal obstructions when someone starts to let go of their thoughts. You must not suppress these things, but simply observe them, and witness them with detachment. That's basic meditation practice.

Many people who practice yoga know of *Patanjali's Yoga Sutras*, which is a foundational book for yoga. The first words in the *Yoga Sutras* are: "This is the teaching of yoga. Yoga is the cessation of the turnings of thought. When thought ceases, the spirit stands in its true identity as observer to the world. Otherwise, the observer identifies with the turnings of thought." The practice of meditation, which is the practice of yoga, is therefore the practice of *becoming detached from thoughts so that the witness transcending the thoughts can be revealed.* Thoughts move, but the witnessing awareness that knows them is motionless and never moves. It is neither in the motion or stillness but transcends both so it can know both. It always transcends the experiences it knows. You actually want to find that witnessing awareness, which is the mind's nature and natural functioning, but you cannot do it if you are clinging to thoughts which mask it.

No matter what meditation method you employ, it eventually involves the two principles of cessation and witnessing, or stopping and observation. You practice some virtuous technique whereby your thoughts die down, stop (cessation), die away, diminish, decrease, dissolve, depart, empty out and so on. Even with thoughts gone, there remains a substanceless (insubstantial), on-going awareness that can never be destroyed. This is what allows you to know thoughts because this is their backdrop, and they are its same nature of consciousness. This pure, empty consciousness backdrop always remains and is what you ultimately are, as a being, but the incessant thought chatter with which you normally identify (cling) hides your ability to experience the purity of this awareness and its vastness. In any case, when thoughts die down, you should always practice witnessing or observing the mental state left behind and examine it carefully. Every meditation technique involves cessation and observation (witnessing) at higher and higher levels until the two actually become one.

The thought chatter of wandering thoughts is the problem we seek to eliminate through meditation. This internal chatter we hear in our heads is like the fleeting images of a movie we see projected on a screen. We can only see a movie if it is projected on an empty screen, and that empty screen is akin to the mind's empty true nature of awareness. It is insubstantial and empty like space. This base essence of empty awareness without substance, which you might also call pure consciousness without content, is primordial. It is the real you-nature, the real self or real stuff of self, and hence is called the "all-base," foundational nature or fundamental self. This is the essence of sentient beings as well as the essence of matter, too, which is something you will discover when you proceed far enough in your cultivation. If you understand this intellectually, and then also cultivate an "empty mind" that allows you to experientially understand this through a direct experience, then you can practice many different meditation techniques safely without fear of attaching to the body. That's the whole point of meditation practice.

The problem with many visualization techniques, especially in the Vajrayana school of Tibetan Buddhism, Hinduism, yoga and Taoism, is that many people cling to the tantric visualizations, identify with their body, or start playing with the energies that arise because they don't understand the basic principles of the practice and what they are ultimately trying to accomplish. Some even get lost in the visualization itself and forget to realize that it is all just a fictitious creation of the mind. The purpose of such techniques is to teach you how to develop one-pointed concentration so that wandering thoughts depart, and then you should, of course, let go of clinging to that visual image rather than remain in a mentally generated reality. That mental visualization is not a real realm either, and can never become anything real no matter how hard you try. It's just a fictitious mental scenario you provisionally create so that you have some object of focus.

After you have studied to attain the correct view or understanding of cultivation and have learned the basic techniques of visualization, only then is it safe to venture further into various tantric techniques where you visualize the chakras and chi channels in the body. Only after you have previously cultivated other meditation techniques as a preparation, so that they have somewhat loosened or opened your chi channels, is it wise to turn to tantric visualizations. Such visualizations tend to release lots of energy from within the body, and that is why few are introduced to them at the introductory stages of the cultivation path. Without having opened up a lot of chi channels prior to this energy release, the energies would usually be quite difficult for most unprepared people to handle. If someone is already prone to strong sexual desires then the results of tantric visualizations can amplify that problem because of the energy release, and they should therefore use breathing practices instead of visualizations.

As stated, if you suddenly open up your chi channels using forceful tantric techniques, without the benefit of having gradually opened the many channels within the body through prior preparatory work, it often releases internal energy currents that are difficult for most people to handle. You can find accounts of individuals in India experiencing painful *kundalini* awakenings after just practicing pranayama techniques, and only pranayama techniques, for several hours a day. This type of focus goes against wisdom because those individuals were never first taught about emptiness cultivation and non-clinging. It therefore represents an incorrect progression of practice. Nevertheless, these cases show that practitioners, in a short period of time, can indeed open up their energy channels from very simple practice techniques performed with consistency and intensity when a variety of conditions are right.

The problem for most practitioners is the lack of sufficient wisdom and the right view in pursuing such efforts, which is why tantric visualizations on chakras and channels are rarely taught to beginners. Without the right view, people often mistakenly believe that they are the body and that the pursuit of physical gong-fu and superpowers *are* the cultivation path, which is why the information in a book like this is ultra-important to such practitioners. Only wisdom (understanding) can guide people to become enlightened, not superpowers or the purified physical body. An example of the need for wisdom is Shakyamuni Buddha who spent years in fervent meditation practice, exhibiting tremendous discipline of practice effort and investigation. Yet, despite his incredibly successful gong-fu foundation, he did not attain enlightenment until with wisdom insight he finally awakened.

If your energies do start coming up from visualization or meditation practice in general, then that's proof positive for yourself that chi does exist, that such meditations are effective, and you can rest assured that your chi channels are starting to open. They will open to the extent that you learn how to let go of those energies and don't become involved with them, but just let them do what they want. There is no need to guide the movements of chi within your body, for how do you know what they must do and where they should go? You don't, even if you read texts that say that your chi should flow through certain meridians in such and such a direction.

As a beginner, you should therefore ignore texts that tell you to try to move your chi in certain ways such as in certain circular orbital patterns. Such practices rarely bring you any type of true progress. You want your mind to settle, such as is achieved through mastering a stable visualization, and then your real chi will arise (called yang chi or *kundalini*) to open up all these routes naturally. One should focus on meditation methods that do not involve more moving thoughts, but encourage thoughts to settle. If you are trying to move your chi energies with thoughts, how can your mind settle?

Therefore, the proper vehicle of practice is to cultivate meditation and simply let these chi energies arise when they do, but ignore them. Stay detached and don't let them pull you into fascination. No one succeeds in the Tao without learning how to let go of their body and its energies, which in turn transform the body on the spiritual path. The health, longevity, and quiet peace of mind that people seek all depend on their ability to awaken these energies through silence, and then let these energies arise and clear out the obstructions within their channels without getting involved in their doings. They will perform all sorts of cleansing transformations that you cannot predict or imagine, and yet this is the natural way of body perfection whose unpredictability matches the unfamiliar stages of going through puberty. When all these occur, you must simply let go.

Martial artists often use the white skeleton visualization to help improve their martial arts skills. The stability of the visualization, which is a quiet state of concentration, causes all of the body's chi to come up, and if martial artists have already worked to open up the chi channels in their muscles from martial arts exercises and other practices such as pranayama, they can then use that increasing chi flow in tune with their muscle movements to accomplish all sorts of amazing feats. For instance, they can learn how to match these rising energies with their muscular movements to accomplish a more powerful striking move, whereas in yoga one simply holds a posture that encourages the energies to open up particular chi routes highlighted by that position.

Some people who reach advanced skeleton visualization progress will also sometimes say they see dancing white skeletons in visions or in their dreams. This is because those skeletons symbolize that the earth element of the body – the densest type of body chi which is the most difficult to purify – is finally being purified and transformed. They might also say they saw dirty things coming out of their body, especially their fingers or toes, after they started consistently practicing the white skeleton visualization. Such visions usually simply indicate that dirty chi obstructions are being ejected from the body, and that their chi channels are becoming cleaned as a result of their practice. When people do mantra practice it is also common to have dreams and visions involving dirty things leaving the body through vomiting, defecation, or anything else that represents purging and purification.

Many people who achieve progress in their meditation practice also sometimes see internal parts of their body glow or brighten. These brightenings within their body are visionary phenomena that reflect upon the chi massing at a particular location, and they represent progress in chi purification. In ancient hatha yoga texts, the authors often say that by concentrating on a particular chakra location you will sometimes see a point that becomes as bright as ten thousand suns, which describes this very phenomenon with a bit of hyperbole. When you see such an internal brightening, which is usually a bright whitish or silver light seen as a visionary experience, this is a time when you should certainly continue doing whatever practices you are following, intensify your efforts, and refrain from losing your chi energies through the emission of sexual activities. That mental image can even become an effective focus of concentration practice just as is the image of an internal skeleton.

It is said in most cultivation schools that your body (your physical nature) is composed of five elements. There is a wind element component, which is your chi or life force. There is a space element, which is just empty space such as the interstitial spaces between your cells and joints. The fire element in your body represents your *kundalini* energy, or yang chi, and the heat of your body. The water element entails your blood, hormones and all the other liquid elements within you. The earth element of your body, which is the densest of all these, includes your muscles, tendons, sinews, flesh and skeletal bones. This earth element is extremely difficult to transform and purify, but the skeleton visualization technique helps along these lines tremendously. When you finally start making inroads into purifying the earth element chi of your body, that's when you might start to see skeleton pictures during your dreams or in visions during meditation practice. Such visions often happen due to meditation progress rather than occur because you used a particular technique. Hence, people who never use the skeleton visualization, for instance, might see a skeleton image to indicate this sort of progress.

As previously explained, you will also see skeletons in countless Tibetan *thangkas* where there is a picture of a Buddha or deity wearing skulls or standing on a skeleton. The purpose is to indicate that people who want to practice the high-level meditation techniques in these schools must always practice the skeleton technique as a preparatory practice. There is no way around this. The skeleton visualization practice is absolutely an essential precursor to these more complicated practices because it helps open up all the body's chi channels, transforms the body's earth element, and because its practice means you understand that you should detach from the body since it is not the real you.

The body is just an agglomeration of various elements and is not the real human being. Without this viewpoint, it is hard to make progress in the higher meditation practices that involve more directly cultivating your mind, and the chi energies of your body. If you were to think that these chi energies were you, or that cultivation means cultivating these energies, you would really be lost, which is why you need the right view before you can engage in any higher tantric practices.

WESTERN VISUALIZATION EXPERTS

As a visualization practitioner, it is nice to discover that visualization practice is not just helpful for spiritual pursuits but has other benefits as well. Visualization techniques in general, even if you do not turn them toward spiritual or health objectives, can result in remarkable mental achievements. In the field of science we find that Einstein used to conduct "thought experiments" that involved active visualizations of various experimental conditions, and due to this ability he achieved many of his famous theoretical breakthroughs. Einstein explained that he learned to think visually and made many mental experiments using a combinatory play of images in his mind.

Another Nobel Prize winner, Richard Feynman, learned how to visualize complicated calculations in his head, and learned how to put different colors on parts of the equations he envisioned to help him perform the computations. In his handling of the thermodynamics and in his formulation of the idea of the electromagnetic field, James Clerk Maxwell showed that he was another famous visual thinker who relied on visual modes of thought. Napoleon Hill, author of *Think and Grow Rich*, was also a practitioner of mental visualizations until he found that they took on a life of their own, whereupon he stopped his particular practice technique. One must always remain grounded in reality when performing visualizations, which is why the white skeleton method is often best.

Perhaps the most famous visualizer of all was Nikola Tesla, a rival of Thomas Edison, who used extensive visualization skills to create incredible inventions including the Tesla coil, induction motor, vacuum tube amplifier, fluorescent lighting, remote control, 3-phase electricity and radio. Tesla, rather than Marconi (who used over a dozen of Tesla's patents), is officially credited with inventing modern radio, as well as radio controlled robots and countless other inventions too numerous to list. He had over seven hundred patents to his credit due to his visualization skills!

Anyone can develop incredible visualization skills like Tesla if they stop tying consciousness to the body. The mind has incredible functional capabilities, such as the ability to think in images and hold them with stability, or the ability to perform complicated mathematical calculations "in the head," and you can start developing all sorts of mental skills like this when you learn, and practice the fact, that the mind can work independently of the body. It takes time to learn how to mentally detach from the body so that the mind operates independently without clinging to the body's chi, but it can be done.

The famous Austrian inventor, Viktor Schauberger, is an example of someone who also learned incredible inventive mental skills by using a special water meditation technique to learn how to dissociate from his body. It was because of this particular meditation, he said, that he was able to discover many of nature's secrets that became the basis of his inventions. It was all due to the fact that he learned how to detach from or disidentify from his body.

When the mind is always bound up with the body, clinging to its chi forces and energies, and when you are always bound to the idea that you are the body, it is hard to recognize that the mind can function independently of the body and can perform endless types of different skills or functions. In other words, it is hard to separate your thinking consciousness from your body-sensation consciousness, which is a wholly separate function. One becomes trapped in always holding onto the body, and one's mental capabilities thereby become greatly limited. When one's mental capabilities become free, all sorts of creative skills then become possible.

Thomas Edison at times employed a hypnagogic state to help his own inventive process, but this was an incorrect meditation technique since it involved cultivating an unclear and dull state of mind. Tesla, on the other hand, learned how to actively visualize his inventions completely with full awareness, including how everything fit together and moved when turned on. He could even refine the inventions in his head because of his stable mental visualization abilities.

Through his visualization practice, Tesla became capable of visualizing all the intricate movement of gears, cogs and motors within all his inventions, and this accounted for his high creativity which some people say has not yet been surpassed. In my opinion, his inventions far surpassed Edison's in many ways.

Einstein, Feynman and Tesla all admitted that visualization skills were important to their inventive thinking and means of scientific discovery. As just these three simple biographical examples show, visualization practice has powerful mental benefits even if one is not targeting the objectives of health, peace of mind or spiritual enlightenment. If I were younger and just starting out, training to become an engineer, scientist, mathematician or inventor, visualization practice would be a primary skill I would work at mastering (even starting in high school) because of the deep benefits it offers.

This would be especially true if I wished to enter the field of science, and I would also strive to learn some of the *super memory techniques* at the same time since they are related and require little extra effort. Though beyond this text, I would also want to learn and practice Altshuller's TRIZ from an early age as well starting in high school. Teaching this inventive methodology to the young could help our societies invent more things that solve our problems, and hence keep our economies rolling forward with creativity.

It is silly that schools do not teach mental skills such as super memory techniques and visualization abilities although we demand the capability of such skills! Therefore as parents you will have to teach them to your children yourself if you want them to excel in the world. Our schools do not even teach children the useful skill of mind mapping for organizing one's thoughts into coherent patterns. If we could teach people how to use the mind in a way that was detached from, or independent of the chi flows running around within our body (to which we are always attached without knowing it), we would truly produce many more brilliant people in the arts and sciences. Of course, as previously mentioned, such training must always remain grounded in reality, for we are not speaking of creating autistic dreamscapes or mental flights of fancy that lead to people living in solitary dream worlds of their own making. If you would practice learning how to detach from the body, by cutting off your habit of clinging to its energies and the idea that you are the body, you would realize that the mind's functions can be totally independent of the body, and that the process of thinking would not have to struggle against the body's internal chi flows.

Mental functions can exist purely in consciousness without depending on the body or the sense organs. All sorts of mental functions can be mastered if you just practice manipulating consciousness while trying to remain detached or independent of the body. Strongly holding on to the view of the body, or strongly attaching to its energies when you are trying to create a stable visualization, is the big problem with mastering consciousness so visualization practice means ignoring the view of the body when concentrating and just working on stabilizing the mental image instead. With independent visualizations of things like Sanskrit letters, Jesus on the Cross, Amitofo's Paradise, mandalas, a visage of Krishna, or the Kingdom of God, you want to ignore the sensations of your body while devoting yourself totally to the provisional mental scenario you create within your mind.

The very highest meditation practitioners often realize that the body you feel is also actually just an appearance within your mind, which is the same case as any visualization you create with your imagination. They realize that this image or view of the body you experience has fundamental equality with a mental image that you mental visualize since they are both made of consciousness. That being the case, you must disassociate from this strong identification with the body as being you, but rather, learn to treat it as just *another appearance within consciousness.* Realizing that the view of a body is also just another item in consciousness, and practicing the independence of other mental functions, one can establish a basis for incredible mental skills, and also be cultivating spiritual practice at the same time.

You must also remember that when you are working to master visualizations you should not be sporting a furrowed brow or clenched jaw or tensing anything during your practice. Just as when sitting in meditation and watching your thoughts, your face should remain serene to indicate that you are letting go of your body while performing this mental practice. Let go of your body and don't hold on to it in any way during practice but forget it entirely. If you feel pressure in the brain from any type of practice efforts, you must recognize that this is usually the chi trying to open up your chi channels in the head because of the success of your efforts. You do not need to push that chi to finish the visualization or hold it in any manner.

Therefore, you need to let go of these energies, feelings and sensations that arise during meditation – from whatever meditation practice you follow—because they are not you, and just let them continue their opening process. The real you is akin to a bodiless awareness that is totally free, without substance, and just functions, but this is something you can only prove after much work at meditation practice. If you are experiencing a real pressure in your head from such practices, it is sometimes because you are incorrectly pushing your chi around rather than independently exercising your mind while remaining free of attachments to internal chi flows. This is what I mean by saying you should remain detached from the physical body, and refuse to push its chi flows or circulate them in any fashion.

One of the challenges with meditation practice is that the body is feeding consciousness with so much input of physical sensations every moment, such as the sensations of its muscles and outer physical form. This feeling information is always present and so predominant that it basically monopolizes consciousness. The other trouble is that our body responds to our thoughts, and so we accordingly tend to take the body as our self. We then begin to get attached to these things and make them into a view of our self through a complicated process of self-identification.

One must learn how to turn away from all this, which means to detach from it. We end up mistakenly taking the body as our self because we attach to all this physical input that always seems to be there. Since these energies even move in response to our thoughts, we get bound up in all this and take this to somehow be part of the "me" whereas the empty awareness that knows this – the true you—actually operates separately from this.

The event of thoughts affecting chi arises because chi and consciousness are linked, and this is the mind-body connection science always talks about without recognizing the existence of chi. There is indeed a mind-body connection, or connection between consciousness and chi, but both are appearing in your mind's true nature, which is what you ultimately are. That is why you must detach from both your body and mind during meditation practice, and subsequently, both will start to transform and purify.

This is one of the key principles of meditation: we always want to detach from the view of being the body. Thoughts and the energies of the body are interconnected because our chi moves when thoughts move, and this interconnection often confuses us into taking the body as our self. Since you feel internal sensations as your thoughts move, so of course you would naturally start assuming that the body is you. If we detach from being tightly tied to the body, then we can eventually get rid of the notion that the body is the self and find where the thoughts really come from or what they arise upon, which is empty consciousness.

To detach from the body, we can start by independently cultivating mental visualizations. It is just fortunate that at the same time we are detaching from the binding hold which body fascination has upon us, we can also be cultivating the body directly due to opening its chi channels. If we focus on finding the nature of the mind by directly looking at consciousness itself, rather than the visualization, we can even begin to understand that the mind is insubstantial and inherently empty. This understanding makes it easier to detach from the view of the body because that view is just an appearance in consciousness as well, and so is not you.

You can realize this by trying to look directly at consciousness and trying to determine what stuff consciousness is actually made of. You can also realize this by trying to create and hold an independent mental visualization and then realize that this mental picture was made of consciousness that is just empty mind-stuff. As your mind becomes empty of wandering thoughts because of your practice, all the things we normally want to happen will naturally occur—your mind will then become empty, your internal chi will stir into awakening, and your body channels will finally open which will start transforming your body, too. All these effects are interconnected with visualization practice.

What comes first in all this, the chicken or the egg? It is all interconnected, which is why visualizations are an effective meditation technique for learning concentration, calming the mind, learning how to detach from the body, realizing emptiness (which is called purifying consciousness), opening up chi channels, and transforming the physical body. The effectiveness of this technique cannot be understated.

Because this meditation technique is so powerful, in some Indian tantric yoga and esoteric lineages, meditation practitioners are therefore taught to visualize an independent image in their mind of a vivid, colorful deity. You also practice to learn how to hold this mental visual image with stability. You "abide in the image," which simply means to hold it steady without having your mind wander everywhere. You just focus on creating and holding the image, and sometimes in connection with an emotional state (or other strong thought) that you try to hold with stability as well.

Tesla could do this with pictures of machines in his mind. His ability to concentrate was so good that he could even visualize moving parts without losing the continuity of the mental scenario he imagined. You don't have to become as good as Tesla, but his example teaches us that you just abide with the imagined visualized imagery and forget everything else, and that's working at developing concentration.

You can also practice the white skeleton visualization in your head like this, too, as Tesla did for moving inventions. You don't have to visualize the existence of bones as they lie within your body. The usual skeleton visualization has you visualize the existence of the bones within your body, so you can actually look at your body and imagine the white bones inside. However, you can imagine a picture of a skeleton in your head, as is done when visualizing a deity or holy figure, so that the image does not connect with your body at all. This is what is done in Tibetan deity yoga, or within any religion that teaches you to visualize some independent picture. It's a totally imaginary scenario you create, rather than referencing the bones (or chi channels) within your body, and hence is a quite related but different type of visual concentration practice.

This is a method of mastering concentration on a purely fictional internal image, and thus once again cultivating mental stability but without connecting the provisional image with your actual internals. With a purely mental skeleton visualization performed independent of your body, you practice exactly as before. You see a body image in your head, and imagine stripping off the flesh of the body progressing upwards from the feet starting with the left toe bone. You progressively visualize an entire skeleton of white bones just as before. What's left is an inner image of a white skeleton that you hold with stability. That's it. You are done. It doesn't even have to be your own skeleton you are visualizing, but just visualization practice on a white skeletal image. But if you are going to go this route, why not just learn how to visualize a moving invention or something else more useful? Alternatively, isn't it better to reap the extra benefit of cultivating the channels inside you?

The point of the skeleton visualization is that you visualize your internal bones as they exist within your body, which is why you study a skeleton model or pictures to get an idea of where they are, and tis practice thereby cultivates both your concentration *and* your body. It very quickly helps to transform the chi channels throughout your entire body, and because of its simplicity, you need not follow the more complicated chakra and chi channel visualization as taught in India and Tibet such as in the *Six Yogas of Naropa.*

Rather than independently visualizing a deity, you can perform this sort of visualization practice instead. Just hold the image for a bit and then release it. Holding the image with concentration does not mean pushing the energies around in your head so that you develop high blood pressure. You always try to remain unaffected by the chi of your body when you practice visualizations. When the image becomes stable, which means the mind has become quiet, then the next step is that you release your hold on the imagined picture as previously explained.

There are many types of skeleton visualization practice, and the particular one I have described is just one of the most popular techniques. The various practices of looking at your body and visualizing the skeleton inside it are excellent for healing because they can help bring chi to those regions. They require effort to master, but all meditation methods require a bit of effort at first. Remember that this technique, once mastered, helps you realize that your body is just a phenomenon in consciousness *and* it also helps you cultivate your chi channels directly. Whenever you develop a stable, steady, empty mind, many of your chi channels will open because your yang chi will start to arise. It's just a principle of science that is made use of in countless meditation methods.

What does it mean to release the visualization after you develop it and have calmed down your other thoughts? Let it go. Let it depart so that there is *nothing* there anymore. There are no images of a skeleton or anything else. Your mind is empty of thoughts, which seems like empty space as the best comparison. This is the same state of cessation, peace, tranquility, emptiness or silence that you are supposed to cultivate through any other meditation technique. You build up this provisional image of a skeleton (or deity) just as a way to try to cultivate this state of emptiness or mental quiet. It is simply a bridge to take you across a river to the other shore, which is to eventually experience an empty mind wherein the experience is like an infinite, boundless empty sky without clouds.

Our minds can perform wondrous functions independently of attachments to the body, such as visualizations. The ability to form visualized imaginations, or mental pictures, is just one of the many possible different functions of consciousness. Endless other functions, or capabilities, are possible. Matter even forms from consciousness, but only enlightened masters cultivate high enough to perceive (and prove) this fact, which they often demonstrate when they display supernormal powers. Various wisdom texts even explain how the original pure pristine awareness becomes the image of space, and then eventually what we know as matter which, in its essence, is still this pure, insubstantial, empty, changeless original nature all the while. Many religious individuals wonder how manifestation, creation or appearances came about, and this actually becomes understood by those who awaken.

Eventually, through meditation practice and internal investigation of the nature of consciousness, which you can do after your mind calms enough that wandering thoughts do not distract you or obscure your capability of insight, you can become able to recognize the base stuff of the mind itself. To directly, nakedly, experientially realize that you are really just the base stuff of what consciousness is, and as a human being are just an ongoing operation of its turning transformations, is self-realization or enlightenment. This ultimate basis is what you truly are, and what matter is, but you must discover this for yourself. You *can* cultivate to realize this on your own and it is a truly scientific investigation. If you don't want to realize it, which is silly, you should still be meditating anyway for all the mundane benefits it brings.

Instead of their internal skeleton, some people try yet another visualization technique which is to hold steady an image of an overly complicated mandala or elaborate description of a heaven in their mind that requires so much concentration that they finally give up, *let go of all their mental functions*, and just rest in emptiness through an abandonment of concentration that was taken to the limit. They tax their concentration and then let go when their mind just cannot hold on to anything anymore. It's like loading a bridge with so much weight that it finally collapses, or running so many programs on a computer that it slows down, and so this technique works at helping you attain an experience of emptiness from yet another entirely different angle or principle.

For this technique, is it important that you be able to visualize clearly and absolutely hold that image? No, because while you do practice to hold an image with accuracy and stability, and while that holding indeed will create mental stability, it is once again that empty state of mind which you are after. You use an overly complicated image because that will tax your concentration to its utmost, and then you abandon it altogether. You are not after the fact that you can hold the specific image with stability. Big freaking deal! So what? If you can, you now have another skill for life, but that's not the ultimate target of the practice.

As always, you are using this sort of a practice as a vehicle to *be able to reach an experience of mental emptiness or quiet.* Emptiness or "empty mind" is always the target of any genuine meditation technique. You want to directly experience what emptiness is so that you finally have a correct understanding of the empty nature of your mind. It just happens that this practice method, and all visualization methods, have the extra side benefit of leaving you with fantastic internal imagery and concentration skills. Such visualization skills may even help you win a Nobel Prize!

You should therefore never feel bad if you fail to create and hold any image with stability because you can always end a visualization practice session, no matter how bad, by releasing it into emptiness, and this is what you practice to attain. Of course, some people will be able to create and then hold with stability incredibly complicated mental images, which is a fantastic mental skill, but if they think that this is the point of the cultivation technique then they have missed the mark by a wide margin. I must emphasize over and over again that it is the realization of a quiet empty mind at the end of the practice, which you want to reach through the vehicle of quieting the mind by visualizing something with stability, which is the important thing. The target of meditation practice is a mind empty of thoughts, which you can achieve through various ways. Visualization practice is only one such technique.

When the mind becomes quiet and you look at it, and try to fathom what is this thing called mind, you will realize that it is empty and insubstantial. It has no substance to it, and nothing seems to be there when you look, but then again it gives rises to appearances. You therefore can't really say it's existent or non-existent. If it's truly existent, then how come it's insubstantial and empty by nature? If it's non-existent, then why are appearances there? It is therefore neither one nor the other, which is its non-dualistic nature.

The true essence or nature of the mind and consciousness is empty of anything phenomenal. There is no phenomenal essence there, and that emptiness is its essence or substance. Yet, appearances arise, but they are insubstantial, ungraspable, impermanent, don't reflect a self-so reality that stands on its own, and simply cannot stay. These words are easy to read and easy to intellectually understand, but hard to truly fathom without a direct experience of the empty nature of consciousness. However, visualization practice may help you make progress towards realizing this and other characteristics of the mind's true nature.

In attempting to master the incredible life skill of visualization, which has benefits that the examples of Einstein, Feynman, and Tesla have demonstrated, you can actually make great headway into realizing what is the underlying nature of the mind and the ultimate substance or essence of the human being. You will not realize it from visualization practice alone, but you can lay the foundation for progress along these lines. You use visualization to try to form a stable mental state without wandering thoughts, you then let that provisional image go to experience an empty mind, and you then examine/contemplate/observe/analyze that empty mental state to begin to understand the mind's true nature.

If I were asked what meditation methods one should consider practicing, I would therefore add visualization practices to the short list of the best techniques. You should definitely add the white skeleton visualization to the short list of methods you might include in a personal meditation practice schedule because of all the benefits it brings. That short list of meditation techniques includes mantra plus the standard mindfulness (emptiness) or witnessing meditation practice, called vipassana, which we previously discussed. These methods all work at quieting the mind, but are based on different principles.

The special benefits of the white skeleton meditation are the possibility of helping to transform your inner chi body at the same time you practice, and the possibility of developing mental visualization skills just for the sake of those skills alone. We have already seen how many great scientists and mathematicians owed their high creativity, productivity and inventiveness to the concentration powers achieved through visualization practice, which we have discovered is basically a meditation technique for calming the mind! Although we did not go into their stories, in addition to the scientists many religious greats also reached enlightenment because they concentrated on creating and holding imaginary internal visualizations as well!

The final meditation method I would add to this short practice list, which could be easily tagged on to the end of any sitting meditation practice session, would be anapana practice. Once you master anapana, which involves watching your breath and becoming aware of the chi flow and obstructions within the body, you could go on to combine anapana practice with white skeleton practice and in this way get the quickest results in meditation. But of course to get those results you must know the basis of meditation practice itself, which is why you must also practice and study the principles behind vipassana, or cessation-contemplation meditation practice.

5

PRANAYAMA AND ANAPANA

All of the meditation techniques that we've discussed so far work on slightly different principles of mental calming. In other words, they all have a different *modus operandi* and attack the objective of quieting the mind from entirely different angles. This also holds true for the last two basic techniques I want to recommend, which are pranayama and anapana breathing practices that come from ancient India.

In the Indian pranayama practices of yoga, you often practice alternate nostril breathing wherein you breathe in through one nostril, hold your breath for a certain period of time, and then exhale it through the other nostril. Alternatively, you might breathe in through one nostril and then, after holding it for a certain period of time, exhale it through the same nostril. In different pranayama exercises there are also various ratios to the amount of time that you spend inhaling your breath, holding it, and exhaling it. If you vary these ratios, you can thereby come up with hundreds of different pranayama techniques. If you add in the fact that you can practice the inhalation, exhalation and breath retention phases in different stationary or moving body postures, the number of possible practices explodes again.

There are therefore hundreds of possible pranayama techniques, and there are even temples in India where all you do is practice pranayama for hours every day. While the techniques you learn are truly amazing, unless you practice emptiness meditation in conjunction with these techniques, I have not found the graduates of such programs to have accomplished much at all in terms of cultivation attainments. They may calm their minds to some small degree but only emptiness meditation, which teaches you to empty your mind and let go of your chi, will enable it to truly open your channels in the deepest, most profound way called a "*kundalini* awakening," that leads to the deepest type of mental calming.

A *kundalini* awakening is simply when the real yang chi of your body finally arises because you've been cultivating emptiness correctly. When you are "cultivating emptiness" it simply means that you are letting go of thoughts, which you do during any type of meditation practice, and then they die down to leave a quiet mental scenario. You stop attaching to your stream of consciousness because you are just watching it with alert aloofness, so thoughts eventually quiet down because you don't feed them clinging energies of attention that push them forward, and your mind thus becomes somewhat emptier or "empty" as attachments die down. In letting go of your thoughts, you also cease holding on to your internal chi currents that are connected with thoughts. When your chi thereby becomes independently free to resume its normal, natural circulation free of the influences of thought attachments, it will start opening up various chi channels within your body.

When enough channel obstructions in the body are pierced, this finally makes it possible for you to open and then feel a full orbital circulation of chi within your body. Your chi energies arise and start circulating through these pathways, and you end up feeling this, which is why it is described in many traditions. There are many such complete orbital paths within the body, but people usually feel the chi going up their spine and down their front first. Thus we say your "chi ascends" because you can strongly feel the circulation of this chi rising along the spine, commencing from below, and then it descends after it reaches the top of the head. When a lot of chi comes up within the body to simultaneously open up many pathways, that, in short, is the full body *kundalini* awakening. The chi is not just felt in the spinal channel, but is voluminously felt everywhere.

The best form of pranayama practice for meditation purposes, which also helps in the objectives of health, longevity and spiritual progress, is one in which you breathe in and then hold your breath for as long as possible before you exhale. This type of forceful breath retention, maintained for as long as is possible, tends to help pry open some of your chi channels, but not the tiniest ones. It is also very helpful for harmonizing your body for cultivation efforts, and for dealing with excessive sexual desire.

I have seen countless "qi-gong masters" visit my teacher in China, and one of the common characteristics of their visits was that many people often felt sick or physically uncomfortable sitting next to them or near them.

This is because their chi did not flow smoothly within their bodies due to the incorrect qi-gong cultivation methods they had used. Those methods evolved from an incorrect understanding of pranayama and anapana techniques, and hence their practice did not lead to a proper balanced opening of their chi channels. As a result, while they indeed started to transform their body from their practices, they did not achieve a harmonious smooth circulation of internal energies, and others could feel this. My teacher would always prescribe the nine-bottled wind practice to help these practitioners, which would quickly help to harmonize their uneven openings (especially around the root chakra from which the chi starts ascending), and then many of these and other troublesome issues for these practitioners would usually go away. You'll be learning that technique in a short while, and it can greatly help anyone's meditation or other spiritual efforts.

To improve your pranayama retention efforts, you should time and record how long you can hold your breath each time you practice. If you record this on a chart, you can see whether you are making progress or not over time, and can use that visual cue as a motivation to help you increase the time spent in retention. You want to be able to hold your breath for longer and longer periods as you progress in practice, but you want to do this while your body is relaxed and you are not straining your muscles because that is actually fighting the practice. As with all cultivation practices, you start gradually at practicing this technique and build up your capability in incremental steps rather than attempt to become a "breath holding hero" in one day.

This tiny act of recording your retention time will help you make a lot of progress at breath retention. One of the tricks I would use to help with my own progress was to watch the clock as I was holding my breath and each time try to beat yesterday's score, or the highest score achieved so far. When you monitor your practice in this way and try to beat a previous score, as do weightlifters in noting the top weight they can lift with multiple repetitions, it becomes a great spur to your practice progress.

THE NINE-BOTTLED WIND PRANAYAMA PRACTICE

Of the hundreds of different pranayama methods you can practice, the best I have ever discovered (which many other pranayama experts have also confirmed to me as their top pick, too, out of the hundreds of techniques they have tried) is the **nine-bottled wind practice** from Tibet that my teacher taught me. While he knows many techniques, and while I know hundreds myself, it is the only pranayama practice that he consistently recommends. Naturally the practice goes by several different names, but they all involve the number nine because you hold your breath nine times when using this technique.

In this practice, you first hold your left nostril shut while slowly inhaling air through your right nostril deeply into your lungs, and then you hold your breath for as long as possible while holding the left nostril shut with one finger. The ribs should be stretched apart during the retention phase, which is accomplished by taking your free arm with an inward curved wrist, and pressing it against your shins to lift the chest and spread the ribs. When you cannot hold your breath any longer after inhaling, you quickly and forcefully exhale the air through the right nostril since it is not being pinched shut. You do this for a total of three times.

Next you repeat the same procedure three times by holding your right nostril shut and inhaling through the left nostril. You slowly breathe in through your left nostril, as slowly and as deeply as possible to fill your lungs to the fullest, and then you try to hold your breath for as long as possible until you just cannot retain it anymore. At that point you forcefully exhale it *as quickly as possible*. You don't let it out slowly, but forcefully shoot it out so like an arrow being shot from a bow.

Most people don't pay attention to this instruction of quick release, or to the fact that the inhalation phase should be slow, long and deep. They also neglect to note that while retaining your breath you must relax your body as much as possible using absolutely as few muscles as possible. If you are straining your muscles to hold in your breath, how can the chi channels within your body, and within those muscles, open? If you hold tightly, you are actually fighting your chi which is trying to open them. They cannot open when you tighten your muscles because it is like twisting or crimping a water hose when you want the water to go through it, so you have to learn how to hold your breath without force even while you are struggling to prevent yourself from taking in more air.

While traditional yoga pranayama exercises usually employ a ratio of 1:4:2 for the amount of time spent during inhalation, holding your breathing, and exhalation, with the nine-bottled wind practice you simply inhale gently for as long as possible, retain the breath for as long as physically possible, and then exhale as quickly as possible. The important thing is to hold your breath, without as little strain as possible, for as long as possible.

The last set of three repetitions in this practice, to compete the set of nine, is then to breathe in through both open nostrils and repeat the same process. This is clearly explained and illustrated in the book *Twenty-Five Doors to Meditation*, but here are the steps once again.

The following instructions simplify the method by concentrating on describing only the important points. It leaves out some of the elaborate hand gestures you make after flicking your wrist outwards and rotating it before returning to pinch your nostril shut, as well as how to hold your free arm in such a way that it becomes locked straight with wrist in-turned while pushing against your shin to raise your chest and spread your ribs. Various videos on the internet are available that illustrate how this is done. In order to practice the basic nine-bottled wind technique, you:

1. Sit in an upright position.

2. Visualize your body becoming as clear as crystal.

3. Close your mouth and using the index finger of your left hand to close your left nostril, press your finger against the left nostril and inhale the air into your lungs slowly through your right nostril. The inhalation should consist of a long, gentle, deep breath—*as long and as deep as possible.* Try to bring the air in down as deep into your body as possible, and compact it as much as possible. Once again, *do not keep it in the upper chest* but try to push it down and bring it as low as possible into the body. While pinching your nose with your finger, your arm should be held in a position that is extended in a perpendicular angle to your body. If you want, during your slow inhalation you can visualize that your body becomes filled with light and that this light dispels any internal poisons, darkness and obstructions. *You continue inhaling as slowly and deeply as possible until you are "full" of breath* and can inhale no longer. As an expedient means, some people find they can inhale more air into the body when they imagine that the lungs have an upper, lower and middle section, and they visualize that they fill the lower section first; then the middle section; and finally the upper lungs. Later they sometimes visualize filling the whole abdomen with breath. Such visualizations can be useful, but are optional. *The important*

point is to breathe in as much air as possible as deeply into the body as possible, and to pack as much as possible into that space.

4. When your lungs become full, relax your body as much as possible while your arms remain extended (one juts out to the side perpendicular to the body, and the other presses against your calf to raise your chest and spread the ribs) holding your trapped breath within. *That air must be held inside your lungs for as long as you possibly can without allowing it to leave the body, and yet you must use as few muscles as possible to retain it without leakage.* If you like, while holding your breath you can fix your attention on the point between the eyebrows, but don't put any mental or physical pressure on that spot. Just place your attention on that region and forget your other thoughts during the duration of breath retention. It is also important while holding your breath that you maintain an upright position without tightening any muscles so that your chi is free to start opening up all the tiny channels in your body that might be compressed as a result of straining your muscles. Think about this fact: if you tighten your muscles with strain rather than relax them, then even if your chi has a lot of force it will not be able to pass through the chi channel pathways in these muscles because the straining will tend to crimp and squeeze the channels shut. If you can learn how to disidentify from the body (and thought activity) while holding your breath, experienced breath retention practitioners can hold their breath for several minutes, even as their face starts to turn red and they pass through a stage wherein they shake, perspire or it seems as if they are about to black out. This stage might be frightening the first time it happens, but indicates that the wind element is opening up the body's tiny chi channels everywhere.

5. *When you can hold your breath no longer, exhale it as quickly and forcefully as possible through the open nostril.* You shoot the retained air out of your lungs, and that exhalation completes one round of this exercise. You must repeat this exercise of slow but deep inhalation, long breath retention, and quick forceful exhalation two more times, for a total of three times for the right nostril

that is open. All the while the left nostril is kept closed with a single finger while the active nostril is the right nostril.

6. Switch hands, so that the right hand now pinches the right nostril closed with the index finger, and the left nostril is left open. Inhale through the left nostril following the equivalent instructions just as before. Repeat this breath retention exercise three times for the new nostril. Thus, six repetitions of this exercise will now have been completed.

7. When the left and right nostril breathings are both done, extend both arms with your wrist in-curled to push on your calves so that they extend and lock to lift your chest, which spreads your ribs. Using neither of your hands, since they are both pushing on your shins, inhale slowly through both open nostrils, hold your breath for as long as possible as before, and then exhale quickly through your open nostrils when you can't retain the air any longer. Do this a total of three times. *Altogether nine inhalations and retentions are performed*, which gives rise to the name of "nine-step" bottled wind practice or "nine bottled winds." As with martial arts, the names for special techniques that have survived over time to come down to us are often very colorful like this.

8. Most people hate this pranayama technique because it forces you to hold your breath, and you really want to let go. Going against that inclination amplifies the emotion of dislike to the extreme, and yet those who persist in the practice find countless benefits such as an improved complexion, clearer thinking, and even, in some cases, weight loss. Yes, weight loss! If you absolutely cannot do all nine repetitions, just do one complete round of three breath retentions (one each for the left, right and dual nostril situations) when getting started until you build up stamina for the technique and get past the dislike.

The important point to this technique is to hold your breath, after drawing it in, *for as long as possible*, during which time you should not tighten your muscles. You should never employ too much force in restraining your breath but simply hold your breath, with one nostril shut, *using as few muscles and as little energy as possible.* It is most beneficial to always practice on an empty stomach and after your bladder (and bowels if possible) has been emptied. The four phases of the process to remember are:

- Slowly drawing air into the lungs.

- Fully filling the lungs as much as possible as if they were a bottle or balloon that had to be packed with compressed air, and so you pack them as much as possible as deeply as possible (many people are upper chest breathers who only inhale into the upper part of the lungs and thereby derive little benefit from the practice). Inhale deeply!

- Holding the air inside the lungs for as long as possible while remaining as relaxed as possible during retention (not tensing the muscles to restrain the air, but keeping them as relaxed as humanly possible). After a while when you are holding your breath during the process, your lungs may begin to make an expansion-contraction movement of attempted breathing. When this somewhat involuntary movement occurs, you should relax as much as possible and just bear it without exhaling or inhaling again, and yet without using too much force continue to maintain your retention if you can.

- Quickly expelling the air from the lungs when you can hold it no longer, shooting it out like the release of an arrow.

You don't have to guide your breath or chi or do anything at all except RELAX during the state of pranayama breath retention. The longer you can learn to hold your breath, which is the breath retention state called *kumbhaka*, the more meditation progress you are likely to achieve though any other methods you use.

It is common during a typical meditation session to eventually reach a stage where your breathing slows down naturally when your mind calms and you truly let go. Your respiration may even become so slight that it seems to stop altogether. When that happens you should relax, try to hold that state of non-breathing with the very tiniest pressure (none at all is best), and at the same time drop any attachments to all your senses (seeing, hearing, feeling, etc.).

This stage, when your external breathing naturally stops, is when the real yang chi within your body starts to arise. Just let go when you experience this effortless respiratory cessation since it occurred naturally without force. If your body wants to take a breath it will, so don't worry about its doings, but just ignore it and let it go. As stated, you can even use a tiny bit of force to help maintain this state of naturally occurring respiratory cessation whenever it happens, and it will appear when you are meditating really well (from whatever technique you have been using) because your thoughts have quieted down. If you use this tiniest bit of effort to maintain this state, it will help to transform your body rather quickly.

If you have to concentrate on something when your breathing reaches this natural state of pausation, just lightly put your attention on the spot between the eyebrows when this occurs, or even visualize a tiny bright circle or flame at that point. If you can practice like this, which is difficult at first but becomes easier after many experiences, this will help your real chi to start to arise within your body. That's what you want! During the time that your breathing seems to stop, your inner life-force starts arising and then begins to open up your internal energy channels, and this is what produces the physical transformation of the opening of the chi channels within your body. Everyone thinks this entails some strange process, but it's a simple as that. Some yoga traditions say to concentrate on the toes, soles or heels of the feet during a forceful retention phase, and to even imagine those areas shining with bright white light, and this is another method as well that encourages the chi channels in the legs to open.

As to pranayama techniques like the nine-bottled wind, the practice of forcibly holding your breath with physical restraint actually encourages your body to pry open various chi channels that make this natural state of respiratory cessation much more likely to occur. Hence, the nine-bottled wind pranayama technique is actually a cleansing or purification practice. *You can even consider it a detoxification practice* because of what it helps do for the body. The forceful holding nature of the nine-bottled wind exercise prepares you for the naturally occurring state of respiratory cessation, which is the real accomplishment you want to achieve.

I must warn you that everyone who practices the nine-bottled wind technique hates it, but everyone who has practiced it sincerely has told me it greatly accelerated their meditation practice. To be sure, this pranayama technique is a bit uncomfortable, which is why everyone dislikes this practice, but if you learn to hold your breath for longer and longer periods of time you will tend to open up constricted areas within your body, and you will move on to a new level of meditation attainment.

If you pass the initial hurdle of learning how to bear the discomfort of holding your breath, and continue with this practice for many months, your pranayama practice will eventually become really effective and the benefits to your body will be tremendous. Pranayama practice alone can often help your real yang chi to arise, and if you have prepared your body for this through prior meditation efforts, it can really lead to substantial results.

You should never perform the nine-bottled wind pranayama exercise while standing up if you have low blood pressure because you may pass out and then fall to the ground. People with high blood pressure should stay away from breath retention techniques as well. They should instead practice breathing mindfulness techniques, called anapana, which we will cover further.

To get even better results from yoga pranayama practices, including the nine-bottled wind, you might reference the breath holding techniques utilized in the sport of deep sea free-diving. These special techniques might be adapted to whatever pranayama breath retention methods you are using, and thus might be used to help you increase the length of time you can hold your breath.

The practice of breath retention not only helps to awaken the yang chi in your body and open up many internal chi channels, but as stated, prepares you for the unexpected event that always happens when people really start to get good at meditation – their breathing naturally slows to a halt as they relax both their body and mind. This, as stated, is when their real yang chi within their body starts to arise, which is traditionally called "internal breathing." This is what really opens up chi channels, not the forced stage of breath retention.

NATURAL *KUMBHAKA* RESPIRATORY CESSATION

The genuine opening of your chi channels is never really accomplished by Indian *kumbhaka* techniques or the nine-bottled wind, for that is just a figurative way of speaking. Chi is what opens up your chi channels, but your breath can activate your chi. Therefore, all pranayama practices help prepare for this truest type of opening, and they can help you expand your lung capacity as well. Traditional pranayama methods constitute a preparatory mechanism of cleaning the body and helping to open some of its chi channels so you can reach this more genuine stage much quicker and easier. How breath retention exercises work to do this is beyond the discussion level of this text.

If you really meditate to a deep level, not only will your thoughts die down, but as noted, your breathing will often slow to a natural halt. Essentially, you will calm your thinking and relax so much, and so many internal chi channels will have opened because of all your prior practice, that your body's need for external respiration will decrease and your breathing will appreciably slow. You can start surviving on the circulation of internal chi alone, which is why the external respiration can come to a halt in the first place. In the state of *dhyana-samadhi,* this is what happens.

At an even higher stage of practice, the beating of your heart will slow and your pulse will stop, too, but this only happens at extremely high levels of meditation for masters and adepts. Many religions talk about these advanced stages of attainment, and if you want more information you can turn to the explanations found within Buddhism, Taoism and Indian yoga literature. If you want to read autobiographical or biographical accounts of such things, you can also turn to the records of the Christian and Muslim mystics and saints, too. Everyone is always accessing the same levels of meditation achievement, so it is natural to find people from within all traditions describing the same levels of achievement.

The results of practice, no matter what road you traveled to attain them, are non-denominational. These are the shared stages of practice. The question for you, therefore, is whether you are on the right road within your tradition and whether you are practicing to attain these stages. If not, what are you trying to attain or achieve, and will you really do so by your efforts? You have to stop and think about this for yourself rather than just accept the words of your own religion, for you must also remember that the world has plenty of other competing religions with quite different viewpoints and teachings entirely. So why should yours be right, and the others wrong, other than the fact that you were born into it and have become accustomed to it and its teachings? "Belief" is not a good answer because you can believe many things that are wrong or which in turn out to be wrong, including viewpoints in physics or opinions that a new Republican or Democratic president will behave in a certain way that turns out to be against expectations. Do you want to put your future outcome in the hands of such belief?

Because it is so unusual for human beings to reach this state of respiratory cessation, this event must be emphasized and explained again and again so that you do not become frightened when it occurs, but instead welcome this progress. When you regularly practice meditation and correctly relax your body while watching your mind, in time, your thoughts and the energies (chi) of your body will both calm down. Because your thoughts calm down, your breath or breathing or respiration will naturally subside and become as if almost non-existent.

This state of natural respiratory cessation is a state of effortless *kumbhaka* breath suspension that you want to *stay in for as long as possible when it occurs, as it will help you transform your body very quickly*. It is just naturally occurs, and during this time your mind – because it is not experiencing many thoughts—can rest quietly in meditative tranquility. Don't' try to move your thoughts when you reach this type of experience, but just remain in the mental emptiness watching.

This is a time when the truly transformative yang chi of the body, which is the only thing that truly opens up your internal chi channels, arises and starts doing its work. Hence, if you can hold this state of respiratory cessation with just a little bit of effort, that's fine because you want to try to prolong it for as long as possible. Try to maintain it by holding your breath with a very minimum amount of effort. On these lines, *it helps to hold the pausation after an outbreath* instead of after an inbreath.

Since during this state of naturally occurring breath cessation your real yang chi will start to arise and start opening up your chi channels, this constitutes a *kundalini* awakening of a gentle sort and you will begin to feel the warmth and energy movement. People don't realize that this is a *kundalini* awakening, but that's what this is since your internal yang chi is rising. That's why you can stop breathing, namely because your yang chi is feeding you energy. After many years of meditation practice, the rising energies will eventually become extremely forceful, and that is when all the major chi channel meridians will finally open from that force. Various pictures of Hindu, Buddhist and other deities are often shown with pokers, tridents, axes and other instruments in their hands to represent the work of that yang chi in prying open closed, obstructed chi channels.

Forcefully holding your breath through pranayama practice prepares you for this natural type of respiratory cessation. In turn, that natural state of respiratory cessation prepares you for this forceful type of voluminous opening. That type of forceful opening, described in *The Little Book of Hercules*, leads to all the major chi channel meridians of the body becoming opened in a very short period of time.

Another key principle to emphasize in this discussion is that this type of natural respiratory cessation occurs due to your efforts at emptiness meditation as you progress even if you never undertake forceful pranayama practice. Forcefully holding your breath in pranayama produces an artificial *kumbhaka* with strain whereas this is a totally effortless, natural result which just happens when you start to meditate very well. If you cultivate an empty mind, it just happens. Artificial *kumbhaka* practice therefore just helps natural *kumbhaka* happen more quickly because it contributes to the health of the body.

As with the daily practice of brushing your teeth, everyone should be practicing pranayama for the purposes of increasing and maintaining their physical health. They should be practicing pranayama techniques regardless as to whether they are meditation practitioners. Pranayama practice helps quicken the purification of the body that is necessary for health, longevity, higher energy, mental clarity and spiritual progress. To get the best benefits from pranayama practice, however, your efforts *should be matched with emptiness meditation* because that enables you to achieve more than just the breath retention exercises alone. The lack of simultaneous meditation practice is why individuals who spend time in pranayama retreats never seem to get the biggest benefits possible from their efforts.

ANAPANA PRACTICE

Related to pranayama practice is the practice of anapana where you sit in the traditional cross-legged meditation posture and, instead of watching your thoughts as in regular vipassana meditation, you switch from watching your thoughts to just watching your breathing and witnessing the internal movements and sensations related to this without getting entangled up with them.

Anapana is the practice of silently watching your breathing, rather than thoughts, and through that practice, thereby calming your mind. Later you will begin to feel energy movements within your body related to your chi flows as you do this, and the method can then expand to include that as well. However, initially you usually won't be able to feel any chi or energies within your body, so at first you just focus on watching your breathing with its ins and outs so that your mind calms down, while also remaining cognizant of any internal sensations as well. Instead of watching moving thoughts with a dispassionate third party type of awareness observation, you watch your moving respiration instead with that same dispassionate detachment.

You don't have to try to feel the internal movements of your lungs because anapana is focused on mental calming, and straining to feel anything will inhibit that calming. *You just notice-witness whatever you feel and you don't try to create any new feelings or sensations.* Anything else you can feel will come with time, and at the beginning it helps to *just concentrate on watching the rhythmical nature of breathing, while also trying to feel your body energy as a whole, to reduce your level of thought distractions and thereby calm your mind.* The point is that you stay focused on witnessing your breathing so that your mind does not get diverted into following other random thoughts as it usually does. The focus stays on your breathing. Instead of paying attention to your thoughts without getting sucked in, in this case you concentrate on witnessing a different moving process, which is your in and out respiration.

Anapana practice links the witnessing function of your mind with your breath by focusing on initially knowing just the doings of your breathing, namely the alternating inhalations and exhalations of respiration, and then later anything else you feel within your body. You only focus on knowing your breathing through the nostrils, in and out, and so your only thoughts become focused on your respiration just as they might become focused on a visualization if you were doing one. Because your breathing naturally calms down as you meditate (which happens when you practice any type of concentration, such as a visualization), through this unity of your calming respiration and your witnessing or following of that respiration, your thoughts will quiet down in conjunction with your breathing slowing down and coming to a natural halt. At that time your mind will be quiet and your breathing will be quiet, and so you will thereby gain an experience of mental quiet (emptiness) while your transcending awareness remains open and alert. In other words, you watch your breathing, your breathing and thoughts will thereby calm down (because breath is connected to your chi and your chi is connected with consciousness/thoughts), and then you try to remain in that state as an effortless observer or witness.

In mantra practice you listen to the mantra sounds and your thoughts eventually die down. You simply concentrate on listening, and then random thoughts eventually die down because you ignore everything except the mantra. Therefore the mind eventually quiets. If you are reciting a mantra while sitting down in a meditation posture, then you will also eventually reach this state of natural respiratory calming, or cessation. Now you can reach it again through a different mechanism, but in this case you tie your attention to the process of following your breathing, instead of a mantra recitation. When your breathing slows down and stops, as it always does when you relax and let go of tying yourself to the stream of wandering thoughts, your thoughts will die down, too. They don't stop totally, but will calm down enough so that you can get an experience of a relatively empty mind. Hence, this is a way to cultivate mental emptiness.

If you sit and visualize a mental image and can hold it with stability, as you begin to attain this state of mental concentration your miscellaneous wandering thoughts must also die down otherwise you couldn't hold the picture with stability but would get distracted all the time. Hence, with proper visualization practice your mind will also quiet and your breathing will slow down, too, just as with anapana or vipassana practice. This calming of your breathing contributes to your ability to cultivate an empty mind. All these methods aim at the same end result.

Anapana targets the final objective of mental quieting by tying your attention to your breathing and your internal body energies rather than to an image (visualization), thoughts (prayer or affirmation) or sound (mantra). You are making use of the principle that eventually your breathing will quiet, so you tie your thoughts to that process of the breath going in and out, and when it is no longer there your mind will have emptied/quieted, too. It's as simple as that, but everybody gets all confused about the practice because there are so many variations and discussions regarding your internal chi energy, which is called "breath" in traditional instructions. With that quieting, you can realize a taste of emptiness, just as you can through any of the other meditation techniques we have discussed.

Here's how you practice. With anapana meditation, you first sit down and start following (witnessing or observing without force or attachment) your breathing as your breath moves in and out through your nostrils. Just know it and ignore everything else like you would do if you were trying to keep your mind on a visualized image. You keep your mind focused on your respiration and just follow your breathing through your nostrils while feeling your body's energies as one whole if you can.

Know when the air is going in or out through your nostrils, and stay focused on witnessing that and any internal feelings that arise within your body as a whole. Whatever you can feel, just keep noticing that along with your breath as it enters the nose while ignoring other wandering thoughts, and bring your mind back to your breathing when your thoughts start to stray. You practice abiding in the transcending awareness that knows the whole body as a single unit, and watch the breathing and any internal sensations you can feel inside it. The body will eventually feel like an empty sack because all the chi channels inside will open, and in cultivating this way without attachment (remember, you are observer like an independent third party observer who is not the body or mind) you enable all sorts of internal chi channels to open.

The great thing about your breathing is that it's a rhythmical process that tends to calm down over time when you become relaxed instead of mentally scattered. Additionally, if you are tasked with watching your breathing, its natural rhythm always has the potential to bring your mind back to the task of observing your respiration so that you don't get lost in following other thoughts, for stray thoughts are sure to arise. Before you get too lost in following other wandering thoughts which are sure to arise, another inhalation or exhalation occurs, and you are immediately reminded to return your focus to your breathing. If you just practice vipassana witnessing, you can think you're not getting lost in following your thoughts, but you usually end up getting entangled with thoughts and distracted anyway.

The rhythmical nature of breathing, and the instructions to have you focus on just that breathing while ignoring other thoughts, partially protects you from this if you practice correctly. You might get lost in some train of thought that arises but woops, all of a sudden you notice another breath, so back to focusing on the respiration you go. You use the natural mechanism of breathing to return you to the act of concentration.

After awhile practicing anapana, you will notice that the body just breathes by itself naturally and automatically. You can let go of the body because there's nothing you need to do. You don't need to imagine how things should feel inside your body either, but just observe the breathing and how it feels everywhere inside as one whole. This dispassionate detachment will help calm your breathing and open your chi channels. You should remain independent and view the body internals as a whole of one feeling (with different sensations inside) bounded by the container of the skin in order to cultivate mental calming. Mental calming or quieting is certainly what happens as your chi and mind then calm down and your chi channels start to open.

Your body will go through many transformations of its own if you just watch it without having to do anything. This is the result of cultivation. This is absolutely correct. Sometimes your breathing will stop and you will just remain in that state effortlessly observing without feeling any pressure or need to breath for a long while. At that time your chi is continuing to open up many chi channel circulatory routes, and you should simply remain clear and cognizant of all these various internal transformations that you feel, while the respiration has stopped, as the opening of the chi channels proceeds.

Whenever your breathing eventually slows down during any type of meditation, your mind will also have become quieted at the same time and this is the experience of emptiness (mental calming) you want to reach. In this case, you simply arrive at it by *tying your attention to your breathing, an automatic process of ins and outs that keeps your mind from wandering, until your mind finally calms and quiets*. Some say the mind quiets or quits, but this just means that thoughts settle down and you reach a state of empty mind.

Like watching your thoughts, this meditation practice doesn't take any special effort other than the effort of deciding to actually do it. You are just mentally watching something that moves, and in this case the focus is on the breathing that is connected with your chi and consciousness because of the mind-body connection, along with the sensations that arise within your body due to chi flows. You don't do anything about these sensations but just know them or feel them. Furthermore, you just treat the internals of the body as one whole, one entire little world that you dispassionately view with your awareness. What takes effort is keeping your mind focused on the breathing and your internal sensations, rather than get distracted by or lost in following other wandering thoughts. We always have trouble keeping our minds concentrated or focused on any single topic for any period of time, and that challenge will arise for this meditation practice as well. Of course, here you are training to get over that wandering tendency by remaining focused on your breathing. In visualization practice we kept our minds focused on something we provisionally mentally created which was to be held in a fixed/stationary capacity, and in this case we keep our attention focused on something moving while remaining detached and independent, so the practice is a bit different. That's the differentiating principle. One has a stable focus of attention, one has a moving focus of attention that in time, because breathing and thoughts both calm down, actually turns into a stable focus of attention that is empty mind.

The main reasons we can eventually relax and realize emptiness this way, by concentrating on something that is moving rather than stationary, is because your breathing is tied to consciousness and because we are abiding in the transcending awareness that witnesses without becoming attached to the body or taking the body as our self.

Your breathing and chi are linked, and your chi and mind are linked. As your respiration naturally calms down because you relax, as that occurs your mind will also calm down to become relatively empty of thoughts. Your breathing will become quiet, so your mind will become quiet because your chi will have become quiet. That's it, that's the body-mind principle of practice this depends upon and from there you can make further progress and branch out into all sorts of techniques once the basic principle is understood, mastered and you develop some gong-fu along these lines.

As with visualization practice, when you reach that stage of quiet, you should just continue to experience the "emptiness" of a mind that seems wider, larger or more clear because it doesn't have too many random thoughts running about. You continue to watch the body and the chi sensations which arise in your body at this time, but stay in the experience of an empty mind as the abiding or transcending awareness. Your chi will accordingly come up, internal transformations will start to happen, and it will all be because you reached a state of empty mind wherein you are not attaching thoughts anymore.

The challenge to this meditation technique is ignoring all the other thoughts that always arise in the mind while you are trying to stay focused on the breathing and knowing your internals. Since that same degree of wandering thoughts is always present during vipassana practice, too, or during any other meditation technique, to ignore these distractions is the challenge of meditation. In this case you are just tying your mind to the regularity of your breathing and wholeness feeling of the body as an anchoring mechanism. You do this instead of following the birth and death of thoughts, so this is just a different way to avoid becoming distracted and eventually achieve a silencing of wandering thoughts due to concentration. During vipassana you just watch thoughts and in this detached watching, wandering thoughts all die down and depart. But in this method you tether your concentration to your breathing and the feeling of the internal chi energies, ignoring your other wandering thoughts, and as both your mind calms and breathing calms then your wandering thoughts will disappear as well. You're relying on similar principles, but using a different technique.

This basic practice of following of the breath can be called "**Anapana Practice 101**." You want to put your mind on your breathing and the internal movements of chi within the body sack, and follow that alone, rather than follow your usual thoughts which are always coming and going and thus busying your mind. You already know from first principles that if you meditate by letting go of thoughts, your breathing will slow down as a natural result, so we're just making use of that principle in this technique.

Once you know your breath is here or there because of awareness, you have connected consciousness and your breath, and so some schools describe this by saying "the two have become one." All these different terms and descriptions confuse people, but if you understand the principles of practice you can help avoid the tendency to get lost by all the poetic ways used to simply describe the fact that you are concentrating or focusing on something. If you know something, or observe it through attention, we colloquially say that "you and that object become one." Hence, some schools say that your mind and your breathing "become unified" because you have put awareness on your breathing. "Become unified"--such confusing terms! Simply knowing the whereabouts of the breath is connecting with it, and at that point your mind and breath become one. When you put your awareness or attention on anything, your mind and that topic become one. Unfortunately, people tried to explain this in the past using the word "unify" and because people always mistakenly thought meditation was doing something strange with the mind, no one realized they were just talking about awareness being focused on some object of observation.

There is absolutely no force involved with this technique. Once again it is effortless. You should not sit with any expectations of anything happening either. As the Japanese Zen master Dogen might say, you just sit in order to sit for no reason at all. Therefore, you just sit to watch your breathing and internal energies, so hold no other expectations. As the Mahamudra expert Tilopa might say, *don't hold on to any expectations, don't try to control anything, don't try to create anything, don't try to think, don't try to examine anything, don't try to imagine anything, don't try to recall anything.* Set aside all your involvements and be natural, letting whatever comes up to come up and pass; let your mind rest. Just sit and witness your breathing and internal chi. You do not do anything other than put your focus, attention, concentration, noticing, awareness, watching, witnessing on following your breathing and knowing whatever you feel inside the body whose perimeter you can also feel as a type of barrier. You relax when practicing, and then eventually your breathing will start to subside whereupon you'll realize a lack of thoughts (an emptiness) in your mental realm. That is cultivating emptiness, or an empty mind. Call it what you will, but that very same result of inner silence happens from prayer practice and countless other spiritual practice techniques as well. They all end up cultivating the same thing.

Once you put your transcending attention/knowing on your breathing and body as from the independent standpoint that you are not them (awareness can know both inside and outside the body), you just keep the attention there without wavering. Don't get distracted by wandering thoughts and start following them, otherwise your mind will not and cannot calm down. You shouldn't try to push the breathing in any way or try to slow it down either. You shouldn't add effort to the practice or try to open up any internal areas where you feel tight or constricted within your body. This is a meditation practice of witnessing, observing or awareness. Sometimes you'll feel the body's meat as if broken into sections, or you might even feel different chi channels, chi circulations or energy movements running from here to there. You just witness everything as one internal whole covered by a sack of skin, and eventually, because of mindfully maintaining awareness without attachment, your breathing will calm down on its own as it always does with most any meditation technique.

You will then "become one with your breathing" because you just kept your attention on its ins and outs while ignoring other thoughts running around. If it calms down – and your breathing will indeed eventually slow down – your mind will start to empty out as well. In other words, thoughts will calm down, too. When breathing and thoughts both quiet, they have both reached a state of cessation. After a long time making progress with this basic technique, your yang chi will subsequently start arising and produce further chi channel openings during the meditation practice session.

All the meditation methods you practice have the capability of calming your mind, and when thoughts die away your real yang chi will start to arise to open up your physical body's channels. Mantra practice quiets the mind whereupon you should rest in that state; anapana practice helps your thoughts die down because you tie consciousness to the breath and it eventually subsides; witnessing practice allows you to detach from moving thoughts directly and they subsequently die down from lack of energetic pushing; visualization practice banishes wandering thoughts due to the activity of focused concentration, and so on it goes. All of these techniques are geared to helping you realize a quieter mental state that is absent of miscellaneous wandering thoughts running around, and this is called mental purity or even "clarity" when the wandering thoughts are no longer there busying your mind and obscuring the clear witnessing. This is good progress, but only an initial fruit of practice and far from the final result.

In that state of empty or quiet mind, it is just a natural phenomenon that your real yang chi, or *kundalini*, arises to open up your chi channels. That's just a natural process which we have gone over. This always happens when the mind quiets. After enough channels open from progress at this and other meditation methods, you will certainly start to feel the presence of chi energy (and channels) within the body. You can feel that your internal energy is here or there, which is basically feeling the results of body purification that start to occur from mentally letting go.

The typical sequence of progress for *all* meditation techniques is that your mind calms down, your chi arises, it opens some channels, and because those channels are more open, your chi can flow through them more freely without blockages or obstructions. Your chi still encounters obstructions in its circulatory flow now and then, which you start to feel, but with so many openings now available its entire flow slowly becomes equalized and harmonious. In turn, because of the connection between chi flow and consciousness, a busy mentality calms down because your chi flow is now smoother. Because your chi flows more smoothly, its circulation is less disturbing to the body and due to the internal harmony of that smooth circulation, your mind can reach an even deeper degree of quiet due to the balance and equilibrium your chi has reached.

This idea of physical progress (the purification achieved by channel openings) and mental progress, in terms of both becoming more pure as time goes on, proceeds hand in hand. Progress in mental calming produces progress in smoother chi flow, and progress in channel openings and smoother, more harmonious chi flow without obstructions produces progress in mental calming. That, in turn, leads to more progress again. This is a principle we have often gone over – the mind-body connection – and we need not drum it to death.

When you reach the point where you can start to feel the presence of chi within your body because of progress in your meditation efforts, anapana expands to encompass the witnessing of these internal energy sensations. Initially most people cannot feel anything inside their bodies but when they can, you should view the entire body as a whole, sort of as a bubble, and just know all those internal sensations as well. You don't need to practice anapana to open your channels and start feeling these energies because all sorts of other meditation methods can help you reach that stage. However, once you can feel these energies, you can especially use anapana practice to make even more progress. Anapana *forces you* to let go of these sensations, and just watch them like a detached third person observer, and so they are left free so that your chi can open up yet more chakras and channels. Only emptiness or detachment truly lets you open up your chi channels, so you are practicing this from the start by remaining detached from internal sensations.

Once you start feeling chi energies in your body you can enlarge your attention to encompass those sensations along with your breathing and try to know them together as one whole. If you can detach from your body and mind while doing this, just as you would doing witnessing practice, this is how to practice. With any type of meditation progress, you will eventually begin to feel either your channels or just the chi energies within your body, or both, and you want to eventually feel everything as one body unit whole. Even if you have opened all your major chi channel meridians and feel the chi flowing through them, which is higher stage progress, there are always sections of the body where the channels have not yet been opened. With higher stage progress, past the level of this book, you can even start to feel the chi within more solid sections of the body that might have felt dead or offered no sensations at all, but this something beginners cannot do for the densest components of their bodies.

If you have received a lot of deep tissue massage to help relax and open up your body, you might be able to initially feel the internal breath energy, or chi, all the way down to your abdomen with a deep inhalation, and even on through to your genitals and perineum. However, with this type of more advanced anapana practice you want to eventually reach the point where you can feel all of the body's internal energies as within one self-contained body unit. The chi within your body may often feel like air, so the sensation of your physical firm can even at times be likened to a balloon or empty sack. You can at times focus on the airy, spacy feeling of chi within the balloon body, and you can also try to feel the body form itself as though it were an empty sack with all these things going on inside along with the breathing. Just watching the whole, without attachment, will help to open up the channels within its entire structure.

That feeling of the wholeness of connected chi, or complete body of breath, is one of the important factors of practice. There are other variants of anapana practice that concentrate on feeling only sections or areas of the body, and the initial basic practice focuses on just watching the inbreaths and outbreaths until you can also feel the energies of the body as a whole in conjunction with noting the breathing. You expand your knowing or attention to the internal chi sensations of the body while also simultaneously keeping your awareness on the inbreaths and outbreaths of breathing.

The body can begin to feel like an empty bag or sack when a lot of internal channels open and the chi starts flowing freely, and it may often feel like there is an empty space within it. Past this practice you can even begin to feel the individual muscles of your body, and try to feel the channels within them, but once again, that discussion is beyond this book.

The basic anapana you need to know as a meditator is to *follow your breathing with your attention, ignore other thoughts that arise while so doing, and as your breathing calms your mind will calm, too.* Then you'll get the same initial final result as with all the other meditation methods we have covered. Next you can extend this to knowing other internal sensations of energy at the same time, but always remaining relaxed, independent and detached from the whole shebang.

COUNTING BREATHS

In some versions of anapana, people are told to count their breaths so that they continue focusing on their breathing rather than have their concentration run elsewhere, but most people miss the point of these instructions. This emphasis on counting neglects the fact that the mind is supposed to calm down. How can thoughts calm down if you are always thinking of numbers? How can the mind calm down if every time it starts to calm down you must keep announcing a number to yourself?

This type of anapana practice emphasizes the *counting* of your breaths, and does not emphasize the fact that your breathing should calm down naturally and your mental state should accompany that quieting. How can your mental state quiet if you always have to think of counting? It is not that counting is wrong, but that a misplaced emphasis on counting misses the whole point of this meditation method. The counting emphasis is aimed at teaching you *how to concentrate* rather than cultivate the gong-fu of an empty, quiet mental state. Once again, it's always the empty state of mind that you want to cultivate so you must consider if the practice you are using will get you there.

If you just want to learn how to concentrate on a moving process, you could choose other activities for your focus instead of your breathing. To learn concentration on moving subjects, you could focus on watching a tennis ball or ping pong ball going back and forth during a long volley. That's one way to learn how to keep your mind on a moving topic without distraction, and to thus learn concentration. The entire modern world seems to be getting better at keeping us away from learning how to concentrate on one topic or task without getting distracted, but you absolutely must learn concentration. You must learn how to make the mind settle so that it can become stable, in order for you to develop *samadhi.*

While it is true that counting keeps your attention centered on the breathing, and thus keeps your mind from wandering, this is not supposed to be a method for just learning stable concentration on a moving target. If you want to learn concentration, you can use almost anything else as the subject of attention rather than your breathing. So why is it that you concentrate on your breathing with this meditation method?

The reason this entire method is based on your breathing is because of the special mind-body interconnections between chi, mind and breathing which allow you to experience an empty mind after breathing calms down, *but many teachers miss this point entirely.* They never let the mind settle because they are always focused on the act of maintaining concentration to count the inhalations or exhalations. Hence, the crux of anapana practice is not so much on building up your concentration skills, although of course they are necessary (and the final state of empty mind is also called a state of concentration). The crux is that breathing and thoughts both die down together leading to a quiet, empty state of mind if you practice in the correct way. This is not a practice for exercising your arithmetic, but a method for calming your mind if you approach it correctly. You focus on the breathing to stop the breathing and empty the mind.

The idea behind this particular meditation technique is based upon the physiological tie-in between respiration and thinking. By specifically following your breathing during its gradual course of calming down, you will surely be led to mental calmness and an empty mind, i.e. an experience of emptiness. All meditation methods want you to realize an empty, quiet, tranquil mind. That is the final objective. We also call this a state of concentration because wandering thoughts have disappeared, but you are not holding on to things during that state, which is why the term "concentration" is sometimes confusing when used in this way. The mind is concentrated, when empty, *because it is not distracted.* Its subject of observation is not a thought or thoughts, but emptiness itself that it continues to enjoy/observe/abide in with bright awareness.

Here we want to achieve that exact same final objective of mental emptiness once again, and so we pursue it by following the breath. We don't pursue it by counting, but by linking our attention to our respiration as it dies down to nothingness. Hence, if you don't need counting as an assist to the practice, then don't use it! If you don't need to count your respirations because you already have enough concentration skills to follow your breathing, then leave the counting out. Furthermore, if you choose the route of counting your breaths, rather than just focusing on them, you don't need to count them for endless weeks of practice. If you are spending all your time doing this, you are probably practicing arithmetic rather than meditation. You've missed the purpose and intent of practice once again.

This discussion reveals a big mistake that I have seen many people make because of poor instructions, which is why it is being emphasized. You don't want to be stirring up thoughts with counting. It was only a method someone expediently invented to help teach people how to stay focused on the breathing. That expedient method has simply been passed down to our times, but people have lost sight of the original objectives.

People who already know how to concentrate for long periods of time don't need to count their breaths but can just follow their breathing until the mind eventually stills as breathing and thoughts both quiet down. If you have a scattered mind which has trouble concentrating, then you might be able to benefit from this sort of counting practice, *or other concentration exercises instead.* After you build up your concentration skills, you can then return to the anapana technique of just following your breathing in hopes of achieving the target of mental quiet.

In the traditional anapana counting practice which is commonly taught, you have many options such as counting your outbreaths or your inbreaths. You usually are instructed to count from one to ten (or some other number), and when you lose track of the count or reach the number ten (or whatever the upper limit is), you start all over again. It's like a visualization in that if you lose the image, you just form it again in your mind but you can just visualize the whole thing and don't have to start redrawing individual pieces. Of course, if you have the time and patience, you can redraw the individual images if you like, and some visualization methods actually want you to do it.

Once again, if you know and understand the principles of practice as I have been teaching you, you can guide yourself accordingly.

If you tend to eat too much, have high blood pressure, cannot sleep, or have lots of miscellaneous thoughts running around in your mind, the general rule is that you should count your outbreaths because those are relieving. If you have a weak or feeble physical constitution, low blood pressure, or weak nerves and/or mental function, you count the inbreaths to help give yourself more energy. For people with bodies that are neither good nor bad, you would typically count outbreaths before noon and inbreaths after noon, which corresponds to when the energies of the day are waxing or waning. These are just general rules the ancients have discovered over time to help people based on the state of their physical constitution.

As you can see, the anapana cultivation method is very scientific, but is primarily aimed at teaching you how to remain concentrated on a single topic, which happens to be your breathing, so that breathing and thoughts both calm down naturally and your inner *kundalini* energies then awaken. The focus on counting misses the whole principle of your breath and mind simultaneously quieting down. In fact, most teachers of anapana don't stress that by counting a practitioner will eventually begin to notice that there is a gap, or pause of respiratory cessation, between the natural inbreath and outbreath. When a practitioner can notice that stationary pause or gap, they should always stop counting and focus on that phenomenon. As the breathing calms down, that stationary gap will extend which is what you want to encourage to happen. Hence, once you reach the stage where you become aware of the pause between the breaths, you should drop the counting entirely and start focusing on following the pauses, which is the period of no-breath. This then becomes the cultivation practice of "following the breath" throughout the body.

In my opinion, most people don't make much progress with this counting method because they don't know the meditation principles of practice and what they are aiming for. They just remain locked in a loop of counting all the time, and thus nothing much is accomplished. The more advanced form of anapana does not use counting at all. You sit there calmly in meditation practice and watch your breathing without having your mind run astray, and as just stated, remain cognizant of the moment between the breaths when there is no movement or breathing. This then turns into the ability to notice internal breathing within the body because the periods of no-breathing will extend, and one's vital energy will then arise which you will definitely begin to feel. You then practice just by watching your breathing and knowing all your internal energies. You always watch or witness your breathing without interfering, as if you were watching a sleeping baby and its breathing. You remain independent of the process and simply watch it calm down.

After you have mastered mental calming and your channels have thus opened to some degree, you can naturally feel internal energies inside you. Therefore the practice includes knowing where and what they are in addition to staying focused on the breathing and the pausation between the breaths so that you do not get lost in following the internal energies. You just know that they exist because you can feel them here or there. You just have awareness of them, or "shine awareness" on them, without attaching to them. Knowing them as *not-you* helps you maintain that independent detachment. In fact, you try to know both your breathing and sensations simultaneously as a type of pure awareness practice of independent physical processes. You want to witness or watch them like an aloof third person observer who isn't attached to either your body and mind. Like a monk, you try to give up or renounce your body and mind and rest in the bodiless clear awareness that is everywhere, like space, but which knows, and the focus of attention for that knowing is on an independent process that you cannot mistake as being you.

When you then know or observe internal sensations within your body, you should not try to move them anywhere or push them in any way, but you just know they are wherever you locate them because of your awareness. That's the correct practice of observing attention. You notice them and remain cognizant of their presence – it's as simple as that. Those energies have arisen because your mind has reached some stage of emptiness, and so they are there because your internal chi starts to move. Hence, this type of anapana practice not only includes your breath but at the same time the knowing of internal chi sensations.

In this type of practice, the target is that you want to eventually feel the entire chi energies within your body *as one whole unit.* By focusing on your chi as a whole while still focusing on the in and out breaths through the tethering point of the nostrils, you will be able to open up more chi channels and dissolve blockages between all the body's chi channels at the same time because you stay detached throughout all your witnessing. In time, many unopened chi channels will then open. You will engender a complete opening of your internal chi circulation by viewing the body as an inflated sack or balloon whose internal energies you can feel as one unit. This may often create a feeling of internal airiness, and at even more advanced stages you want to concentrate on simultaneously feeling the unopened muscular regions of the body, and later even denser parts of the body.

While it is true that the pressure-less, effortless shining of your attention-awareness on the energies felt in a specific area of the body will tend to open up the chi channels within that region, doing this alone is another form of meditation practice rather than the anapana practice of watching your breath while simultaneously feeling all your internal chi as one whole. The danger to this technique of just witnessing/observing internal sensations is getting carried away by the sensations, and then following them just as you might follow thoughts and get entangled in some stream of thinking about something. It's hard to remain detached and independent so that you can refrain from getting caught up in thoughts and lose your state of presence. Some type of mechanism must still be utilized to prevent you from wandering off into some thought world rather than remain focused on a practice that helps to calm your mind and further open up the body's channels.

At the earliest stages of progress for this and many other meditation techniques, it is common for practitioners to begin to feel like their body is empty inside, like an empty sack where the bones have dissolved away. *Sometimes it might feel like the bones have disappeared altogether*, and that is because your chi encounters a stage where it flows through a relatively free circulation of relatively complete channel openings you've established. However, afterwards it will eventually move on to opening up more obstructed channels once again. Thus it is a temporary phenomenon. After the channels at that level of progress have opened, one will regain the feeling of internal solidity once again because this is only a temporary sensation. Onwards the chi then proceeds to opening a complete circulation at a deeper level of progress. Advanced meditation practitioners may often bump into this "dissolved bones" phenomenon as just described. All you need to know is that it occurs because you have made progress, and it is a sign that your channels and chi are transforming.

There is also a meditation principle that wherever you put your mind within your body, your chi will follow. Your chi life-force will go wherever your mind internally focuses, and that chi will therefore try to run through (and thereby open up) the channels in the region if it can. When you focus on two different regions at the same time and try to form a bridge, your chi will try to flow between the two areas. This is something we need to know in order to employ a practice called **dissolving blockages**.

At the beginner's level of meditation practice, you don't try to do this sort of practice because you want to ignore all internal sensations within your body. With anapana you only focus on the target of having your breathing and mind calm down so you can get the initial result of experiencing what an "empty mind" actually is, and during anapana you know internal sensations but don't play with them or try to move any internal energies. If you've had the experience of emptiness and know what "empty mind" means, you can understand that many chi channels have already opened for you to have been able to experience this, and to reach a yet higher stage of gong-fu you must cultivate a greater degree of detachment from these sensations.

Most schools just tell you to cultivate an empty mind and you will naturally achieve this higher stage of gong-fu. Those instructions are correct. However, the esoteric school concentrates on transforming your physical body by cultivating your internal energies, so it says you can reach that higher stage by cultivating your chi and channels more directly. It is certainly true that you will achieve a higher stage of emptiness attainment when you achieve an even greater degree of channel openings and smoother chi flow circulation. So how do you cultivate your chi and channels *directly* to achieve this? You can employ the practice of following your breathing while sensing your internal body of chi as one full whole, and that will help all your internal channels to open. Just use anapana! If you are good enough you can do this from the start, but I am just breaking the practice into pieces so that you can understand how to combine various methods.

If you are not tethering your attention--in a detached, third person, transcending or independent observer sort of fashion--to the regularity of breathing when you are also noticing certain areas within your body and the internal sensation within your body as a whole, you are actually practicing yet another different meditation technique that focuses on noting internal body sensations. Without the focus on the breathing, this meditation practice becomes a form of inner observation, or even inner viewing, and the problem with this technique is the possibility of getting lost in thoughts once again. You can start feeling things within you, lose your independent bearing, and then get sucked into various wandering thought streams.

There are indeed variants, but anapana practices usually require that your attention remain focused on the nostril breathing throughout the process to avoid this possibility, and when the breathing stops you still remain aware and alert and continue viewing the internal scenario of the body as a whole. After awhile there will be a bit of breath coming in again, and then after another long interval an exhalation will go out again as well. Sometimes you will remain in the state of respiratory cessation for a minute or longer without trying to hold anything, and it will just happen naturally. Just because you can feel the internal energies within your body during meditation, however, does not mean you are practicing anapana. Many inner witnessing meditation practices from Taoism and other spiritual traditions employ this capability.

This ability to feel your body's internal energies is very interesting. Your body's chi is often compared to a blind man who can move about, while your mind is often compared to a lame man who cannot walk. If the lame man sits on the shoulders of the blind man, however, he can direct the blind man to go wherever is required. Thus, wherever your attention is focused within your body, your chi will immediately go to that area. Your mind can direct your chi.

By simultaneously shining attention on several different areas of your body, you will therefore tend to open up all the chi channel routes between them. You can sometimes establish a better connection between them in this way. You simply bring your attention to energies that you feel within disjoint regions of the body, and that will help link them into one whole after the chi passes between them. Or, you can shine your attention on an area you cannot feel, staying with it but without pressure, and that will tend to help open it. Of course, this is an inferior sort of practice because it has nothing to do with searching for the basis of consciousness and the mind.

DISSOLVING INTERNAL BLOCKAGES

In any case, this discussion is the actual basis behind the popular martial arts technique called "dissolving blockages" for advanced practitioners who have already somewhat opened up their internal structure of chi channel orbits. Some schools say you just "shine awareness" on the blockages (chi obstructions) you can feel. Some say you "release" the blockages. Some say you should "offer them away." Some say just to "let go" of the blockages you feel inside you.

No one can predict which of these phrases will work best in helping you to let go of the obstructions you feel, but they all mean the same thing. As each person responds best to different words, you should try each of these meanings to see which one works best for you during your practice.

This is not anapana practice, but a special type of chi cultivation practice to release restrictions or blockages within your chi flow. It is a type of physical calming, or physical adjustment, which is achieved by just watching your chi in different areas and having it link, or sometimes even manipulating your chi. Thus it belongs to the category of inner energy cultivation work, or *nei-gong* practices. Even so, it is still very related to some variants of anapana and inner witnessing practices for calming the mind. There are many types of chi cultivation like this used for transforming internal blockages and cultivating inner energies.

Even if you don't meditate, there will be times when your body might feel uncomfortable inside as if there were an energy blockage somewhere within. Sometimes this is due to meditation progress, and sometimes to illness or the weather. If you know there is an obstruction in an area because you feel the chi stuck there, people normally try to push it open with mental effort, but that doesn't usually work. What is usually more effective is that you can also try to release it with the outbreath, or offer it away, or just focus on it as a type of grabbing (or without the grabbing) and then try to dissolve it by letting it go. When there is pressure-less attention on an area it will tend to open the blockages and may release the obstruction after a time, but if the discomfort is painful, people usually don't want to wait that long and want to actively try to dissolve it. Hence, you can also try imagining that the area shines with light, or that you shine light on it which dissolves it. There are all sorts of active imagination methods that may or may not work. The big method is to find it with your attention and then try to somehow mentally release it so that it goes away.

Shining passive awareness that is fixed on an area will tend to slowly help the chi pass through it (which we already know happens during an internal white skeleton visualization). However, releasing an obstruction in tune with an outgoing breath will also help dissolve that blockage and the uncomfortable feelings that accompany it, usually at a faster pace.

There are many such techniques one can try that attempt to release energy congestion in an area using the outbreathing. The most popular technique is perhaps the practice of the **Six Taoist Healing Sounds**. These are specific sounds you make upon exhalation, for six different organ systems, when your energy feels stuck or obstructed in those particular body regions. This type of practice – of exhaling your breath while making a particular sound and simultaneously shining/focusing awareness on a specific body region—is another *excellent life skill to learn for managing your body*. It will help you learn how to harmonize your body's energies when you feel uncomfortable in any fashion.

You always have access to many different forms of internal energy practice to help you solve the problems of feeling uncomfortable inside. They can all help you reach more meditation progress and experience physical relaxation. Anapana gets you started on feeling your internal energies as one whole, but all these other internal energy cultivation methods can be used when circumstances require. I only mention them so that you see the large variety of methods available for dealing with internal body energies which you will eventually feel when your meditation becomes good enough. *There are hundreds of methods you can employ for cultivating your internal energies. There are also hundreds of methods one can use for cultivating the breathing.* Whether you choose to cultivate your internal chi energies or breathing, the mindfulness method of anapana is the basis for many of these techniques.

I personally recommend that you practice anapana and try to at least reach the stage where you feel that your body is like a large empty sack filled with chi and the bones have dissolved. Naturally the bones are always there, but a distinct feeling arises as if they have suddenly gone missing when your level of gong-fu becomes high enough. You can head towards that accomplishment, which has been mentioned by several masters such as Tsong Khapa, if you try to feel your body as if it were just an outer covering that is empty within.

If you ever arrive at this feeling, and all your bones inside feel as if they are no longer existent, you should once again let go of your thoughts, forget about your breathing, and just remain in an aware state that's relatively free from thoughts when you reach this stage. Whenever you let go and abide in emptiness during any stage of gong-fu, it always helps more chi channels open so that you can progress to the next level of achievement. At higher levels of achievement, you will better understand how to cultivate your chi, channels and internal energies. I am only introducing the basics, and mixing various topics to help you quickly move forward.

If you are a yoga student who practices any alternative nostril breathing forms of pranayama, you can use some of these external witnessing principles to make better progress with your practice. For instance, if you are breathing in through your left nostril and are holding your breath, you can also practice feeling your internal chi energies in the left side of your body at that time. When you breathe in through your right nostril, you can use that opportunity to try to feel the entire chi in the right side of your body.

This is combining pranayama with the inner witnessing of chi sensations, and can help you quickly cultivate your chi and channels. As previously mentioned, you can also practice feeling the chi of your entire body, or any particular section, by itself but you always want to eventually try to link any disconnected sections with the one whole by feeling the body as a whole. This will enable blocked regions to link automatically.

The final objective is to feel all the chi and channels of the body as one whole unit without any disconnected regions. With yoga practice, there are so many opportunities to link various practice principles together for meditation and thus spiritual progress. If you practice forced *kumbhaka* pranayama techniques, you can concentrate on having shining toes at the same time so that your chi tries to go through your legs and open those downward leading meridians. As a yoga student, you can even use visualization practice on target muscle groups in conjunction with your stretching exercises to help open specific body regions, too.

THE IMPORTANCE OF STRETCHING EXERCISES

People who are ardent cultivators always think that sitting meditation practice is the only important thing and exercise is not important, but many of these internal physical sensations arise (such as feelings of blockage) because people are not healthy or have not been exercising enough. If you don't do a lot of exercise then your muscles may be tight, and it will probably be harder to open up the chi channels in any region regardless of the meditation methods you use.

You absolutely need to soften the body through exercise and stretching if you want your chi to flow more smoothly and if you want to remain soft, flexible and pain free on through to old age. Meditation is about mastering practical life skills, and while it helps soften the body by itself (because it opens chi channels), *anything else you can do along these lines would be beneficial.* It would be beneficial if meditation practitioners always practiced some form of stretching exercises to help keep in shape, and that will make the task of opening their chi channels much easier.

The first Zen master of China, Bodhidharma, ended up teaching the monks of Shaolin temple how to practice muscle and tendon stretches and martial arts exercises because their bodies had become too weakened from concentrating on meditation alone. This lack of exercise constitutes incorrect cultivation practice. Regardless of the benefits to meditation, we all need to exercise our muscles to keep them in shape, so we need not discuss this fact since it is readily understood. The question is, which types of exercise match with the objectives of meditation and good health in general?

One can easily practice hatha yoga into one's advanced years, so this is a possibility. However, it is even more beneficial to master the art of stretching during movement, such as found in martial arts or dancing. If you can learn how to feel your chi during the specific forms of deliberate physical motions and movements which are designed to activate or open certain chi channels, this joint combinatory type of chi and movement practice is fantastic. My preference is for people to learn the martial arts, and yoga secondarily.

At advanced stages of internal chi practice, you must particularly try to link the upper and lower torsos of the body, especially the upper trunk with the legs or the arms with the chest, by trying to know the energies in both those sections at the same time. The more stretching exercises you do for the body, such as yoga or the martial arts, the easier it will be to open up your chi channels in those regions and link them. You can keep your awareness focused on an entire section of your body and that section will open to some degree according to your level of practice.

Shining awareness on two sections that seem disjoint will also tend to open the chi channel circuits that pass through both regions, thus helping to link them. Eventually the channels will open all the way through and feel like one united whole.

The leg channels are particularly difficult to open, and the chi channels in the areas of the shoulders, buttocks, and knees are also difficult challenges for meditation practitioners. Any exercises you do for these areas will help to differentiate their muscle mass so that the chi can more readily pass through them. This would be of benefit to all meditation practitioners, and is just smart for good health anyway.

When a meditation practitioner practices anapana very well, they can eventually switch from focusing on the breathing going through the opening passage of their nostrils to feeling it in the center of their nose, and later they can proceed upwards to feel the breath through the upper bridge of the nose just between the eyebrows. Some spiritual schools believe that just keeping one's mind on the spot between the eyebrows is a wonderful meditation practice and the best way to reach *samadhi*. This, too, can also become an exercise in unwavering (and effortless, *pressure-less*) concentration, but has to do with the location of a chakra point rather than feeling the breathing pass through the nose at the upper bridge. Perhaps one can use the chakra locations in some form of advanced inner anapana practice, or learn how to exercise the chi and chakras directly in some other way, but that possibility remains for higher practitioners to discover.

The respiratory action of inbreathing and outbreathing is always naturally happening for the body as long as it is alive and consciousness remains. However, your breathing and chi rarely become unified during life unless you practice meditation and then move on to internal chi cultivation. When someone finally gets around to cultivating their internal energies, they can learn to do remarkable things. During meditation practice, you are giving your consciousness and your chi the opportunity to both calm down together and become one/unified because you want to get rid of thoughts. When this happens through anapana practice, it means you are practicing correctly. When this happens your true yang chi will arise, your channels and chakras will start to open, and you can eventually proceed on to various inner chi cultivation practices that the Taoists call *nei-gong*.

This joint cessation of the breath and quieting of the mind cannot happen if your mind is still wandering, which is likely to happen when you put the focus of attention on feeling the energies of the body alone, so you always have to bring your mind back to the breathing as it enters the nostrils, or middle of your nose, or at the passageway between the eyebrows. Our respiratory process is an automatic, autonomous process that is always there independently operating, so to prevent the mind from wandering by getting trapped in internal energy sensations (rather than feeling the internal energies as one whole unit), you must stay aware of the breathing to help prevent this. Your breathing, and the task of feeling your inner body as one whole, becomes the tethering line for preventing your attention from getting lost in scattered thoughts. A new inhalation or exhalation always brings your mind back to the state of presence to snap you out of getting lost in following wandering thoughts.

The mind always gets diverted into all sorts of random topics and thought streams, and easily becomes distracted if you let it just follow the wandering thoughts which always arise. If you practice an external witnessing concentration like this, as if you are not the body or its internals but just viewing them, your mind can calm down and your breathing will calm with it. All those random thought streams will die down as well. When your thoughts calm down, then you must still let go of your body and mind and rest in the emptiness as you do with all other normal meditation techniques. That, in short, is anapana practice. You can even hold to the feeling of the entire body as a shell, with internal energies, by remaining tethered to the breathing, but you must remember that any meditation practice follows the principles of cessation and observation, so adjust yourself accordingly to reach that desired state of cessation (quiet) while maintaining alive rather than deadened awareness. You want to reach a state where random thoughts *cease* and the mind is empty, and you want to remain in that state with awareness witnessing or *observing* the full visage of the mind.

Once again, when you are just getting started at anapana practice you usually cannot feel the internal energies of the body at all, but only some of the movements of the breathing. However, if you introspect and notice, you will discover that you are always feeling the entire outline of your body as a whole, and while the internals of this body cannot yet be felt except by some sensitive individuals, this is actually akin to feeling it as if it is one solid block of meat. The entire body all feels like a single block because the internal channels are not yet open, but one is, nevertheless, feeling this obstructedness! You are feeling it because of the sluggish chi within; without chi you could not feel anything, but even so, the chi channels have not fully opened in the living tissue. This is something you must come to recognize.

As the channels open you'll start to feel all sorts of energies inside the body, and the airiness of the chi energy itself. That's why you can reach the stage of feeling that the body is like an empty sack. That feeling arises, and the feeling of bones being dissolved away, because the body finally begins to fill with chi in the channels. As you progress in meditation, later you will begin to feel an internal airiness and lightness to the body which is another chi phenomenon as well. Many such phenomena will arise as you start to make meditation progress.

INTERNAL ENERGY SENSATIONS

Over the years I have found that people often worry when they start feeling unusual energy sensations within their bodies like this, which is one of the reasons we discussed the method for witnessing internal chi sensations without involvement. A thousand books could not describe all the different energy patterns one might internally feel, although general patterns do exist for the most important phenomena that are usually encountered as a result of meditation practice.

Sometimes you will feel the chi moving here or there, sometimes the body will feel hot or cold in certain regions, and sometimes the complete channel openings called meridians can be felt. Sometimes the body will feel heavier, lighter or even taller. Sometimes, after a complete channel orbit finally opens, you can even feel the chi revolving through that particular chi circulatory pathway. These are all great signs of progress when they occur. They mean that your chi channels are opening and your internal chi is transforming, which is the true breath or life force of the body, and when this occurs then your body is transforming to a higher stage of purity, too.

There is a natural progression to the transformations that occur within your body that involve chi transformations and channel openings. It is your chi along with the water element of your body that first start to transform due to meditation practice. Eventually your chi channels next start opening, and then the muscles, bone marrow (the soft inside of your bones), tendons, bones, and hair progressively start to become transformed in that general order.

The entire body is not transformed all at once. It takes well over a decade to open up all the channels throughout the entire body and totally transform it *after all the major meridians have initially opened.* To cultivate your chi and initially open your channels is just the start of this process because then you have to cultivate the denser parts of the physical form by opening the channels within those structures, and liberate their chi flows. To open the major meridians of the body is challenging, but this stage of transformation to affect the entire body's structure is even higher.

It might take years of beginner's practice to cultivate your chi and channels to finally open up the major meridians, as described in *Tao and Longevity* and *The Little Book of Hercules.* Whether you achieve this quickly or slowly depends on the meditation methods you choose to use, how consistent and ardent you are in your practice efforts, whether you continually lose your vitality during this process, and whether you even understand the correct principles of practice so that you are always meditating effectively with a detached, open mind that does not cling. As the cases of many Zen masters show, if you know the principles of practice, the principles of mind, and know how to let go, you can become enlightened before the body has finished these transformations, and then afterwards can go into retreat to finish the process. As my teacher often said, the principle is emptiness cultivation all the way. Enlightenment is a wisdom attainment, so if you can detach from your body and consciousness, you can get the Tao and then work on having the physical transformations catch up to achieve something truly remarkable at the highest stages of spiritual attainment. Naturally you will always need to establish a certain foundational basis of practice, which requires a certain amount of chi and channel transformations, to be able to see the Truth, which means to attain enlightenment.

There are many types of internal energy cultivation techniques that can help to speed these transformations, and help you reach a more empty experience of the mind. There are also different techniques you can apply at different stages of practice. An important practice principle is that your meditation technique can, and should when necessary, change according to the circumstances. For instance, if you feel internal discomfort, try shining awareness on the area or try practicing one of the Six Taoist Healing Sounds to help relieve that pressure. If the skeleton visualization gives rise to too much sexual energy, then switch to pranayama and anapana practices instead. If you are watching thoughts and you find your respiration subsiding, then remember the principles of anapana wherein you want the two to become one, and then stay in some stage of emptiness when your breathing stops. Or just practice anapana in terms of viewing the whole system dispassionately, in a detached manner, as a whole while cultivating awareness. Sometimes a deeper stage of emptiness feels less comfortable than a lower stage of attainment because more chi channels start opening, which produces a greater degree of initial discomfort, but you have to understand such principles of practice to realize this is progress, and let go.

Switching between meditation techniques when appropriate, and practicing a particular technique in a different way every now and then, is also a principle that helps prevent you from falling into the rut of clinging to an incorrect style of practice. It helps prevent you from incorrectly practicing a proper technique, and thereby wasting your time, which would lead to little progress at all.

Unfortunately, after the chi in your body starts to move and you obtain all sorts of internal physical sensations from correct meditation practice, most people tend to forget about all these various practice principles and will start focusing on their internal sensations. They forget about the principle of cessation and observation. They forget about empty mindfulness. Only the detachment of witnessing (observation) helps you remain unbiased and allows you to remain unfettered. However, in following the internal sensations of chi movements, meditators sometimes get lost in the world of running after these sensations. They start attaching to these things or pushing around their chi, which is the same thing as attaching to thoughts, and their meditation progress then goes out the window.

The anapana technique, which teaches you to know all your internal chi sensations as a single whole, in an independent detached fashion, always prevents you from getting lost in the sensations because you are always viewing from the third person standpoint, and always brought back to the breathing so that you don't get lost in wandering thoughts. If you start getting attached to some thought or internal sensation, along comes a new inbreath or outbreath whose occurrence helps remind you to release your attachments. Then you can resume your viewpoint as internal and external awareness. A new breath will always come, and with awareness focused on the inhalations or exhalations you are always prevented from losing the presence of your mind and falling into wandering thoughts.

You therefore should learn how to detach from both the breathing and the internal sensations through the external witnessing of pure awareness. However, because you are still focused on knowing internal sensations, too, which represent areas of internal chi channel obstruction, those areas will still tend to open. Just knowing them, with detached awareness, will allow them to open more readily. Hence, you will still be refining your chi and cultivating your channels. In fact, knowing all the internal sensations within a body felt as an empty bag, and refusing to attach to them, all the chi channels within your entire body will start to open via a different mechanism than how the skeleton visualization accomplishes this feat.

Because you always return a focus of attention to your nasal breathing while simultaneously feeling internal sensations of chi, you can successfully practice dispassionate viewing or watching without becoming attached. Always try to feel the body as if one whole, and as if you are awareness that is also outside the body rather than just in it. This is how the body becomes seen as an appearance within consciousness, and becomes easier to cultivate.

The great thing about this technique is that you are cultivating the internal opening of your chi channels while also cultivating inner peace and clarity since you are resting in the independent observing awareness, which is an abiding by non-abiding. Through this transcending meditation method your breathing will subside, your thoughts will subside, and you will eventually experience an empty mental realm that is free of thoughts but clear and illuminated, and always capable of knowing even though there are no thoughts on the horizon. That's the experience of awareness. As with the white skeleton visualization technique, you then end up cultivating your body at the same time you are cultivating a mental detachment from thoughts, and will reach a state of empty clear awareness this way, namely "empty mind." Your thoughts will die down, so your mind will become empty and clear.

Clear awareness (pure consciousness) always prepositionally stands behind thought consciousness, and with miscellaneous thoughts now absent, all that is left is the clarity and purity of this awareness which you eventually find is boundless. Naturally you continue to see the world around you with your senses because perceptions always arise, but it now seems as if awareness has become larger, and is somehow more clean or pure, because countless useless thoughts have now departed. This often gives rise to the notion that the radiance of the mind has become brighter, but awareness has not actually become more clear. It is just that false thoughts have dropped away so you start to get an understanding of the underlying emptiness of the mind. That boundless empty purity you discover is the true nature of your mind.

In other words, thoughts drop out so that your mind becomes clear/empty, and since the awareness that knows this is always clear, you end up *cultivating clear knowing* because there are no longer many wandering thoughts remaining that are screening, polluting or obstructing you. You thereby end up cultivating your abiding awareness (that can know everything that arises in the mind) when there are no longer a lot of wandering thoughts running about, and so your observational scenario becomes clear, vast and pure. Once again, we accomplish the same end objectives of other meditation systems but through an entirely different mechanism. If you can do this directly, such as by cultivating the "seeing the light" meditation method, then fantastic, but most people cannot do this until after they've already accomplished a lot of chi and channel purification work.

I hope you can see how the various meditation methods all aim for the same objective. Most people don't realize this because they never fathom the interconnections between chi, thoughts (consciousness), breathing, the difference between consciousness and awareness (pure consciousness), the opening of chi channels, the coarse or smooth flow of chi circulation within the channels, empty mind, and the purification of the body and mind. They are all interconnected, and as your experience builds with meditation, and as you reflect upon these principles, you will start to more deeply understand the connections. Meditation is all based upon simple scientific principles. Those principles, and the results they engender, constitute the science of meditation progress.

Once again, the basis of anapana practice is that you are simply simultaneously observing, witnessing, watching, knowing the doings of both your external breathing and the internal energies of your body, too. You are cultivating the awareness that knows, and the object of focus is this entire body of yours with its breathing and internal chi movements. *Whether your breathing is long or short, shallow or deep, just stay with it as the focus of your attention.* Stay with the knowing, or observation of your breathing until your mind quiets and empties. From this alone you can attain the experience of a quiet, empty mind and eventually a mind truly unblemished that abides as imperturbability.

This is why the Taoists, Sufis, Buddhists, Shintoists, Orthodox Christians, Greeks and many others used following the breath as an initial spiritual practice technique. Following the breath is the basis of many internal energy cultivation techniques, too, such as *kundalini* yoga and qi-gong. You basically follow your breath with attention until it becomes very subtle, and then your body starts generating its own internal energy in response. That internal energy eventually ignites and opens up all the body's chi channels in response. In other words, when one-pointed concentration on the breath combines with the breathing, the flow of air in and out of the lungs stops, thoughts die down, and the body opens up its internal chi channels to come alive with its inner yang chi. This opening of the chi channels thereby paves the way for higher spiritual states such as *samadhi* attainments. The cultivation route is that you simply become fully aware of the distractions, or movements, of the wind element within the body to achieve this.

As to the internal sensations of chi that will eventually arise from your various meditation efforts, it is also often taught that you should *know where they are hot or cold, long or short, and so on.* Basically, this just means that you know wherever they are and whatever they are like inside the body, including where they feel blocked or stuck. This is therefore a stage of cultivating your chi channels. By knowing they are there while remaining detached, they will further open simply from the focus of attention/awareness/knowing paid to their existence. Just keep cultivating emptiness, let your body fill with chi, and they will open. Because your chi channels will then open, your memory will improve, your alertness and mental clarity will improve, your energy level will improve, and in general your overall health and brain function will improve, too. This is why many poets and artists would commonly practice breathing methods in ancient times. However, in order for this to become a spiritual practice rather than just a method for practical health improvements, you have to focus on the empty nature of the mind during this technique, and you can gain hold of that by focusing on the non-moving interval gap between the inbreaths and outbreaths of your respiration as you practice.

How do you practice? One starts by focusing on their external breathing, and notices the gaps between the inbreath and outbreath during this watching. Eventually this gap will widen as the breathing and thoughts calm down. You focus attention on the gap while remaining cognizant of the comings and goings of the breath. Eventually the coarse breathing will subside, the mind will become quiet, and internal breathing will take over. The internal breath, or chi, will start to move and so the body will generate its own energy that will literally fill it entirely. When your chi starts to move in its own form of inner respiration it will start to open up your chi channels, and then eventually circulate through those channels everywhere.

One can leave this process to automatic, but there are also various techniques whereby one can also proceed by further refining this chi or tempering this internal energy once ignited, and the number of possible methods explodes from there. It all starts or becomes possible by initially focusing attention on the quiet, empty interval of pausation between the breaths, and then allowing that empty quiet interval to gradually extend. When your breathing and mentation both calm down, we say they "unite" and you experience some degree of emptiness or empty mind because neither thoughts nor breathing is there, both are absent. With thoughts absent, your thinking or discriminatory processes quiet down, afflictions decrease and you can enter a high meditative state called the first *dhyana*.

While the general rule for meditation is not to try to move your internal chi, actually, sometimes you *should* do this to try to relieve any internal imbalances. The principle of "shining awareness" on an area, without pushing it, is always taught to prevent you from getting caught up in playing with sensations, but sometimes you will find that a gentle push is correct and proper. Similarly, while you are taught not to use effort but remain natural, if you can deliberately stop your breathing with a tiny bit of effort when meditating, and remain in that state, it can help you quickly transform your physical body. You do this because you must transform your physical body's chi channels in order to be able to attain the Tao, and this technique can help you achieve the greater objective when you apply it appropriately.

Such instructions to use energy when the general rule is avoid this thus seem contradictory, but you have to recognize the spirit in which they are given. If it was taught that pushing internal energies is always proper, people would do it all the time, get lost in constantly pushing their chi around, and never make any progress. However, sometimes you *should* give your chi a nudge, and you'll eventually realize when you should do this based on the results you get. Sometimes you should try to stop your breathing if you can. You must comprehend the fact that all these instructions are themselves expedient methods (such as *counting* the breaths), that the rules of meditation practice are flexible, and they require the application of some discriminative wisdom to determine when you should use a little effort now and then.

People think that meditation instructions should be like an inalterable cookbook recipe with things precisely measured out, but as you may well know, recipes have a lot of leeway as to how they are actually prepared. Adjusting your body in meditation is like cooking food over an open fire; you always have to adjust the cooking to take account of the strength of the fire, the amount of water in the pot, the food to be cooked, and so on. You have to learn when to adjust matters from experience because everyone is different. You start out by knowing the general instructions, and as your progress grows, with wisdom you will know when to adjust the general rules. You always need to guide yourself in meditation practice though personal wisdom, but according to well known principles. The more you practice, the more your wisdom will grow and the easier it will become for you to adjust your body and mind.

Another important principle you should know is that when you can feel chi energy in an area, that sensation actually represents friction or blockage rather than the smooth flow of the chi within the region. If the chi flow was smooth you would not feel it at all but would just feel comfortable, as often happens after good sex. We can feel the chi only because it is bumping up against some barrier within its flow pattern. With anapana and internal chi cultivation methods, you recognize where your chi flow is errant and your effortless attention to the problem helps to open the channels in a very gentle way. You become aware of obstructions without becoming attached to them, and in taking the body as one whole you free up any pressure on individual channels, and allow them all to open at once. You become able to view the body and its energies as one giant phenomenon within consciousness, and that detachment, achieved by resting in the transcending clear awareness, allows all its chi channels to open.

Every time we start to meditate correctly our chi starts moving in response. That moving chi eventually encounters frictional obstructions within our outer skin which, because we then feel the outer shape/form of the body, we mistakenly take as our self. Because we can feel the outer shape or form of our body, and because we can move the body or its energies in response to our thoughts, the limited size of our body thus becomes the size of our idea of the self. This is not only incorrect, but very limiting to say the least! As an enlightened master once said, if people could recognize that the body consciousness – feeling the shape of the body and the sensations of energies within it – is not your true self but just another phenomenon that appears within your bodiless true mind, you would be half way to enlightenment already. People have an incredibly hard time separating body consciousness from thinking consciousness, which is why I stressed this fact in visualization practice.

In anapana practice, you are basically just following your respiration until your chi flow smoothens and thoughts subside. Some schools call this result a state of harmony, balance or equilibrium, but it just means that your chi channel network has opened to some stage of completion without obstruction, and all your chi is flowing smoothly through that network to that degree of opening. This is what causes wandering thoughts to subside. This is why you can relax to the extent that your breathing slows to a halt. Your breathing can calm down because your channels have already opened to some degree.

During that eventual state of respiratory cessation, you should abide in that state of mental emptiness and physical stillness just as you should upon reaching it through any meditation technique. You don't have to worry that you have stopped breathing because your body would not decrease its external breathing if it needed it. Trust your body – it knows what it is doing, so give this state of respiratory cessation no concern when it occurs. When it happens, your body is surviving on practically chi alone.

It is said that some people, after sexual relations, can totally let go of everything because their body becomes extremely relaxed and comfortable, too. If we can just let go of the body and mind completely without holding to thoughts anymore at that time, but without falling asleep, this will also do wonders for our stage of cultivation. Similarly, during the state of respiratory cessation, just remain relaxed and let go of your body and mind. Just remain detached during that state of respiratory calming. Your mind will start to empty as your breathing calms, and then your breathing will naturally subside, but ignore all these events and just let go. Eventually you can realize a state wherein your mind is empty, but you remain aware yet detached, always practicing clear witnessing.

If you practice anapana or internal energy cultivation techniques, the benefits of opening up your chi channels and transforming your physical body will extend to the achievement of more energy, more alertness, better memory, less sickness, long life and good health. An even greater achievement is to eventually recognize that empty bodiless awareness that knows, which is the awareness capability of your real self. This awareness is your mind. All of the ingoings and outgoings of breath and movements of chi that you notice are phenomena happening in the mind's pure, clear nature.

Prior to this type of realization, you start out by simply observing whatever energies appear within the body while remaining tethered to following the breath and especially the gap between the respirations, which should slowly extend with practice until respirations softens and seems to halt. When your external respiration slows to a halt, that's when the real chi or vital energy of your body will start to arise and circulate, and sometimes you will feel a type of internal pulsing (a pumping sensation) deep in the abdomen when this happens. This is the arising of real yang chi which starts opening up the major chi channel meridians. This is when people often feel the pumping of the chakras, but after all those channels opening, you will rarely feel pumping afterwards.

In any case, as meditation practitioners we must strive to reach the stage where we can actually feel this internal yang chi vital energy, and only then are we doing anapana correctly. If you can reach the stage in your practice wherein you can feel your internal chi or vital energy, then in connecting with it and unifying with it, you can end up opening up all your chi channels and achieve *dhyana-samadhi* extremely quickly. Then one will be sure to achieve all the possible promised fruits of meditation.

ANAPANA AND INTERNAL CHI CULTIVATION

Shakyamuni Buddha knew hundreds of cultivation methods from ancient India, many of which have survived until today. When practicing as an ascetic, he used countless techniques but in particular, he extensively relied upon anapana. He discovered it was one of the top techniques you can use for quieting the mind, transforming the body and cultivating pristine formless awareness.

When Shakyamuni went on personal retreats during the rainy season after his enlightenment, he would also practice anapana for his cultivation. When Mahakasyapa (one of his principal students who became his successor) asked for meditation instructions, Shakyamuni Buddha taught him anapana practice. When Buddha's own son also asked for a meditation method he might practice to become enlightened, Buddha also taught him anapana practice by which his son attained *samadhi* within two weeks!

After your major channels have been opened from establishing a base of cultivation practice, there will be fewer disturbances in your mind because the chi circulation in the brain and body will have become smoother. You typically feel your chi when it hits something in the body, and as these obstructions disappear your chi flow will smoothen because its circulatory routes become cleared. Ripples in chi flow, however, become disturbances within consciousness, namely afflictions and irritations, all of which appear as thoughts.

Anapana helps open up so many obstructed channels that the resulting smoothness of chi flow, after all have been opened all the way through, enables you to experience extremely pure states of mental peace and equilibrium, including emotional calming, and if one uses insight analysis to introspect during those periods, one can easily attain the Tao. This is why Buddha's son, Rahula, could make such great progress in so short a period of time.

Confucius explained cultivation in terms of the awareness practice of watching your thoughts, and noted that in time thoughts will die down just from the process of witnessing them with awareness. From that state of cessation you will experience internal peace, quiet and stillness. He said that your mind will become transparent, pure and clear without afflictions. Because of that inner peace, he said that your body will start to transform so that you eventually experience a physical bliss. This physical bliss, of course, occurs because your chi channels start to open. It is a result of your inner energies stirring just as happens from anapana practice, only in this case you reach this stage through a different meditation technique.

This is the actual sequence of personal cultivation practice everyone non-denominationally experiences, which is why Confucius could describe the very same phenomena we have been reiterating. Because of this transformation of your body, your mind will continue to purify, your wisdom will arise (you will attain the ability to see what the mind actually is), and you will start to obtain the deep fruits of the path such as more energy, mental clarity, spiritual progress, health and longevity.

Once again, even if you do not travel the pathway to spiritual enlightenment, you should be meditating on a regular basis to get all these other benefits. For the person with non-spiritual objectives, those are the results of meditation practice, and they will indeed occur if you practice. In this poisonous day and age, meditation practice is also one of the few things that can help you internally detoxify your body of poisons to produce health and longevity through its ability to open up your chi channels. No other method can open up your chi channels and push the poisons within them out of the body.

The Confucian meditation practice of watching your thoughts not only helps you reach some stage of quiet mind, but helps you to reduce your desires (for money, fame, power, etc.) as well. With mindful introspection you are always checking your thoughts to see whether they are good or bad, clean or impure, and this allows you to manage your thoughts and actions in order not to give people hurt or harm. It prevents you from losing your head and doing something for which you are later sorry. If you take off the religious covering of Christianity, you will find that much of its instructional teachings on mental purity and self-behavior match perfectly with the teachings of Confucianism!

Mencius, who followed Confucius, explained cultivation matters differently by simply saying that you can cultivate your body's chi to a state of fullness, and then eventually your mind can become as boundless as the universe. This is something we actually have already discussed. The awareness capability of the mind, being formless and empty, is exactly like this. Taoism said that through breath cultivation your chi will fill Heaven and earth, and your mind will become as vast accordingly.

That state of chi fullness is something you can achieve through anapana practice or by watching thoughts (since they will both open up your chi channels), but it can only be reached when all your channels open up. This usually corresponds to several years into the "completion stage" of Esoteric Buddhism, or Vajrayana, which stress that practitioners must learn to cultivate the vital energies of the body for its transformation. Esoteric Buddhism places a great deal of emphasis on directly cultivating your body's chi and channels in hopes you can reach this stage, whereas Confucian cultivation approaches its achievement by watching thoughts and telling you it will produce physical body bliss. Zen Buddhism brings you to this stage by having you jump out of attachments to the body and mind altogether, from which the channels will open as a natural result of that detachment.

In Taoism you are taught to cultivate your mind so that thoughts calm down. When your thoughts calm down, your chi will arise and open up all your channels. After they are all opened, you can reach a state of fullness. Your chi will be full and thoughts will die down so that your mind is empty of random wandering thoughts. At that time you can start cultivating *shen*, or the clear awareness of which we always speak.

Cultivating *shen* is akin to cultivating the experience of pure consciousness itself rather than being caught up and entangled within the moving thoughts of consciousness. If you remain abiding in *shen*, without attaching to thoughts, your internal thought environment will eventually decrease of busyness and clarity will arise. It will become so empty and clear that you finally reach a stage of true emptiness, and the mind will seem to extend into boundlessness. Even the thoughts of being a self will drop out, and you will also eventually attain the Tao in this way. Then you can continue cultivating that realization and proceed up the ladder of progress to perfect and complete enlightenment.

There are so many different routes and approaches for proceeding through these stages to reach the attainment of self-realization, and the different cultivation schools of the world all champion one or the other. You already have the basic meditation techniques that they use, and it's up to you whether you want to put them into practice. In Islam we have the repetition method of *dikhr* similar to mantra recitation, in Christianity we have Hesychast stillness prayer, in Judaism we have kaballah contemplation … every genuine school, religion or tradition has techniques to cultivate spiritual states of quiet mind that, with wisdom, can eventually lead to enlightenment if performed properly.

While some of the world's spiritual schools place a big emphasis on transforming your body through meditation, most do not. Most religions do not even mention this will happen, and adherents are left at a loss when this happens. There are many reasons for this, including the fact that most religious functionaries who lead the public have never experienced their internal vital energy, have no clue to its existence and don't know how to cultivate it, and in general know nothing about the general correct principles of spiritual practice and its common results. Even so, meditation practice can help you transform your body to a better state of health, so this is indeed a possibility. And it is indeed a possibility for you to be able to cultivate the internal energies of your body.

Meditation can help you eventually get rid of the view of being a body *because* your chi channels finally open, your mind becomes peaceful, and with better chi circulation you can then detach from the feelings of the body and the view of the body. With enough progress, you will stop holding on to the false idea of being your/a body. You will stop taking the body as yourself, and so we say that you will detach from the body notion; you will disidentify from the body, ignore the body, or achieve an "empty view of the body."

There are lots of ways to say this, such as "forgetting the view of the body," but they all refer to the fact that you stop identifying with the body as your real self. You know this is incorrect, but you still end up taking the body as your self anyway. Of course there is a body there, and you know it is there, but now you know it is just an appearance in consciousness like everything else rather than the ultimate *real you, the* fundamental pristine awareness that ultimately is the essence of this consciousness enjoying the appearance of your body right now.

Right now you still think that a permanent, self-so, self-existing soul or entity or sentient being or something like that shines through your body using it, but this is because (1) you have not analyzed the situation carefully enough to determine what the assumed soul/entity/self really is, and (2) you have not realized enlightenment whereupon – through direct experience—you *realize and incontrovertibly know* what you really are that is appearing through the visage of this body and mind and turning into the ideas of being a small, independent self in the world at large.

"Emptying the view of the body" is a definite wisdom achievement, and being able to cultivate your chi to a state of fullness helps you achieve this wisdom attainment. You can attain it because with sufficient chi cultivation your body and mind will both purify. When they both purify, it becomes easier to finally detach from them both and have a direct realization of the Truth, which is the nature of your true mind.

ACTUAL ENLIGHTENMENT VERSUS INTELLECTUAL UNDERSTANDING

An intellectual understanding of these facts is not enlightenment but just an understanding. Just because you cultivate your internal chi energies to a highly refined level, and just because your mind becomes pure, and just because you intellectually understand the Truth does not mean that you are enlightened. Self-realization is not the acquisition of something material or physical, *or knowledge*, or a mental realm. It is more of the nature of an understanding that arise when a state of purified gong-fu is achieved, where thereafter you can perfectly let go. You cultivate high enough to finally attain a "recognition of It" through direct experience, an empirical realization, and then you shed all final attachments to ignorance that separated you from a realization of your original nature of pure consciousness. You suddenly have insight of what the true nature is, that you are the true nature and always have been, and then that understanding is never lost because you let go of final attachments and thereby achieve attainment. To say "you become It" is only a manner of speaking because you cannot become something you already are and you cannot attain or acquire something you already have; you simply stop identifying with everything else that is not It, and so you abandon polluting obscurations that shield your realization of Truth. Some say "you come home," but once again this is just a manner of speaking because you are always home; It is always you, you are always It. Every moment is It for all of us, every step you take is your home, the entire universe appears in the moment.

There is a well known story about the famous flying Taoist Lu Dongbin that can give you an understanding of this discussion. He had achieved all sorts of tremendous energy gong-fu, which means his chi and channels had been cultivated to a very high stage, and of course he had achieved an accompanying purity of mind (consciousness) to match such incredible vital energy accomplishments. However, even though he could fly around from here to there and exercise various miraculous powers, he still had not attained self-realization. He was lucky enough to meet a Zen master, who engaged him in conversation, whereupon he took a moment to look within at the nature of his mind, and then suddenly realized the true nature of consciousness and the falsity of his imputed self. That's when he became enlightened, or "attained self-realization."

He had done all this internal energy work to cultivate his body, refine his internal energy and purify his consciousness, but prior to his enlightenment he had still believed that he was an independent self. Then the Zen master Huanglong pointed out what his mind/consciousness actually was. Lu Dongbin looked within and immediately realized that what he thought was the "he" (him, "I" or himself) was actually the underlying Self of us all. The forms of body and consciousness are all the manifestations of the one original nature, which is the case for all of us, and he realized that the nature or essence of his mind was his true self, and it was also *That One.* He finally "saw it" and so he was able to let go of any remaining subtle vestiges of an assumed self that we all create through conceptions. He had cultivated to such a high stage of mental purity but all the time had missed this realization about the true nature of self-consciousness, but now, based on some prompting, he finally saw it. This shows it takes wisdom/understanding to experience the awakening of self-realization. You can do all this internal energy work cultivation, and get all sorts of incredibly high results including a highly purified empty mental state, but without wisdom you may never awaken. In the modern biography of a Hindu master named Papaji (H.W.L. Poonja), there is a story about his meeting with a young adept in India who also possessed many superpowers, and through a similar brief verbal lesson Papaji was also able to help him awaken.

In the annals of Zen there was also a monk who lived in the remote mountains, named Fa-jung, whose mind had become pure (empty) because of his excellent cultivation of years of refined meditation work. The Fourth Patriarch of Zen, Tao-hsin, came to engage him in a conversation, which also prompted Fa-jung to awaken and recognize what he had always missed despite years of meditation work for purifying his mind.

These examples all show that you can cultivate these high states of mental purity and physical purity (because your chi and channels transform if you've gotten to a high level of mental emptiness), but if you don't have wisdom, you will still keep holding on to pure consciousness without realizing where it comes from and what it is. You will still take it as a small and independent self-so self without realizing the substrate of your mind, which is what we all are. Shakyamuni Buddha even warned that you can cultivate all the major realms of *samadhi* and still remain unawakened, or non-enlightened.

All things appearing in consciousness have fundamental equality in that they are all equally consciousness. It's all the same stuff of consciousness appearing in different forms/shapes that you are always experiencing. When you finally get the thought to turn around and look at the consciousness itself, and at that moment realize the source essence of that consciousness and the fact you are only that source nature, you can abandon clinging to the forms of consciousness altogether and finally realize what you are, what you have been and always will be. Thus we say "you come home."

Enlightenment, therefore, is a wisdom realization. You are already It, the original nature, but don't realize the fact. You just need to awaken to the fact from a direct realization that sees this with direct experience. Hence it is said, with one thought you awaken. You finally "see it" or "understand it" and awaken. Then you can finally fully let go of any last remaining attachments you have to the concept of a being and self.

You are always the empty fundamental essence and the functioning of that wonderful fundamental enlightenment, the Source, but think you are a separate self and don't realize it. When the mind clears it is as if thick curtains drop away and the boundless sky empties of all clouds, but this is just an experience of mental purity. It is just an experience of the underlying natural purity of consciousness, or awareness, when discriminative thoughts settle. You still have to know, you still have to introspect and realize that you are an underlying pure nature that has the miraculous factor of consciousness or awareness. You can rarely realize this, however, unless your mind clears enough to reach a high stage of purity where most thoughts are absent. *Only meditation practice allows you to realize that purity*. Study will not bring you to the Truth. Memorization of holy scriptures will not bring you to this Truth. Worship will not bring you to the Truth either. However, some people have wisdom so high, such as many Zen masters who reached enlightenment at an early age, that they understand the Truth immediately upon hearing it, and can just detach from the view of the body and mind directly to realize their mind's nature once they hear of it. Such was the case of Hui-neng, the Sixth Patriarch of Zen.

The other route, for those of us without such high wisdom, is that we can also attain realization through the road of study and meditation practice, as you are learning here. In terms of study, you have to cultivate an understanding of what your mind and consciousness actually are, which is why you can read books on Zen, Vedanta, Buddhism, Mahamudra, Dzogchen, the Great Perfection, and the like. You must intellectually understand what they are saying to understand the view of enlightenment. Then you have to cultivate meditation to clear your mind-stream enough of afflictions so that thoughts calm down and it becomes empty and pure. Within that state free of mental pollutions and obscurations you have a chance to *realize* this understanding and authenticate it.

Passing through stages of progressively quieter, calmer or emptier stages of mental purity, your chi and channels will change as you make progress towards this end, and eventually your mind will become very empty, pure and clear. There is an ever present clarity of awareness that can know the realm of mind, and the random thoughts which normally obscure it will have departed from the mental scenario. The mind will then seem as if it is both empty and vast. In this stage of clear awareness—without any thoughts or thought attachments—when the right circumstances come together you might suddenly realize by insight that you are the original nature. You might suddenly, in that realm of mental purity, understand what *It* is, which means *what you are.*

Prior to this sort of realization, typically you pass through many stages of spiritual gong-fu. You also will experience many intellectual understandings. One of the first understandings is to realize that you are not a body, and to stop clinging to it in consciousness. You want to stop binding up the existence of a body with the views of a self.

This realization that you are not your body is different from "emptying the view of the self," which is a yet higher wisdom attainment. Nonetheless, when you finally realize that the idea of being your physical body is false, and that it is just an experience in consciousness, with more insight you can realize that space, time, phenomena and other experiences are all in your mind as well.

These things are mental experiences, or "appearances" within consciousness, and hence they are mind-stuff. Being equally mind-stuff, they are fundamentally equal. Realizing this fact, one can try to learn how to detach from them (and all other mind-stuff) while letting them appear, for you don't try to suppress anything. If you can learn this detachment, you will be cultivating awareness. With experience or proficiency of abiding in just pure awareness or pure consciousness that knows/views but does not attach, you may be able to "turn around" to realize their source, which has no self or thoughts in it, and that is called enlightenment.

When because of meditation practice you have a direct experience of your original nature that does not have any conceptual overlays, then you will have an insight that is really, truly yours. It will be a wisdom understanding derived through experience rather than study. Your personal authentication by direct experience is what makes it real and genuine. This is what proves or authenticates the path and everything we have been discussing – direct personal experience of the Truth and knowing it is so.

You cannot just read about these things in a book, understand them, and then take that intellectual understanding as a "realization." Genuine "realizations" about your true self-nature prior to enlightenment always correspond to certain mental stages that involve your chi and mind and which are attained through meditation practice. You must reach and directly experience those stages yourself to claim those insights as your own.

That is called proving, authenticating or verifying the path. This is why meditation practice does not produce a purely philosophical result, or a religious dogma that can be argued over or which you are taught to swallow.

It is all very logical, there are no holes in the complete explanations, and most of all *you can and must prove it through personal experience* rather than have to just accept these notions on faith. You actually can experience these things directly if you cultivate high enough. You can directly experience the truth of this reality if you work hard enough at cultivation practice, namely meditation efforts. So many individuals have succeeded in the past this way, they have left similar records of the same final result regardless of the fact they came from different religions, and that authentication trail is open to you, too. In fact, this is what religion and spirituality is supposed to be all about but most people are not following this Way at all!

Once thoughts further die down ("empty out") from the view of the body, you can eventually realize that the "you" which you take as your self is just an experience in consciousness, too. It is a set of ideas or conceptions rather than the primordial illuminating Self, which is what you actually are. You certainly have self-awareness right now, but its actual origins – for you, and me, and all sentient beings — are a boundless underlying awareness or pure consciousness that is not a thing or substance or mental experience. The purity of this base consciousness is obscured because of our attachments that have developed in taking our body and mind as our self. Whatever is ultimately behind consciousness, whatever transcends it, whatever has the capability of awareness must be the real you. That infinite awareness or base consciousness of pure consciousness *is you* if you can go no further beyond it but find it as the foundational state. We are all That, and you can actually, genuinely realize this original nature on the road of meditation practice. Once you do, there is no mistake of self-delusion anymore.

Of course, sitting there right now you have self-awareness and thoughts of being an "I," but these are just ideas. Do they have an ultimate reality to them? Are they true because they certainly seem so?

You think those ideas are real, but they are not since they evaporate when you cultivate high enough and find that there is no difference between you or anything else, and that you don't feel separate from anything because it is all one. Nevertheless, no one believes this, so you have to prove it not through logic but through personal experience. In the proving you don't create anything new, but just let go of thoughts, and if they are false they can drop out to leave what is true and real as remaining. The stage where there is no more dropping possible is It. That's what everyone tries to reach – the true self or original fundamental nature.

These notions of being a fixed soul or self or personality entity, with an independent self-so nature, are eventually seen through as being false when there is high enough wisdom and meditation progress. With great meditation progress, all such thoughts slowly drop out. The Hindus say "*neti, neti*," or "not this, not this" to indicate that everything you can know or identify is not It, but when you let go of all thoughts and conceptions you can finally realize It. It is like the *Tao Te Ching* which says, "The Tao that can be named is not the unchanging Tao." If you can identify something in the mind, which is "naming" it, it is not the original nature (but rather a phenomenon instead).

Hence, the view, thoughts or conceptions making up the idea of individuality dissolve away, too, by the fact that you eventually see through this ignorance as being untrue. When you attain enough clarity and purity from meditation progress, you will see through many such errant concepts (including many espoused by various religions) and recognize their falsity in a direct experiential fashion. When that happens, many schools call it liberation, but it is far from complete enlightenment or self-realization. There are actually a number of stages between initial realization – a stage like Jesus or Mohammed – and complete enlightenment such as with someone like Shakyamuni.

Just by study and logical investigation alone you can also come to an intellectual understanding that there is no solid permanent "you" that you can call a self-so independent being, but with meditation progress you actually experience the dissolving of all the thought concepts that make up the assumed self you take yourself to be with the "I-thought," and so we say they become extinct. Since they can dissolve away, you realize they were not necessary or real to begin with, and the Truth can then be known. The idea of there being a solid you, self, "I" or observer within your life has always been formed by the overlay or agglomeration of interdependent factors within consciousness. As those factors purify from meditation practice, the false ideas surrounding the self-sense simply drop out like ice melting in the sunlight. Those notions were just a big false assumption. Without it the world still works, and nothing changes at all in fact except you now live with freedom and non-suffering.

This is a remarkable discovery that few ever believe until they actually achieve it. That is why so few Western philosophers or religious professionals have realized this or discuss it. They never took the road of meditation practice and cultivated far enough to achieve this, or anything else substantial along these lines. Go search and you will not find any philosophers even talking about chi, chakras or channels because they never even got to the stage of activating their internal vital energies and cultivating any internal gong-fu they could feel. People almost always discuss gong-fu when they start making inroads into truly investigating the nature of the mind, and yet not one of them has achieved anything along these lines, but these are the people whose thoughts we study. What a topsy-turvy world! Without attainments, their ideas as guiding principles are therefore just that – mental thought constructions that lack any basis of true reality. Amazingly, rather than a path to liberation or Self-realization, this is what the Western world of philosophy always studies. Many religions are actually deficient in this respect as well, and postulate all sorts of inferior notions as final states of salvation or liberation.

There is nothing that is a personal "you" which independently exists as a solid basis for being the ultimate experiencer of thoughts and consciousness. You cannot find any truly existent personal entity like that. You can encounter various states of consciousness that you can experience, but any states that can be returned to prior causes are obviously not the permanent self-so you.

What you are is not an invisible soul or *atman* or self, but actually the original nature itself in the guise of an agglomeration of types of consciousness which produce experiences, and within them the idea of a personal self arises. Consciousness gives birth to consciousness, namely thoughts, and so these ideas arise within consciousness. Ideas are just consciousness transformations. However, everything is just that original fundamental nature which is why some religions say the original nature is just expressing itself in all these false forms. The entire universe is all just the temporal manifest fabric of the one original nature which Itself always remains unmanifest. All the unenlightened living forms capable of consciousness within this manifestation take themselves as separate independent units because of mistaken thoughts or ignorance rather than recognize they are the one Source. We are not truly existent living beings or souls but just *That One.* The awareness functioning/characteristic of the original nature shines through endless constructions of consciousness, some of them "living" that we call beings, and they take themselves as independent units rather than recognize what they truly are. That is, each non-enlightened personal consciousness takes itself as a separate being; those consciousnesses wrongly take themselves as separate independent beings.

What we call a person is an agglomeration of types of patterns that are ultimately animated by a true one, and the thoughts given birth by this set of patterns do not belong to a soul or ego but to that pattern set, which is itself made up of consciousness. Consciousness is just spinning thoughts to consciousness, itself, and there is no really existent person, self, soul or entity inside. There is no true being within it because the animating force of pristine awareness or pure consciousness is what it and everything else is, including the seemingly independent thinking. So nothing real is actually happening from that aspect. Consciousness is *That*, individual consciousness is *That*, the entire realm of all manifest consciousness is *That*. The absolute nature no one can know, all-consciousness is its function, individual consciousness is an artificial delineation within the all-consciousness (manifest consciousness), and there is no actual individuality within the all-consciousness so there are no such true things as truly existent separate sentient beings, entities, living beings, ego identities, personalities, souls, or selves. The absolute nature is not anyone in particular but is everyone, as well as everywhere.

The pattern set of individual body and consciousness has the capability of consciousness/thoughts because it is consciousness, and through incorrect notions of consciousness the pattern set has spun thoughts wherein it takes itself to be a true self. When those thoughts dissolve, the true underlying self is finally known, and this finding is liberating. You abandon all the obscuring transformations of consciousness to find the true, pure consciousness that you really are; previously, in focusing upon the manipulations you obscured recognition of your true self. Hence, this is what is rediscovered at the apex of meditation experience. The discovery, returning home, brings purity, bliss, peace and non-suffering.

This is why you cultivate. The purpose of meditation is not so that you can achieve a blissful state, but so that you can cultivate a clear mind of wisdom that, because of its clarity and wisdom, can detach from and thus transcend the manifest realm of the cosmos and thereby end suffering forever.

THE SEQUENCE OF MEDITATION PROGRESS

The traditional sequence of this meditation progress runs as follows. When you empty the view of being a body you still have thoughts, so this is an incomplete achievement. You must then experientially realize, because thoughts die away, that what you call the "I" or "ego" or "self" has no self-so, independent, homogenous existence. This is the higher attainment of "losing the view of being a self." It is a direct experiential attainment. There are no presuppositions or conceptual overlays to this. You experience this as being directly so.

As a direct experience of truth, this realization does not fall into the realm of constructed theologies and religious dogmas. It is so real that you cannot deny it, and *thus this result belongs to all religions.* It has been achieved by many spiritual greats regardless of their religion, which is why they always speak about this. Do you really expect the truth to be denominational as Jews, Christians, Muslims and others might purport, or rather, to be non-denominational as I'm describing?

When the false notions of being an individual self drop out, this is called "seeing Truth" and some take it as final enlightenment when it is only initial enlightenment. Christianity tries to point you in the direction of this attainment by teaching you to be selfless. Taoism wants you to realize this through the naturalness of letting go of thoughts. Judaism, Islam, Sikhism and Hinduism all have their own teachings on how to realize this. Some traditions, such as Buddhism, teach you how to realize this truth very directly.

Because there is no real, permanent center of a person, being, life, self, "I" or entity in our experiencing of the flow of consciousness, the thoughts of a self, called "the view of a self," die out when we spiritually advance. It's just been a reflexive construction of thoughts that entirely depended on one another without having any solid or real supporting basis, like a complicated illusion that appears in the air but which lacks any solid basis/support of fixed reality. When meditation proceeds far enough, the idea of the "I" as the center of perception slowly disappears. It is discovered that there is something that has a capacity to perceive but there is no actual center to experiencing, and this clear awareness extends infinitely without outer boundaries. You don't create this clear awareness without the "I-notion." You find it to already be there, primordial and pure, when you let go of the polluting obstructions of the mind. So you are not creating anything new, you are not creating anything artificial. You are discussing what is really so.

As stated, this stage of realization, wherein the view of having a fixed true self drops out, does not count as complete self-realization. You start to become stabilized in pure consciousness, but the riddle of the presence of phenomena is not yet resolved (the union of emptiness and interdependent origination). There is no self, but you must reach the state where there is no other (non-duality), and this realization is not instantaneous. As one stabilizes in consciousness, or awareness, further things must happen as you expand into the manifest. Nevertheless, it is only due to the fact that the small ego stops that the real Self can appear.

To some religions and individuals, the loss of the small ego/self idea is their stage of final salvation because the self/personality becomes liberated once it is found not to truly exist. Even so, the final spiritual result is still far from being achieved at this stage. The view of being a self can disappear (we say it becomes "extinct" or you achieve the "*samadhi* of extinction"), but this is only realizing the emptiness of the self rather than the emptiness of phenomena, which still appear. That's what's incomplete about this stage of realization. There is no small independent self, but what about phenomena? Are they really there as independent self-so things?

Phenomena, or appearances, also have no independent self-so nature but are also just interdependent constructions of consciousness. The manifest all arises together as one whole within consciousness. You've dissolved the mystery of the existence of self-consciousness, but not the continued appearance of all phenomena, or the manifest nature, and now you discover their source. What are phenomena? What are appearances? What is Creation, or the manifest phenomena?

Phenomena do not exist from their own side and by means of their own independent essence, but are also manifestations of the pure original nature of consciousness. They also do not have a really existent independent nature of their own, but you have to prove this once again through cultivation and then direct experience, too. *If you can finally realize the inherent emptiness of both the self and phenomena, that's what's called spiritual enlightenment.* That is the final achievement. It also entails various other attainments such as special powers and *nirmanakaya* and *sambhogakaya* accomplishments mentioned within Buddhism, but their discussion is once again beyond this introductory text.

How does this tie-in to the simple practice of meditation? Most people never travel this trail far enough to discover these truths, but just settle for the mundane benefits of relaxation, more energy, better health and peace of mind. However, you can travel a long way to attaining some of these stages of realization, and in shooting for this higher result you will surely get all these lower benefits, too.

From meditation, your mind will start to empty and your chi channels will start to open. Your chi and consciousness will both begin to transform to a higher stage of purity, which is why your mind quiets or "becomes empty." After all the major energy meridians in your body first open, it will take many more years before the hundreds of thousands of other channels all over the body completely open, too.

You can only reach a higher stage of this opening due to a continued and yet higher detachment from clinging to thoughts. That's why you try to cultivate witnessing, which is resting in the awareness that stands behind thoughts without entering into them so as to get lost or entangled. You can achieve this higher stage of detachment, which matches a higher degree of mental purity, by cultivating a variety of meditation methods. You can also cultivate insight analysis. Insight analysis, such as used in Zen or Vedanta, is one of the top approaches for detaching from absolutely everything ("*neti, neti*") and discovering your original nature. However, anapana practice is the king of practices for transforming your physical body.

At these higher stages of channel openings you don't talk of chakras or specific chi channel meridians anymore. After the major meridians open, so many other channels will open that you cannot describe the process with a specific detailed sequence, and so the best you can do is summarize all the transformations by saying your body is becoming full of chi, your channels are all opening, your body is becoming transformed, the physical nature is becoming purified, your five elements are becoming harmonized and balanced, and so on. These are all synonyms, or simultaneous happenings. Hence, in describing the progress, Mencius (who followed in Confucius' footsteps) just referred to large stages rather than specific details as you usually find in Taoism or Esoteric Buddhism.

Every spiritual school describes this type of gong-fu progress differently. Your chi and channel cultivation can become so good – in other words, the smoothness of your chi flow circulation can become so good—that your physical body progressively feels lighter and then almost non-existent because of the harmonious chi flow. This perfection is the real potential of the physical human body rather than the excellence represented by athletics, sport or bodybuilding.

As these stages of channel openings occur, which we can alternatively call stages of "chi cultivation" or "internal energy work" instead, your thoughts die down as previously explained. There are no longer many thoughts or ripples in consciousness that correspond to obstructions or attachments, and it seems as if the head empties out from the quiet. This is why we say that the mind purifies.

Some people describe it by saying there are no thoughts, or they just call it the stage of "no thought." Because there are no thoughts, the mind is not limited but becomes boundless and free, formless in being empty of all content. With wisdom, you can then realize the nature of the awareness that is what you are, but if you still hold on to the subtle idea of being an ego/self having that experience, you cannot end up knowing its boundlessness. You have to cultivate the a stage absent of thoughts and abide in the awareness to experience that the awareness is pure, clear, formless and boundless, everywhere.

At that point the personal mind eventually ceases to be because consciousness exists in its own nature as consciousness, and that is *pure being.* This is why the great Mahasiddha Tilopa said don't recall, don't imagine, don't think, don't examine, don't control, but rest your mind and thought processes. You can arrive at the pure being of consciousness just through the practice of purely witnessing the mind until all its machinations die down, which is why witnessing and cessation are the two principles inherent within all meditation techniques. When consciousness eventually loses all notions of objectivity (because thoughts die down), it merges in itself losing its separate identity as personalized consciousness, and resumes its identity as pure being. It achieves single, non-dual, *self-identity.* This pure consciousness or pure being is what is experienced by a sage, which is an "awakened" or "realized" one. Once again, this is not an experience you create, but the foundation of your beingness itself which you discover only through meditation practice.

When thoughts die down "in the head/mind," it seems as if the body is there "without a you" anymore. You begin to lose your deep habitual identification with the body as your self, and your body seems as just something that can be used as a function of your mind, which itself becomes empty and vast. Thus you can finally become thoroughly detached from the body, which is the natural progression of practice.

Mencius called the stage where your channels start to fill with chi, after many of the major chi meridians have opened, the state of "beauty." It is a state of cultivation wherein your chi starts to feel rich and full throughout your body. As your cultivation progressed even further, the state of chi cultivation then became what he called the stage of "grandness." These stages are the target of anapana practice taught by Shakyamuni Buddha, and this type of achievement enables you to attain *samadhi.*

At this level of attainment, the chi of your body as one wholeness can be felt and one eventually switches from chi cultivation to *shen* cultivation, which is akin to becoming expert at cultivating the non-moving awareness that knows thoughts because it transcends thoughts. There is always awareness (pure consciousness) that stands behind thoughts in order to know them, and now thoughts have quieted to such an extent that you can finally recognize the existence of this underlying awareness and can rest in that empty, invisible, always present awareness rather than in the consciousness of thoughts and appearances, which is what it sees/experiences. At this stage you truly know how to detach from the doings of consciousness and be the transcending pure witness that is always present (it's not something you create), so you start cultivating the awareness which transcends or stands behind consciousness (thoughts/the mind) allowing you to know it. That awareness never enters into consciousness to interfere with it, and does not falls into either the motion or stillness it observes. Consciousness, accordingly, calms or stills to reach a level of no thoughts, or cessation, where the mental realm is truly empty.

At this stage your consciousness is still connected with chi, but if one rests in the witnessing awareness alone while staying detached from the body and consciousness, your mind becomes emptier and emptier. We say your consciousness becomes like the empty space of the sky or entire universe. We say it becomes boundless. Mencius talked in terms of chi, rather than consciousness, so he said that your chi eventually becomes so grand, large, formless or big that there's no boundary to the mind, which Mencius then called the stage of a "saint." Your consciousness becomes so empty or pure that you realize the transcending pristine awareness which is empty, formless or boundless, and that's what he called the stage of a saint.

In this stage of attainment the idea of the self no longer exists but the real Self awareness is still actively shining through what we see as that person. You, he, I and everything else are that original nature, but just don't know it. Everyone, regardless of their religion, school or tradition, eventually arrives at this practice result if they proceed far enough, and it all starts from the simple road of meditation. The teachings of Zen, for instance, constantly speak to this revelation.

Past this stage of the saint, Mencius said that if your cultivation level becomes so high (because of no thought) that nobody knows how high it is, that's the highest accomplishment. This is the stage of an enlightened sage. The sage does not even take pure consciousness or pristine awareness as being real. He considers it a guest rather than the host, or original nature. He considers it a functioning of the original nature and therefore practices the Middle Way of not attaching to it.

This is correct, but I like to use the terminology of pristine awareness or insubstantial pure consciousness, rather than the absolute nature, to help people understand, and when they get far enough to realize that the universal consciousness is just a function of the empty absolute nature, I trust that they will have enough wisdom to recognize what is the absolute or fundamental nature. Let me explain it another way: to attain realization you must cultivate an empty mind free of thoughts. Then you should not cling to this mental freedom, and you must also become unmindful of this concept of freedom, too. Then awareness is functioning, but you have no concept of functioning including no concept of self as well. That is how one proceeds.

THE IMPORTANCE OF ANAPANA

The question arises as to how you get to this stage, and it all comes down to personal cultivation. It all comes down to personal meditation practice rather than Church going or temple, synagogue, or mosque attendance. What meditation practice do you use? As we can see in the case of Shakyamuni and his prime students, and as we can see from the story of Mencius who talked about cultivating one's chi or internal energies, one can not do wrong by cultivating anapana.

After I had made significant progress in my own meditation practice without ever using anapana, my teacher called us all together in the main Zen hall where he gave us an important lesson saying that he wanted me to know the top cultivation method of the Zen school used by masters both before and after their attainment. He then taught me anapana, and said he wanted to make sure I knew this was one of the top methods, which he himself had proved after many decades of practice. He said that he was sure no one would tell me this fact, so it was essential that he take pains to call attention to it and point it out, and in turn I'm transmitting his emphasis of that importance to you.

Even after they achieve enlightenment, masters sit and practice anapana meditation to make further progress. It is a way of cultivating the four *dhyana* quite easily, but no one ever tells you these facts. It always helps to maintain your progress and keep transforming your body to a new stage of purity. You can reach states wherein your respiratory breathing totally stops for long periods of time while you remain totally open and aware in clear vast (bright empty) awareness, and an internal chi circulation commences and then continues inside while that external respiration ceases. This constitutes a high *dhyana* attainment. At a higher stage you can reach and remain in a stage where your pulse also naturally stops, too, because your heart slows to stop beating. This is an even more advanced *dhyana* attainment (the third *dhyana*) you can reach through anapana, and it is attained through perfect relaxation rather than force. It just naturally happens from letting go rather than from performing some strange yoga where you try to make your heart stop beating using force so that you might decrease oxygen consumption and enter into a trance.

In Esoteric Buddhism practice you will often encounter instructions to cultivate simultaneous emptiness and bliss, or co-emergent emptiness and bliss, in order to attain *dhyana-samadhi*. The various stages of emptiness-bliss cultivation actually correspond to the four *dhyana* of Orthodox Buddhism, Taoism and the Hindu yoga traditions. In fact *they are the genuine four dhyana* although some in the Esoteric school do not admit it because they want to help preserve the uniqueness claims of their tradition or actually believe its cultivation methods produce higher stages of realization than the methods of other schools. This can be confusing to many ardent practitioners, so let me give my personal take on these matters.

When you reach the stage through your cultivation that all your major channels have all opened and your mind has so quieted so that it seems extremely empty, we say in Taoism that you have moved from the stage of cultivating chi to cultivating *shen*. In this stage most all your wandering thoughts have died out, and so you can finally attain an understanding of pristine awareness. Once you understand this abiding awareness, you can cultivate a genuine experience of emptiness by letting go of all thoughts (including those of the ego-notion) until they die out, which is why Taoism says that *shen* transforms into emptiness. It just means you can cultivate a true emptiness realization wherein the thoughts of the self drop out, and you realize some degree of the Tao. This is the initial enlightenment of Hinayana Buddhism.

In Vedanta, for this same stage of practice you are said to be cultivating pure awareness because your thoughts have emptied out, and so the observing mind is empty of thoughts. That overriding pristine awareness that is always there now is now recognized and seems vast like space, namely boundless and empty. You remain in that clear pristine awareness and by abiding in it, by just practicing witnessing without attachments or efforts, in time thoughts drop out including the thoughts of being the body and self. Personal consciousness, without objects, has no other objects to be aware of other than consciousness, so we say it merges into itself and resumes its identity as pure being. This non-dualistic experience of self-identity is called "beingness" in Vedanta and is the awakening attainment.

Some schools call that ever present witnessing factor of the mind clarity or awareness, and others just call it mind without thoughts. Various other terminologies also abound such as that you are cultivating clear witnessing, empty clarity of mind, no thoughts, pure consciousness, or clear illumination. At this stage, they all mean approximately the same thing because most of your discriminative thoughts are gone, your mental scenario is extremely empty, clean and pure, and it seems endless like the infinite expanse of empty space. "Boundless" is how Mencius described it, so once again, every school ends up describing the same natural states of Tao attainment. Thoughts drop out, including those of the ego-concept or self, consciousness then becomes pure because it only knows itself, and that state of pure consciousness or beingness is a liberating attainment.

In Buddhism we just say you are cultivating emptiness, or empty mind because the awareness or pure consciousness still exists, which is what mind is, but its contents become empty when thoughts leave. Consciousness discovers that it is itself pure when empty. What's the sequence of practice for this realization? You cultivate meditation, your thoughts die down, your channels open, your chi flow becomes better, more thoughts drop out, more channels open … finally with enough practice all your major and most of the minor chi channels within your body become open and all your chi flows become smooth, you aren't holding onto mental scenarios so much anymore, and you finally reach a state of pure, empty mind where wandering thoughts have departed, discriminative thoughts seem non-existent and the mental realm therefore becomes clear like crystal. This is when we say you are cultivating empty mind, or thoughtlessness, or *shen*, or emptiness, or no-thought, or pristine awareness. This is when you can finally cultivate *dhyana*, and you can use anapana to do it.

The stage of cultivating awareness (clear witnessing mind) along with your vital energy is what you are practicing with anapana, and this is what helps you to attain the genuine *dhyana-samadhi* attainments. You eventually abide in the transcending bodiless clear awareness that knows and seems everywhere, and you know all the transformations of your breathing and the internal chi and channels within your body because you are watching them. Boundless awareness knows the subtle remaining mental thoughts and internal sensations. Most thoughts are empty/non-existent, and the physical body feels wonderful because of all the chi flowing through opened channels in a harmonious fashion. Hence, you experience co-joined emptiness-bliss as stated by esoteric Buddhism. You can cultivate this through anapana practice!

Raising the thought of joy, you can cultivate mental joy while feeling physical bliss and remaining empty and relaxed. In terms of your physical body transformations, you are already watching, knowing or witnessing the internal sensations of your chi movements and chi channels with anapana witnessing, so you are cultivating your chi to achieve the foundational physical bliss aspect of *dhyana*. You can feel your body and know all its internal channels are open and can feel all this chi, and that is the wonderful feeling of physical bliss you can cultivate. Your mind is empty, and that is the emptiness characteristic of the *dhyana*.

As to the factor of joy, if your mind is very empty then joy does not arise as a distracting mental disturbance. However, at a lower stage of emptiness you can be cognizant of thoughts of happiness, joy and pleasure if you want to cultivate them in conjunction with the knowing of your body states and the fact that your mind seems very empty at the same time. If you let go of these thoughts of happiness/joy, and your chi flow then becomes better/smoother/more harmonious, that's how your mind becomes emptier and how you progress to a higher *dhyana*. Hence in anapana you cultivate witnessing, empty mind and chi, and in time this can lead to internal mental and physical transformations so that you eventually end up cultivating the four *dhyana*! This is why I encourage everyone to practice anapana.

Sometimes with my own cultivation I always seemed to be coming late to the game, so I'm hoping this advice and these explanations can help people make progress much quicker than me, and that you learn how to practice witnessing and anapana. It all starts from learning how to abide in the clear witnessing of thoughts while remaining detached rather than getting caught up with thought flows and losing yourself. If you do this, not only will you be able to make progress in meditation and change your personal behavior, but as often stated, your chi channels will start to open and you'll get all the energy, health and longevity benefits promised. As your face and body fills with chi, you'll even look younger and better, too! It all starts with desire to learn how to correctly use this thing we have called consciousness, or mind. None of this is religion; you are simply learning how to *correctly* use your consciousness. People don't get this point. You are, in essence, an aggregate, knot, ripple, wave or stream of consciousness (however you want to word it) within a manifest universe of Only-Consciousness, and that aggregate that's you will always flow on forever continually transforming, so you better learn how to use your functions of consciousness correctly and wisely. This is why you need to learn logic, wisdom, and skillfulness starting in this life while you now have the teachings.

People always want to know how to cultivate the emptiness, joy and bliss of the four *dhyana*, and it is accomplished easiest through anapana. Anapana is not the only way, but is certainly extremely effective which is why my teacher bothered to stress to me that this is one of the absolute top methods in Zen, and why Shakyamuni taught this to his closest students who thereby awakened through its practice.

I hated anapana when I first began to practice it. As with most meditation methods that ever benefited me, there always seemed to be a barrier to anapana meditation that discouraged me from really delving in and trying to master the practice. If that happens to you, you must strive to break through that barrier, as I finally did, to confirm that anapana is one of the fastest ways to cultivate the body and open up countless other chi channels including *after* all the major meridians have already opened.

To open up all the major meridians is already a daunting task, but to progress past that stage one can, should and must turn to anapana. When you read stories of ancient masters whose internal energy work was so good that they could fly through air or live incredibly long lives into the hundreds of years, you can surmise that they were usually practicing some form of anapana and internal energy cultivation since they can help you open up even the tiniest chi channels of the body beyond the large meridians.

Even after you open up all the major meridians, it takes years to complete the transformation of your physical body, which is effectively done through anapana practice. One will continually, time and again, reach a state of respiratory cessation just by watching the breath and focusing on the periods of respiratory cessation with anapana. During that state of stillness the yang chi will sometimes seem to arise again just like it did the very first time for the initial *kundalini* awakening, and will then work to open up more chi channels at finer and finer levels due to your cultivation. This continues to happen in cycles for years after one completes the initial completion stage yogas.

Some ancients have used sexual cultivation to further help open their chi channels and transform their body after sufficient degrees of progress, but the difficulties of finding a qualified partner with suitable chi cultivation and karmic affinity, the risks of pregnancy, or the fact that the successful practitioner might be a monk or nun, make this an impossible route for most. Nevertheless, this is also a route for transforming the body quickly by dissolving channel obstructions in a different way. The correct form of sexual cultivation practice can act as an adjunct to anapana practice for helping to transform your chi channels. One should know about this fact if they ever open up all the body's main chi channels, such as detailed in *The Little Book of Hercules*, and are faced with the task of completing the body transformations quickly. Few, of course, ever reach this stage of qualification or are even qualified to enter into an intelligent discussion of the matter.

In addition, the more you stretch your muscles through yoga, martial arts or other forms of exercise, the easier it will be to open up the chi channel routes along the lines of muscular definition through anapana, especially if you learn how to combine your exercising with your breath. It is very hard for chi pathways to open up through undifferentiated muscle mass, which is why martial arts and stretching exercises are very useful to cultivation and health in general. At advanced stages of meditation practice, you can practice anapana while assuming various yoga asanas (or special postures you create yourself) to help further transform your body. As usual, you must strive to detach from the body and sensations while doing this sort of practice, otherwise your chi will have difficulty passing through your channels which are being stretched through the unusual positions.

Advanced meditation practitioners often close their lips and teeth and curl their tongue backwards to touch the roof of their mouth as far back as possible when practicing, which is said to prolong life, and this is another tip you might want to apply during meditation sitting practice. You can even do various upward pushing or twisting tongue exercises in such a position, while looking upwards, to help open up the throat region of the body which otherwise is very difficult to open.

Together the anapana and white skeleton visualization practices allowed Buddhism to enter China without much opposition because local practitioners kept getting marvelous results using just these two meditation methods alone. The two methods can always be practiced together, or with other techniques for the best results, and practiced together they have enabled many people to attain better health, peaceful minds as well as incredible physical skills and even enlightenment. Together they help you to quickly realize a stage of empty mind and cultivate your chi and channels. When all your chi channels clear through, you will not only have transformed your body so that it does not decay at death, but will have made great strides in achieving mental purity. All sorts of beneficial physical and mental results will come out of this success.

The intelligentsia that disliked Buddhism's arrival in ancient China could not oppose its entry into the country when many practitioners of anapana and the white skeleton visualization commonly attained *samadhi*, enlightenment, or developed superpowers from their usage. People in yoga, Taoism and the esoteric school all talk about opening up chi channels and chakras using elaborate meditation methods, but combining these two techniques is perhaps the simplest and most powerful route of them all. If you combine them with mantra, insight meditation and just the simple practice of watching thoughts, you will have a killer combination. The results of such practice will be extremely beneficial, and what you do with the results of practice is totally up to you.

Some of the basic teachings on anapana practice have been left to us by Shakyamuni Buddha in the *Anapanasati Sutra* and the more important *Dharmatara Dhyana Sutra* first translated by Buddhabhadra into Chinese. This sutra was essential to the formation of the Zen school, but paradoxically, no one has bothered to translate it into English. Such an important foundational work, which was pivotal to the establishment of Zen practice, never made its way into Tibet either! This is why the Tibetan meditation tradition never developed an effective anapana practice vehicle even though the works of Vasubandhu and Asanga discuss this practice technique. Tibetan Buddhism has relied extensively on pranayama instead, and other methods of internal energy cultivation from India and China.

Having explained as many details as possible, I think you can see that anapana practice is yet another meditation technique that should definitely be added to your practice schedule if you really want to make meditation progress. It can be practiced by itself, or in combination with other techniques, and it is also easy to combine with any type of meditation practice session. It's just another technique to help you calm your mind (and open up your energy channels), and it works through yet another entirely different principle or mechanism. In fact, from the examples provided, you can see that some of the highest of masters succeeded because they relied on anapana practice.

You should know that in the esoteric and yoga schools, most practitioners build their practice foundation on pranayama first before they ever proceed to cultivating internal energy work. The secret of Tibetan Buddhism and its many unusual practices is that most of them rely on the cultivation of the breathing and then internal energy, and you have just learned two of the premier techniques for doing so. In fact, yoga, *kundalini* cultivation and qi-gong all depend on breathing practices as their vehicle of attainment. Countless spiritual traditions focus on the breathing process, such as "watching the breath," "refining the breath," and "tempering the breath" in order that it becomes so subtle that it almost stops and the body starts generating its own inner energy to take over. That's the arousal of *kundalini* or yang chi, which is called different names by different traditions. That is the beginning of the transformation of the body necessary for you to be able to attain the Tao.

Pranayama practice, on the other hand, is a technique which you can use to help purify your body and prepare it for receiving the benefits of anapana and other meditation methods. You should think of it as physical detoxification exercise. In holding your breath you are also trying to trigger the real chi latent in the human body, and prompt it into arising to help clear out your chi channels. As does the exercise of stretching, this will help open some of the physical structures of your body, such as expanding your lung capacity, and chi channels as well. People who practice pranayama often report an eventual balancing of their physical body, better memory, higher alertness, and more clarity of mind, too.

With anapana practice you don't use force at all. Instead of watching your thoughts, you remain aloof in the clear awareness and watch your breathing by focusing on the period of pausation between the breaths. You also turn to witnessing the sensations of your internal energy inside your body, and then allow your chi to arise and channels to open while detaching from both body and mind.

With time and progress in using this technique, your breathing and thoughts will calm down just as they do with all proper meditation methods, and you will start cultivating your internal energy in such a way that eventually leads to high meditation achievements. At the point where thoughts die away when using this practice, you should try to entirely forget your thoughts and body and just abide in that emptiness with awareness which you will be able to do without much discomfort because all your channels will have opened. Thus you will be able to naturally experience an empty mind without using effort that will lead to even deeper states of peace, clarity, chi purification and chi channel openings.

6

SETTING UP A PRACTICE SCHEDULE AND RECORDING YOUR PROGRESS

People often ask, "What is the best meditation method?" but there is no such thing as a "best" meditation technique. One just starts meditating with what they know, from whatever stage they are at, and adapts by trying new methods all the time. The key is just to get started and to progress from there.

The question is like that of people who don't exercise and ask, "What is the best exercise?" Well, there is no "best exercise" or "best type of exercise." The best exercise is the one you'll bother to do since you are not initially doing anything at all. Once you get started exercising, however, you start laying a foundation of experience. Once you lay this foundation, you can then ask about the best way to move forward for progress and improvement.

That same reasoning or principle holds for meditation. The key is how to get started, and for that purpose you need to pick a meditation method or methods that you will practice. After you get into the habit of meditating, then you can ask about the best form of that particular practice, or other meditation practices you might try. Because of different propensities, for everyone the answer will be different.

Over the years I have found that the best way for people to make progress at meditation is to get started and record their daily practice results in a practice log. The actual activity of monitoring your progress by recording your practice results on a piece of paper definitely helps you establish new habits. You get to see how far you've progressed, and the formality of filling in a schedule at the end of the day can be made into a review of the day's efforts as well. *People respect what they measure and measurement ends argument, so that daily review will help you remain aware of how you are progressing, and will help you stay on track and committed to progress.* This is something I have written about extensively in my book *Your Destiny is in Your Own Hands*, also known as *White Fat Cow*.

As to scheduling the time of day you should meditate, by all means schedule a specific time if that helps you. However, if you are the kind of person who will skip the practice effort if you miss your scheduled time slot, you have to rethink that strategy. The point is to somehow make meditation part of your daily life in some way, so you must work it in however possible. Just get started regardless as to however little time that initially amounts to, and in time your commitment will grow as will your progress and the benefits of practice.

Adults brush their teeth because they were taught as children to form this habit. Muslims pray five times a day because the Islamic tradition forces them to adopt this habit. If you don't have such a tradition or habit, you must use willpower or some other method to help get you started in making meditation part of your life. *Scheduling and monitoring (record keeping) help you establish the habit of practice.*

Some people will start meditating as soon as they wake up in the morning. This gives your body time to allow your chi to start harmonizing throughout the channel orbits, and that helps you start the day feeling balanced and comfortable. My teacher immediately meditates sitting on his bed for a half hour or more whenever he wakes up in the morning, and of course he meditates at other times during the day as well. But he always told me that he never leaves his bed in the morning until he feels well from meditation, which (after sleeping) reestablishes the smooth harmonious flow of chi throughout his body.

Some people will meditate right before they go to sleep. Some will wake up in the wee hours of the morning, like Christian monks who get up around 4:00 am to say their prayers, and meditate at those early hours. Some will take a few minutes at lunch time, or on the subway, or before dinner. If you practice right after a meal you'll tend to become sleepy, so you should practice before eating rather than immediately after a meal, or wait about one to two hours afterwards to meditate.

As to other opportunities, whenever you can fit in some minutes for meditation, that's a good time to accumulate some practice time because results come from the cumulative hours of your practice. If you are standing idle for ten minutes or so, who says you cannot use that time to do the skeleton visualization? It only takes but a few minutes! Who says you cannot be practicing anapana and watching your breath for a few minutes at any point during the day? Who says you cannot drop thoughts immediately? You don't have to be sitting in a cross-legged lotus posture to do that. Who says you should not be watching your thoughts all day long, which is witnessing practice? And any idle moments can be used for mantra practice, as you well know! Many of these opportunities don't have to be scheduled.

In short, you have to use whatever time works for you and you must try to initiate the habit of practice. However, although spending more time in meditation is better than spending less, you don't want to neglect or ignore your worldly obligations and responsibilities. If you want me to mention a specific amount of time, it's best if you can do at least forty-five to fifty minutes of continuous practice for each session when you sit down to cross your legs and meditate.

Forty-five to fifty minutes of meditation per hour in a group session will allow everyone to have ten to fifteen minutes to stretch their legs or exercise; this is important when you are meditating for a long period of time in a super marathon session. Many advanced practitioners will find they only start to make chi progress only after two continuous hours of practice, but it is difficult to sit continuously for two hours, and so they must break up that practice time into sections. Some people, when they first get started at meditation, cannot even sit for fifteen minutes, but in time this can always be lengthened. How so? Once again, it just takes practice which brings you the capability.

No one can give you a rule for how much time you should meditate, or when, because everyone is different because everyone is at a different stage of practice. This is why everyone experiences different results at the beginning stages of meditation as well. Really, it's all about what you can do versus doing nothing at all, so don't get fixated on the number of minutes you must spend meditating.

If, when getting started, you cannot practice several meditation techniques in a single day because your schedule does not permit, try devoting yourself to just one of the big four methods per week – mantra, anapana, visualization and vipassana. Just focus on practicing one method per week and cycle through all four during the course of one month. As the story of Hercules and the Twelve Labors suggests, in about thirty days of devoted work an individual can awaken their yang chi and start getting the results of practice. The *Hatha Yoga Pradipika* says it only requires about forty-five days of devoted practice for a celibate individual, and then his or her *kundalini*, or yang chi, can start to arise. Whether it is thirty or forty-five days, the key in this short time period is devoted (deep), proper, consistent practice.

In a little over a month's time of true practice effort, you will have broken much of the resistance you feel to the act of meditation, and will have dissolved quite a few barriers that have always prevented your chi from starting to move. You'll then be on your way to greater health, longevity, stress-free peace of mind and happiness in life. You will also begin to lay a stronger foundation for whatever religious spiritual practices you already follow. Of all the activities you can do in the world, meditation lays the strongest possible spiritual foundation and provides the support for genuine spiritual attainment.

THE BENEFITS OF MAINTAINING A DAILY PRACTICE LOG

What I used to personally do to force myself to practice and make progress was record my daily meditation efforts on a piece of paper. I'd bundle up the pages and keep them in a binder, which I would refer to from time to time to see my advancement in progress. Today you can simply go to a computer, open up Microsoft Excel, and easily create any type of recording schedule you want, including a schedule that can also become a journal or goal setting mechanism for any area of your life.

I like to plan my life activities for the week, so I would create one sheet of paper for each week in the month. My schedule would have rows for each day of the week and columns for each type of practice or other activity that I wanted to do each day. There would also be a Totals row that would count up how many times I did the practice represented by each column, or for how long, or totaling any other criteria that was relevant.

How did I categorize my columns? The first column was always the number of mantra recitations I completed that day. As I mentioned, there is no excuse for not doing mantra practice, especially because mantra practice does not have to be scheduled but can be done during other activities. You will commonly read the stories of countless masters who recited *millions of mantras*, and if you wonder how that was possible, it was because they simply made mantra recitation a constant, unscheduled practice. They were going about their worldly activities and reciting mantras all the while. In other schools the masters would simply recite prayers, but as stated, choose such prayers carefully. Because the sound of the prayer is not the important thing, the meaning, or thought you hold to, becomes important because of the impression it can leave on the mind. If you choose the wrong thought, it can have psychological repercussions that you'll have to deal with in subsequent lives when you may not be born into that religion!

After finding out the natural number of mantras that I could recite during a day, that amount became the first target objective for how many to recite on a daily basis, which I slowly increased over time. I am told that many Christian monks recite four hundred prayers before they sleep, and because of my own natural habit patterns I eventually ended up targeting three thousand full Zhunti mantra recitations for each day. I would keep track of my recitations using one of those metal clickers people use to count visitors coming into a store. I never liked using mala beads or rosaries for counting, but some people like that method, and you should use whatever works best for you. Others simply know how many mantras they can recite per unit of time, and use that to estimate their counts which they record their progress at night before sleeping.

As you can see, there are no fixed rules or methods for doing any of these things. I therefore can only offer some simple advice. You must choose what works best for you, or develop something on your own that is particularly tailored to your own private situation. That is the way it always is in life with everything. You should just use whatever method will get you started and keep you going, that's all. In my own case, I would always try to recite my minimum target amount of mantras per day, and if I failed at this target I would make sure I did more the next day to make up the difference. It just became a personal objective to try to increase that daily count over time for no other reason than I knew it was important, I had faith it was helping (because nearly every genuine tradition recommends it), because my teacher had recommended it, and because I wanted the results of practice.

Another column was filled in with a check mark if I made a nightly offering to the hungry ghosts, which you'll find out about later. This is something I would do the same time every night before sleeping, and it only took about three minutes of my time. I also had columns as to whether I did good deeds for the day to increase my merit-making, similar to the methods that Liao Fan and Ben Franklin used for this exercise in self-improvement.

I scheduled and dropped many activities over the years, so the names of the activity columns changed over time. There might be columns on my practice schedule that were to be checked off if I did yoga stretching exercises that day. The box to be checked off might mean that I read a spiritual text that day, was abstinent in some manner, or it might represent a violation of certain behaviors I wanted to eliminate from my life. I had columns to check if I avoided certain bad behaviors or boxes to be checked if I performed good behaviors I had selected. You can make your columns represent anything you like that is important to your own goals and situation.

I had columns to represent the completion of pranayama practice that day, the white skeleton visualization, anapana efforts and yoga. I even recorded the number of times I meditated along with the total minutes involved. All these columns changed over time, so do not get the idea that I was doing hundreds of practices simultaneously. Like everyone else, I had a normal life to live with job and family responsibilities, but to make sure cultivation was part of my life I scheduled in my meditation efforts. You respect what you measure, so monitoring yourself in some way will help you.

What you use as a recording system, what activities you decide to do and for how long or how much, and what design works for you best is totally up to you. However, I do recommend that you create an Excel spreadsheet type of practice schedule. Make it official, and "report your progress to Heaven" in the evening at the end of each day to keep yourself honest in your commitment. It is said that the knights of King Arthur's Round Table had an obligation to undertake one quest every day before its end, and you might consider your own heroic quest the recording and analysis of this self-improvement journal for the day!

In one of my columns I wrote down my breath retention times for the nine-bottled wind practice when I was practicing that strenuously, and on my wall I even had a chart recording my average and best times for the nine-bottled wind. I eventually got to holding my breath over four and half minutes (free-diving experts can hold their breath for seventeen minutes), and would never have gotten that far had I not posted this chart on the wall and reminded myself of my most recent personal best right before I sat down to practice. When suffering through that breath retention phase, I would keep my eye on the seconds hand of the clock and try all sorts of tricks to hold my breath for just a little bit longer in order to surpass my best prior record. Remember that when holding your breath you have to relax your body as much as possible, and you'll find that very few muscles need be involved in actually holding your breath!

In any case, every evening I would record what I did during the day, if not immediately after a practice (such as pranayama), which is a habit I duplicated after reading the stories of Liao Fan and Benjamin Franklin. At the end of the week I recorded the totals. That weekly summary also gave me time to figure out the mundane things I wanted to accomplish in the coming week, and I always made a list of what I wanted to accomplish for each month as well. Sunday became a time to review the week's efforts, and to write out goals for the week ahead.

Most people never write down what they want to experience or achieve during life, but when you write down yearly goals and then break them down into monthly and weekly goals, your chances of actually accomplishing those goals and desires skyrockets. You will actually end up doing what is important to you in life – before the lack of money, time, health or opportunity slips by – and will be a happier person for the effort. Your meditation schedule that includes goal setting can therefore become the basis for an effort at self-actualization, self-improvement and self-fulfillment. I implore you to consider using this technique because of the great benefits it brings!

Everyone has their personal interests or limitations regarding how much they can practice meditation and how they can work it into their life. I had my own private targets for mantra recitations and for some of my other meditation objectives. Accomplishing those objectives is something I did not always accomplish on a daily basis, but I definitely tried to accomplish them despite a busy schedule.

Let's be realistic. If you have a job and family or other heavy responsibilities, there is only so much time you can devote to meditation, which is why scheduling and recording things forces you to see whether you are doing what you want or not. If you aren't, it causes you to think about how to fit what's important into your life schedule. You are only scheduling, and recording, what is important *to you* in life. This is for you, not me or anyone else, so figure out how to make it work. You are the one who should be disappointed if you're not doing what is important to you! Recording your daily efforts and goals forces you to think about such things, and will therefore help you in so many ways.

What was important to me was that I always wanted to see mantra practice being done absolutely every single day because there was no excuse for not doing it, and in that way I ended up reciting millions of mantras. It took some time to accomplish that task, but it's simple to do – you just begin, keep at it, and soon the goal is accomplished. I also expected, as an absolute MUST, to see a check mark in the final column of my sheet showing that I did an offering to the hungry ghosts every single night, and some type of mark showing that I did meditation practice that day even if only for fifteen minutes.

Whatever is important to you in life can and should be worked into such a schedule to keep you doing it. After all, you are the one who selected it as an objective of importance. After a habitual routine is established, perhaps you won't need a schedule anymore. However, to initially get started you need to set up a practice schedule, and try to combine it with a weekly and monthly schedule of life goals and things you want to do. I am a firm believer that recording your efforts will make you more aware of what you are doing and help you achieve your personal goals in life.

HOW TO SELECT YOUR BASIC MEDITATION PRACTICES

One more word about meditation practice: I have found over and over again that the exercises we dislike, or the meditation practices we dislike, or the activities we dislike in life, are usually the ones that tend to help us the most. We hate them because they irritate us, and they irritate us because they are not our natural inclination. They irritate us because they stretch us and cause us to grow, and that hurts a bit. What causes us to grow helps us to make progress, but that stretching most often causes a bit of a challenge and discomfort, which explains why we might psychologically dislike those activities. Hence, *those meditation practices we dislike often tend to be the very ones forcing us to change the most, and therefore are usually the ones that help us attain the most progress.* This is not always true, but is a principle to keep in mind.

When some activity is forcing you to change, it is causing you to push against your normal behaviors and go past your standard limits, and that progress produces the blowback emotion of dislike in response. Change always produces resistance, and progress challenges the status quo, which naturally opposes it in some way or another. Hence the tendency for dislike often arises. Do not let this stop you from making meditation a part of your life. Any dislike you feel is probably because it is helping you in more ways than you can count.

Therefore, if you have trouble sitting down and watching thoughts, stick with it for a month or so to get started. If you cannot concentrate in forming a visualization and hate it, that's one of the methods you might want to especially work on because you need those skills of concentration. If you hate reciting mantras, that's precisely the practice you should perform! For instance, my teacher said that he initially hated reciting the Zhunti mantra, as especially did I, and he therefore knew it was extraordinarily powerful and producing positive changes because of that dislike. If it was not working to help transform his consciousness, that emotion of dislike would not have strongly arisen. I also came to the very same conclusion, and this principle applies to many other meditation techniques as well. The ones I hated, and thus tended to avoid, were the ones that usually ended up helping me the most, but of course this was just for me and may not be that way for you. It is just a tendency that I often noted but is not a hard and fast rule.

If you love doing some particular meditation practice, you should keep doing it so that you are always engaged in one you like and therefore continue practicing meditation. However, please remember that it's the one that challenges you which often produces the most progress. If you can do a yoga pose without strain or effort, are you making progress or are just involved in maintaining flexibility rather than increasing it? When your muscles stretch beyond their previous bounds, that's when you feel the strain (or "burn") because that's when you are making progress. So those meditation methods that cause us to develop will often be the ones we tend to dislike "because of the burn." In short, don't let dislike be the cause for dropping your commitment to meditation practice altogether, or for letting that commitment falter, or for avoiding a particular practice.

Hence, a principle I want to leave you with is to try to maintain a meditation practice that you love, and try ones that you hate. But don't veer off track and pledge yourself to some strange unorthodox meditation practice that few people ever use just because it's new or different, complex, hard to perform, or because you hate it. That's twisting the principle entirely. We're talking about orthodox practices – if you hate mantra recitation, do it! If you hate visualization practice, try it! *You usually hate it because it's difficult, and therefore you usually need to develop those particular skills.*

The big four methods that I encourage everyone to practice are mantra recitation, watching your thoughts, visualization practice and anapana. This entire book is written to help you master these four techniques. Whether or not you add yoga stretches or martial arts, pranayama, seeing the light meditation, celibacy or sexual cultivation and others on top of this list is up to you. If you achieve the state of ultimate emptiness then there is no method anymore, but since people have not achieved this they need some methods to practice. Don't get transfixed by a particular method, however, for in the end you have to give up even meditational methods to attain enlightenment. For instance, the *Surangama Sutra* lists twenty-five methods used to attain enlightenment, but they are all just expedient means to help you arrive at discovering the root source of the mind.

As a further helpful hint, every now and then *try practicing a particular meditation technique in a different way* and *try switching to new techniques altogether* to keep your practice fresh. Please also remember that you should always vary the cultivation method you use according to circumstances, such as how your body feels at the time. This is important. You have to become flexible when you set yourself on a course of self-cultivation. The practice you use at any particular moment, and how to employ it, should always depend on the situation.

I suggest that you set up a daily practice schedule, with an initial minimum amount of involvement, in the following way. First, find the steady state amount of time you can comfortably spend in meditation activities. Next, schedule that involvement as your daily quota of practice commitment. Lastly, work to slowly increase that amount if possible. If you do this, you'll be able to look back at the end of the year and say, "Wow! Look at all the work I've done and the progress I've made." Most people who look back at the end of each year have trouble citing any significant accomplishments at all in their ordinary life unless they set up goals for every week and month, as explained, and kept working at them. This method insures that you do just that and accomplish what is really important to yourself. Your life will become full of useful activities and progress if you adopt this routine.

Whatever you want to do in life is up to you, so no one can tell you how much you should practice or whatever other goals you should target on a weekly basis. You have to decide what is important to you and must determine what you personally want to achieve in life based on your own vows and objectives. I can only show you what worked for me, Liao Fan, Benjamin Franklin and countless others who have found that recording your goals and deeds, and monitoring your behavior on a regular basis, helps to keep you on track at accomplishing *whatever is important to you*. You set the priorities, not someone else, because it is your life! The time limit for accomplishing anything of significance in this life is your life span and since that time limit has already been set, if you do not use it then this opportunity will be lost, and no one can guarantee you'll have such an opportunity in the future.

VARIOUS SIGNS OF MEDITATION PROGRESS

Another thing that keeps people on track is seeing the signs of progress from their meditation efforts. Every type of meditation has its own special signs or marks of progress, and of course they also differ by individual. Therefore you should not expect to experience what someone else experiences, or even expect to experience any signs of meditation progress at all. This often frustrates people, but it is the plain truth of the matter. In fact, many masters who succeeded never ever experienced anything mystical, strange or unusual at all during their practice years, and then suddenly they succeeded. This is really what you should expect rather than catching hold of the idea that you should feel certain energetic sensations, see visions, develop clairvoyant dreams and things like that. You are searching for the root source of the mind and not looking for sensational outcomes or unusual events. You are looking for something permanent, pure and infinite.

Nevertheless, you will sometimes find that mantra practitioners will often reach a stage where they find that the mantra seems as if it is being recited by itself automatically, and is even there when you sleep. Many people after a certain amount of mantra repetitions will have special dreams symbolizing their progress at mental and physical purification. They'll often experience symbols of physical purification in their dreams such as vomiting, dark colors changing to bright colors, defecation, cleaning a house or rebuilding it with new construction, and so forth.

For those who mantra on chakra locations, such as those who recite the Prayer of the Heart over the heart chakra, you might even see a little flame on that chakra after a certain period of intensified practice effort. When this finally happened to me after doing millions of Zhunti mantras over the heart chakra (I often visualized Zhunti Buddha, a point of light, or small moon at that location), my teacher immediately called me up to his apartment and then gave me several teachings and a set of special Zhunti clothing to recognize this accomplishment.

With regular meditation, one of the signs of progress is that you start noticing your thoughts for the first time, and when this happens, after a while you might begin to think that your practice is backsliding because your thought volume seems to be increasing. This is like an optical illusion in that what appears to be true is not actually happening. It results from the fact that you start seeing your thoughts for the first time, which you never did previously, and because of that new level of clarity you mistakenly think their volume is increasing.

The phenomenon is akin to the fact that you can see the tiny individual specks of dust and dirt in a glass of dirty water only after the silt finally begins to settle. Prior to this settling you could not see the individual particles of dirt, so in noticing your thoughts and thinking that they are increasing in volume it is because they are finally beginning to disperse. It's actually because you are making progress, not because you are backsliding! You are finally seeing the impurity only because a backdrop of some purity has been achieved. Hence, this phenomenon appears because you are finally noticing all the thoughts that are arising in your mind. Previously it only seemed that there were fewer thoughts running around in the mind because your mind was muddy, and so you simply were not aware of all its scattered content. Most people are not aware how scrambled their mental state is until they start to meditate.

When people get proficient at the skeleton visualization, some people report that they can sometimes see their own skeleton or the skeletons of other people. This is usually a temporary vision and not a stable capability. Images of skeletons might also appear in your dreams as well. As explained in *The Little Book of Hercules*, and illustrated in Tibetan Buddhism and several Greek myths, there are many stages wherein you can experience visions of skeletons that represent the initial transformation of your body's earth element.

With pranayama and anapana practice, as you get proficient it becomes easier for your respiration to die down and seemingly crawl to a halt when you are meditating, which is always an excellent sign of progress. Once again, it is also common to experience dreams which symbolize some form of internal physical cleansing or purification after you make progress with breathing practices. Basically there are all sorts of phenomena that mark signs of excellent meditation progress.

It is not necessary for you to experience any of these signs, nor should you necessarily expect them. On the other hand, you should not stop practicing when they occur because you become fearful you are doing something wrong. That would be a big mistake and unfortunately happened to me in my youth so that I lost many years of possible progress. Meditation means resting your mind (because you no longer hold on to thoughts), and when that happens your yang chi will start to arise, and when it arises it will start poking through your acupuncture meridians or energy channels. That will produce all sorts of unusual and unexpected physical results and sensations as well as mental phenomena, but they are all the natural results of physical and mental purification. Don't get frightened when this happens. It's just a natural event from starting to become really healthy in body and mind.

Meditation progress is really a very simple sequence to understand: you meditate, your yang chi subsequently arises in response, it starts moving through your chi channels and obliterating obstructions (encountering friction throughout the process), and you experience various physical sensations as the channels open from the chi working through them. Here is the problem: because they were never told this, people get worried about the internal energy sensations they start to feel, and always think they did something wrong. Then, out of fear and misunderstanding, they stop their meditation practice. They stop at the very moment they start making significant progress because they didn't know enough. They didn't know these simple principles.

People excitedly send me hundreds of letters each year with extremely detailed descriptions of all the sensations, visions, and physical phenomena that occur due to their meditation practice, always worrying that something is amiss, but all those descriptions and concerns never go past the simple stages of chi and channel purification. People always get worried about experiencing strange physical sensations of energy movements within their body (from meditation) because it's so strange and new, but all that it does is prove that chi is a real phenomenon and that your channels are being opened. Congratulations! The way to have things stop is to meditate with even more intensity to more quickly pass through those openings, but never cling to them when they occur or try to suppress them from happening. As soon as particular channels open, those sensations stop because there is no longer any friction to the movement of chi within that area.

It is a catastrophe when people stop meditating because they mistakenly believe meditation is making them ill, or they believe that they are doing something wrong because various purification phenomena start appearing (due to the arising chi) such as skin rashes, perspiration, feelings of warmth, internal movements of energy, or external physical shaking. Nothing harmful is happening at all – your body is purging itself of internal poisons that usually cause illness if left inside. Your chi is finally moving them out of the way so that it can circulate freely. *This is what you want to happen* and what must happen as your energy channels clear of impacted obstructions, but because people don't have the right information or understand the correct principles of practice, they don't understand that thousands of different purification reactions can occur when you start to practice correctly.

In the hundreds of letters I've received from people elaborately detailing their descriptions of chi sensations, body movements, dreams, visions and other phenomena connected with the chi channel openings within the body, the authors simply cannot believe that anyone has ever previously experienced such things. They just don't know enough – these results are all mundane phenomena at the very lowest purification stages of the cultivation path. Everyone thinks their own reactions are universally unique and high stage phenomena, but they are simply low stage results due to the stirring of chi within the body. The cleansing of their chi channels has finally commenced because their meditation has gone on long enough and started to become effective. Once again, however unique they may seem, the results they report *never go past rudimentary stages of physical cleansing.*

It takes years of such meditation efforts to really produce substantial physical progress, as the cases of Shakyamuni and many other masters have shown. As detailed in *The Little Book of Hercules*, when these reactions occur it is because our body is simply reacting to the release of chi energies that arise when we finally let go of thoughts, which are bound to the circulation of chi energies within the body. When those energies become free they start detoxifying the internal obstructions within your body that would, if not for your meditation efforts, later develop into severe illness. Meditation thus heals you. Due to meditation your yang chi starts moving, it pokes through obstructions to find latent illnesses, pushes out the poisonous culprits, and thereby begins the process of healing from within. This is why it leads to health and longevity.

FINDING A TEACHER

I also often get letters from people asking how to find a "master" so that they can achieve this type of progress more quickly. If you are a person who only devotes lackadaisical efforts to meditation practice right now, do you think you deserve an enlightened master? A realized master is the most important person in the world, and rarest, and doubtless quite busy helping those who are working hard. He or she can help you in many ways, the highest of which is to point out your original nature to you. He or she can help teach you the right view, but you can and should start to study the materials I have already recommended so that you can make as much progress as possible by yourself. You always still have to do meditation practice yourself. In fact, *lots of meditation practice.* You still have to do everything yourself even if you have an enlightened master, so you might as well get started at the self-effort of helping yourself by studying more and practicing more.

If you are just interested in having someone guide you as to the best things you can do with your money, power, status, time and energies in life to help make the world a better place and relieve the suffering of people, an enlightened master can definitely guide you as to the correct courses of action, but first and foremost, he or she wants you to cultivate meditation and awaken. A teacher can teach you so many things, such as how to look at history and psychology to derive wise rules of behavior for the world, how to behave with others to form harmonious relationships, and how to change your own behavior, but the primary relationship is to get you to start cultivating to attain self-realization yourself.

History shows that enlightened masters are, without compare, absolutely the very best advisors for the great and powerful on issues of politics, economics, social issues, military matters and most every other area of world concern (because they are outside the whole realm of consciousness, transcending the entire field of manifestation that includes all such events and concerns), but even with respected positions they always still encourage their patrons to practice.

If you are not working at meditation to establish a good basis of practice, a master cannot do much for you except teach you how to live a better life, practice better behavior, and practice meditation so that you learn how to let go and start experiencing all the various benefits of self-cultivation. When people tell me that want a master, in those cases I recommend that they work hard at their current practice *and mantra for help in their quest.* You mantra while holding on to the thought of finding a master just as you would hold on to the thought encapsulated in a prayer. When the karma is right, a connection will arise because of the merit of your practice effort and sincerity of your request, so that is the best advice I can offer. Even if you do not find one (because an enlightened teacher is rare and hard to find), my meaning is that you should still practice meditation because you have to do everything yourself anyway. Do not avoid meditation practice because you have to do it by yourself, or surrounded by people who make fun of your efforts, or without a teacher. A master cannot make progress for you, and any progress you achieve is due to personal meditation efforts. This life represents a time limit that has now been set for you, and if you do not use this opportunity to properly cultivate meditation practice, the opportunity will be lost and no one can guarantee that you will have any such opportunity in the future. So once again, get started at effective practice as I have been describing.

It is said that there are four difficult things to achieve in life, namely to be born as a human being, to be born in a civilized land, to come in contact with real cultivation teachings, and to meet a genuine teacher. Even if you have enough wisdom and merit to find an enlightened teacher, afterwards you still have to practice deep meditation to prove the truth of enlightenment teachings yourself. It is all about yourself awakening. It is therefore best to start on that road of personal practice even if you do not yet have a teacher, and then much more can be accomplished when you eventually find one. This little book gives you everything you need to know to get started, which is why I encourage you to give copies to others who want to learn how to meditate, too. I've tried to reduce everything down to just four basic practices, and the basic theory, so that anyone can get started.

Since you have to practice meditation yourself, and since there are no secrets to meditation practice, you should be putting your time into practice right now instead of waiting for a teacher to arrive. At the start, a teacher cannot do anything more for you other than teach you the basics you've already been learning. This is why personal study and practice together are so important as a matched pair. If you have a great foundation from your own self-effort, a teacher is sure to appear and can then help you a lot. Your hard work may even draw one to you. How? *Study a lot, practice a lot, mantra a lot, look a lot.*

I often compare the situation to a banker who is presented with the possibility of having poor clients and wealthy clients. Bankers will run after wealthy clients because they already have a lot of money, and therefore have a lot of options available which they can guide. For poor people, the banker naturally accepts them as part of his clientele and certainly looks after all their needs, but has to wait patiently while poor men and women accumulate some money. Otherwise, he cannot help them in any substantial way because they simply lack the funds with which to do anything. You must, therefore, establish a solid practice foundation to be worthy of a teacher.

This is where the importance of religion and culture lay in teaching the masses how to be good people, spiritually cultivate, and establish that foundation. In the East people know that this foundation requires meditation practice, but in the West this idea never took hold because religious institutions typically promised "salvation done for you" in some form or another. Of course, you should realize this is just impossible because you are the one who has to discover, by personally looking, the actual fundamental base of your self, soul, personality, life or mind and finding out that you are not what you take yourself to be. Those who have discovered this have all left us a similar description of the result.

Nevertheless, the background culture of a family, country or religious group is so critically important in teaching people the fact that they need to practice meditation. Truth be told, without the influence of a culture stressing spiritual practice, most people would entirely succumb to materialism. They would lack the wisdom to even know there are spiritual truths to which they can and should aspire.

YOUR TRUE BEING IS BEYOND YOUR INDIVIDUAL CONSCIOUSNESS

Few realize that the entire world is all just a transient appearance not just in your consciousness but in a universal consciousness, and that fundamental consciousness is the *true self* that animates all, extending to all, and that the All is just that one true self. You are not a real sentient being but just *That*, but you have this idea of being a real independent being or self because of thoughts which are just the power of *That* to generate a thing we call consciousness. Without consciousness in the universe, the cosmos would just be an inert existence. Ordinary people think they are independent self-so beings experiencing the rounds of reincarnation, but they are just ever changing formations of consciousness through which that original consciousness shines. Those formations, wrapped up in manipulations of consciousness that they are able to do because they are in essence consciousness, never turn around to discover what they really are, but get wrapped up in all those transformations of consciousness and remain blinded in suffering because they don't recognize their source. However, because they are consciousness, they can awaken!

For human beings to awaken – for these transformations of consciousness to have the realization thought/understanding/insight that they are their source – these aggregates of consciousness must have cultivation ideas available through the vehicle of culture and religion. Otherwise, becoming overly caught up in their own self-thoughts and lacking wisdom about the nature of their own being, they would rarely strive to search for a method of self-realization that would liberate them and free them from suffering, and would not even know how to correctly search for answers (other than spinning thoughts) about the nature of life even if they decided to devote themselves to looking. Those answers cannot be obtained by thoughts or consciousness, but by gradually experiencing the purified realms of consciousness, called empty mind, which fall out of the deep practice of meditation. Then consciousness has a chance to realize itself, or realize the Truth, and awaken. With a glimpse one knows and understands, and that is enlightenment or awakening. That is why Lu Dongbin or Fa-jung in a single moment awakened. Their minds were purified, someone pointed out the Truth to them, they looked, realized it was so, and then finally awakened upon that insight understanding.

There are no secrets to meditation and spiritual progress. You just have to practice meditation with consistency to experience the results you are seeking, just as you have to do if you wish to master any sport or skill. In other words, you have to lay down a solid foundation of cultivation efforts to gain the results of meditation such as peace, long life, or health and energy. Thus, you can and should lay down that practice foundation yourself. If you sincerely throw yourself into devoted practice of the meditations within this simple book of instructions for three or four years, you can lay down an excellent foundation.

People mistakenly put all their hopes on a teacher for meditation progress and then do little to no meditation work at all other than just read books. They forget that no one can save you but yourself, and a teacher can only show you the way. This holds for everyone from Jesus to Krishna, Confucius, Lao Tzu or Buddha. *You have to save yourself (liberate yourself) by your own efforts* by purifying your mind and then looking within, with analysis and logical reasoning, to discover that fundamental substrate of the universe which you ultimately are. Once found, you can find that it encompasses all beings and inert matter, and because it is the base state, just by a switch of attention one can experience the kind of consciousness that any being has, and can be the inner witness of that thing since they are all inside the Self. As the base, one just knows directly whatever one wants because consciousness is all one, and you know everything within your self. Reaching the basis, which is the seed essence of *all* matter and mind, all sorts of marvelous functions become possible which are the basis of spiritual superpowers and the miraculous feats demonstrated by sages.

One is all things, and discovers just as Jesus said, "I and the Father are one." Krishna said, "All are my expressions." Al-Hallaj said after his self-realization, "I am the eternal Truth." Shakyamuni Buddha said, "I alone am the Honored One." Upon enlightenment, one becomes the conscious presence of the total manifestation without the stain of any individual characteristics, and so in considering itself as the conscious presence of the total manifestation, all individuality is lost. One loses the individual identity and knows oneself only as the Absolute. There is no you, I or anyone because all is the original essence of primordial awareness (original mind) and thus, being the original nature announcing itself through the guise of the human being, Jesus, Krishna, al-Hallaj or even Buddha could all equally say what they did, and it was true.

Samantabhadra said, "Because I, the All-Creating Sovereign, have created you, you are My children and equal to Me. Because you are not second to Me, I am present in you ... Oh all you sentient beings of this threefold world, if I were not, you would be non-existent. ... Because all things do not exist outside of Me, I firmly declare that I am all." Jesus also said, "I am the Way, the Truth and the Light" and "I and the Father are one" because in losing the small self through his cultivation, he, too, realized that he was simply the original nature. Jesus was not unique, nor were his words. Unfortunately Christians do not realize this. Anyone who attains enlightenment knows their true nature and can say this. They just realize what they actually are when the thought conceptions of being an independent self, so self dissolves away and personal consciousness becomes infinite, pure and clear to match with the original fundamental awareness. Then consciousness can recognize itself.

There is not and never has been any such thing as an actual (independent) human being, or any sentient being anywhere in the universe, for all sentient beings have been the original nature from beginning to end. All you are ever seeing are transformations of one single consciousness, and yet that, too, is not the original nature but just its function. Upon realization you realize you are the absolute original nature and it has always been that way, even before you were born, but through life after life and endless transformation after transformation you have continually thought of yourself as a separate, independently existing, self-so sentient being. Those are just wrong ideas of consciousness, that's all. These are just false thoughts which do not change the truth even though you believe these false thoughts are true. Whether you have them or not, they do not change the truth. The blessing in life is when you discover the Truth so that you can awaken. Hence these words are rare to hear and hard to find.

Your manifestation is essentially just a transformation of the base consciousness – a minor part of one single consciousness wherein everything is interconnected. The one which gets liberated upon enlightenment is consciousness, not a sentient being, for there is no entity inside it. All that is functioning is the consciousness, for no entity is involved. There has never ever been an individual with consciousness, but rather, *the one consciousness has been assuming innumerable forms that think they are individuals.* Consciousness simply, after enough meditation and spiritual work that purifies it, finally recognizes its true nature and ultimate source – the host, absolute nature, *dharmakaya*, Father principle, source essence or true Self – and then gives up clinging to wrong notions such as the idea of being a small independent self.

What is the exact nature of the ultimate host, or original nature? The nature of the host can only be realized while the guest is present because consciousness is the only thing that can have thoughts; the host itself is without personal consciousness so must give birth to consciousness to know, and that consciousness must awaken. This is why enlightenment is called a wisdom attainment. It's not an actual becoming, but actually a realization, recognition or insight into what you actually are, and which some refuse to accept. The ideas of the small self drop away, one realizes (through thought) their inherent unity with all phenomena, and as the mental realm further purifies one gradually reaches the stage where one just functions without clinging to consciousness, and therefore becomes totally free because they are always in a state of perfect presence, or pure beingness.

Shakyamuni Buddha also explained, "I know the minds of all beings," because he attained pollution-free realization of the fundamental substrate without any remaining ignorance stains that might obscure, pollute, or eclipse the full underlying awareness. He spoke of the stages of this in the *Surangama Sutra*, if you are interested. That omnipresent pristine awareness, which is the stuff of everything, is like a mirror in that it can reflect the internal mode of sentient beings – whatever they are experiencing—since the internal appearances within the mind-stream of each sentient being are included in this one underlying mind substance. One is actually both the experiencer and the experience, but there is no person as the experiencer and actually no experience or experiencing – it is all mind substance knowing itself through transformations so nothing is actually going on outside of the whole system. In other words, nothing real is ever happening. The original nature has consciousness or awareness as one of its functions, and that function (being consciousness) can recognize what it is through the understanding of wisdom which is just itself a transformation of consciousness. Knowing what it is, consciousness can let go of clinging to itself and resume being the pure source without stain or pollution.

A mirror just reflects everything that appears within it, and so an enlightened one can know the delusions of all sentient beings because their minds/consciousness are not independently separated from the foundational base nature awareness but appear like insubstantial reflections within it. They are just *That* in an apparent manifestation – a very tiny part. In other words, one can reach the state where they can witness the total functioning of the universal consciousness, or any part of it, because you are the base awareness functioning through the vehicle of individualized consciousness. It is just that since beginningless time, what you take as the "individual you" has evolved to become individualized consciousness whereas some things in the universe have no self-consciousness ... or do they? If the entire universe is consciousness and all things are made of consciousness, does an inert "insentient" rock have consciousness in some form we cannot know or understand, even at a subtle level? You must cultivate to reach enlightenment to find out. In any case, the underlying universal base awareness, which shines through the medium of the individual to power individualized consciousness, can cultivate to finally realize what it ultimately is, which is its identity as the Source. So Jesus, or Buddha or anyone else can say "I and the Father are one." Don't be deceived, however, for there are complete and incomplete levels of this achievement, and Shakyamuni Buddha represents the complete level.

As Shakyamuni Buddha also said in the *Surangama Sutra*, "You do not know that the physical body, as well as mountains, rivers, empty space, and the great earth are all within your wonderful bright true mind." He was using the term, "wonderful bright true mind" to describe this original pristine awareness, or pure consciousness, that is what you and I are as its manifestations. That pristine awareness is like a mind, hence the term "bright true mind." It can know all universal appearances just as your mind, right now, can know all worldly experiences or appearances in front of you. In Tibetan Buddhism it is called the "clear light," or clear illumination because this pure, pristine, infinite awareness is the source of all knowing, and thus illuminates all mental objects as light does. It is also like a bright, empty mind within which can appear any content that arises through the interdependent transformations of consciousness.

In the Zen school that pristine empty universal awareness is still considered a guest rather than the ultimate host, and the ultimate host is *unknowable true original nature or essence.* It is unknowable by thought and indescribable because you can only be It, but as It (the absolute nature) there are no thoughts, and thus It cannot know Itself. Only as individualized consciousness can you gain some understanding of It – what you are. You can gain this understanding if you cultivate meditation and awaken on your own without any teachings, which is hard, or if you study the correct teachings that introduce you to the proper dharma, and use them as a stepping stone to awaken much faster. Much, much, much faster.

Unfortunately, the organized religions tend to hold these teachings from the public, so life after life people endlessly revolve through higher and lower states of destiny, all involved with mental pains and karmic afflictions. Why not? It is just consciousness undergoing transformations of various forms, with no individual beings truly involved, and so there is no justice or injustice to the process. It is simply like a chemical reaction where nothing is really happening except a process of transformation. This is why people need to learn how to police themselves and cultivate better states of rebirth.

When, through meditation progress, your identification with your individual body-mind complex slowly diminishes, you will not only lose the feeling of being a separate entity from everything, but your individual consciousness drops out (or we can say "expands without borders" so that it is no longer individual) to reveal the underlying pure universal consciousness because that is what it truly is. That is what individual consciousness or awareness is made of, that is what it is. It is just that thought attachments, since beginningless time, have been holding you back from realizing this as your realness or real being. Only now, this very moment, do you have the teachings in your hand that can help you awaken.

Upon enlightenment, one then knows oneself as all matter and all beings, all life, all consciousness … which is the unified message of religions when they talk of the fountainhead or source of Creation. You are actually the total presence, the total manifestation and not a particular you or any self-existing individual. Because of the wrong thoughts of being a small self, you have limited your perception and your consciousness has become cloudy so that it no longer recognize what it is. You are essentially consciousness-only.

You can look back on history and know there was no person called Krishna, Jesus, Buddha, Socrates, Confucius, Mohammed, Abraham, Moses, Nanak, and so on – there was only consciousness of a particular form at a particular point in time. *In other words, in the universal consciousness there are no individuals.* Consciousness simply assumes different forms, shapes, or transformations which the consciousness within these forms individualizes. This is why Krishna said to Arjuna, "Never have I not existed, nor you, nor these (others). And never in the future shall we cease to exist. Indestructible is the presence that pervades all this, no one can destroy this underlying reality. Our bodies are known to end, but the embodied self is enduring, indestructible, and immeasurable." Krishna said this because you, I, everyone and everything is just this indestructible original essence that has awareness as its nature. There are no real individuals within this One-without-a-Second.

Of the three Western orthodox religions, it is actually Islam which expresses this the clearest, but even there these teachings are unclear to the public because they require a degree of spiritual wisdom to be understood. Mohammed's audience lacked the requisite attainments to understand much, so there is very little he could say about higher matters to a society for which his ideas were so new. Confucius was presented with the same problem, as was Jesus. You can only reveal so much for the level of your audience, and you must teach in respect of the needs of the time. It is only when someone like Shakyamuni Buddha arrives, *who had hundreds of enlightened students and students with high samadhi spiritual attainments*, that a fuller dharma could be revealed since the audience was mature enough and skilled enough to comprehend it.

When speaking to the uneducated, ignorant, and immature, most awakened teachers have taken the expedient path of simplifying things or dumbing them down to whatever could be accepted within a culture or tradition but which would still lift people up and help society progress. As Buddha said, he himself left out much that had nothing to do with cultivating pure conduct, attaining peace, and enlightenment. Much always had to be left unsaid for most spiritual teachers, otherwise the bulk of the message would be rejected because some tiny truth might turn the public against one. Hence Zoroaster, for instance, could only speak of "right and wrong" or "good and evil" rather than teach of many higher realities despite his attainments. He addressed the call of the times and responded to the level of his audience, and actually prepared the way for Islam.

It is strange that those divisions within the three Western paths which do stress true spiritual cultivation practice and the definite states of spiritual achievement for the Tao -- such as Sufism, Hasidism and the Eastern Orthodox Church – are usually ignored or directly and immediately dismissed off hand as "mystical" or irrelevant when they are the very ones pointing out the highest paths. It is thus the fate of this lower world that Western societies are rarely exposed to the highest spiritual teachings that might help them. Furthermore, the aggregation of misleading dogmas over the centuries, along with common misinterpretations or additions intellectual or charismatic but deluded religious individuals, ends up with many people believing in fantasies passed from one generation to the next. Such is bad karma.

A sage, such as Jesus, Krishna, Socrates, Buddha and so forth, has transcended individuality because of realizing the Tao. That personalized consciousness, finally abandoning the incorrect ideas of being a small personal self, eventually abides as the universal consciousness since that is what personalized consciousness always is and discovers itself to be. After enlightenment, the ignorance or pollutive thoughts of thinking it is other than the underlying nature, and the clingings to the transformations (streams) of consciousness that obscured a clear realization the original nature, no longer exist because they have been purified away through the indifference of non-attachment, whereby they have naturally subsided.

What is enlightenment? The universal consciousness expresses itself through a particular body and personalized consciousness that is the sage, as it always has done even when the self-consciousness was unenlightened, but upon enlightenment the pollution of ignorance that is usually held onto, such as ideas of being the individual, finally drop out. One discovers the base state of both the mind and matter which is the fundamental ground state of personal existence. That is what you ultimately find yourself out to be, and the sages of all religions discover this same universal awareness. By resolving one's actual unity or identity with the underlying source nature then internal peace, purity and bliss as well as all sorts of marvelous functions become possible. As a functioning transformation, you still exist and thoughts still arise but you don't cling to them nor to the original essence. The question, then, is what do you do? Some leave for better heavenly realms of existence that have far less suffering, and some choose to come again and again to try to help the masses awaken via their enlightening influence.

If at the stage of enlightenment you let go of the universal consciousness, or manifest consciousness, or knowingness of the pristine fundamental awareness, you become just the absolute itself, the host in the midst of a functioning. If you abandon every possible clinging, and no longer identify even with the manifestation of total consciousness, you are just the absolute nature. One can say that this is the highest, wherein there is no thought of identity with even the total manifestation, and that is the true identity as the absolute nature performing Its functioning. However, one must not cling to this but must practice the Middle Path.

In cultivation, one should not cling to notions of emptiness, the absolute nature, or block any of the manifestation of all consciousness. One should properly function according to the Middle Way and cling to neither existence or non-existence (an empty state of mind), all-consciousness or the emptiness of the absolute essence without thought consciousness. You should not attach to pristine awareness (and its contents) since it is a guest, nor should you cling to the emptiness realization of the absolute nature. You practice non-holding, non-abiding or non-clinging while abiding in the fullness of awareness via non-abiding, which we can call true existence or beingness or presence.

Your true being is beyond individual consciousness, and so you are the endless expanse of consciousness in which innumerable, uncountable beings appear and disappear in endless succession. You are actually all of them because you are that underlying pristine awareness, the pure consciousness, but you mistakenly think of yourself as a tiny self because of ignorance and confusion that has limited your view. That allness is what you are. They are that, too, rather than sentient beings. You are the fundamental substrate that truly exists while the manifestations that appear within you are like a dream that represents no solid, true reality. It is only because you have personal consciousness that you can have this knowing.

A teacher can point this out to you, but you have to progressively attain and then transcend various states of mental purity, achieved through meditation practice, until you can finally experientially realize this base condition yourself. You must cultivate to realize the presence of fundamental pristine awareness which is so obvious – because it is stationary or non-moving — that you never even notice it even though it is always present.

That which knows, which serves as a back drop to the known, must itself be empty and changeless. Because it is empty, and because it is changeless and never moves, you never ever notice it even though it is always there. Only when the mind purifies, because of meditation, do you create a chance to recognize this underlying awareness, which is why enlightenment is considered a wisdom attainment of understanding after direct knowing. You only attain it by finally *seeing the Truth*, understanding it and then letting go to finally relinquish any remaining ties of attachment to the body, self and consciousness *to be just That* without pollution or stain, always abiding through non-abiding in the immediate presence with perfectly pure and free functioning as is right. That's what you are, so there is nothing to worry about in letting go and being that way.

In other words, you – consciousness – can only recognize your position as consciousness – what you are, when the realization arises as an understanding. That understanding can only arise after you directly, nakedly experientially experience this truth, and that can only happen after your mind has become purified of wandering thoughts (that normally would obscure such a recognition) through meditation. The Zen school would explain this using an analogy that the original nature is the host (something that never moves) and your consciousness is a guest, and you can only recognize the host while the position of the guest is there. Without the position of the guest (individual consciousness) that can recognize the host, you would just be the host looking at the host, and so there would be no knowing at all. In the host looking at the host, there are no thoughts at all, so how could there be any awakening or even knowledge of Its own existence? But just because personalized consciousness exists, it doesn't mean that it is truly a separate self-so independent being. It is just a small speck or part of the entire consciousness tableau that imagines borders and limitations because of being bound by ignorance and mental clinging. Free yourself of that ignorance and clinging, and you awaken to your true nature in an instant.

Such realizations, and even simpler mundane attainments, all come down to the need for personal meditation practice to get the results of an emptier mind and the transformation of the physical body that leads to better health, longevity, freedom from stress and spiritual results. Some people really understand the theory of settling the mind and then detaching from the veil of consciousness to find their original self, but without cultivating the requisite gong-fu of mental purity, it becomes impossible for them to attain enlightenment. Therefore, your study of any sort of spiritual or religious matters needs meditation practice to attain any great results.

From understanding the theory of meditation/cultivation, you can intellectually understand the truth about the nature of your mind and self and be clear about the truth of matters. However, for actually realizing this to prove it is so, you absolutely need to cultivate meditation. You must meditate, which purifies your chi and mind, and from that basis you can eventually awaken. Without that basis, you cannot attain self-realization. While awakening, or enlightenment, is a wisdom realization, that awakening requires the foundation of wisdom and mental purity, and the gong-fu of mental purity is achieved by cultivating meditation step-by-step.

Once you begin to get some signs of progress from your meditation practice, it confirms that your meditation efforts are having a result, that chi does indeed exist, and that science – because it doesn't even recognize these phenomena – is not something you can turn to for answers when it comes to cultivation. You need to turn to teachings from meditation-rich cultures to help guide you through the various stages of meditation progress.

POSSIBLE ADDITIONAL STUDY MATERIALS

For this type of wisdom understanding I always recommend Buddhism, Jnana Yoga and Vedanta. There are the teachings of Shakyamuni, Nagarjuna, Hui-neng, Shankara, Nisargadatta, Ramana Maharshi, Gaudapada, Tsong Khapa and many others who arrived at very high stages of realization.

Tao and Longevity, *The Little Book of Hercules*, *Twenty-Five Doors to Meditation*, *Internal Martial Arts Nei-gong*, and *How to Measure and Deepen Your Spiritual Realization* were all written with the hopes to help guide people through the various phenomena that typically arise on this path of investigation when you meditate. As an author I have never chosen the route of popularity but instead the route of service, and so I have always worked to put more of this type of information in my books than you can possibly find anywhere else, and to address countless questions that other literature has left unanswered. Otherwise what would have been the point of writing?

The Eastern spiritual schools are very much cultivation oriented and will explain many of the more advanced phenomena that appear on the path as you progress, such as feeling like your body is an empty sack without bones, tasting sweet saliva, seeing tiny visionary flames on the top of the head or shoulders, feeling two protrusions on the left and right side of the head, seeing lights or silverish brightenings within the body that blaze like the sun, feeling individual chi channels, having so much energy you cannot sleep for days, feeling so full of chi that you are not hungry for days, having clairvoyant or precognitive dreams, hearing sounds within the body, feeling various energies within the body, and so forth. Roman Catholicism has catalogued many of these same cultivation phenomena, too, but the best explanations behind their appearance come from the teachings of Buddhism, Taoism, Vajrayana and the yoga schools.

The Eastern traditions definitely tend to explain more of these non-denominational phenomena than the Western religions, so you should readily borrow from the best and refer to them for your own efforts. These explanations tend to come from the personal experiences of men and women of attainments, who continually re-confirm what others have also discovered across traditions through their own personal meditation efforts. If you just guided yourself from Western teachings alone, however, you would be absolutely lost even though these are all scientific, non-sectarian, non-denominational phenomena.

Of course, you only get the results from meditation like this if you consistently practice with patience over time. The ability to maintain that commitment to meditate on a daily basis can be maximized when you use some scheduling and monitoring system as just discussed. The idea of recording your progress in meditation, such as how long you can hold your breath while doing pranayama, will help you progress tremendously. The actual design of that practice schedule, in the end, and the activities you deem important enough to record, are totally up to you but recording them will, indeed, help you experience the signs of definite meditation progress.

7

MIXING STUDY, ANALYSIS AND WISDOM WITH YOUR PRACTICE

The whole purpose of meditation is to help you develop a quiet mind. A quiet mental state is not something you plaster on to the mind, or something you produce by suppressing thoughts to prevent them from arising. It is something that is revealed after your thoughts gradually die down, but it appears while you are awake rather than sleeping. That silence is inherent in the naturally aware reflective state of your mind underneath the streams of consciousness. It is already there because it is the true unpolluted nature of the conscious mind. The real nature of your mind, which you can discover after all the thoughts clear away is empty, calm, unperturbed, tranquil, serene, peaceful, unmoving, stationary, quiet.

You don't know that your natural mind is always peaceful and quiet because you always busy yourself with thoughts and self-identify with them, and so you never encounter the real nature of your mind. When you do, you become happy and peaceful and free of stress. You need to practice meditation to learn how to let go of thoughts and unmask the true ordinary mind of consciousness. If you practice meditation enough, not only can you learn how to deeply relax to get rid of negative self-talk and the thoughts of stress and anxiety, but you will start to reap health, longevity and spiritual benefits, too. These results all depend on how much you choose to practice and how well you practice. Many people do not fully practice according to the correct principles, and so they never get far along these lines at all. However, if you meditate correctly, your wandering thoughts will indeed die down and you will discover what "empty mind" means because it is always there, and therefore always within reach.

After your wandering thoughts finally die down from meditation practice, you will discover that "emptiness" is the natural state of the mind that has always been there, and that emptiness is accompanied by an ever present awareness. Awareness, also known as a clear ability to know, luminosity or illumination, is the nature of the mind. However, the natural state of the mind also is that it is empty of content. No particular thought can be the mind's natural state. No stream of consciousness can be its natural state. The natural state can only be silence, without thoughts, and the essence, substance, nature or body of the mind's natural awareness cannot be a thing such as chi or energy or anything substantial you can know.

Empty primordial awareness, clean and pure, eternal and non-moving, is the reflective source of your personal individual consciousness. In the final analysis, this is what allows you to know your mind of consciousness, meaning thoughts and sensory appearances. Our fundamental original body is naturally manifest awareness, a self-arising primordial awareness. It doesn't come from anywhere else, such as having been made by a Creator. It just was, is and always will be. It is self-so, unconditioned, unproduced depending on nothing else for its support. That's just the way it is and since beginninglessness it has always been that way. You can say that this pristine nature is empty of content, and so you might say that it is beyond or transcends the phenomenal. This means it is just empty or void – it has no phenomenal characteristics or features at all, but is not an non-existence as opposed to existence.

When you cultivate meditation, at first you will find that your mind of thoughts starts to calm down and becomes quiet. This absence of thoughts is like the quiet achieved when you turn down a stereo but don't totally turn it off; there are still sounds there but they are barely perceptible. The sounds seem gone but there is still a mental state there. The silence you experience in your mind is still a thought conception because it is an image of silence, and so to the mind the image of quiet is still a sound phenomenon.

As you move to higher stages of progress, which happens as your chi and consciousness further purify, you will become able to separate from even these quiet states of consciousness characterized by "thought cessation" to discover that consciousness is known via a clear witnessing function, and that clear awareness is itself motionless and quiet. You will discover that real quiet or stillness is the pure consciousness of pristine awareness itself where no phenomena are present. That body of self-arisen pristine awareness is empty. Or, we can say that our absolute original nature (of true beingness) is empty of everything in terms of contents *and* essence, and yet that transcendental nature has the functioning capability of awareness. The trick during meditation practice is to try to abide in the aloof witnessing awareness until even the most subtle, imperceptible thoughts and conceptions within consciousness drop out, and then one can achieve a true state of emptiness or imperturbability. Within that state of emptiness, discriminative thoughts are gone and the mind therefore seems to expand and become boundless without borders, so some describe this by saying it "fills the universe." This just means that thoughts drop out -- including the thoughts of being a self which act as a afflictive filter through which you experience all other thoughts - and thus the mind becomes truly empty, pristine, motionless, changeless or clear. There's always a clarity aspect to this natural clear illumination. In any case, during the realization of a motionless clear mind you might be able to realize that the mind's actual nature is formless, infinite, boundless — which is essentially saying that underlying awareness is formless, infinite, or boundless when not constrained by thoughts. This is what you discover to be the ever present mind which is always there and which is the awareness functioning of your true self.

Our natural mind is empty, appearances always arise/appear within it, and because you always attach to them you then never notice its empty true nature. Therefore we say it is empty by nature yet gives birth to the wondrous existence of thought appearances. Furthermore, everything that appears within your consciousness is a *transient* reality (meaning the world/universe) and therefore an *illusory* reality since all mental phenomena lack the unassailable, stationary, changeless, motionless, permanent, immovable characteristic of the underlying fundamental essence. Everything experienced is an illusory reality because nothing perceived exists by itself but always exists by depending on something else, but this alternative definition of a non-real or illusory nature is something we'll have to skip for the moment.

In meditation practice, first you start to cultivate mental calming, and then your body's chi and channels will start to open and purify. From this opening and better circulation of chi, together with mental detachment, you can then in turn reach a higher stage of mental stilling/calming. Together your mind and body will progressively purify as you remain in the detached witnessing function of awareness and let go of clinging to thoughts. Because you let go of thoughts, you give your body a chance to transform. At a sufficiently high stage of mental purity, which corresponds to all your chi channels having become opened and the chi flows through them having become regular, harmonious and stabilized, your mind quiets substantially and then it is said that you begin to cultivate *shen* rather than chi. Your mind is so empty and quiet that you realize clarity in your mental realm, and you begin to recognize that knowingness originates from an ever present, always in the background, always clear awareness. You become able to recognize that an underlying or transcending awareness is always there and has always been there behind thoughts and consciousness enabling you to know them.

Once you discover this always present thing, pristine awareness, which you can only finally see/realize after the mind sufficiently quiets and purifies from your previous meditation efforts, you can begin to cultivate the pure beingness of that awareness by abiding in just that awareness rather than thoughts. You have always tried to cultivate that awareness through detachment and witnessing meditation practices previously, but now *you can more effectively* abide in the witnessing awareness partly because you now better know what you are doing. Now you know how to view the manifest consciousness as a whole without attachment, and in time, from this practice, you can reach an even deeper stage of non-clinging empty mind. In fact, *you can practice doing this from the start, but thought attachments are so obscuring and so many transformations in your chi, channels and consciousness happen that almost no one, except people of extremely high wisdom, can avoid mental clinging to all the mental states of transformation that happen to consciousness.* Everyone, except very high spiritual individuals, get caught up in the stages or thoughts of consciousness.

Unfortunately in terms of realization, this continually present awareness is so silent, peaceful and unmoving that hardly anyone ever notices its presence. It is pervasive, empty and stationary, so you almost never recognize it. This is why people take thoughts to be the nature of their mind rather than this empty, invisible, clear clarity that really is not anything at all we can point to as a phenomenon. You must cultivate an emptiness of mind to become able to discover it. We try to get at it through various types of witnessing practice that stand behind thoughts watching them, and hence try to detach from the flow of consciousness. People can learn to do this during meditation practice, but it is often difficult to bring this clear witnessing practice into the regular world and integrate it with our personal daily behavior unless we also practice worldly integration as well. But that's what it's all about, isn't it? Eventually this is accomplished, too.

In any case, we need to cultivate meditation to finally reach a quiet enough point where we "get a glimpse of it," understand it's there, "realize" it abides as the witness, etcetera. We follow the path of meditation practice to produce internal quiet, and if we proceed far enough past the purifications of our chi and mind, our mind will eventually empty to a profound degree and we can discover the existence of that pure background consciousness called pristine awareness. If we keep cultivating this way, we can eventually discover ultimate peace because we will drop all thoughts of being a self, and then we will always be in a timeless state of direct cognition and pure presence, and we can then penetrate through to the actual substrate of the mind. We are then one with that eternal peace without all the disturbing afflictions; we resume being our true nature without any pollution. That underlying nature does not come, it does not go and that substrate is discovered to be the same substrate of all minds in the universe, and all matter as well.

The whole universe is that substrate, whose functioning nature is awareness, and that is what you truly are and discover yourself to be. One can find the awareness but cannot see or know the absolute nature or original essence itself because to realize It consciousness would have to be It, and in being It there would not be any thoughts by which to ascertain any of its qualities. Hence the absolute nature that has awareness as its functioning is ultimately indescribable or inconceivable and cannot be fathomed or reasoned.

Here's what happens. We discover, through the road of meditation, that there is this boundless thing called pure awareness that has always been there as our mind. It is pure, infinite, boundless, empty and clear. It always exists. It extends across the universe for the universe appears within It. Even when we didn't exist as individuals it always existed and has always been there and always will be. Even without any life in the universe it exists and is there. Somehow a living body came upon this pure awareness – let's not speculate as to how and why just now — and shone through that body unit to produce self-awareness and individual consciousness. That self-awareness, that idea of me, I, and so forth, is just the expression of this ultimate one that ends up being expressed/experienced through individual consciousness. But individual consciousness, being consciousness, can awaken to understand what it is. It can generate a thought recognition of what it is so as to understand the truth of the matter, but only when the mental realm of consciousness becomes so clear (and looks at consciousness itself rather than thoughts) that one can gain some inkling of the Self. Once the individual (consciousness) gains some inkling of this, which is called *prajna* wisdom or insight, it can then fully let go and become the pure presence of the source awareness without any more pollutions such as incorrect ideas of being an individual self. It then always abides in a state of enlightenment, or pure presence, which it has always been from the start, even when not aware of the fact.

You therefore need to know this key distinction—the inherent underlying emptiness of your mind is not something that you create but something that you reveal, find or discover, and that inherent emptiness has the ability of awareness/consciousness. The two are inseparable, and awareness is the basis of a living being rather than there being a permanent soul or self. The boundless underlying awareness is just one, and shines through the filter of uncountable living beings to become their individual minds. One pure consciousnesses, via unreal transformations, assumes all these individual forms that think themselves really true, self-so independent beings.

You can say that awareness is the functioning, characteristic, or capability of this inherent original emptiness, or in trying to communicate the idea of co-emergence you might say that the nature of the awareness is inherent emptiness. Hence, you are not creating anything new through cultivating meditation but simply discovering what has always been already so! There is no religion in this. There is no reason to fear hearing you have no true self and are not an inherent soul but This One, and in discovering the truth or in refusing to look, nothing changes at all. The only thing that changes upon realization is freedom from afflictions, pain and suffering and realization of peace and bliss. Shakyamuni has already explained this, but most people misinterpret his teachings.

Some schools say that the nature of the awareness is emptiness to describe a unity, but the Zen school goes even further and considers that the awareness itself is still a guest of the host, which is the absolute nature. No Zen master holds on to the entire realm of manifest consciousness as a really existent thing, or identifies with it as the Self. Zen students try not to attach to the pristine underlying awareness and its contents, or to the inherent emptiness of the host which is absolute, lacking of everything.

This Middle Way is the correct way of cultivation, and the highest Way in existence. However, in a beginner's book ~~this~~ ~~this~~ I like to stress the functioning of awareness to help lead people to its cultivation as this helps them realize what they are in a form they can most easily accept. If they cultivate so far as to realize their underlying pristine awareness, I am hopeful they will have enough wisdom to understand this is itself a functioning of their absolute essence, which is the original fundamental nature or True Self.

All consciousness in the universe forms out of pure consciousness (awareness) – consciousness cannot be anything else except that same "substance" – so moving consciousness has to discover that it is actually that pure, clear, stationary fundamental pristine awareness that is totally empty or insubstantial. This is why it transcends everything. Once a mind reaches a deep state of calmness and purity, it can give rise to the sudden insight of its true nature and awaken to the Truth. Then it recognizes "home," "host" or "Self." Otherwise, it continues spinning around in the realm of false thought involvements continually undergoing countless transformations and thinking they are all real, and does so for eons throughout the endless unreal transformations called "lives." The real thing is the underlying one, that's all. You must therefore cultivate meditation to realize your true Self because if the mind is busy, clouded or muddy, it can never reach this realization.

Meditation practice can progressively lead you to this Self-realization by teaching you how to stop holding on to your thoughts so that any unnecessary mental chatter naturally dies down, your mind purifies, and awakening becomes possible. That's a first step. Because the nature of the mind revealed after thoughts depart is quiet, empty or non-moving, it's free from stress, pollutions, worries, anxieties, stains and afflictions. Experiencing this peaceful state can rejuvenate you just as sleep does, and this is a wonderful mundane result that we are all after. In sleep you forget yourself as an individual, and this ability to forget yourself during sleep is what brings you refreshing peace and rest. Meditation brings that rejuvenation to you during the everyday real world, and by regaining the pure state of presence, everything always appears fresh, vibrant, joyous and new. Everyone is always looking for peace and happiness in life, but you will never truly find it until you discover that you are that ultimate underlying peaceful one.

Meditation is the only practice that allows you to turn around and find that peace and bliss that is already existent because it is what you are. This is why it fulfills all longings. Meditation also causes your chi to arise and flow smoothly, and this gives you boundless energy and physical comfort as well as healing energy. These are just some of the initial mundane benefits of meditation, but there are far more.

A quiet mind is actually a mind empty of wandering thoughts. However, in this quiet state your awareness is not blocked or shut off, but still functions to be able to instantly know whatever streams of thoughts actually arise. Nothing is blocked. Actually, you can never shut off awareness—even during sleep – for awareness continually operates. It's always there and always has been there, even when there was no body, and simply needed a body to become individual consciousness. Consciousness in a living being is at times discontinuous and may often seem to come to a rest to disappear, but witnessing always continues through all those states. It happens purely by itself without any effort since it is always there as the natural state. *Whether or not there is anything to be aware of (thoughts), whether you remember any objects of consciousness, or whether you remember clearly are other issues entirely.*

If you meditate to attain the deepest possible levels of mental purity, you will indeed discover that there is a primordial awareness of pure consciousness that is always there. You discover yourself to be a universal functioning awareness that has omniscient capabilities because it knows the essence of reality, the source of all consciousness and phenomena. I am not making this up because you actually discover this, which is why it's called "seeing Truth." This is not a religious dogma you have to swallow because you actually prove it by having it happen, and though hard to discuss, many religious greats have spoken of this to confirm the same finding.

When you search the spiritual texts of countless religions, and the autobiographies of many religious greats, you will find that they commonly speak of this same truth and as usual, often use different terms to relate this. If they proceed far enough in their efforts, they all eventually find this *underlying one.* As to how far they can let go of thoughts to become the Truth without any remaining stains of ignorance, it all depends on their efforts at letting go of functioning consciousness. It all depends on their stage of attainment, and *there are indeed different stages of attainment.* They also often tell us that we have been ignorant for so long, wrapped up in thoughts of the self or ego and constantly attaching to the phenomenal appearances that arise in our minds, that we should not simply accept their words. They tell us we need to achieve this realization of the true self to actually prove it. Meditation is the way.

The nature of your mind is insubstantiality, or emptiness, but it is the functioning of the mind/awareness/pure consciousness that produces existence, and that existence or appearance of the world entails afflictions if we attach to the phenomena we experience. This is why we choose to meditate in the first place, which is to reduce mental afflictions. Meditation is the one medicine that can help us get rid of mental afflictions and suffering, especially the self-imposed sicknesses of the mind.

For instance, many of us want to change our personalities because we don't like certain things about them, but we don't realize that our chi, which is conditioned by our body, helps determine our personalities. Only meditation helps us open our chi channels and purify our chi flows that are connected to our personality. And also change our bodies which affect our emptions and personalities as well. Behavioral change is therefore only achieved, in the deepest sense, through the practice of meditation because of what it accomplishes at the levels of chi and consciousness, or body-mind.

It is strange that psychologists and psychiatrists immediately turn to pills and counseling rather than tell people they must learn how to meditate to help truly change their personalities and learn relaxation. Only meditation teaches you how to let go of thoughts, so this must definitely be part of the cure for the deepest of mental issues. In purifying your mind, *and thus the chi flows upon which consciousness rides that play a role in determining habits and the personality*, one can finally start to dissolve mental problems at their root. Habits will change as well, as will the personality for the better. This takes time, but it can be done. Consciousness will always arise, so one must learn how not to get entangled with the thoughts of consciousness so as to eventually purify one's reactions to the appearances that arise. You see, it's all about behavior in the end!

In time, the consciousness (thought reactions) which arises will itself become pure but you still have to work at purifying your habits and behavior to have this happen. It doesn't just happen that your mind becomes empty and then you always react in a kind and compassionate way, or anger never arises, or wonderful things like that. You have long seated, deep habitual energies that still exist after enlightenment, but now your awareness is so clear, and you are always in a higher state of presence, so you have a chance to purify your normal behavioral inclinations and reactions.

Conduct in life comes down to two kinds: that to be followed because it is wholesome, and that not to be followed. The task of self-purification therefore comes down to purifying your mind and behavior in the end so that it is virtuous from moment to moment and free of delusion, which is why I always recommend cessation-observation practice to everyone. Your consciousness always turns into the outward behavior of words and actions, and you have to learn how to purify them so that they become more wise, skillful and compassionate.

THE TEMPORARY CALMING OF THE MIND

When your thoughts calm down and you reach a realm of relative quiet, that emptiness is not the emptiness of the mind's true nature but just a relative stilling of thoughts. In Buddhism they call this a calming or "stilling of the sixth consciousness." It is still a thought-image of silence rather than a real silence of perfect thought absence since a thought image of silence is still being perceived and since there is still a perceiver of that silence. Let's talk of hearing instead to make this more clear. When you can distinguish between a sound and the silence without the sound, it is an abiding awareness of hearing which enables you to do that. That awareness is always there even when sounds are not there, hence that empty awareness is what you have to find as the source of your mind. That awareness is what is really empty. It is fundamentally empty, clear, pure or we can say silent and quiet.

This abiding or transcending quiet is never ever bad for you. On the contrary, to realize any type of quiet is mental resting. It always leads to health and rejuvenation just as sleep or a vacation does. Fewer afflictions arise when your mind becomes quiet because many of those afflictive wandering thought streams have been dissolved away. However, this initial result of thoughts calming down to produce mental quiet is not an experience of the mind's true essence. It takes years of meditation practice to be able to arrive at such a self-realization where the mind is empty and there aren't even any thoughts of being a person there anymore. This is called "self"-realization because one finds, after this effort, that the empty substance of your mind's true essence (which is behind awareness) is what you are, your true self. This is what is your self, and since that inherent emptiness extends everywhere and its awareness is like a single light that powers the consciousness in all beings, it is discovered to be the True Self.

Since this is the one true Self of us all, sometimes I write it as "Self"-realization rather than "self"-realization (with a small "s") when I am trying to communicate a particular emphasis. These are all synonyms once again. Everyone uses words and words to try to point to this original nature of ours, and yet many communications fail because people don't want to hear it or believe it and because it's really hard to write about it in a way where people easily understand since their minds are filled with so many false notions. Since the masses usually don't understand, in the past many sages just gave them lower teachings of doing good, avoiding evil and things like that which were, essentially, just "lighter weights they could carry." It really takes a lot of merit to be able to encounter these higher teachings, believe in them, and then practice to prove them. To accept them is not enough. Unlike in religion, you must prove them to claim them as your own.

As you make progress with meditation practice, your mind will continue to empty of countless thoughts and its underlying crystal pure clarity (lucidity) will gradually be revealed – something that is always present. Consciousness is naturally clear, it is empty of content, but it can perceive. That's its ability – cognizance, knowing or perception. You always can have cognizance, awareness or knowing and so you will always still have insights, understanding and knowing available because awareness is always there for whatever arises. It's just that the thought volume of the distracting internal dialogue or "monkey mind" (so-called because a monkey races from branch to branch just as our mind jumps from thought to thought) dies down and is not so profuse anymore. Awareness, lucidity, illumination or knowing (however you wish to word it) never leaves you, but simply becomes unclouded, unpolluted or unobstructed by mental attachments that depart. Once again there are lots of different ways to say this. Usually we just say that *false thoughts drop out*, and thoughts are called "false" because what is real and true, unbreakable, inviolable, unmoving, pure, clear and peaceful is the original nature. Because it is pure, eternal, and unchanging it is called "real" in juxtaposition.

There is no such thing as an annihilation of consciousness possible because the base awareness is empty but always there and always ready to know thoughts, which will always appear. Consciousness simply becomes more purified rather than annihilated on the road of meditation. When thoughts die out we call it a state of extinction, but awareness is still present and never obliterated. There is and always will be awareness, or pure consciousness, ready to know thoughts. Thoughts and sensory perceptions will always arise in whatever realm you land in, and you will always know them. The realm of total consciousness never departs just as the original nature of empty awareness never departs either. What appears is like an endless show which manifests across an empty, stationary base awareness that never changes but has somehow given rise to the personalized consciousnesses that can view and know such as what you are now experiencing. This personal consciousness of yours is just a small part of the entire manifest field of consciousness, and personal consciousness will always know some type of thoughts or appearances. The key stages of practice are to first discover the entire manifest realm of consciousness, and then pure consciousness, and then the absolute nature. However, one must cultivate to reach these attainments.

Most random thoughts die down from consistent meditation practice, but whenever thoughts become necessary for situations they will still always arise because consciousness is not annihilated. You should therefore never try to block thoughts from arising in order to experience the quiet mind that is the target of meditation practice. If you are sad, then just be sad and if you are happy then just be happy, but without clinging to those states. If a good friend passes away you will be sad but you don't cling to that sadness forever, do you? If every moment you experience whatever arises, but never cling, then in every moment you are living in a state of presence, which is the fullest, richest type of living experience possible. You just don't believe it because you've never attained it, and think that by trying to hold to thoughts or the concepts of the self that you avoid missing something or somehow become more real.

What is the state of presence when one has (forgotten the self and) discovered their original nature and cultivated attainment? Let me recount a Zen *koan* to explain. Once the students of Zen master Tozan asked, "How can we escape the heat and cold?" Master Tozan replied, "Why not go to where there is no heat or cold?" When the student then asked, "Is there such a place?" Tozan replied, "When cold, be thoroughly cold, when hot, be thoroughly hot."

The stream of consciousness will flow on forever, always undergoing transformation endlessly from moment to moment. It is impossible to get rid of experiences, just as you cannot annihilate all the phenomena of the universe. Some consciousness experiences just arise naturally in response to situations (such as saying "Ouch!" to a minor pain) and some arise because you call for them when you have the intent to think and consider, such as in pondering what to do to solve a problem. This is fine because that is the proper functioning of consciousness; consciousness has all sorts of possible functions and you never try to obliterate them but instead, try to master them. Since you are a stream of consciousness that lasts forever, you better learn how to purify it, master it, and use it correctly.

The trick is to learn how to remain in the pure awareness, which always knows the immediate present, that is ultimately detached from the flow of thoughts when using consciousness, for in being the awareness, without attaching to the thoughts, you are liberated and free and are no longer their doer or slave. You thereby transcend the world while living in the world, and become free of the mental karma of the world. Yes, experiences continue to arise but there is no small self of individuality who suffers them.

This is actually the highest level of spiritual practice, much higher than being involved in religious functions and worshipping activities such as going to church or the synagogue. You can attain to this state of emancipation by dissolving the habit of mentally clinging to thoughts, after which your mental realm will purify and then be entirely different than it was before. This is what the ancients have discovered and what people consistently prove when they start making progress in their meditation practice. People say their mind becomes cleaner, more purified or emptier, like a sky without clouds. They always attest to the fact that it becomes clearer or more pure, so this is a proven result of meditation you cannot challenge. This is what we are after and you don't have to go all the way to enlightenment to attain this. It does not take a lot of skill or time to experience this. You just have to cultivate a bit and you can achieve this and all the other benefits already promised.

When you directly, experientially realize that the nature of your ordinary mind is actually pure and clean, entirely empty of thoughts – when you experience this for yourself due to the purifying results of meditation and the fact that you look directly at your now purified mind rather than just read this result in a book—you will then realize that this emptiness of the mind is always present. It never undergoes any addition or deletion; night and day it is always the same, and it is always able to know thoughts or a state of no thoughts. It knows them without ever getting polluted itself or losing its clarity, but in becoming focused on the wrong thing, mental busyness proliferates and we lose sight of its existence and what is really so.

THE BASE OF PRISTINE EMPTY CLEAR AWARENESS OR PURE CONSCIOUSNESS

For example, when you watch the stream of thoughts in the mind you'll notice a sequence of thought-silence-thought-silence-thought-silence, etcetera. To be able to see this means you already transcend it. The you who sees this is already beyond it. You have to already be beyond this to see this stream of thoughts. That being the case, what/who is it that is seeing this stream of consciousness?

What is seeing thoughts is pure, clear awareness or we can say pure consciousness that is like a mirror. It is an awareness substrate of pure non-moving consciousness that knows transient consciousness. It's like a mirror in that they appear as a clear image within its reflective nature without polluting the mirror one bit, which itself never changes.

Ontologically you can only, then, be this pure awareness that has no substance and which never leaves. Better yet, you can only be whatever ultimately gives rise to it. You are only this pure reflective awareness which in essence is always empty. It is totally pure consciousness, so pure that transient consciousness is not there. It is self-arisen or self-existent, so there is no substance (like chi) or content or causes (like energy) or conditions supporting it, and yet it can arise as the knowing of something. That's just its self-so nature. If you sufficiently cultivate meditation you might be able to suddenly recognize its existence — which has the nature of simultaneous or "co-emergent" emptiness and awareness—if you start actually looking at the mind itself and suddenly have an insight about it. You can only fail to reach such results of understanding because you don't generate sufficient states of mental quiet/purity and don't try to inspect your own mind.

Over and over again sages non-denominationally try to get people to look at the nature of their own minds just to prove to them all these truths, but no one wants to do it. Socrates would say, "Are you not ashamed that you give your attention to acquiring as much money as possible, and similarly run after reputation and honor, and give no attention to truth, understanding and the perfection of your soul?" Everyone is lost in following their false thoughts and chases after them their whole life with glee, and hardly anyone turns within to discover the nature of their soul/self and what allows them to actually know these things. Actually, it's not even that you are the clear awareness. Actually you are the empty essence, or absolute fundamental nature, of which it is a function. No one wants to believe this or cultivate to find *This One*. The consciousness of individual beings want to believe they are something permanent that is a small self, soul, *atman*, entityship, but it just isn't true.

What the higher beings know and therefore believe in the higher Heavens is much different than what humans believe in this lower realm of consciousness (the human world) that sages compassionately come to again and again in order to try to relieve suffering and help liberate the sentient beings within it. As Shakyamuni Buddha said in the *Lotus Sutra*, "All Buddhas want to enable sentient beings to open up their enlightened perception and make it pure and clear, and so they appear in the world. They want to show sentient beings the perception of the enlightened Buddhas, and so they appear in the world. They want sentient beings to awaken to the perception of the Buddhas, and so they appear in the World. They want to enable sentient beings to enter into enlightened perception, and so they appear in the world."

If you have a thought, that thought arises and is experienced within a pure base of awareness. An individual thought is called a "thought," "concept," "conception," "notion," "consciousness," "mind," "mark," "sign," "phenomena," "appearance," "image," 'idea," "manifestation," "manifest consciousness," "a product of consciousness," "a phenomenon in consciousness," "a consciousness phenomenon," "a ripple within consciousness" or an "appearance within consciousness." However you wish to word it, the thoughts of consciousness are experienced by, within, and because of the purest awareness that is so pure that it is insubstantial of anything. It is so pure that there is no chi or energy or anything as its base as there is with ordinary consciousness. It is totally beyond that or anything within the phenomenal realm, which is why it is described as empty, void or insubstantial. That is also why it is pure, boundless, infinite, permanent, stationary and eternal. It transcends everything, and exists independently self-so.

We are saying it "exists," but can we use that word to apply to It? We are borrowing the word "existence" here but since this word applies to the phenomenal realm, we cannot even apply it. We should not use the word "non-existence" either, which has another fault in that it suggests emptiness as inertness without this capacity for awareness that we have. Some therefore call it pristine fundamental awareness, and some call it pure consciousness to emphasize its aspect of fullness, manifestation, consciousness and life. Some also call it "original *mind*" or "fundamental *mind*" because there is the knowing capacity of awareness just as with your mind. Since everything is that one base emptiness-awareness, it is also called the "one mind," "true mind," "bright mind," all-consciousness and so on. You can call it different names depending on what aspects you are emphasizing, and also depending upon what level of its manifestation you want to refer to.

Consciousness, which means thoughts and sensory perceptions, is experienced by pure awareness or pure consciousness. It is experienced by a background of pure awareness that provides the knowing. You may think the thoughts are doing the knowing, but it is the clear mirror-like awareness that is doing the knowing of thoughts, and you don't understand it because you never cultivated that far enough yet to have thoughts drop out enough so you could see/realize your unity as this base without pollution or stain.

Once again, if you call awareness a form of the most purified consciousness (that has no objects or support), then you can say that working, ordinary or moving consciousness is experienced by purified consciousness wherein "consciousness" means thoughts and "purified consciousness" means no thoughts. The purified consciousness is so pure that nothing is there as content or substance, and so it is stationary, empty, pure and never moves. Never moving, nothing ever happens to it and it never changes. If nothing ever happens to it, it is permanent or eternal and must also be infinite and pure. Insubstantial, it is not anything but transcends the phenomenal.

When you know a thought, this pure consciousness is therefore just experiencing itself because thoughts are also a manifestation of that pure consciousness; everything is all happening within the base of consciousness itself. There is no inside or outside to this because the entire realm of what we call existence is just This. Consciousness is just its knowing of Itself, and during this activity of knowing the very purest nature of consciousness itself is never sullied by knowing some version of itself that is constituted in thoughts or images. The knowing takes place as a sort of reflection, like an image which appears within a mirror's surface without ever staining or changing the mirror one bit. So in effect, nothing truly real is happening at all. The true nature never changes one bit throughout all these false appearances. It might sound contradictory, but it is so. It never enters the realm of manifestation, and yet that realm is there although it lacks the characteristics of the absolute nature. This is not some thought experiment or exercise in logic because you can actually cultivate to realize all this.

If you cultivate to the point that all thought attachments go away, your thoughts then resultantly decline and you become no longer entangled with thoughts. Eventually, you will find that you are only a base awareness of impersonal pure consciousness. There is no individuality in this fundamental nature of ours, or memory "I am this or that." There is no beneficiary or experiencer of an "I am." There is no perceiving self within It, and there are no "others" being perceived. Everything arising is ultimately a transient appearance within primordial awareness, empty of true substantiality, and when analyzed we cannot even find a tiniest fraction of time where those appearances are stationary at all. Hence, those appearances all lack any true unchanging existence. They therefore have to be unreal down to the tiniest sliver of time in order to be able to arise within a base that never moves; if they were not illusory they could not arise within it but would conflict with its unmoving nature.

There is no inside or outside to all these appearances or perceptions because all is It. It is All. It extends everywhere because everything is It; everything is happening within It because everything is It. It is infinite and things are not self-so, self-produced, independently existing phenomena. They are not real like It is and when analyzed sufficiently you can also find them to be empty consciousness. The transient world of appearances we see lacks any self-so fundamental validity but is simply like an illusion or mirage. It's only our thoughts which make us think the external world is real in the sense of being something other than It. The manifestations we take as solid matter are insubstantial and transient, and are just fleeting appearances. They are like agglomerations that can be broken into tinier and tinier units that end up being empty space, and that space is knowable consciousness. Discovering your unity as the original nature of pure consciousness, then, which is what you are, you finally become free of suffering caused by clinging to matter and consciousness. It is not that they do not occur/exist in a conventional sense, but in finding the identity with your true self and detachment from the false self and false mind of consciousness, you are detached from them and therefore do not suffer.

Sages of countless religions commonly tell us this is so, but people normally become fearful when they hear the truth that they are just a consciousness aspect of *This One*. Then again, most people think they were created, and never bother to think about what they were *before creation* if that's really the story of their existence. If they thought about it deeply they might get scared about this notion of creation, too. They typically don't get scared about the past, however, but usually get scared about the future. The great thing is, upon enlightenment, self-realization, awakening, or liberation, that future begins to gets better in all aspects from what it would have been. So why is there discomfort, fear and trembling? Because in knowing the truth, your consciousness already starts to transform or purify and this provokes a reaction. Whenever you hear the Truth that you know to be true, consciousness starts transforming and that often provokes an uncomfortable response as consciousness tries to shed the wrong ideas it has clung onto. That is why it is extremely useful to often expose oneself to these matters and study them again and again.

Discovering one's true nature, one attains liberation from the false world of thoughts and finds peace and bliss, and yet one does not try to destroy the world of thoughts but simply effortlessly functions within it with skillfulness, wisdom and compassion. You are the original nature and you are also the functioning essence, so that's what you continue to do – skillfully function forever. Now, however, your realm of possible manifestation is larger, mental afflictions are absent, and there is always a freshness and newness to it all while also a peace and freedom from suffering.

There is no place of ultimate rest in the universe, no Heaven you can go to and permanently remain in at the end of a journey, so in continuously functioning forever the task is left to continually strive to improve your behavior throughout all this, and to make it more compassionate, wise and skillful. You can take on accomplishing, through your own vows, whatever objectives you like because you are the original nature, and so you can also accomplish them. You are the original nature, so nothing is forbidding you or stopping you except your own commitment and application of effort. Everything is open to you but remember that there will be consequences for everything you do since everything in the material temporal realm follows the laws of cause and effect. This is why one cultivates virtues rather than selfishness or hedonism. Nonetheless, everything that happens in the universe is just a transformation of consciousness, including yourself, so you must keep working at improving your skillfulness of activity to improve the effectiveness of your consciousness in bringing about good results for the world, and you should continue working at purifying your consciousness so that it becomes virtuous every moment.

The inherent nature of your mind reading this right now is this primordial fundamental awareness, which is all of us. The stream of thoughts that flit by are the objects of awareness; they are appearances, or the shapes/structures of consciousness that are cognized or known by your individual consciousness that is also this pure awareness. Call them appearances or manifestations, it's all the same thing. Thoughts are temporary so they always go away, and meditation is the technology that helps us decrease this volume of wandering thoughts that bothers us. Our ability to cognize or know is our ability to understand so it is sometimes called "wisdom" whereas the original pure awareness, being stationary itself and empty of content, is sometimes called non-conceptual wisdom. It is because of the base of pure consciousness that we have individual consciousness, knowing or self-awareness, yet all these individual experiences within sentient beings are essentially transformations or turnings of that one source. Everyone has the very same fundamental enlightened nature, and so an enlightened Buddha is no different than an ant in this respect because their original minds are the same, but the differences in individual manifest consciousness are infinite.

You can comprehend or understand, such as having the ideas of existence and life, because of the arising of understanding or "wisdom" which entails thought constructions within the rubric of consciousness, and yet you must recognize that these are just thoughts. You created them, and they don't match anything that is a fundamental reality. Actually, the only real thing is the empty absolute substrate, without substance or phenomena, and the phenomena that appear are like a miraculous display of consciousness which is only shining to itself, presenting itself to itself, and that radiance is empty of any true phenomenal steady beingness. It is all a falsity, meaning it lacks a true existence, and yet it miraculously appears as an appearance or manifestation in consciousness.

Since mental appearances constitute thoughts that come and go, and since the emptiness always stays (it neither comes nor goes), the underlying empty, non-moving, permanent, stationary awareness is real whereas thoughts and conceptions are unreal. So stop holding on to them! You cannot hold on to them because they are ungraspable, they won't stay, and they don't represent the true reality of your original nature anyway. Let them calm down by refusing to cling to them. They represent a transient realm of suffering that always changes. Just use them, function with them, but do not try to grasp them and you will be fine. You will then be reflecting the inherent freedom of the absolute nature. They represent an *ungraspable* reality anyway rather than a true, solid reality that always stays and does not change. They are like a mirage that appears to be there as a reality, but on close examination is found to be nothing but false images. The solidity you thought they showed was not there at all.

Is there such a thing as life? In truth, there is only this thing – underlying empty pristine awareness that is itself a function of the empty absolute nature. Everything else, namely the cosmos and everything within it, is all its various functions, manifestations or forms. All the appearances experienced by your consciousness are just the stuff of consciousness. Consciousness just knows consciousness-stuff. However, if you say there is then no such thing as true life you are neglecting this factor of the world appearance and conscious existence (appearance or manifestation) that appears right before your eyes this very moment all around you. There is a universe of manifestation – manifest creation or phenomena – that is a realm of manifest consciousness as a whole even if it is transient and lacks a solid reality for any single moment.

A conventional world of "wondrous existence" does indeed appear to be there even though it originated from the highest, purest, clearest. You cannot negate it nor should you try to negate it even though it is not the true nature. You just have to learn how to function better within it, recognizing that you are essentially just consciousness yourself. That being the case, there is no reason for emotions such as greed or hatred because there are no true beings involved.

If you also take the extreme of trying to shut off the flow of consciousness to just abide in the underlying emptiness of the absolute nature without thoughts, this type of clinging to a conceptualization of emptiness by trying to blot out thoughts or cling to non-existence is wrong. It's beyond this text, but there are many ways consciousness can go wrong even after someone experiences very high stage realizations, and they are called the fifty *skandha* Mara states explained within the Buddhist *Surangama Sutra.* I always feel a bit apologetic when I mention Buddhism because I try to include as many spiritual traditions as possible to show the non-denominationality of the meditation path, but Buddhism differentiates itself from other schools and religions because it is the only place you can find the highest stage wisdom teachings on all these matters. As a result I have to reference it time and again just as I must continually reference Confucianism and Christianity when it comes to teachings on purifying your self-behavior.

The middle road of not clinging to either the stationary empty true nature or transient flowing consciousness is therefore the correct road. The middle path of detachment, of not clinging to thoughts, is the task of what you must actualize in life, and that's what you try to do when you try to discover and abide in the transcending awareness that knows thoughts. That is the specific non-attachment taught for meditation. Whether it is in this life or another life, you must start to master this in order to become free and liberated. *This road leads to the highest fortune and highest merit.* It is better to start mastering it now, and to initiate a karmic relationship with this path now while you have this rare good news in front of you.

What happens when you abide in this way, the way of non-clinging? That is really the truest, highest and best form of meditation practice – the effortless method of no-method—but no one can do it at the start. Only fully enlightened individuals explain the final result of this sort of practice, which just means you end up being perfectly effortless and natural since you gave up clinging, but we have to leave that discussion aside because this wisdom finding is beyond the level of this book. This book only teaches you how to meditate, but to help with those instructions we have dipped our toes these more serious topics of ontology and soteriology just a smidgen. These are topics people rarely encounter in their entire lives, or in many lives, and that's why I've bothered to discuss them with you.

WHAT IS LIFE?

You might ask, and rightfully so, then according to this what exactly is the human being, or life? An underlying pristine awareness is always existent everywhere as the function of the one body of Reality, but personal manifest consciousness needs a living bodily form, with chi, by which it can arise. Otherwise infinite pure consciousness never has any thoughts and perceptions, and cannot know Itself or anything. A physical body along with its chi supports the arising of personal consciousness which is, in its essence, the original consciousness since that is what animates it and is what it is made of. Once you have life with self-consciousness, it just goes on functioning until the life force is no more, and then that consciousness stream undergoes transformation to appropriate another bodily form again. It always changes and undergoes transformations, and this is what is called "life after life in the stream of transmigration." However, the personal consciousness going through all this can, with insight, determine what it actually is when a mind becomes pure enough, looks within at itself, arouses the correct wisdom/understanding, and suddenly surmises the truth in an instant. Consciousness can realize that it is the original nature.

This is called sudden enlightenment. With one glance or glimpse you awaken to the truth which has always been and always will be. Your personal consciousness is not the real self, but your real self is the stuff of which consciousness and all else is made. Your real self or original nature can be described as co-emergent emptiness and pristine awareness that has the characteristics of purity, permanence, and bliss (freedom from suffering). This is what we call the Self, *true self*, fundamental nature or true existence.

In short, the pure infinite underlying awareness of the universe becomes self-awareness (in an individual body and mind) when the filter of a living body arises. The self-awareness starts serving as the witness within it, but the witness is not a person. The thoughts of that consciousness make it think it is individualized and it thereby, becoming bound to and enmeshed with those thoughts of individuality, loses its understanding of its connection with Itself. The witnessing, shining, or functioning of the original awareness, when it shines through the medium of a body, becomes the experience of self-awareness. Because of thoughts it takes itself as a separate "I" until it also, through thought, realizes that it is just that original nature and can let go of all such mistaken thoughts perfectly to awaken. Then it can resume being a pure functioning of the original nature (which it always is and always remains) but *without the ideas of being a separate self or individual.* It will function as it always does, but no such thoughts arise just as is the case for beings in some of the higher Heavens. In other words, the universal awareness, which has no body, becomes manifest when a body comes into the picture. *The universal awareness has no thoughts or ideas, but in becoming personal consciousness then thoughts, concepts and ideas can arise within that consciousness, which thereby are its expression or functioning.* Consciousness can realize what it is and then awaken. If the consciousness of a sentient being does not awaken, it remains unenlightened and can continue on and on and on through eons, if the merit is lacking, in ignorance until it awakens.

Why do the thoughts of being a separate "I," ego, entity, or life arise? Perhaps that doesn't happen so much in the highest Heavens, because within them consciousness is so pure and thought entanglements are so little. However, for the stage of the human being we can say that thoughts arise to this consciousness, the consciousness gets mixed up entirely with these thoughts and loses its bearings— taking them as a world of their own—and loses recognition that it is all the Source. There is nothing inherently wrong with thoughts, or their functioning, or the world they create. That is their purpose, so-to-speak. They just are, and the world is just so, and consciousness serves the purpose it does. The world created by consciousness will always go on, turning and transforming, with no real individuality inside it. The harm is the unnecessary suffering of the individual consciousness thinking it is alone, separate, real and therefore ever clinging to the painful manipulations, twistings and turnings of consciousness which are simply effervescent appearances.

We are that original underlying non-conceptual wisdom, or pure original emptiness-awareness, that powers self-awareness, but not a permanent soul or entity that possesses individual self-so awareness. We are essentially the underlying awareness, not the little being we take ourselves to be. How could it be otherwise, and yet you have to prove this.

That assumption of being a little self-contained self is all a mistake made due to incorrect clinging to the forms, appearances, thoughts, transformations, twistings, manipulations, etc. of consciousness and the wrong use of the individual mind that is ultimately powered by this base awareness. The consciousness of any sentient being is a functioning of this base awareness, and in essence it is no different from this base awareness, so it is this base awareness.

People who hear that there is no small self, ego, or soul often become frightened, and want to immediately deny it or run away from the hearing, but that doesn't change the Truth. How could it? While some people become frightened, those who cultivate and directly discover that there is no self *all become filled with joy at the discovery, and find great peace and bliss due to the freedom from suffering and misery that this brings.* They always tell us this — every single one. It is not a living thing, but just co-emergent emptiness-awareness that we essentially are. In India this is *sat-chit-ananda* or existence-consciousness-absolute bliss (peace).

Why should we fear being what we are, or fear finding out what we are? People sometimes call it God with the notions of a living being, but it is not a god. It just is what it is and will always and ever be That. Nevertheless, fear of the Truth is one of the many reasons why the true cultivation teachings are hard to take hold of in societies. No one wants to hear this because everyone wants to believe they are a truly existing independent being, or especially chosen, destined to be saved and all sorts of other fictions. Unlike in the Heavens, when teachers in this particular world speak the truth to help liberate others and relieve suffering, they are often killed or persecuted, especially when the teachings of Truth threaten the views of organized religions.

Yes, conventionally speaking there is a body and life and person there, and conventionally speaking reincarnation does exist, but what you take yourself to be because of your thoughts is not what you really are. If you trace your self, ego, *atman*, personality, soul or consciousness back to its base, you will find that you are this awareness that is everything, or you can say you are everything because it is all appearing within this all-base awareness that you are, and thus you are All. You can say "I and the Father are One" or "I will never leave you" because it is true for every sentient being who realizes their underlying unity/existence that they are the fundamental essence, and that the assumed ego-self is a false collection of thoughts. But have you reached that actual stage of realization accomplishment where you know this, and can speak as the Source like this because the thoughts of being a small self or ego have vanished? It takes meditation work to be able to reach that stage.

When you read of masters who can speak to animals or even plants, see the past and future, or create fire in the air or walk through walls, it is because they have cultivated the purity of their minds far enough to reach this fundamental base nature and can then access many of its miraculous abilities. The pure awareness of the base nature has innumerable functions, such as being the minds of all beings or becoming matter, too. This is the only reason why these miraculous abilities become possible, for the universe is just consciousness in various forms, and consciousness has many possible manipulations.

You can think thoughts or internally visualize images, for instance, and these are just some of the possible manipulations of consciousness (which I'm sure might seem miraculous to animals), but there are far more than that. Life itself is a manipulation of consciousness, as is the existence of a rock, the laws of chemistry and physics, memory, inference, extrapolation and so on. Who knows how long it took to develop these things, these interrelationships within the world of phenomena? How many eons did it require for these things to come to be through interdependence? It has been turning since beginninglessness, and always will.

Is there a stop to it? Only Buddhas, fully enlightened ones, speak about this. When you find the source and detach from false views/thoughts we can say it (illusion or ignorance) all stops or becomes extinct, so ignorance has an end even though it has been there since beginninglessness. What does it mean for ignorance to cease for the enlightened mind that becomes totally and absolutely the source without stain? What does it mean to have "no outflows" or cultivate "nirvana without remainder"? You must cultivate yourself to find out. Buddhas have left us the instructions, and most of the highest stage teachings can only be found within Buddhism, but it is for you to find out. The answers are not to be found in a little introductory book like this.

Accomplished or enlightened masters arise in every school and tradition because they cultivated practices that purified their mind so that they could reach *This One.* After enlightenment, some leave the world, some go into retreat to improve their stage of attainment, and some take on the suffering task of teaching to help others awaken despite the fact that there are few genuine seekers. They commonly taught peace and ethics and good behavior for this on-going realm of consciousness wherein sentient being consciousnesses take themselves as individualities. They also dumbed down the highest teachings knowing they would find little understanding or acceptance. The assumed individualities of the audience (non-enlightened sentient beings) always prefer their own thought-constructions rather than the correct wisdom teachings that might help them awaken. The non-enlightened are entangled in incorrect thoughts and views, and few want to improve their stage of mental purity, how they interact with the world, or even awaken out of fear. The highest wisdom they can usually generate in their thought streams is to prefer dogmas, rules of discipline, worship, ceremonies and things like that as spiritual practice whereas these are all turned away from their true source. And so, life after life, transformation after transformation, they remain non-enlightened and continue to suffer and produce bad fortune for themselves, others and their own future.

People usually prefer religious worship, ceremonies and disciplinary rules because no one ever taught them these dharmas, which are rare to be found or received. Nevertheless, *they can be proved, which is the differentbetween these teachings and religious dogmas.* Their truth becomes self-evident through the personal authentication of meditation practice that proceeds far enough, and in certain traditions people arrive at the Truth through a commitment to cultivating other additional spiritual practices than the ones already mentioned. When people finally cultivate their minds to a state of purity and discover the Truth, they also find they have *become free* and find the internal bliss they have been seeking and running after their entire life. It is just due to a lack of wisdom and effort that people do not awaken to realize the true nature of reality, or Truth. The way is barred to no one because everyone is that fundamental true nature.

People always speculate how to make the world a better place. Think how much better everyone would act if they learned the truth about their own existence, and believed it. This is far superior to just telling people to be good, don't lie or cheat or steal or kill and so on. One needs a way to untangle the bad karmic propensities of greed, anger, hatred, pride, arrogance, envy, enmity, vexation, malice, deceitfulness, guile, hypocrisy, stinginess, shamelessness, indolence, sloth, carelessness, forgetfulness, too. Even after awakening, one must cultivate their consciousness to untangle such habits and cultivate more purified mental states. As stated, it all comes down to behavior in the end, which means there is a need to purify the endless stream of consciousness that gives birth to behavior. Meditation practice does this.

That underlying awareness is always ready to know the effulgence or radiance of its (empty) appearances that arise due to consciousness. It never fades out, it never sleeps; that is what you truly are – a pure consciousness or insubstantial awareness that has always been, never departs, which has no body or substance to it, and which is shining through you right now giving you the experience of self-consciousness. It is pure because it is undisturbed, motionless, stationary, at rest, empty and perfectly clear and therefore easy to miss. Self-consciousness is just the knowing of appearances to the mind which are themselves transient and insubstantial, but flow on unceasingly. Without the consciousness of sentient beings that gives rise to knowing, there is no such thing as knowing anywhere in the universe despite the fact that it is essentially pure consciousness.

Your mistake is in thinking that your awareness is somehow originating from a small soul self that is an independently standing sentient being. But it is just that the apparatus of a body has come upon the original essence, by some process consciousness has risen inside it, and this consciousness has lost recognition of the Source yet spins thoughts of being an independent sentient being. It is as if you turn directly away from the light because you are lost in a world of thoughts and cannot recognize yourself.

Therefore, the pure consciousness, apparitionally polluted by the filter of the body and ignorant thoughts of the individual mind (without being polluted in essence), mistakenly takes itself as the apparatus of just the one tiny body and private consciousness. Because of holding to the wrong thoughts and notions, and because of using the mind wrongly, it assumes it is the body, or the thoughts of consciousness, or the "I." This happens because of the compelling power of ignorance, which is something that only pertains to consciousness and not the clear base itself.

Basically, the pure clear self-nature assumed/appropriated/shone through a body producing personalized consciousness, that consciousness came to identify with this body and its thoughts and call itself "I," and now the binding ignorance must dissolve. This wrong attachment of self-identification, or ignorance, is what one ultimately becomes liberated from through the path of spiritual salvation whereupon one finds the Truth. Most people think spiritual salvation is to die and then go live in some Heaven forever, but spiritual salvation or liberation is to discover your true self. The true you stands apart from everything phenomenal.

Even though there is this involvement with non-awakened states, all beings are this underlying one in equal measure. They are like endless bubbles which it shines through, animating all matter and life, and upon enlightenment you realize that you are this one essence and its total functioning throughout all these forms. Their bodies are It, their minds are It, their awareness is It, you are It because It is All. In substance, essence, functioning and appearance, they are all It. There are no "other universes" outside of It.

There is no beginning or ending to It, no top or bottom, no inside or outside of It. It is infinite, boundless, everlasting, everything, All. It may sound strange, but this is what the "I," ego or assumed self actually is. You are not what you imagine yourself to be as an ego, soul, "I," personality, being or self. If you meditate very well, your mind will purify and you have a chance to "awaken" to discover what you are, and this is what you will fully fathom.

Have you not ever wondered who you are really behind all your thoughts? Have you ever wondered what is the real you like? It is not a result or finding that you artificially create, or a dogma that you must believe, but is actually something you can experientially find out. *This proving, in the sense of finding out what you always were – infinite formless awareness essence—is the basis of true spiritual practice.*

The idea of self-existence, presence, beingness or self-awareness is the "I am," but once again, what powers this idea is this primordial base awareness, the experiencing of the fundamental nature. Before the world was, you were; and after it is gone, you remain. Jesus already explained this when he said, "Before Abraham was I am." The fundamental awareness announces itself in the individual body as self-consciousness, which is expressed through the word "I." This is the "I am" of self-awareness, beingness or presence. The "I am" in this therefore points to the ever present original awareness, which Jesus was and which we all are.

Being the eternal absolute nature, you actually existed prior to your birth, so were never born. With this birth you simply attained conscious knowledge that you existed, but you have still not recognized your original self-nature – the fact that you are only pure insubstantial consciousness, rather than a person, and the all-consciousness that you are is just the functioning of your absolute original essence. You are that absolute nature. On your pure absoluteness this concept of self-existence – the "I am" within you – has arisen because of this physical body and mind, but you are neither this temporary physical body or its attached personal consciousness but that underlying original nature. You are the absolute nature in which the "I am" concept of self-existence is absent.

This is why the concept of the self just drops out when you proceed far enough with meditation. It just drops out because it was a falsity or illusion to begin with, and that's why it can leave. Because of meditation practice, consciousness purifies of all sorts of false thoughts and this set of thoughts also drops out. They are not pushed out, but in resting the mind of attachments they simply disappear naturally on their own because they are discovered to be false or untrue. *We say that the views of being an independent self "suffer extinction," but this does not mean that the personalized consciousness is annihilated.* Rather, it is transformed so as to abandon ignorant views and that transformation is called a "revolution in its basis."

You don't have to try to erase this I-concept but simply let go of all mental attachments, and what is not the true you will always eventually leave (since thoughts always depart) while what is the true you is permanent, and therefore it will stay. What is really you must be permanent, *so it must remain.* Therefore if something drops out, it was a falsity to begin with! This is the nondenominational path of awakening.

Since the ideas of being an independent, truly existent, self-so self, entity, personally, soul or ego – rather than the original nature that you are – are all false, they will certainly depart. They were not there before you were born, they represent pollutions within pure awareness, and so they are destined to also go away. When that happens, what one discovers abiding is their unchanging True Self beyond which one cannot go. Nothing transcends It. It is the finality, and also the beginning of everything. It is real, true, absolute, peaceful, pure, eternal and lacking of suffering. That original absolute nature of ours is what we essentially are, and has the power of miraculous awareness. From that awareness comes all consciousness like the waves on the ocean's surface that originate from the deep unmoving stillness below. The idea in each and every sentient being that "I exist" or "I am" is that pure consciousness in the form of self-consciousness. This knowledge, in every sentient being, *is you.*

Unfortunately, people never understand Jesus' words because they don't know he reached a stage of self-realization, and don't know what this actually means. There is no such thing as an individual being the only God-stuff or God-son because everything is equally God-stuff, and the substance of man is not different than the substance of God or the universe. Our ground of being is not different that the universe's ground of being.

Christians have simply adopted these illogical notions due to the writings of individuals who lacked enlightenment and even *samadhi* attainments, so how would they know how to interpret things correctly? To help you understand Jesus' message, I have just actually touched upon issues pertaining to the explanation of "The Kingdom of the Father is spread upon the earth, and men do not see it." In the *Gospel of Thomas*, Jesus also said, "There is a light within a man of light, and it lights up the whole world." This illumination or light is the same teaching we find in Buddhism that there is pristine awareness that is behind self-awareness and consciousness, and it extends to the universe. Zen master Yun-men said, "In the universe, within time and space, there is a treasure which is hidden in the mountain of form; it cognizes things, emptily shining, empty inside and out, alone and still, invisible." This awareness illumination is the awareness functioning of the original nature, it is you.

You were never born nor will you ever die because you are this non-moving base awareness appearing in the vestiges of a "sentient being," which is just a manner of speaking. There is only a personal knowing (cognition) of "world appearances," which we call "existence," because there is the filter of the body of a "sentient being" that has intercepted universal awareness to produce personal consciousness. Individual consciousness is a development of the universal fundamental nature into a consciousness knowing mechanism, but there is no real being inside this. There is just the original awareness that has intercepted the filter of a body and mind, which we conventionally call a living being, and that body and mind function without knowing their true nature until that self-consciousness awakens to realize the Truth.

Our personal consciousness of being a self or person can be traced all the way back to this stationary universal awareness that can know all with omniscience because it is All. Regardless as to the names religion call this, this is what you essentially are. That is YOU. Everything is *This One.* This is what you must discover on the road of religion in order to become free, liberated, saved, emancipated, awakened, enlightened or however you wish to word it.

CHARACTERISTICS OF THE BASE NATURE

We call this universal awareness the absolute nature or ground basis, and we also call it an essence or substance to denote the idea of a body – the body of reality. The idea of a body is misleading because it is infinite (boundless or formless), so this is only a manner of speaking in order to talk about it. What is there, true and real, remaining and always ever present, is absent of all substance and content, and that insubstantial emptiness is its essence or nature. That is its body, which in the best manner of comparison is like endless space. Awareness, in the best manner of comparison, is like sunlight or moonlight that is everywhere in empty space though invisible while in space, and yet can illuminate objects when it strikes them. Those are just analogies for our absolute fundamental nature is not empty space, and our pristine awareness is not light.

You cannot say there is something there as our absolute essence because there are no substantial characteristics to it – no color, form, shape, space or anything to grasp. But it's not a total non-existence or non-being or inert existence because we have a world of appearances that arises in the mind, which we call miraculous existence, creation, manifestation, appearance, consciousness or reality. You therefore cannot believe in any ideas of non-existence because you see things arising in the universe. The inherent emptiness arises as awareness, illumination, knowing, consciousness, cognition or lucidity of a world, and all of these synonyms are words trying to capture this idea that knowingness is possible of some form of manifestation or appearance that, even though empty of unchanging self-so reality, seems to be there and functions with interdependence between all its parts. Hence sages explain that *there is co-emergent emptiness and awareness that just independently shines as all of Reality*. In the highest form of meditation practice, you therefore should neither cling to the extreme of emptiness (having no thoughts) or awareness (the phenomena of consciousness) to realize It.

Our original nature, or fundamental essence, is like the truest, purest, clearest essence of awareness or illumination – a primordial self-so lucidity that is not dependent, caused or conditioned like relative existence, but stands alone without any support—that is empty of subjective substance, so who can say what it really is? Its functioning of knowing is "existence," "manifestation," "appearance" or "creation." Thus, it is said that "the nature of pure being is awareness," "the nature of pure being has awareness as its characteristic," or "empty pure nature has the functioning of awareness" and other similitudes that try to point to this idea of co-emergent or co-joint inherent emptiness and purest consciousness. There are lots of ways to say it to try to get you to realize what we are talking about. There are lots of name tags we can use, but all the naming and talking is like a finger pointing at the moon. You should be trying to understand the meaning by seeing the moon rather than fixating on the finger of expression.

That clear beingness-awareness is what you are; what you know as "objects" are phenomena and therefore, because you think you know a personal self due to notions, this cannot be the *real you* because it is just a phenomenon, too. If you are in a position to know the mind, you are not the mind. If you are in a position to know consciousness, you transcend consciousness; you are out of consciousness. If you know the waking state, for instance, you are not the waking state. If you know the dream state, you are not the dream state. If you know or think of a self, you are not the self. As the *Tao Te Ching* says, "It is nothing that can be named, It is nothing that can be described." You, too, are not a phenomenon that can be known, but the source behind the consciousness knowing.

Call it what you like but when you think about it, this must be you. *Whatever is "you" must be behind your awareness, and awareness must be its function.* Whatever is you must be some homogenous underlying beingness that has the capacity for awareness. Now, with this understanding, your job is try to find *That One*. You cannot do it other than through meditation.

You are not matter, nor energy, the body or your consciousness (thoughts/mind). There is a knower or witness, and we call it the self, ego, I, personality, *atman* and so on, but those are just names used for the purpose of communication because the true homogeneous-you with the power of awareness is not a thing with shape or form. You have never realized this fundamental awareness, which is the fundamental equality of all consciousness beings, simply because you never used your mind correctly and so you have remained ignorant or your greatest treasure.

Being a bunch of thoughts, this idea of a self, entity, soul or personality never identifies the *real self* of a person. The ego-self is a totally fictitious creation of ideas. Your personality is also just a set of changing consciousness patterns of thoughts, habits, desires, emotions, behaviors and memories bundled together but through which this self-illumination shines. This self-so illumination of the underlying awareness—the real you—has no individuality or pattern. There are no individuals within It. It is totally unconditioned, boundless and free, but when it shines through the vehicle of causes and conditions called a living body, then self-awareness and all these thoughts can arise. There is no ultimate goal or purpose to It, for It remains infinite, pure and unchanging. Consciousness, and thus awakening, has simply appeared as a potential within sentient beings. Who knows if it was possible eons ago?

If you are fixated on the idea of evolution throughout this time, which is the idea that we are always evolving to something higher or more perfect, this is not correct at all because the aggregates of the self making up the personality fluctuate moment to moment and in going from life to life, so that is simply *transformation rather than evolution.* No state reached, neither the higher or lower, is permanent either, and hence there is no plan in it except the fact of karmic transformation brought on by the efforts of that life. You become what you choose to cultivate and attain it according to your merits. Consciousness may become more or less purified with each moment or state of being, and hence you cannot call this any evolution with a purpose.

Along these lines, however, you can view the idea of self within the aggregate of consciousness like the hard seed of a plant that always survives but is carried along from season to season without ever germinating. Then one day, when all the right conditions come together, the seed finally suddenly cracks open, its covering falls away, and it realizes the knowledge of its true self. If it then lets go and becomes perfectly natural without holding to anything, this leads to the highest state or merit that is beyond states or merit. So in one sense you can say there is evolution *but this evolution can only happen if you choose it and actively cultivate it,* otherwise you will simply be tossed about by the comings and goings of the universe.

Awakening is the result of studying cultivating teachings to develop wisdom, accumulating merit, and cultivating meditation practice. If you call this evolution, then the peak of evolution is something you must choose to cultivate as your goal because it can only be achieved by *active cultivation* of wisdom, merit and meditation. If you just wait eons for it to happen, however, the seed case will never break open and you'll never discover your true reality or truly find what you are seeking life after life.

REINCARNATION

What gets passed from incarnation to incarnation, in the conventional sense, is just this aforementioned bundle of inconstant consciousness patterns, which is why habit energies do get passed from life to life and we must therefore work to purify them. Buddhism explains that the aggregate of consciousness gets passed with likes, dislikes, behavioral patterns and so on left as energetic seeds or impressions within what is being passed. Habits and memories are retained in the continuity of what passes from life to life, *but it is not a person that flows from life to life.* It is just consciousness that is being transformed. This is why, from one aspect, you can deny the existence of reincarnation. You can say, "there is no such thing as reincarnation."

Then again, from a conventional standpoint, something is being passed with continuity, and so you can also say that reincarnation *does exist.* Of course that apparent continuity is like the flickering of a flame; a flame appears to exist as an unbroken continuance over time, but it is actually changing from moment to moment, and hence there is nothing permanent or fixed within this passing vehicle. There is no real being or fixed self; there is only constant becoming.

Those who deny reincarnation exists are not usually speaking from the first vantage point, however, but from an inferior understanding of the actual workings of the cosmos. For the benefits of society, it is best to teach the idea of reincarnation and karma and the necessity to purify consciousness and behavior because in the conventional sense, as in the conventional world around you right now, it is so. It does exist, and it teaches self-responsibility. It accounts for your good luck or bad luck and steers all the transformations of your life. It makes sense of life and the process of universal change that affects all beings.

However, you must understand that what passes from life to life ("undergoes transformation" is a better way of speaking) is just these selfless changing patterns through which the light of the original nature shines, so-to-speak, animating them with the idea of self-consciousness. If not purified, those habits and energies in this unending stream of consciousness will create problems and suffering in this life, and afflictions in future lives as well. Even if they do not create problems this life, it is inevitable that they will eventually encounter some situation or situations in the future where they end up creating incredible troubles and sufferings for others, including misery and affliction for the false self it imagines itself to be if they are not purified.

There is no solid person, soul, entity or self within this passing net of memories, habits and consciousness constructs. What is passed *does not belong to the same person but simply supplies energy for a new person.* Thus memories are passed, but since the animating one is the absolute nature which lacks individuality within it, who says that a self travels from life to life? There is no such true thing as a person, being, soul, entity or life in the absolute nature or conventional cosmos; there is only the original fundamental awareness shining through all these various patterns, some of which take themselves to be independent consciousness beings. Those patterns are consciousness, and a small speck of consciousness is the thing that falsely assumes a self.

Consciousness, which arises when there is a suitable bodily form, mistakenly creates the false idea of a self due to ignorant thinking. Since these ideas are false (incorrect, delusional or mistaken), one can win liberation from this ignorance and find out what one actually is. Thought attachments can dissolve away if one practices to learn mental detachment and hereby allows consciousness to purify so that one can recognize the true self. False thoughts can drop away, just as thoughts always depart, if we realize those notions are wrong and let them go without stubbornly holding onto them. Some will just drop out by themselves as the mind purifies, and you don't even need to dissolve them by realizing they are wrong to abandon them.

Thus, you can say that reincarnation does not truly exist because there is no such thing as an unchanging *atman,* self, person or soul that gets passed from life to life. Something definitely gets passed in the conventional sense, and it thinks of itself as a real truly independently existing soul, person, entity or self, but that is not what it is. It is just another subset of consciousness agglomerations, within the entire realm of interdependent consciousness or "manifestation," which is all operating through the infinite interdependence of dependent arisings. It is all animated by the shining of the ultimate awareness, but there is no ultimate personal doer to everything, which is why liberation is possible. As consciousness, you simply must choose to cultivate to discover what you are. You must want to cultivate liberation or self-realization and then cultivate to attain it, and only then does it become possible. You must first want to awaken. The awakening to enlightenment sets you free from all pain and suffering. Furthermore, in rediscovering your inherent unity with the base of All, marvelous miraculous functions also become possible that, directed by wisdom and compassion, can be used for the salvation of all beings.

The witnessing that shines through you is the same common pristine awareness that is all sentient beings, and all matter as well. Yes, *it is also all insentient matter.* That is a problem that one must resolve at very high stages of meditation. You may not know about these issues yet, but these are all matters you can investigate and then directly find out through personal confirmatory experience rather than just take all this discussion on logic or as a tenant of faith. After solving the issue of the assumed self being a false assumption, for complete enlightenment you also have to solve the issue of the existence of phenomena you see as well. What are they? Do they really exist there outside of consciousness? How can you find out? You must start by reading this type of wisdom study material, which is called the stage of studying cultivation teachings to accumulate wisdom and understanding, and then you must cultivate meditation to find the answer as a direct realization.

Our pristine base awareness, or original nature, is empty of all chi, phenomena, or content. Yes, even chi is not there. Chi energy is linked to ordinary consciousness, but there is no chi involved with the original nature. There is no energy of any form either, which Hindus might call *shakti.* There is no movement, no material or phenomena, nothing that can be called an anything. It is just itself, complete in itself, a One-Without-a-Second, a pure unborn, unmanifest potential. It is a pureness that needs nothing because it is complete, perfect and whole in Itself. It is a true voidness of everything phenomenal, which is why it is pure and changeless, so we say it is empty in the sense that nothing is there as its body or essence. It is unexcelled, it is perfectly pure and clear, it is permanent, everlasting, motionless, stationary, unperturbed, changeless, infinite and eternal. It is nirvana. Because it has the nature of awareness, it is the universal factor that makes all perception/perceiving possible for all beings. Our substance or essence is It.

Why is it like this, being empty but having awareness as its nature? That is just the way It is. If it wasn't that way we would not be here because the universe would be an inert, static existence. As sentient beings, we would not be having this discussion because we wouldn't be without the existence of awareness. Instead there would just be an inert, dead, static emptiness instead of wondrous existence created by consciousness. The nature, beingness or presence of underlying original awareness prevents a one-sided non-existence which we typically call nihilism.

This awareness or consciousness of ours is the beingness within experience. Just as colorless light is present in all colors and is how we see them, so it is in every experience and yet it is not an experience. One cannot see the rays of light in space, but just what light illuminates and you cannot know any experience without invisible pristine awareness. You are, in essence, what makes experiences conscious. You are what is the mind, and the mind is essentially empty awareness. Think about this … are you not whatever it is that gives birth to your mind?

Try to fathom what this means. To find this fundamental thing-you-are, you must travel the path of meditation and end up becoming aware of your essential nature. As often stated, this is science and there is no religion or dogma to it. You can call it "human being science" if you like. After your mind and attachments purify to a remarkable degree due to meditation practice, you can discover what remains after all thoughts depart and abide as your true self. At that time, marvelous functioning capabilities will open up because of recognizing you are *That One*. The fact that it is stationary, pure and clear is why you always fail to recognize it even though it is right in front of you, and until you let go of the stains of perception you normally cling to, it is easy to miss its presence and the recognition that this is what you ultimately are.

You must really understand this discussion if you want to attain the highest possibilities of meditation progress. While you can't say there is some *thing* there -- because this base essence lacks substantial characteristics and is therefore not a phenomenal thing -- yet you must admit there is awareness shining or you would not be experiencing a world of appearances. So you can call it "non-being" in the sense that it is not a substance, phenomenon, phenomenal existence or anything in particular, or you can call it "pure being" to denote the powering existence of pure cognizance or pure consciousness that gives you the experience of beingness. This aspect of the pure awareness is sometimes called its illumination, effulgence, radiance or lucidity (because it can become appearances). Perpetually calm, pure and clear, this illumination is like infinite and boundless light, and that is the original pure substance of the mind.

When you think about it, the real nature of reality has to be like this wherein there is no duality or dichotomy. This is the only thing that satisfies such requirements, and that is what you actually discover to be so if you cultivate far enough. You might think these are all verbal arguments, or just exercises in logic, but these are also *the actual descriptions from people who have cultivated meditative spiritual methods and finally reached some stage of attainment.* Their descriptions are similar and consistent, and when analyzed are totally logical from all angles. There are no holes in the logic or explanations of this as there are within religious dogmas. You can find saints and sages of various religions actually pointing *to* this Source or fundamental Self if you bother to investigate and read their words beyond the normal religious dogma involved with worship. That commonality of proof requires yet another book in itself.

Our original fundamental nature is therefore not merely empty like an inert non-existence, for at the same time there is clear cognitive lucidity, illumination, clarity or awareness potential. That's why we say "beingness." But it's not a substance and transcends the phenomenal so we say "emptiness," void, non-being or non-existence to denote the lack of anything we can normally know such as any type of conscious experience. But it's not the nihilism of absolute nothingness because there is the appearance of awareness. Do you see? It is two sides of the same coin.

We say it is self-luminous, radiant, self-effulgent or has self-so illumination (the ability for cognizance or awareness) because that functioning of awareness is its own natural state. That is its fundamental nature. It just exists self-so and always has been eternally infinite and pure by nature free of pollutions. The existence of foundational, primordial awareness comes from nowhere else but is just there as the absolute basis because that is its self-so nature. That's where the universe comes from and it has always been present.

The beingness of the self, soul or individual can be experientially traced back to pure consciousness, what we also call the capacity for awareness or knowing or appearance manifestation. That's all it is. That awareness functioning is primal and inseparable from its nature of emptiness because that is just what it is, so it is original, primordial, foundational, fundamental, primal, original, self-existent, self-so, non-dependent, uncaused, beginningless, unborn, unproduced. We can call awareness a functioning, quality or characteristic of the absolute nature but it is also the true nature, however, we must even detach from clinging to this awareness aspect to attain perfect and complete enlightenment. What mentally arises you simply let arise without making attachments, and you function effortlessly without making distinctions so that you are truly empty and at one with the Source, the absolute nature. Thus, emptiness and awareness, or emptiness and manifestation-appearances co-exist. This Middle Way of non-attachment is the highest way to practice, the highest way *to be*. This is the highest, purest, clearest of perfect functioning. That is why the Zen school says that the awareness of the mind's true nature is also considered a guest rather than host. It is in essence the host, but if you treat it like guest you won't cling to it and make it into a falsity.

When we cultivate meditation, we start coming closer and closer to realizing this base awareness of pure consciousness that is absent of everything, but which gives us the power to know thoughts. Thoughts are just things (turnings or transformations of consciousness) that arise in your field of awareness, and they come and go incessantly. They lack substantiality, which is why they can exist within it. That is why the world can appear solid but is not, for that insubstantiality does not conflict with the ultimate underlying nature of unchangingness. Without emptiness as the nature, there would be no room for anything to appear and no place to disappear. The world is like a magical illusion – its solid appearances are not real but just give the appearance of a solid reality, like the appearance of a ring of fire when a lighted stick is quickly twirled in a circle.

Those coming and going thoughts are not the ultimate you since what is you knows them. If you know something, then those thoughts cannot be you because to know them you have to be beyond them. You must transcend them to be able to know them. Something stationary must stand behind something moving in order for the moving to be known, and you are that formless, empty stationary transcendence. Thus, consciousness is not you, but is experienced by the you, and that "you" or self or "I" is this awareness when it is traced back to its most fundamental origins. The particular thing that knows the coming and goings of consciousness is ultimately you, your true nature. You therefore stand apart from them, and thus you can detach and let go.

It is hard to realize this empty awareness even though it is present in every experience. You can only realize it if thoughts die down enough so that your mind becomes pure, clean and stable. This just gives you the chance to introspect and become aware of the Truth, and possibly catch an understanding of It, but does not assure the event. If at the right moment you introspect, with wisdom, to examine your mind, you might be able to realize what is this thing called consciousness/mind.

It is hard to recognize that the mind's nature is empty with the luminosity potential of realizing a world it creates. Only after a lot of meditation effort and cultivation effort that purifies the mind (so that a high degree of wandering thoughts drops out and the mental realm starts to become crystal clear) does such a realization become possible. Along the way your mind has to calm down, your chi and channels have to transform, consciousness has to empty out, and you have to cultivate the right understanding or wisdom to awaken. The words I am giving you are like a priceless gift in that with the right conditions, are like a seed that might one day sprout to produce for you an awakening.

THE GREAT IMPORTANCE OF STUDYING CULTIVATION TEACHINGS

There are many stages of awakening after the first simple finding, from meditation, that your ordinary mind of mentation is naturally empty, but since this is a beginner's book we'll have to leave more complicated sequences aside. You can turn to *Tao and Longevity* or *The Little Book of Meditation* for such information. However, you should know that what we have already gone over are called "wisdom teachings" to help you awaken. *People can go for many lives without coming across such information, and to come across them requires great merit.* To accept them and put them into practice requires something more--wisdom. The purpose of this book is to help you get started at the practice of meditation, so it cannot go deeply into these higher wisdom teachings which are best left for other books. Nevertheless, the principle for deepening your meditation practice is studying such issues because an understanding helps you let go of thought attachments.

Logic, analysis, reasoning and "wisdom" helps you understand these discussions and apply them to your meditation practice. The fact that you cultivate wisdom, or understanding, also helps you avoid the habit of clinging to any mental realms you cultivate because you now understand you shouldn't do that. In letting go, nothing changes except that you are more effortless and free, fewer afflictions arise in your mind, and personal suffering accordingly decreases. So the world does not change at all in any negative way, except that everything gets better for yourself. In fact, your behavior can get radically better in a fantastic way. Our behavior as it now stands is like some character in a video game who only has so many limited options for how he or she can act when confronted with a situation. As your mind becomes unconditioned due to non-clinging, because habitual thought tendencies and habitual thought patterns drop out due to meditation, you stop falling into your usual set patterns of habitual conditioning and become totally free to respond to situations in any way warranted. Think of the breakthrough possibilities this brings. Think of the brilliant solutions that become possible, as illustrated by the history of the Zen masters, when you therefore cultivate to enlightenment.

To heighten the excellence of your meditation practice – which means results in terms of health, peace of mind, and spiritual progress—*you should always study the theory and methods of meditation together, and join your understanding with your practice so that you are always making continual progress over time.* One without the other, study without practice, is like a bird with only one wing who can fly nowhere.

Without study, you almost always end up clinging to mental states without recognizing the genuine nature of consciousness. The highest form of study is to read, ponder and try to bring the results of spiritual wisdom teachings, such as we have just discussed, into your practice results. These teachings are rare because they are only stressed within most Eastern traditions which have grown up along the practical and realistic principle of investigating the mind. When spiritual heroes of other traditions discuss them, such as in Judaism, Christianity and Islam, the public tends to ignore them, dismiss them, criticize or twist them, misunderstand them, or as mentioned, persecute the teachers. No one bothers to protect these teachers even though, just as in Socrates' case, they are the very finest members of society.

History shows that many people become enraged upon hearing the Truth because their false notions start to become shaken, and although one can factually prove the Truth through direct experience without resorting to artificial dogmas (as is the typical case characterizing the practice of religion), they still end up killing their best spiritual leaders.

This is the experience of history, but let us put this history of human behavior aside. What matters is that everyone still desires happiness, health and wellbeing, energy and peace of mind. Therefore, you should know how meditation works and practice it to obtain these results, even if you do not pursue it to the very highest stages of self-realization mentioned. It still produces all these wonderful benefits if you don't progress that far and even if you don't believe in those statements.

Meditation should become a lifelong practice for all the benefits it brings, and so you should know how to properly practice, why your chi starts to arise and purify, why your mind calms down, how your body is likely to change, and you should understand the phenomena that typically arise when this all happens (as well as all sorts of other things) if you really want to make great progress. Furthermore, you should recognize that *this type of progress along these lines, and nothing else, is the most genuine form of spiritual or religious practice.* Going to the church, mosque, synagogue or temple certainly has social benefits and the benefits of hearing spiritual messages, but only this type of personal effort constitutes the truest and highest form of spiritual practice.

Knowing all these various things can help you learn how to let go of your habit of self-identifying with the stream of conscious thoughts arising within your mind. By becoming free of mental entanglements, while letting consciousness always arise, you will definitely make progress in terms of health and relaxation and will additionally become able to recognize the underlying basis of your mind. The key is learning meditation so that you stop getting stuck in self-identifying with thoughts.

You must learn how to let go of all existing phenomena. You are always tying your consciousness up in knots and thereby losing sight of your clear basis, which explains why you are not enlightened. It is all due to maintaining thought attachments together with incorrect assumptions and wrong views. Emptiness is one type of phenomenon, and existence is another type of mental phenomenon as well, so you must learn to let go of mentally grasping to either of them. This will bring you all the benefits you seek.

Grasping is a functioning of your mind, but the only functioning you should support is not really any functioning at all, rather, the natural, effortless, frictionless shining of original awareness. In effect, by practicing the effortlessness of non-clinging to mental states you thereby accomplish the highest form of meditation and spiritual practice. This is the naturalness represented by Lao Tzu and Taoism, but you can only achieve it if you cultivate meditation attainments. To live you must do everything you are required to do in the world, but do not take yourself to be the doer and simply function as you must without mental attachments to situations. This is the naturalness that Krishna taught Arjuna on the battlefield in the *Bhagavad Gita* as well. Everyone with enlightenment ends up teaching similar lessons because they discover this is the correct way to live.

Because you have a tendency to grasp at consciousness, you have lost the state of no-effort and have gotten attached to thoughts, and now it's hard to free yourself from following thoughts and getting caught up in thought entanglements. You end up getting lost in consciousness without knowing you are lost within consciousness, and this habit obscures the possible perception of your true self-nature. If you let go of thoughts, however, at the very minimum they will calm down and you will start to experience more peace and inner quiet. That's the initial objective of meditation practice. The highest objective is discovering your own true nature. Once you begin the practice of meditation, you are on your way to this possibility.

In Christianity, we call this initial calming result of meditation practice a state of inner peace, silence or tranquility. Christianity also calls it a state of holiness, charity (since you are *giving away* thoughts), renunciation (giving up thoughts) and poverty (no thoughts are there). If you cultivate a state of no thoughts and if thoughts of a self therefore don't arise, you can call it selflessness, egolessness or even humility, too. These are all the Christian virtues we are taught to cultivate, and you can see that their true meaning is linked to the highest possible results of meditation and spiritual cultivation practice.

Some schools call this peaceful silence reached though meditation a state of no-thought. Other traditions simply call it a state of emptiness. Some call it a state of *fullness* because you can accept the whole of miraculous functioning reality without limiting thoughts to bar this boundlessness. This is why it is an optimistic, happy, joyous state full of life rather than a negative state of nihilism. Furthermore, when your mind becomes empty then your chi or life force starts to come up, and everyone can feel this energy when it arises. You therefore become a blessing to those around you in many ways like this. Internal silence is a very natural phenomenon, but some people end up putting religious notions on internal peace when it is not necessary at all.

The big point is that your mind, when discriminative thoughts are gone, becomes so empty that it can accept the entire universe without suppressing anything or clinging to anything. Without the presence of internal wandering thoughts that might limit its attention and thereby restrict it, the mind becomes so empty that it effectively becomes boundless. You can start to live as if in full reality as you are truly meant to do.

Taoism calls this resulting quiet a state of internal peace and harmony, or equilibrium. Confucianism and Buddhism call it a state of "cessation," halting or stopping since random thoughts disappear or stop, so naturally they have "ceased." Some call it a state of "no effort" or effortlessness since no clinging is going on as the mind clams down. Some call it equanimity. As stated, some schools call it a state of selflessness if it proceeds far enough that even the bundle of thoughts of being a self or person drop out, but that is a more advanced stage of practice than the simple attainment of internal quiet.

Everyone is naming the same preliminary end result in a different way to emphasize one or another of its characteristics, but people are always reaching the same initial state of a tranquil mind. It is only the people who proceed far enough past this who can talk of the enlightenment matters we have discussed. You can work your whole life at meditation and never become awakened because it requires a lot of meditation effort along with exceptional wisdom and merit attainments. If you are never introduced to wisdom teachings, or never study them, it is hard to awaken just by your own efforts. This is why such teachings are to be treasured wherever they are found because they can free you from the endless suffering rounds of reincarnation that go on forever. What worldly merit can compare with that? None can, none at all in the entire cosmos because all states of enjoyment are temporal felicities. Cultivating meditation to find the root source of life, mind and matter enables you to become free of these rounds and control them, which is a great achievement because there is no permanent place of rest you can go to in the universe.

There are all sorts of ways that you can indicate the initial quiet mental state achieved through meditation. The quieting is simply a natural phenomenon that occurs when you meditate and detach from consciousness. If you meditate and let go of thoughts while remaining aware, rather than falling asleep or forcibly trying to suppress thoughts, you will reach this state of internal peace and your chi will calm with it. *It is like a law of physics that if you meditate and watch your thoughts while refusing to hold on to them or follow them in a way that gives them extra energy, they will die down and your mind will become tranquil.*

Your breathing will also eventually quiet down and slow to a halt as well, which is a state of respiratory cessation that ends up matching your state of thought cessation. And then, as the real chi of your body starts to arise in response to this quieting, it will produce all sorts of chakra and chi channel openings that lead to countless other beneficial results in their wake. We need not mention chakras separately because chakras are chi channels, so when we say that "channels open" the idea of chakras opening as well should be understood. When enough channels open, it is as if your internal chi energy takes on a life of its own because it arises and you can begin to feel the rotational circulation of chi within all the energy meridian pathways of the body, which open in a particular general order and sequence.

This is what prepares you for being able to access high spiritual states called *samadhi*, and while the Western religions describe these energetic feelings and the *samadhi* states by clothing them with religious words about God and the like, you have to turn to Eastern sources to understand all their characteristics in a scientific or clinical fashion. One concentrates on following the external respiration to reach the stage where these internal currents arise and are thereby set into motion. You only use the method like you use a match to light a fire, and after the fire starts you don't need the match anymore, so you don't need the method after the result is achieved but then let it proceed on its own and detach from the results. Thereafter you let the body transform on its own, and concentrate on cultivating the mind to attain higher states of natural emptiness clear witnessing.

In any case, you can gradually detach from the view of being a body from this sort of progress, and then detach from the view of being a self, and finally you can also detach from the view that phenomena are independently separate from your true self and are a self-existence all their own. You discover the truth of phenomena as well, namely that they are also consciousness, and their manipulation then becomes possible. These final steps of achievement require a lot of deeper meditation work and purificatory transformations of consciousness so it can reach the basis without stain.

All meditation methods are designed to help you achieve this initial state of emptiness, empty mind, quiet thoughts, silence, peace or tranquility – however you wish to word it. You achieve it by refusing to hold on to your thoughts and then, if practiced with consistency, streams of wandering mental chatter will in time gradually die away. That's why you meditate in the first place.

Reading spiritual books on meditation topics can also help you attain this inner peace because they may teach you how to practice to attain it. Your study of meditation matters can help you learn how to detach from mental entanglements so thoughts die down. Studying can also teach you some new practice technique that helps you to let go, or just from study alone you can realize something that helps you let go.

It is very hard to break the mental habit of clinging to thoughts, especially when this tendency has become so ingrained that you don't even recognize that you are always doing it. Only when you are free of this habit can you recognize that you have been blinding yourself through an unnecessary stickiness in mental functions. You have always been using your mind wrongly, and that excessive mental engagement has been blinding you from realizing the underlying clear awareness that is essentially your mind.

Studying spiritual wisdom texts on the nature of the mind, and then looking directly at your mind to analyze it with this new understanding, can help you break this habit by mastering dispassion. Dispassion does not mean that emotions do not come up, for you should never suppress them, but means that you do not cling to whatever naturally arises. You will still function, act, or react exactly as you did previously (unless you have purified some negative tendencies of your consciousness, such as a tendency to get angry quickly), but just won't be sticky about it or remain stuck in the past. You will always remain in the freshness of the present. This will bring you effortlessness, capability, openness, freedom and peace. You will learn a frictionless freedom of behavior that brings you a deeper level of effectiveness, vigor and tranquility in all you do.

The study of spiritual books therefore gives you the tools to be able to both analyze the cultivation path and analyze your mind. From that information, you can make progress at meditation and attain the deep mental states which many sages and saints have written about. This is why people study the enlightenment teachings of Zen, the teachings of Vedanta, Mahamudra and Dzogchen, the self-perfection methods of Confucianism, the naturalness and no-effort teachings of Taoism, Buddhist teachings, the consciousness teachings of Yogacara, certain Hindu *Upanishads* and so forth. More than the Western religions, these schools give you the tools and teachings which enable you to more readily find the root source of matter and the mind by penetrating through the barrier of consciousness.

This is not something that can be found through blind belief or achieved by following disciplinary rules, performing rituals and ceremonies, making sacrifices, or engaging in some type of worship. When you achieve self-realization, you will find that all beings are just worshipping their own thought constructs, and in essence, they *are* what they hope to be worshipping. Actually, from the absolute standpoint, conventional beings engaged in worshipping activities are only worshipping their own Self, so what is the need of worship?

People rarely bother to find out who/what is the ultimate creator of what is being worshipped. Since that creator is their true self, what need is there for worshipping your own true nature? It just is. What you need to do is actually cultivate meditation *to find that ultimate creator* and work on transforming your mind and behavior for the better as its perfect expression. That would be a worthwhile activity that would bring benefits to yourself and the universe. Unfortunately, the organized religions become furious when they hear this, despite its logic and the fact that *It* can be known.

Let me provide an example of external intellectual or academic study of the kind that can help you, and then an example of direct contemplative study of the mind, and show how both can assist your meditation practice. Both types of study effort should be used to help further your meditation progress.

With academic study you might read a spiritual book. It might point out that when you say, "my body is mine," you are acknowledging that your body is not an "I" but belongs to the "I" or "you." Also, the body itself cannot say "I," so clearly the physical body is not you. It is not your self, but *belongs* to your self. Now that you know this, you now have the problem of finding out what your true self is.

Are you the consciousness that runs through your mind? If you say "my mind" in a sentence, then for the very same reason you are therefore acknowledging that your mind is not the real you either – it belongs to you.

The real you stands apart from it. So what is the true "I" that owns or uses these things? Where is the ultimate self that announces itself with the word "I"? In fact, since you know something, don't you have to be above, beyond or in some way transcending consciousness to know it? If that is the case, what are you ultimately since can do this witnessing or knowing? If you say witnessing is your function, but not your self, then what are you? How can you describe your true nature?

Just thinking about these issues, because you read them in a book, is an example of external study and discriminative analysis. You read something, follow the train of thought, think about it with a bit of some discrimination and logical analysis, and come to a conclusion. You should definitely read teachings about the nature of your mind, but you must not confuse any intellectual understanding you reach with a direct experience of your mind that is free from the overlay of concepts.

This sometimes happens that the ideas you have been studying arise as thoughts during meditation, or afterwards, and you take those thoughts as a "realization." A genuine realization is actually when you achieve a direct experience of the nature of your mind from looking directly at it rather than remaining fixated on the appearances/thoughts that arise within it.

One such realization is discovering insubstantial emptiness as your mind's true nature. You don't need any *a priori* theology or religion to see this, but can just discover this as a natural result via a direct experience of looking within. You cannot refute the result! You see it, experience it, or directly perceive it, and that is a realization. This is why religious greats say that the ego or self drops away. It happened to them; it happened to countless saints in countless traditions, and they have spoken of this as a direct experiential event. Hence, you can gain an actual knowledge of the mind and direct experience of this type from cultivating meditation work or spiritual practices, and an "insight" is our intellectual understanding of that direct experiential knowledge.

This path of searching and discovery is scientific and humanitarian, practical, logical, universal, non-denominational and non-sectarian. There are no assumptions necessary as in the case of religious dogmas. You simply cultivate and discover how things really stand because the results just naturally fall out, and then you know them from direct experience. This scares the heebie-jeebies out of religious functionaries holding on to dogmas, especially when they suspect their tenets are wrong, for it is like the Catholic Church finding out that Galileo is saying that the planets do not revolve around the sun. He's right, but they feel they have to crush him anyway, and so they do because they do not have the right religious view. If you mix religion and politics, for instance, another result is that you always get politics rather than Truth.

The responses you take may mask the Truth, and you can imprison, kill or just persecute the truth-giver, but all these manipulations are useless in the face of reality ... and they win you incredibly bad karma as well. The sutras always tell us, without exaggerating, that to harm an enlightened individual in any way brings more karmic suffering than harming millions or even billions of people, and from prior discussions you might develop an inkling as to why. Without an ego-notion, they are the most perfect expressions of the original nature possible, and the merit they are issuing forth to others, even when silent, is immeasurable. In studying wisdom texts left by those with attainments, we are simply trying to be like Galileo and also discover the real truth of ultimate reality, but in a quicker fashion by standing on the shoulders of giants who have gone before us and left some teachings for us.

This type of direct realization from looking straight at your mind and analyzing it is what you try to achieve through meditation practice and wisdom analysis. You can start achieving such realizations only after you start successfully calming your mind's scattered nature, calming your chi, and penetrating through the haze of wandering thoughts that screen your mind's true nature. Without that basis, this is hard to accomplish.

The basis of higher attainments is first calming your mind and body, and then cultivating a purified mental state that is relatively empty. With that emptiness achievement, your body will also become more comfortable because your chi is flowing smoothly and harmoniously throughout all its channels. When your chi circulates without any obstacles, then you won't even be aware of your chi or body energies since it moves so freely without friction and, therefore, you will attain a sense of great physical wellbeing. This wellbeing can serve as a basis for cultivating mental detachment, which further smoothens the harmonious flow of chi throughout the body by allowing the opening and emptying of even more chi channels. Hence, the personal cultivation route of meditation not only gifts your body with great benefits but prepares you for great spiritual awakening.

Hence, you can read about the true nature of your mind, and then cultivate meditative states to prove those teachings so that you can confirm them. There is nothing hidden in this, no dogma you have to accept that you cannot prove. *This approach of study AND practice is therefore one that can bring the highest attainments.*

As often stated, not all past saints and sages reached the same high levels of spiritual attainment. In fact, Buddhism has described ten stages to differentiate the attainment of enlightenment, called *bhumis*, that vary in terms of perfection. Many of the past saints and sages from various religions did not achieve as much as they could have, especially in the West, *because they lacked all sorts of relevant wisdom teachings that might have helped them make further progress.* While it is possible that you can meditate to cultivate highly purified mental states, starting without any expectations or wisdom teachings, and can then observe the mind and reason out its nature using your independent powers of insight and understanding that are unbiased by any previous teachings, this is difficult and requires an exceptionally talented individual. Therefore it is always recommended to study spiritual texts that discuss the true nature of the mind, and there are all sorts of topics you can study like s*amadhi, dhyana*, Consciousness-only teachings, Middle Way teachings, and so on. This is why the foundational stage of religious accomplishment is always referred to as a stage of wisdom and merit accumulation. You start by study, and you build by engaging in meditation practice.

You can start with a known result and then prove its truth through the results of meditation practice. You can also start out knowing nothing (without any assumptions) and then cultivate until you realize a result that sages have already explained to us, thus once again proving it. *The necessity for personal proof is what is key in all of this.* Like Shakyamuni Buddha said, you should not take any spiritual matters on faith or belief alone, but must prove them. "Don't even take my word for it out of respect for me," he said, "but prove everything and authenticate it for yourself."

What religious dogma can stand up to such scrutiny? Most of our beliefs that we adopt in religion are not based on reality at all, and in fact are based on totally false information. To the degree to which we accept religious ideas as true they then become true to us, and so our religious beliefs (even if based on false information and opinions) have an important impact on our lives. When we view our own religious upbringings we should not necessarily cling to tradition or to the ancients and what they said unless it is tested as Buddha said. Furthermore, we should emulate science in that if some superior understanding comes along that contradicts a religious view, we should follow that, shouldn't we?

Even if you reason out the nature of your mind through logic and intellect on your own, or even accept everything that has already been said, you must match a purely intellectual understanding with meditative accomplishments wherein the nature of your mind is directly experienced and becomes known. This is how you can correct your errors of understanding. Most of the strange philosophies in the world arise because people spin thoughts, become attached to them, but never bother to prove them. For instance, people often point to various modern Christian splinter sects to illustrate collections of unusual ideas that people can come to believe in without any proof except claims of truth, such as in Mormonism. A long habit of not thinking something wrong gives it a false appearance of being right. Accordingly, in many religions people end up holding on to all sorts of false notions and assumptions or artificial creations, and sometimes even call them "revelations" to give them an air of credibility which they lack. That cannot be the road of true cultivation practice.

Study, reasoning and logical inference are not acceptable by themselves, although they are good for a start. You must experientially authenticate whatever you reason out, and prove what the past saints and sages have told us through your own definite meditative attainments. Then the results will be truly yours. Then no one can cheat you with strange religious dogmas and false notions that lead nowhere. Then you can find personal liberation and an end to suffering, as well as the capability to compassionately help other beings. The results are all achieved in your own mind. If you look for spiritual liberation outside your own mind, it is called an "outside path."

We want to use meditation and other cultivation techniques to quiet the mind, and thereby get rid of the thoughts that mislead us about its true nature. This is simply an expedient approach we use so that we can realize the answer to the question, "What is this thing called 'mind' or 'consciousness' that we are using every day?" Somehow the answer is tied up with our concepts of self, being, entityship, existence, experience, perception, personality, consciousness, presence, "I," awareness, and soul.

What is this thing called "mind" and "consciousness," who or what is actually experiencing it, where was it before you were born (became existent), and what happens to it after you die? Prior to your conception in the womb--before you recognized your own self-existence as you did after your birth--you were in a peaceful, quiet, blissful state of non-knowingness, so why did the concept of "I exist" arise for this personal body and consciousness after birth, and where is your original state now?

If looking for these answers is not spiritual inquiry then nothing is. This type of questioning and search touches upon the foundational roots of our being. The public is rarely taught lessons that approach this great matter, and it is not taught how to investigate these questions. The religions of the world hardly ever ask you to question or prove anything, or give you a method to prove anything. However, a personal pursuit and experience of Truth is the only "great learning" we should treasure. If you devote your time to memorizing religious texts as your spiritual practice, or engaging in ceremonies and rituals of worship, this is far from what can actually win you any measure of liberation or salvation. It can only win you a minor amount of good or bad karma.

Therefore we have the practices of meditation and internal contemplation available for this type of learning. Contemplation is the type of discrimination, analysis, or investigation you perform by looking at your mind and examining it while you are sitting quietly in meditation. While sitting there in meditation, you contemplate your mind by looking within and analyzing the actual nature and doings of your consciousness. What is it? How does it function? Where does it come from? Where do thoughts come from and where do they go?

This type of observation and analysis is also often called insight analysis, inquiry, or wisdom analysis, and it means you stop focusing on external objects by turning away from the appearances of the external world to instead start actually looking at your mind itself within which they appear. You are using your mind every day, and yet no one ever bothers to look at consciousness and analyze it. People, it seems, are always focusing on the external world of phenomenal appearances that manifests inside consciousness, but never look at consciousness-stuff itself or inquire as to who is the ultimate perceiver and try to trace things back to that source. They never realize that whatever *is* cannot be anything other than consciousness, so we should examine consciousness rather than just the doings of, or appearances, within consciousness. Hence, to contemplate the mind, you have to turn away from the objects appearing in consciousness, and straightly, directly look instead at consciousness or mind-stuff itself.

As one example of contemplation or wisdom analysis, referencing the teachings of Buddhism you might sit there and try to identify which "skandha experiences" are arising within your mind, and ask how you might detach from them. You might try to notice all the separate senses operating and flooding consciousness with input (because you are seeing things, hearing things, feeling the body and so forth), and might try to discover how they are arising. You might try to think about how your body, as an appearance in consciousness, is constructed of various elements. You might try to fathom what the true nature of those elements is, in their ultimate form, if they are matter that is somehow known by consciousness.

Is it not strange that matter can be known by consciousness, and so how can that be possible?

THE "SEEING THE LIGHT" MEDITATION TECHNIQUE

Here is an example as to how a pondering can even be turned into a meditation method. You might, as another instance, sit there during your practice with eyes shut and notice that you still see darkness even though your eyes are closed. Connecting this with teachings on the seeing consciousness from Buddhism, you can recognize that the eye (seeing) consciousness is still operating even though the eyes are closed. Why can you see blackness? It is because there is an awareness of the image of blackness. That awareness itself which lets you known blackness has no color but is clear. Blackness, or darkness, is an image in the mind that is known because there is an invisible clearness that it becomes known within. To know blackness within the mind is like blackness being illuminated by sunlight radiating within space that no one can see until it suddenly hits an object and its existence thereafter becomes inferentially known.

The operational awareness of "I know blackness" has clear lucidity at the base of the realization/knowing. That clear lucidity is another term for pristine clear consciousness; because of that clear consciousness there is awareness of the knowing of blackness. We say "pristine" or "pure" awareness but awareness is pure by nature, so we really don't need that adjective. It goes without saying, but we put it in there to emphasize the fact that it's really hard to understand that this pristine empty awareness is actually there as what's really reflecting the knowing of the thoughts in the mind.

If you can realize that the empty clear lucidity is the power of knowingness, and you can then stand apart from the consciousness itself and rest in that clear awareness while letting go of its object, you have turned an investigation into a meditation method. In other words, if you can learn how to stand aloof from consciousness and just witness it with alertness, like a third person observer, you are getting closer and closer to just *being the presence of that clear awareness without pollution.* This is a great meditation practice.

There are no gradations in awareness, and no questions of pure or impure awareness. If you remain in the awareness that knows all the states that arise within consciousness, you are cultivating in the highest possible manner. This is the basis of a meditation technique called "seeing the light" or "drinking light" wherein you try to realize the pure, clear, pristine awareness that lets you see things, even blackness, and try to rest/abide in just that. You abide as the invisible witness that is like unseen light in space, and try to have your mental realm become like that.

Awareness is not a physical light, but because it is like the light of the sun which appears invisible in space, and is everywhere, the analogy of light or illumination is used to help you realize this abiding awareness you must cultivate. It's just a term for pure awareness that is clear and stands behind knowing. If it wasn't stationary and clear you could not see the world, so it is just like a stationary empty movie screen which must be there for you to be able to see the projected moving pictures.

Empty, stationary and clear, you always miss it and don't see it although you use it every moment. The whole world appears within this boundless awareness of your mind. This is what you are. It is not *out there* but rather, you are it. Like a child who is sitting in his mother's lap but doesn't see her because he is turned away from her body, you remain deluded because your eyes are fixated on the external images and miss the presence of the awareness.

As another popular example, while sitting there in meditation you can watch your thoughts appear and disappear and can then start searching for their origins. How do those thoughts arise? Where did they come from? How do they cease? Where do they go when they end? What exactly is this appearance and disappearance of thoughts we call experience? Is a thought a solid thing? Does a thought have a duration and if so, what is it? How does a thought deteriorate into nothingness? How is the perception of thoughts coming about?

You can look directly at your consciousness to answer such questions and ponder whether it has a definite form, or any form at all. If it has a form then it has a shape, so what kind of shape does the essence of consciousness have?

These are all the types of questions you can contemplate. Buddhism, in particular, catalogs all sorts of ways you can examine your mind like this.

Other religions often take a stab at some aspects of this, too. Who said you had to turn to Buddhism alone to analyze matters, or Vedanta? The questions are equally valid from any perspective. The answers must hold regardless as to any religion, too. I am only pointing out that Buddhism has a lot of literature available on this type of wisdom analysis if you choose to pursue it for the benefits it brings. Once again, Buddhism is so full of such detailed information because its teachings were given by a fully enlightened sage to a wide audience of enlightened individuals who could verify everything, and thus countless higher teachings could be given than in most other situations. If the audience is immature, however, there is very little that an enlightened individual can teach, which has been the situation that the founders of most other religions have encountered.

For true spiritual practice you must look directly at your mind and question what it really is that is giving you all these experiences. Look at it directly. Investigate it! That is internal contemplation, which is the process of trying to fathom the nature of your mind from directly analyzing it. You contemplate, or reason out, "what is it?" This is a personal investigation, and you can see there is no theology to it. There is no artificial philosophy to it either, or random speculation. You are looking for natural direct results without resorting to any artificial dogmas. The results must be self-evident without need of any strange assumptions or artificial theologies.

Where is there any religious aspect to this? *There is none at all*, so just start doing it. Even if you say you used Buddhism, Advaita Vedanta, Jnana Yoga or Kashmir Shaivism teachings to help, that doesn't mean that the search or the results are sectarian, or that what you are dong is Buddhist, Vedantic, yogic or Shaivist. You are simply being curious and scientific. *Furthermore, the results must hold for any religion, so they are not against any religion and therefore it shouldn't matter what religion you use to get started with the matter.* If you use the Talmud or Koran to awaken, then you awaken and the source of inspiration doesn't matter anymore because you used a raft to cross the river, and now you can leave it behind. Additionally, if the results of such a scientific investigation run contrary to assumed religious notions, then it is those notions which have to change just as the Catholic Church had to eventually admit Galileo was right. It is your mind you are using every day, so take some time and actually analyze this thing called mind, consciousness and self for your own benefit, and to your own satisfaction.

The inquiry or probing is very humanistic, naturalistic and scientific because you just want to see what's ultimately there behind the human being

– what's behind the "you"! To gain the highest and best fruit of meditation attainments, you should start out with the big four exercises I have gone over, but then turn to this type of analysis for the next phase of the journey after your practice becomes really good. You must really examine consciousness itself by actually looking at it like this. You have to try to develop a "wisdom understanding" of the nature of the mind, and this specific type of wisdom is called *prajna transcendental wisdom.* It is the wisdom obtained after directly looking into, analyzing and then understanding your mind's true nature. The Zen masters, in particular, talk about this a lot. Because we are talking about matters that transcend matter and consciousness, they are "transcendental." You may attain a realization or insight about the true underlying nature of consciousness and that's *prajna* wisdom.

Even Confucius said we should trace all things back to their root source to gain understanding, and through these words he was also pointing out the necessity for us to investigate to discover the nature of our mind. We use it every day, but few of us have ever bothered to look at it and truly investigate it. We turn our telescopes to the heavens, our microscopes to the world of the small, and use analysis devices on all types of matter, but hardly anyone ever looks at their own mind-stuff and subjects it to analysis. They study thoughts, as in psychology and psychiatry, but not the nature or essence of consciousness/awareness itself.

This, frankly, is why few people have ever become spiritually enlightened. People think that if you say enough prayers, do enough good deeds, follow enough rules, worship long enough, make big enough sacrifices or even meditate long enough that they will attain good fortune or go to Heaven, but these are actually just material affairs. Spiritual enlightenment is a wisdom attainment that transcends all this, even the fact of being reborn in Heaven. It requires meditation work along with wisdom for awakening. You must learn how to first cultivate clean mental states, which previous saints and sages have done through a variety of practices, and then you have to realize what it is that is being perceived, and what/who is the perceiver. Doing so, one can pass beyond the realm of phenomena to function as the Source without the stain or pollution of individualistic thoughts claiming a self-so ego.

Because self-realization is a wisdom attainment of understanding achieved after a direct insight of the result that becomes possible because of a purified mind, if you don't learn how to progressively analyze the states of purified consciousness you reach by spiritual activities of purification, you probably miss what is always right in front of you. When you read the stories of Zen masters awakening, they work for years at meditation to purify their minds of wandering thoughts, and so their mind streams eventually became extremely empty and clean. But many still did not attain realization. And then, one day, they finally relaxed and *totally let go*—like making a leap of faith to release your fingers that are suspending you from a cliffside--and suddenly realized what had always been right in front of them.

Letting go of even that recognition, they then passed through to the "other shore" of awakening to forget self and phenomena completely, and realized their unity as the original nature without stain. It's not that they became the original nature, because you and I and they are *It* already and have always been *It* from the start. This is just a manner of speaking to help you understand the topic of realization. They awoke to realize what they were, and then dropped all remaining vestiges of holding and false identification. Awareness functioned fully and freely without constraint.

They simply dropped the last notions of being an independent self which had polluted an effortless functioning. When their minds thereby became pure from letting go, they then abided in perfect spontaneity wherein they were nowhere darkened, confined, polluted or obstructed. This perfect spontaneity from perfect union with the original nature without any pollutive stain is the final fulfillment of all spirituality and all religious teachings. It is the final aspiration of all effort by humans and others to find meaning and happiness. The Bible says, "Ye are Gods," and this is being God in the manifest sense. It means being perfectly natural, effortless and ordinary. Without notions of a self, and being just what you are, the original nature is perfectly shining through every moment of beingness without stain. It is achieved through the calm extinction of body and mind achieved via the road of meditation practice.

EVERYTHING YOU EVER EXPERIENCE IS JUST YOUR OWN MIND

Let's go through another deeper example of insight analysis, or *prajna* wisdom analysis, to show how looking at your own mind and analyzing your consciousness can help you understand what it actually is.

Right now everything you are experiencing or perceiving – the room you are seeing, the body you are feeling right now, the sounds you are hearing around you—is your mind. Everything you are perceiving or knowing is happening inside your consciousness, but you forget that fact and assume it is a real world you are *directly* seeing. It is just your consciousness, and only your consciousness, that you are ever experiencing. Please stop and take a moment to recognize this – please prove it to yourself—and don't move on until you know this is so.

Everything you are experiencing through the perception of the senses, as well as your internal thoughts, is not actually an external world but replicate images seen within your consciousness, and nothing else. In fact, your consciousness is all you can ever know or experience. Whether it is a copy of a truly existing external world or not, you must admit that all you can ever know is your own consciousness. Is this not so?

Think about this for a moment. You cannot argue with this – it is fundamentally true. Is it not true that all you are ever experiencing, though it looks like an external world, is just thoughts within your own mind? Your eyes translated light into mental images, and that's what you experience internally when you believe you see an external world of pictures. Your ears translated sounds into something experienced by consciousness, and so it is really just your own consciousness that you are knowing/experiencing when you hear a sound. You are hearing something within your mind rather than actually hearing an external world. In fact, the world you are seeing at the same time is also a set of images in your head, so you are only experiencing your own mind. Even body sensations have been translated into conscious thoughts for you to know them.

You have developed this incorrect habit of perception, which has become a habitual mistaken perspective or viewpoint, that you have a mind that is looking out at an external world which is somehow separate and outside of your perceiving mind. Sorry, but the world you see/experience is within your consciousness! It is therefore no different in essence than a world seen in your dreams, and you already understand that dreams are entirely consciousness, too. Things are perceived as if they are external to you just because of habit, namely the habit of clinging to false perspectives of a "me" and "others," but they are all happening inside your mind. The things or appearances that you know are basically just your mind. They are just various transformations of your consciousness, and so the "others" are just another part of your perceptible world as well.

Thus, the whole world of "what is seen out there" is actually an internal experience within your mind. That world arises within you! If there is no mind, then the world does not arise. The outer objects of perception are appearing internally as mere mental appearances, but you mistake it for an external world rather than a mental realm. As to thoughts, they are a *direct* internal product of your consciousness, which is easy to understand, but that external world you are now seeing this very moment is also just your internal consciousness.

The world of appearances or manifestation is an internal product of your consciousness; the world you perceive is made of consciousness only, and so every item, phenomenon or appearance within it is equally the same – consciousness-stuff in some form or another. It is amazing that consciousness can take on all these various forms, but that's why enlightened masters say the mind's functions are truly infinite. Consciousness can be all these things, all these experiences. They are all just consciousness that you ever experience.

Your entire realm of experience, the entire universe you experience, is just the contents of your personal consciousness. Call it experience, appearances, phenomena, manifestation, creation or whatever; it is all just the functioning of your mind which you are knowing. It is something created by the mind. There is no inner or outer to this external world because it is all within your own consciousness. When you look at your body, that body, too, is just an experience within your consciousness. It is an experience within consciousness, *so awareness has a body appearing within it rather than that the body has awareness.* It is only because of the body that personal consciousness can arise powered by transcending infinite awareness. The right question is, who or what is ultimately doing the perceiving if this is all consciousness and there is an apparent "I" being sensed as a self which some say exits, and others say is just a collection of thoughts? What is the true nature of the perceiver and the perceiving?

Since all you are ever experiencing is just your own mind (and I am emphasizing this because it often takes years for people to "get" this point and "see" it), then right this moment everything you know, see, experience – however you wish to word it – is just your consciousness rather than an external world. There might be an external world out there, *but what you see and experience* is truly just a world composed of internal consciousness; that being the case, can you ever truly know an external world if it is all just your mind? Can you ever know an external world if the only thing you can know is consciousness, namely your own mind? No, you can only be knowing your own consciousness and never anything else, ever, so once again, *it becomes imperative to find out what/who is experiencing this thing called consciousness*—a flow of thoughts. Who or what is the "who" experiencing this?

You already know that thoughts are your own internal creation, so that part is settled. Let us leave aside the existence or non-existence of real objects on the other side of your visual, auditory, tactile and other sensations that appear in the mind. Let us leave aside the question, "What are the external objects on the other side of my consciousness? Are real objects there? Is my consciousness creating an accurate image of a real external world, or mimicking it in any way?" Let us put this issue aside for the moment and only analyze your own aspect of personal knowing. We are trying to get to the awareness that is your real Self experiencing all this, and we are going to do it by tracing back consciousness.

In terms of personal experience, you don't really know any external objects directly; you only know your own consciousness that has images within it of external objects. You think it's an external world, but now by reading a few logical sentences, which you cannot deny, you can realize this is a false assumption. This is not like Mormonism, Christianity, Islam, Judaism or other creed-communities where you must believe in something which someone else asserted. Here we just need to follow the logic and confirm whether or not it is true. The confirmation from meditation experiences comes later, for this is simply a mental exercise of wisdom analysis without yet the meditative attainments to also back it up. And yet, so far everything is true and you cannot deny anything.

Whatever it is that you think is the "you" is not experiencing a real world, but only ever experiencing a transient consciousness whose contents are always turning and transforming, never staying the same for one moment. Then again, it is your own consciousness that you are experiencing, so what you are seeing is therefore somehow part of your own being. The entire universe you perceive is within your own mind and thus is your own mind, and so the entire universe you are perceiving must somehow be you.

This is a very important realization in *prajna* wisdom analysis. The problem with human beings, though we cannot say this is true for the residents of heavenly realms if they exist, is that we don't realize that we are not experiencing an outer world but an inner world. This is because we've become trapped by attachments and have become entangled by self-identifying with what we see. We think it's a real world "out there" that we're seeing rather than our consciousness self, whatever that is. We also forget that all these experiences are impermanent and cannot stay, but we grasp at them anyway and cause ourselves pain, anxiety, afflictions and suffering in the process. We have become so lost in wrong thoughts and wrong thinking, in so many ways, that we've even lost recognition of our inherent independence from these views.

Within all our mental experiences and perceptions, there are many problems of ignorance, falsity, illogic, pollution, obscuration and attachment. One particularly large problem is self-identifying with our physical body as our self since it appears in nearly all our clear states of perception. First of all we forget that this body is an image in the mind. Then, we take our body images of physical feelings and sensations as our self. We mentally create the idea of a body self with external "others" opposed to it. This mistakenly becomes an assumed real world "out there," and the problems cascade on and on from there. It does not necessarily happen in this precise order (Buddhism, Vedanta and some other spiritual traditions fill in the details), nevertheless the problem is that the whole field of experience is only happening within our consciousness, and we become ignorant of this current understanding through false assumptions and attachments. We not only perceive this consciousness but *are it* in terms of being it. It is somehow part of us, is it not?

A deeper problem is the notion of being a self or entity. All ideas/concepts are products of consciousness, and these ideas of being an independent self, "I," being and so forth fall within this field of consciousness. They are just ideas; they are just a set of notions or bundle of thoughts. There is definitely self-awareness going on, but where is our true self behind it? What is becoming aware?

The true self or self-nature is not consciousness because we say "my consciousness," so we stand beyond it. So it's not the consciousness or mind, and that's why we assume a soul or self having consciousness. But when we look for a soul or self we cannot find one, and analyzing matters in detail (which is beyond this text) we cannot find an unchanging one either. We want to find the true self transcending consciousness that is actually experiencing everything and that gives rise to the perception/idea of self-awareness. The body we assume is us is just one tiny part of that field of experience called mind/consciousness, and the thoughts of being a self are one tiny part of that field of experience, too. Where is the true perceiving self behind this? Even if you say this is all fictional, there must be something real in all this fiction that's always flowing, so where is it?

Since the whole field of experience is our consciousness, and because we say "my" consciousness, we've already established that consciousness is not you, but somehow belongs to your true self. There is something still, silent and unmoving, something real that is experiencing consciousness which we identify as the "witness" behind everything. Isn't this so? We say "my" consciousness because consciousness is witnessed by the self. There is witnessing or awareness going on, so who/what is the witness?

Because we become unconscious during sleep (or during a coma or from fainting, etc.) after which we become conscious again, *that alternation of conscious and unconscious states implies an unbroken substratum of continuousness beneath them*. There must be something continuous, as a backdrop, to register the discontinuity of the workings of the mind. Consciousness always suffers various types of gaps and yet there is a continuity of identity that's there, and it exists because of something transcending ordinary consciousness with its comings and goings. The particular thing that knows the comings and goings of consciousness is "you," your true being or true nature. Even if we have no thoughts, a continuousness must still continue to be there for things to pick up again and if you think about it, that continuousness must be the real you.

Whether we call it pure consciousness or clear awareness or emptiness, that continuous substratum must then be connected to the true self if that is the most reducible aggregate we can find. It must be something homogenous that does not change whereas inconstant streams of consciousness appear on/in it and come and go without ceasing. Consciousness appears on/in it without altering it or destroying its purity just as an image appears on a mirror's surface without altering it in any way. Pure awareness empty of content is that body in which everything is appearing, and it never suffers a transformation of its pure nature even though what appears is also of the nature of awareness. The more empty, clean or pure the mind's mirror becomes, the more clear the appearance become, too.

Now think back to when you were a child and your body was smaller and younger. Your body has changed since then and millions, billions or even trillions of thoughts have gone by, or more! Your personality has changed and the world has changed during this time, too. Your body has aged, your memories have accumulated, habits have altered, your personality has grown up and the scenery has all transformed. Your mindstream and personality have indeed changed throughout this time so nothing has remained the same. In that sense the "you" of a personality has changed. However, throughout all this there has been an unchanging base for perception there with an insubstantial non-fluctuating nature, and that inalterable base has been serving as the constant functioning of your ever present awareness capability. It is empty in terms of having/being a body or essence that is a substantial something, such as a phenomenon, and so it is somehow like an infinite pure boundlessness that has always been there. Some schools call it "self-liberated natural presence," and it has always been there behind the comings and goings of thoughts.

Your thoughts have come and gone, but there has been something constant and continuous throughout all this time as an unchanging witness or presence. In spiritual realization we have to find that unmoving one that announces itself with the thought "I." That is the highest goal of meditation practice. This unmoving awareness, or self-liberated natural presence, is the goal of meditation practice and we find it by non-clinging to thoughts while practicing to witness them like a detached independent observer.

When you realize that all you have ever been experiencing is just your mind/consciousness, you can realize that *all* your perceptions and mental contents, including the external world you are seeing, are therefore fundamentally equal because they are all consciousness. They have a fundamental equality to them, and have all been appearing within your mind of awareness. Even your ideas of being a body or self are just consciousness rather than a realization of the real thing you are, which is what you have to turn around to find. All these things are made of the same mind stuff, and so they are equal from the viewpoint of being the same "substance." Awareness, however, is what allows you to know this mind stuff. You have to find the transcending awareness, which is the ever present natural state.

The feelings of your body, sounds you hear, images you see, and your internal thoughts are all fundamentally equal because they are all equally consciousness, and *from that standpoint nothing is more valid than anything else.* That being the case with all things experienced being equally consciousness, you don't have any need to attach to any appearances within consciousness, including the idea of being a self, since everything is fundamentally equal and destined to come and go. You certainly have to function properly and according to situations, but there's nothing that needs to be attached to more than anything else. You don't need to try to hold on to anything. What you need to know will always arise, so don't have any concerns on that part when you are trying to learn detachment. There is always going to be the birth and death of thoughts, so you don't need to attach to this realm, but you should try to find the unmoving awareness that allows you to be aware of the birth and death of thoughts because it transcends them.

There is no necessity to attach to anything because all these appearances (namely ideas, concepts, notions, thoughts, conceptions, perceptions, images, experiences or however you want to word them) are equally the same substance of consciousness, and in fact you cannot make them stay even if you try. Nothing in the realm of experience is more real than anything else, and nothing can stay, so *just keep functioning properly but let go of mental grasping while so doing*. The flow of consciousness will go on, but you don't have to grasp at it and tie yourself up in knots to experience suffering. Remain in the transcending awareness that knows and be free. In letting go, nothing fundamentally changes except suffering goes away.

There is no *real* outer referent on which you need to focus, or which deserves thought-binding attention to the extent that it obscures the source awareness. Everything seen is all your own mind known by your unmoving awareness. It is all equally unreal and ungraspable. Therefore just do what you have to do to live, and remain unattached all the while as you attend to all your affairs and duties and accomplish what you want or need to do.

As to those affairs and duties, kindness, compassion and all the other virtues still reign supreme, for **you do not want to do to others what you do not want done to yourself, and you want to do for others as you would want them to do for you**. Confucius said don't do to or impose upon others what you don't want them to do to you, which has you practicing restraint from harming others such as by using power wisely. Jesus said to do for others what you'd like them to do for you, which encompasses active ideas such as generosity and compassion. Shakyamuni Buddha said, "Don't do evil, do good, and purify your mind." Why shouldn't these still hold? It always holds! Even after enlightenment, one is not immune to karma or the necessities for good behavior.

Consciousness is a realm of interdependent origination, dependent arisings, or cause and effect, and that still holds and always will. There will always be effects to your behavior. After awakening, everything is the same as it was before except that your behavior might become better in terms of wisdom and compassion, and you will probably spend more time trying to improve it. Nevertheless, as the Zen school pointed out, to make a living you still have to afterwards "chop wood, carry water." The conventional universe does not change upon awakening, and mountains will still be mountains and rivers will still be rivers. The Zen school therefore had this famous for monks, "Before enlightenment, chop wood, carry water. After enlightenment, chop wood, carry water." You can achieve enlightenment, but afterwards you still have to do everything you previously had to in life to survive. Eat, sleep, shit, drink … it's all still there.

Now if all experiences/perceptions/thoughts within consciousness have the same equality of the nature of consciousness, there can be no genuine center to this perception that is itself a product of consciousness. The center must also transcend consciousness itself. In fact, it must be boundless if you think about, and that implies homogeneity or sameness throughout its nature. If you assume there is a center – a self – than a genuine center cannot exist within manifest consciousness because even the thoughts of being a self are within the realm of manifest consciousness. Even if you became the whole of universal, manifest consciousness itself, there would still be no center in it, and in becoming that you would have no identity as anything in it in particular. There is only the original nature itself that is the true ultimate source, and consciousness cannot know that absolute nature because it cannot turn around to look at its source just as an eyeball cannot turn around to look at itself. If consciousness tries to turn around to look at itself, all thoughts drop out and one enters a state of non-knowing. Consciousness can understand there is a source, but the source itself is imperceptible or unknowable. You can only be It but not know It with thoughts or images, nor should you try to conceptualize It.

Now since manifest consciousness is all one whole, there is also no inner or outer to it. There is no inner or outer because everything is happening within the one realm of consciousness only. In terms of your limited personal consciousness or mind, you may think you are viewing a really existent external world, but it is really just your own consciousness you are experiencing, and so all the images or pictures are within it along with your thoughts about it. They are all consciousness. *Even scientists have come to acknowledge this fact that you can never truly know an external world, but only experiences of a world that appears within your mind, and that is what you are always enjoying.*

If there are no outer referents that you are perceiving, it follows that there is no real person within consciousness perceiving them either because the thoughts of being a self are also just consciousness. There is witnessing or awareness, but no real person or things that we can find within consciousness itself when we look at and examine its contents. The thoughts of being a person or self are just thoughts, and whatever is the true self is not that bunch of thoughts. The true origin or center of perception behind everything cannot be a bundle of conceptions. Those thoughts even die out after much experience at meditation, and that proves this, too, as well as the fact they aren't needed. When that idea of being a person or self then drops out without clutching to an assumed center, and with the mental realm having had to become extremely empty in order for this to happen, the mind seems to expand and become boundless like space. But does the mind become boundless, or was it already boundless to begin with but hemmed in by thought attachments that limited it and made it previously seem bounded?

The saints and sages of countless religions tell us that the thoughts of being a person or self disappear if you practice hard enough, and your mind will become empty and boundless like space while still operating whereupon you can come to know all, but why is this so? Realizing that the idea of being a "you" within the experience of consciousness is also the same stuff of consciousness, but the real you must transcend this, the ideas of being a "you," personality or self eventually drop away just from the fact that you recognize this ignorance and finally totally let go of it. Ignorance gets destroyed when it is seen through as being untrue, whereupon we let go of those errant thoughts and the ignorance just dissolves. It is like holding a false belief, you see facts to the contrary, know your assumption you've been holding is untrue, and then those thoughts (no matter how strongly you have been holding on to them), pass away. You think you see a snake on a path, you hold to that thought as you approach the "snake," but when you get there and see it's a stick then you realize you were wrong and abandon that snake idea. Poof, ignorance departs when you wake up to the truth. You stop holding tightly to those wrong notions and they depart, dissolving away. Prior to the awakening to enlightenment, you always hold on to the idea of being a self until you one day see this isn't true, *let go* of those thoughts and awaken.

This is why people who attain high stages of spirituality – and this is common across the genuine religions--say there is truly no real thing as an independent ego or self, and why those same religions tell you to cultivate purity, egolessness, union or selflessness. They are not telling you to become selfless in the sense that it creates a new reality, but rather, they are telling you that the true nature of things is that you are not actually a small self, and thus should abandon those ideas. Those are just false ideas, thoughts, concepts or notions you should abandon, and all of them are wrong, incorrect, mistaken, errant, ignorant. As you meditate and your mind becomes emptier, all sorts of false ideas drop out, and then true reality eventually becomes known. When all falseness ceases, there is enlightenment.

So what is there to worry about when you hear that the false ideas of an ego self drop out? You simply awaken to what is true and has always been true even if you didn't previously recognize it, know it or even refused to acknowledge it, and nothing changes with your acceptance of the Truth except that you are better off in multiple ways. The world doesn't change and you don't change since you are essentially whatever you were before the acceptance of the Truth. The only thing that has happened is that ignorance departs, and *so does any of the pain and suffering that exists because of those false notions.* Your existence or functioning in the world remains of whatever you truly are, and in fact the life experience increases to a wondrous fullness and vividness never before imagined. You become a real man, a true human being who lives in the state of presence, and that is the definition of an awakened one.

You can actually experientially achieve these realizations, and you can read the accounts from Christianity, Judaism, Islam, Buddhism, Hinduism, Taoism, yoga and so on to confirm this. You discover this; you do not make this up or create this as you create other notions. You uncover the Truth; you realize what has always been rather than create a new idea for yourself that you mistakenly hold to be true.

You just need to stop attaching to consciousness to eventually experience this, and then consciousness itself will purify of all sorts of thoughts and pollutions which cannot stay since they are not real. You are not forcibly forbidding thoughts in your mind. *They just drop out from the "no effort" of resting the mind.*

Prior to this, one of the necessary stages of progress is that you must realize that everything within the realm of consciousness is fundamentally equal – it is all consciousness! That is a good starting point and is true regardless of any religious notions to the contrary, so start there. This fact even explains why a master with realization can actually manipulate the material of consciousness. It is good that you first understand this intellectually, as is being explained to you, but then you have to see it experientially and prove it. All perceptions are equally inventions of the mind, they are all constructions of/within consciousness. They are all the stuff of consciousness, and so being of the same nature of consciousness they are all of one taste. Being of one taste, everything experienced is therefore one.

It is the underlying or foundational *essence* of consciousness which is therefore important, and what you must search for, rather than fixate on clinging to the ripples of consciousness that we call thoughts, appearances or experiences. To see this and understand this equality of phenomena within consciousness experience is a definite wisdom achievement. It is an understanding of equality that there is just a manifest oneness being experienced. All sentient beings, too, are exactly equal in having the same Self-identity – nobody anywhere forsakes the fundamental self-nature for the pure ground of enlightenment shines equally in all beings. Once again, we find that the differences between things are in appearance only, rather than essence or substance, because they are all just forms of consciousness. However, this is not yet awakening because understanding the equality of all things within consciousness is just an intellectual wisdom realization prior to awakening. I can explain this with a famous Zen *koan.*

Once there were two Zen monasteries, one in the North and one in the South. A student traveled from the northern monastery to the southern monastery, where the (unenlightened) master there said, "My southern monastery is no different than the northern monastery." The student then returned to the north, and the (more advanced) master there said, "You should have told him that I am ready to enter *nirvana* (achieve enlightenment) any day." Obviously the southern master had only realized the equality of the contents of consciousness, but had not cultivated further past this to go beyond.

THE UNITY EXPERIENCE AND THE PROGRESSION OF PRACTICE

Sometimes people without any meditation efforts, but due to the merit of past lives, suddenly experience *an intellectual realization of the unity of everything* (because it is all only consciousness that you are ever experiencing), and sometimes see it as if in a vision, but then they lose it. Sometimes poets and writers speak of this visionary experience as having suddenly come upon them one day. Most who experience this view do so as a result of meditation work, and from devoted meditation practice they eventually bump into this realization as an attainment, but then they lose it, too. Other people both study and practice and then eventually achieve it as a continuous view.

There are further stages past this type of understanding. Not only do you eventually experientially realize that the idea of being an independent self/soul is empty of true existence, but phenomena are empty of true existence, too. An assumed difference in essence between sentient beings is seen as non-existent. The view of the self not only empties out, but the view of self different than others, and of phenomena as independently self-existing on their own also drops out with enough practice. The Japanese Zen master Dogen summarized matters saying, "To study the path to enlightenment is to study the self. To study the self is to forget the self. To forget the self is to reach the realization of all things. When you reach this stage, your body and mind and the bodies and minds of others drop away. Eventually no trace of (the thoughts of recognizing this) enlightenment remains, and this traceless enlightenment continues endlessly."

When you stop grasping at the ideas of being a self, the idea of "others" which arises in opposition to the idea of "self" also diminishes. *Without the idea of being a self, you can find nothing that you feel separate or apart from, and thus you eventually develop a wisdom of equality which becomes the basis of further progress.* With meditation progress from this foundation, one eventually discovers an identity as the base awareness underlying all existence. To discover that basis means dissolving attachments to all thoughts, even the thoughts of enlightenment. It's not an intellectual realization you reach because you become the basis without pollution, and simply function as what you really are. You don't actually "become that" as a type of transformation because you are actually already that – it is what we all are, so this is a manner of speaking to tell you that you shed ignorance you have been holding to from beginninglessness. The barriers of ignorance fall away and this is what you realize your consciousness or self to be. "Become that" is just a manner of speaking used in order to communicate the idea. The base nature, or fundamental essence that is the nature of awareness, is what all the sages point to as what we naturally are. At that stage of realization, you can find that phenomena are also the absolute nature, too, and you can discover how they came to be.

This realization of enlightenment is achieved through meditation work. Along this route of cultivation, as you progressively let go of clinging to your body while also letting go of thoughts, your chi and consciousness will purify due to the non-clinging, your thoughts will calm down and your mind will quiet, the thoughts of being an independent self will disappear, and then you can begin to actually experience this type of unity and equality every moment. As long as the I-sense or I-notion is still there, however, you have not "gone beyond" or transcended consciousness and the total manifestation of the universe. If you cultivate further to go beyond consciousness to where there is no mind left at all, there will no longer be any link between you and anything else. In that case, you will finally reach your original nature and attain enlightenment. How can you do this? Through no effort, through effortlessness, by being totally natural and straightforward. This is what is called having a straightforward, non-crooked mind. Simply by refraining from the wrong mental habit of clinging to thoughts you will stop holding onto ignorance and thereby, in letting it go, it will depart on its own.

It sounds so easy to attain this, since the route is one of letting go, but it is actually difficult to achieve this progress because no one wants to let go of thoughts attachments and the mistaken views which they have turned into ingrained habits. They actually become fearful of experiencing the true reality because they think "no self" means extinguishment or annihilation. Not so. Once again, you are not creating anything new, or adopting a view that is artificial. You are only finding out what is already true or so, and hence, what is the worry?

While it is true that the incorrect ideas of being an independent self drop out from correct cultivation, identity still remains. An identity still remains with our true self-nature since that is what we are. Furthermore, one becomes free or liberated in finding this identity. Since you are the original nature, all of manifest reality (consciousness) then can be known by switching the attention, and you recognize that you are this. Furthermore, as you approach these higher realizations, suffering and afflictions begin to disappear because you don't need to identify with them anymore. They occur but they don't happen to a "you," and so you can function naturally as you always would, but without undue mental strains, pains or frictions, always without mental suffering and internal peace. The *real* you is still there. However, the false thoughts you have been holding onto are gone, so you are internally at peace and free, alive every moment, happier and even more effective than other people. What harm has happened? Nothing at all. What was lost? Only the ignorance of false thoughts. What was to be fearful about? Nothing, so the enlightened always jump for joy and bow to their teachers after awakening to the Truth because they cannot thank them enough even if they had 100,000 eons to do so!

This is not fictional theory because countless prior spiritual greats have achieved this, they have reported of it, and you personally can experience it, too. The sequence is that your thoughts die down, the thoughts of being the body die down, the thoughts of being a separate self experiencing the world die down, and the thoughts of phenomena truly existing as something other than your true Self also disappear.

The world still functions as before, and everything still operates perfectly but without painful clinging or stubborn friction. You won't hold on to anything specific more than anything else appearing in the mind, including an identification with the body or idea of a self, because they are all just appearances within consciousness without any self-so solid reality all their own. What has departed was ignorance which was false to begin with, and if it wasn't false it couldn't depart but would stay. The perceiving also has no center, and thus your attachments to consciousness dissolve so that its real base can be realized. Awareness can then become universal, boundless, or infinite across space and time. It is not that awareness becomes that way, but that you find out that awareness was always like that but you bounded it by clinging to thought conceptions. Past and future can both be known to an extent that is dependent upon your stage of realization.

Sometimes people bump into this oneness experience as a vision, and realize that "everything is one," or "I am That." What they are actually saying is, "All that I experience within consciousness is just the substance of consciousness, which is just one unity because it is all a single mind substance. I am that consciousness." They therefore realize, "I and all things are one. Everything is one unity." You realize that there is no external world that you are experiencing, but simply your consciousness that you are viewing and all its contents of the universe are one whole. However, the true Self is not that universal consciousness but the absolute nature which transcends it. *That* is the *True One.* The awareness and its contents are just a function of the absolute nature or fundamental essence which is the true source or True Self.

This is just an understanding when it is not a permanent view, and many mistake this intellectual knowledge as enlightenment itself. At this stage it is just a wisdom understanding, but with enough cultivation you can eventually perceive this as a naked, direct, living experience. If you can detach from even this – consciousness in aggregate and total — so as to realize the transcendental original nature, then you can say "I am all things" and be speaking from the stage of realization. You can also say "I am always with you" or as Krishna said, "all beings worship me." They are all valid statements if you shed the concepts of being an ego-self and awaken to enlightenment to discover you are the Self of everything.

Hence, this is an example of the kind of wisdom understanding that meditation and personal cultivation eventually brings, especially through insight analysis when you actually bother to investigate your consciousness. The actual experiencing, realizing or seeing of this is not the result of "study" where you read about some fact in a book and move on after several seconds of comprehension. It's not like memorizing some facts for a school test and thinking you've got the necessary understanding. You have to think about this information to understand it, but it only becomes an insight, revelation, realization or genuine "aha!" moment when you actually truly understand it by directly viewing, knowing and understanding your consciousness by having a direct experience of it. You close your mind during meditation, look at your experiencing of your mind and ask, "Is this really so?" and then see it to be true.

As your chi purifies from such meditation practice, your chakras and channels start to open, your mind becomes clean and quiet, and if you introspect then you can actually experientially see this rather than just intellectually understand it. You realize you are the awareness that knows consciousness, that underlying awareness is non-moving and empty, and it is eternal. Since most people rarely understand this at first, they have to revisit the teaching again and again as their mind purifies until, through insight, they can get it. Hence, the spiritual journey starts right here by reading this universal result.

The importance of understanding this material is why it has been repeated for you from different angles. As an old saying runs, "Wealth and high position are just like dreams. There is no Immortal (someone who has achieved the Tao) who does not study." If you are not introduced to these things, then it is harder to detach from thoughts, and harder to make use of your meditation practice for the highest possible result, which is to awaken. Very few people have the merit to even come upon these teachings unless they cultivated in past lives, so they are rare to be found and should be protected by your own efforts.

In pursuing wisdom or insight analysis, you should inspect your mind and always ponder what it is you are really experiencing. You must prove any understanding derived through the study of wisdom sutras and wisdom teachings by directly examining your own consciousness with discrimination, and determining if what the teachings say is actually true. You are trying to determine if the teachings are true after hearing/reading the results, therefore you must check them, verify them or authenticate them with the practice results of meditation and the personal attainment of mental states of pure consciousness. You cannot take the results on faith like people do in swallowing all sorts of strange religious or political dogmas. You must prove everything with naked, direct experience.

Some discover these sorts of things on their own without being told, which means their transcendental wisdom is incredibly high, but the idea of insight analysis is that you can take the results which prior sages have left us and, using these teachings as directions to shorten the path, examine your own mind to see if what they said is truly so, and thereby jump many stages of progress. Of course, another method is to simply keep looking for the self underneath all experiences, and then you will eventually penetrate through many realizations such as this until you find the ultimate, absolute, unchanging true self basis.

To cut the time short, it's better to start with a well-known result and then use that to help yourself awaken. In any case, when you read a result like this (which you can find from studying Buddhist wisdom sutras or Vedanta teachings which both analyze the mind), you have to fathom what it actually means in the realm of personal experience. You cannot just read this, think you understand it, and move on within seconds. Please take some time to stay with these issues, which in addition to their precious value, are reasons they have been repeated.

As stated, some people arrive at such realizations through the meditation practice of watching thoughts to let pure consciousness clarify without pondering any special mental investigations. With meditation your mind eventually empties of miscellaneous thoughts running around, and then all of a sudden, because of relative mental purity, you can suddenly see something and "realize it." That is such an insight. You cannot "see the real" as long as you are looking at the constructs of consciousness, so as consciousness purifies you get a chance at experiential realizations.

Some people realize many high level teachings just from skillfully examining their experience of consciousness and questioning what this fabric of consciousness is that is there every moment of their lives. This is how the teachings were derived in the first place, which is from a combination of direct observation and logical discrimination to understand and intellectually comprehend them. Having left us those results, you and I can read such observations, understand them, and then close our eyes in meditation, inspect our minds, and analyze them according to this guidance to confirm or disprove these understandings of our consciousness.

I am hammering this home again and again because you can greatly benefit by this practice. I was confused for years on what insight analysis meant because all the books I read contained misleading translations and used the wrong words, or were so boring I lost interest or simply didn't get the point. Thus, I lost years of possible progress in being able to let go of thoughts and cultivate highly pure mental states because no one ever bothered to explain this all to me in plain English. I do not want that same fate for you so I've been giving you as much as I possibly can in such a simple book. The even higher topics we will have to leave for later.

Even if you do not pursue meditation for its ultimate possible achievements, you should still think about these issues because that consideration will, in some future time, always bear fruit. It will always bring positive results, whether in this life time or another. You therefore need to plant the seeds of pondering and aspiration now because the chances to plant such seeds of wisdom are extremely rare.

If you look around to examine what people take as religion and religious practice in this world, you will see that hardly anyone is studying these matters or practicing in a way that approaches the heart of the matter, and thus you can understand this rarity which masters always emphasize. I keep emphasizing Buddhism and Vedanta, but even in these schools the real cultivators are rare to be found. The teachings on how to find your ultimate essence, from which everything has arisen, are also not only rare but more precious than gold or diamonds or anything you can think of. People want to go to heaven, live forever, or worship the idea of a god to receive blessings, but none of these felicities will last or solve the problems of suffering and impermanence. The biggest issue of all is never resolved until you discover your underlying unity with the source nature, as the Source, because you are the Source that is empty of substance but has this inherent, self-so awareness-cognizance capability that comes from nowhere else because that is just its essence or nature. It is self-arisen beingness or presence that lacks any concepts of beingness or presence.

This is the primordial base. This is what you, I and everything else is. There are no such things as sentient beings for "sentient being" is just a figure of speech. There is no *why* to our fundamental nature of what we ultimately are either; it's just the way it is – co-emergent emptiness and awareness that is always pure, stationary, peaceful, and eternal. All the gods and men originate from this same fundamental nature, and are It. All sentient beings in all realms and dimensions are united in one fundamental identity and exactly equal without exception, without exclusion. That fundamental ground is our only true self-identity. There is thus no fundamental difference between a god, Buddha, insect and you. There is no purpose to It and no creator, but there are indeed karmic results in the realm of manifest reality due to unbreakable cause and effect in the realm of manifest consciousness, and hence it behooves us to always work at purifying and perfecting our behavior since that will be with us always.

After enlightenment or *self*-realization, for it is your true Self that you discover as the treasure, you will abide in peace, freedom, joy and bliss. Having put an end to mental projections (they just eventually die away from the correct meditation of no-effort witnessing since this dissolves attachments), you will have freed yourself from the delusions that once separated you from recognizing/realizing/being the purity of this underlying awareness. You will still know all the delusion-based appearances in the universe, but now they will arise and be perceived without attachment. Think of how much easier that is – that's the only thing that has changed. Life is still there, phenomenal appearances are still there, your duties and responsibilities and requirements for living are still there, ... nothing is annihilated except ignorance.

It may take numerous lives, but everyone will eventually become enlightened by discovering their own substance, so we might as well start shortening the journey right now because the road of suffering is extremely long and at times seemingly unbearable until our true self-nature is found. If you establish a relationship with the wisdom required to awaken, several masters have stated that this time requirement for enlightenment can be substantially shortened to *at most* three lives. However, the attainment or achievement of self-realization requires that you learn and practice meditation. It absolutely requires meditation practice, but you now have the practices necessary to begin the journey for this target, and I recommend just four of them so that your efforts are not scattered everywhere.

If not for this highest objective of enlightenment, you will still gain the fruits of the other worldly objectives if you practice meditation, and so from the aspect of the mundane world, it still offers all the benefits promised. Meditation is an incredible technology with innumerable, almost uncountable benefits.

From ancient times until today, everyone has been trying to answer questions about the self and the universe through philosophy, religion and even science, but only a direct investigation, done by you, will find the answer *for you.* Through deep meditation practice and insight analysis you can ultimately arrive at the answer, but the completeness of this particular discussion is far beyond this beginner's book. We have only been introducing the idea of *prajna wisdom* insight analysis with a few small examples to show what is ultimately possible.

Prajna insight analysis, as a path or way of cultivation, is so profound, so useful and so penetrating that it deserves a book in itself. It can lead you to finding your true self when you combine it with meditation practice that helps you first purify your consciousness of the countless miscellaneous thoughts running around. Only then, with mental purity, clarity and then careful investigation, can you actually penetrate through this haze of attachment objects to realize the self.

What I can tell you is that a final result has been continually reaffirmed by sages of countless religions who cultivate far enough. I have spent many decades collecting the writings of saints and sages and comparing their teachings with one another, as have many others. One of the commonalities is that there is no such thing as the small self, but there is a true greater Self. That underlying or fundamental True Self encompasses all things, and its realization brings peace, bliss and freedom from suffering and afflictions. Within It there are no true individualities or separate consciousnesses. There is just a total functioning through innumerable sentient (and insentient) forms. There is no "I" or "you" but all the functionings of consciousness still exist for the individual upon realization, and can be used as required, because they are part of the universe and consciousness never becomes annihilated or deleted. You are only waking up to find out what you have always been.

In fact, if you understand this you will realize that the idea "I am a living individual" is wrong right now, too. All thoughts, including everyone's thoughts of individuality, are collective thoughts and belong to the one collective manifestation of consciousness, which is one whole of creation or manifestation that is impermanent, transient, temporal, ever changing. This is continually stressed by sages as well, which is why they tell us not to spend so much time pushing for temporal riches and honor but to work on liberating ourselves to find the Truth behind these temporal things.

The first step in cultivation is to reach the stage where thoughts calm down. Next, you must disidentify from the body. Next, you must reach the point where the imputed or assumed small self drops out of your thoughts and you eventually recognize the emptiness of the pristine awareness itself. Proceeding further, nirvana and samsara are found to be no different than each other. Inherent emptiness and interdependent arising are one and the same. You discover that behind the assumed self has always been an original wakefulness or pristine awareness, without center or borders, that is all pervasive, and primordially empty, free and clean, intrinsic and self-existing complete in itself. This original nature abides beneath or transcending false consciousness and manifestation. While always transcending the birth and death of thoughts, yet it can manifest all things without changing; being temporal and dependent in nature, none of these things are real. You discover an equivalence between inherent emptiness and the realm of manifestation or dependent origination which is a realization we call enlightenment, or self-realization.

RELATIVE NAMES AND LABELS LACK ANY TRUE REALITY

Your consciousness is therefore essentially the same as a turtle's consciousness, or the consciousness of a ghost, butterfly or Buddha. It is all consciousness-stuff in total that you believe has been segmented out into separate independent pieces, but only because you cling to imaginary barriers of your own making. Drop those barriers, those artificial constructions that you furiously cling to, and the underlying all-consciousness can be known.

As to the individual personal consciousness that you are now experiencing, what's being perceived in that consciousness are relative names and labels (definitions) we have made up ourselves that all depend upon one another. They are relative interdependent definitions that work perfectly for helping us navigate the world, but they have no fundamental absolute validity in themselves. They are just experiences/appearances within consciousness, identities we have assigned for ourselves, and thus not the real thing we are after. They point to an impermanent, transient, ever changing world that is itself a construction of the mind, and which lacks self-so validity.

As humans, we have created a false world all in our heads. As children we start creating and then eventually share many of the same names, labels, words or definitions for similar experiences, but the net of interlocking relative definitions we build up – what is blue, red, hot, cold, love, hate, space, time, consciousness, magnetism, electricity, atoms, etc. as just examples – are totally dependent upon one another without a single one resting on an absolute basis. They are also interdependent arisings. Nothing has a self-so nature that is independent of everything else and not defined by the co-existence of everything else. And neither the individual names or labels, or this whole interdependent net itself, ever ultimately rests on (revolves around) anything that can be called an absolute standard. This is the filter through which we view the world, which in turn becomes yet more of our own making when we add in personal likes and dislikes and memories of other experiences that are thrown on top of any clean perceptions that greet us.

In other words, we build up a net of internal definitions within consciousness that are mutually interdependent or self-reflexive, and thereby create a system that "works" but it lacks any security of an absolute basis. It is all just a large set of fictitious constructions within consciousness, like the illusion of a giant net floating in the sky, and we revolve around within this self-created net of dualistic names and labels while mistakenly calling it reality. It operationally works because everything is connected through interdependence, and thus this explains why there are cause and effect laws of functioning that link everything together, but we go too far in calling it reality. Everything we presently experience as an appearance in the mind is all just a set of names and labels we create within this interpenetrating net of relative definitions that has no solid ground to stand upon.

Anything you try to grasp in this net is not what it was a moment ago because things are always changing, and not one moment of time reveals anything of stability. Therefore everything you ever experience is not only impermanent, but *ungraspable* and impalpable like a dream, mirage or illusion. These are all good examples of unrealities, and the waking state is actually an unreality just as well.

You are actually rotating between expedient names and labels in your own self-made interpretive perception of the world, these names and labels and definitions lack any absolute reality of their own, and it is really all just a construction of your own mind that you are experiencing. You are not the forms you perceive or names you construct but stand alone, shining independently, unconditioned by names and forms. You must find *that unchanging one* which transcends this moving realm of births and deaths. That is your true self or true nature.

What about the "I" that sees this or experiences the world? What you think of as the "I," ego, soul or entity you take as your small self, when analyzed, is also just a set of names and labels (ideas and conceptions). It is also just a bundle of networked thoughts within consciousness, a self-reflexive creation of relative name and labels all bundled up together and to which you cling. That net of interdependent definitions through which we experience a world is composed of an agglomeration of interlocking, interconnecting experiences that lack a true self-so center. We are seeking a homogenous thing beneath them that never changes as your true self, or real I because the constituent parts that make up a sentient being lack a self.

When people always call themselves a personality, soul, being, entity, ego, *atman* or self, they are always trying to refer to something that they somehow know must be a homogenous beingness. These terms therefore cannot refer to the physical body, or even some type of higher "astral body," because it is not homogenous but made of parts. The body is not one thing. It is a unity or agglomeration of different pieces. The *real you* cannot be an agglomeration of parts but must be one single entity, wholeness or unicity, otherwise we have not reached its ultimate substrate nature. If it was a composite of parts, rather than a homogenous whole, you could progressively take away the parts or separate them, and then you would not have a permanent self. We are looking for something fundamental or foundational that is an unchanging homogenous whole serving as the true self. Everything else we can find, not being that permanence, must be an agglomeration of transitory parts.

The real you must be something that underlies all the things that change, so it must be something stationary, eternal, permanent and unchanging. We're therefore looking for one homogenous substance that never changes and that is the real you underlying this idea of a soul, entity, ego, being, self or life. There must be an underlying substrate that is absolute, foundational *and final* beyond which you cannot proceed further.

The search using meditation and inquiry – to find this underlying one—is what spiritual striving is all about. It is not about subscribing to some religion or theology. It is not about rituals, dogmas or disciplinary rules, but about *finding the unchanging real nature of what you call your "self" by discarding everything that is not your true self.* You let go of *what is not you*, you let go of falsity, you let go of ignorance and errant views and what can depart and you are finally left with what is true, real and unchanging because it cannot be discarded, cannot leave, cannot be reduced further, cannot depart.

Your true self cannot be thoughts because they come and go; they only appear within consciousness to your awareness. Your true self cannot be consciousness because you say "my consciousness," so your true self must have consciousness as one of its functions. As explained, the real you, "I," self, soul, or entity cannot be a composite agglomeration of parts either. The real you must therefore be something unchanging, whole, and permanent rather than a fictional relative construction of names and labels, something impermanent that moves, or a composite agglomeration of parts.

Think about it – is the *real you* something that has parts, or should it be one whole solid thing? It must be something whole and homogenous without change, and pure in nature throughout its wholeness. That requirement for changeless unity or wholeness means it must be infinite (because that's the only thing which satisfies the requirement), and because there is no change it must be eternal (because any change would mean impermanence). If it had edges or borders that would mean it could change, so through analysis we just figured out it must be infinite, boundless, eternal, permanent, pure, and unchanging. Is that God? The Eastern spiritual schools call it the original nature, *dharmakaya* or True Self. If you say it is God, why do you then think of God as a person or being, which clearly this is not? Somewhere your ideas and notions have become mistaken, and now is a chance to correct them.

All spiritual practice is aimed at having you attain a direct experience of your/the underlying absolute nature that is pure, unchanging, eternal, infinite, real. It is sometimes called Truth. Sometimes it is called Self. It is empty of all phenomenal substance, which satisfies those requirements since all substances are impermanent, inconstant and conditional. It has the capability of awareness or knowing, which is why appearances arise and we seem to exist, but that awareness is empty and unchanging ... which satisfies our criteria once again. It is *pristine* or *pure* fundamental awareness that is complete in itself, beyond the realm of thoughts and conceptions, and yet it can give rise to appearances without ever changing or losing its purity. This is the fundamental nature, original essence, or true self.

This absolute foundational self that sages discover and then teach about is indeed single, pure, motionless, homogenous or unity. It is "pristine awareness" because it is empty and clear but luminous in the sense of possessing the functioning capability of awareness, cognizance, illumination or wakefulness. It is therefore the nature of awareness, or pristine awareness that is empty. It is infinite and has always been, and thus is beginningless, unborn or unproduced, and since it never actually changes it remains unmanifest and unknowable by thought as a vehicle of seeking.

This is your true self rather than any consciousness or bundled agglomeration of things that give rise to consciousness. You are seeking a direct experience of *This One*, and you can definitely arrive at this through meditation. Enlightenment comes from meditation practice, achieving higher stages of mental clearness or emptiness that are states of pure consciousness, and probing those experiences with wisdom, analysis and understanding to ultimately discover that the ultimate perceiver is this self-illuminated One-Without-a-Second.

THE HUMAN PATH

Enlightenment is therefore a wisdom accomplishment of discovery. You see the truth of that reality because you have a direct encounter with that Truth, and you recognize it. After this recognition, you can let go of all your concepts of a small self and self-contained personal existence and start to proceed effortlessly forward from there.

There is no theology or religion to this quest. There is no philosophy, political theory, or social theory in this at all. Not only can you experience this, but all the logical discussions about its nature (of which I personally might not have been very good at expressing) match up perfectly without any holes or deficiencies, *unlike the artificial dogmas proposed by various religions.* The search for who and what you ultimately are is therefore a very natural and scientific investigation, and requires no prior special assumptions. You don't have to abandon logic as you must in various religions that tell you to "have faith and just believe." You do not have to wait until an afterlife or wait for some special time in the far future to understand this or realize it, but can awaken right now if you choose to cultivate the path of meditation to its fullest extent.

Just as sunshine melts the solid ice of a lake to reveal the water underneath, meditation will melt the ignorance that obscures the recognition of this ever present empty clear base of awareness. In history, countless individuals, both Eastern and Western, have found this base after cultivating their mind. It is a non-denominational finding, and to find it is to become enlightened to your own essence. To realize the pure ground of enlightenment is the goal of all spirituality, not just Buddhism, Taoism, Confucianism, Sufism, and Vedanta. As the Fifth Patriarch of Zen said to the Sixth Patriarch after his enlightenment, "All your spiritual striving and practice, all your religious activities and moral activities and cultivation are useless unless you discover This."

This is what everyone is after on the road of spiritual striving. If you believe in such a thing as evolution, this is what you get around to finally realizing after deciding to purify your mind and behavior but it does not just occur to you for you must cultivate to realize it. Your accumulated merit may afford you opportune circumstances to both encounter the teachings and to cultivate, but to realize it always takes cultivation effort and striving.

Once again, there is no theology, faith or belief involved in this investigation, which is why it frightens the orthodox religions which have created all sorts of artificial dogmas they impress upon people – it's just a scientific investigation that is followed through to completion, and it all starts by investigating the mind. If you only investigated matter you would never find the ultimate source of consciousness because it transcends matter just as it transcends consciousness. In looking at matter you are looking at the wrong direction. The most you can do with matter is keep dividing its particles into smaller and smaller units until you find an emptiness like space that in its purest form is ultimately empty of everything, so is non-moving and perfectly pure because it is empty of self-substance. You can, however, quickly find It by tracing consciousness to its source. This route is valid because consciousness is of the same nature as the ultimate self.

You must have a deep urge to know your self, and therefore start to trace consciousness back to its absolute roots to find *This One.* If it was impossible to find the final substrate then that would be fine, but countless individuals from different traditions have discovered – *continuously over time* — that you indeed can trace things back to an everlasting, absolute, final substrate that has awareness as its nature. We are that base awareness; there is no "we" in actuality because all those individual ideas of being a separately existing "I" are just false thoughts that screen our recognition of being It, and what we take as our independent selves are all that one beingness in manifestation.

Actually, we are the absolute nature that has awareness as its function, but I always word this loosely to bring you further along. There is in actual existence only one thing, and we can discover that we are that one thing and can understand what it is because we have knowing. We are *the* primordial pristine pure consciousness that sees itself as personal consciousness, and consciousness knows through thoughts of understanding. We can have thoughts of understanding of what we truly are, and thus awaken. We can have a direct experience of our inherent emptiness-awareness, conscious recognition of that, and then awaken.

That is what you are, and finding it, you find you are everything. You can know reality to the fullest extent. Shakyamuni Buddha explained all the omniscient qualities you attain by achieving this realization, some of which enlightened masters often display for our benefit, but they never go overboard with this in order not to mislead people into thinking that cultivating these powers, or the phenomenal world, is the way. In teaching, enlightened sages often explain having the ability to understand the mental perspective of others, meaning they can know the minds of all beings (what they are experiencing as if inside them). It is because a sage is all beings (the source of all beings), and because all beings are just the one pure consciousness, that this is possible.

There are no beings; everything is just that one foundational awareness-essence. So you are all beings, too, because you are this universal awareness appearing in the guise of a being and taking yourself as that assumed being because you wrongly cling to that identity. I am trying to wake you up – you are the original nature! The fundamental nature is what we are and what the manifest (and unmanifest) universe is as a whole, but being consciousness we have mistakenly come to believe we are these separate individuals because consciousness has become entangled in false thoughts and the source of that consciousness has become screened by incorrect fixations on the false.

We are speaking of the omnipresent root source of matter and mind with innumerable functional capabilities. Penetrating through to this source, which some call God since it underlies all matter and mind, we say you attain self-realization and become a saint, a sage, a *jnani*, a *mahatma*, a self-realized one, an enlightened individual, true man, or a "Buddha." The pathway of investigation and then realization to find our source or true nature *is* the spiritual path for human beings. Think about it … what else would it be, especially with countless saints pointing us in that same direction?

After self-realization, many enlightened individuals often teach out of the compassion to help alleviate the unnecessary suffering in the world. Everyone teaches in their own individualistic fashion, in response to the needs and circumstances of the times, and eventually the common people wrap those teachings with expedient structures in order to keep the enlightenment teachings alive with a vehicle of transmission. Usually these teachings, because they are so high, become lost.

The most common structure of preservation is the one of religion, but over time its original purpose gets lost, and other things get mixed in and attain prominence. Certain teachings attract an independent following and eventually take on a life of their own. Dust collects on all things and as time goes forward, expedient guidelines become fixed rules of behavior, and personal cultivation effort is replaced by the activity of worship. The original impetus is lost and a priestly class takes over. Religion eventually mixes with politics and the end result is politics. In time, the original body of teachings becomes embedded with all sorts of other stipulations on human affairs such as diet, marriage, clothing, politics, warfare, ceremonies, and behavioral rules of comportment and so on.

These are all expedient teachings rather than absolute rules that must be followed, and they have nothing to do with the main goal which is to find your foundational true mind, non-transformational true self, your underlying illuminating nature. Smart people see through all this other stuff and say "orthodox religion is bullshit," but they, too, tend to miss (or dismiss) this fundamental, natural human search for the ultimate essence of the human being – the fundamental self-nature. They recognize that organized religion is like a slave master, but they themselves also eschew the practices of meditation and the personal striving for awakening.

This search for the Source is non-denominational and the result is non-sectarian as well. It is a universal result common to all sentient beings. *It should be that way.* There should not be a special salvation for one specific people, or to people who hold to a certain belief, do a certain thing, worship a certain way, follow a certain teacher, and so on. The Path should be universal. If there were beings on another world and it didn't hold, or if it did not include the realm of animals, then it cannot be a true path of liberation. If it did not encompass both great wrong doers and saints, or hold in the past before religious teachings were given, or hold for people who could not possibly even even know of the teachings, *then it cannot be a true pathway of liberation, salvation or awakening.* Think about it. If your religion requires such things, it is absolutely incorrect and artificial in its doctrines. The organized religions don't tell you this, or ask you to think about it, because they fail this test most masterfully.

This searching for the Source nature is what it's really all about, and meditation is the method that starts you on this journey. Everyone has the Tao and everyone can awaken if they simply learn how to rest their mind, and that resting is not an artificially derived activity. This world is lucky that we therefore have enlightenment teachings left to us by the awakened. Rarely will you find a realm where this search can be most fruitful such as in this world where there is a mixture of good and evil, joy and suffering, and the incentive for awakening. The first stage of the process is to help you quiet your mind, and whether you want to proceed further after that it is all up to you. Even should you decline to start actively investigating your own consciousness using internal contemplation, once you learn to quiet your mind from meditation you will begin to reap all of the physical and mental benefits previously mentioned. Meditation practice is a win-win situation no matter how you look at it.

During this investigation of self-discovery your chi will start to change, your energy channels will start to open, you will become healthier, mental problems will disappear, your personality will soften, your reaction speed will increase, you'll have more energy, your body will become warmer from the better circulation, internal health problems will begin to heal, your wisdom will blossom, prejudices and negative self-talk will drop away, and you will begin to experience peace and tranquility even in the midst of the difficulties of karma. You will learn how to detach from pain and suffering so that you always abide in a state of internal peace while handling the difficult affairs of the world that always surely arise.

Some people will attain special clairvoyant abilities, or the ability to see past and future lives, or special gong-fu that lets them demonstrate extraordinary physical powers and abilities. These are all possible functions of the mind, but not the original nature. What seems supernatural is just as natural as anything else, only it involves a deeper layer of physical reality. These are all non-denominational results of cultivating your chi, your mind and the deeper functions of the mind. With progress in meditation, you will be able to banish wandering thoughts so that you can concentrate on anything with clarity and patience, and therefore you will also become able to achieve more than was previously possible when you set your mind on accomplishing any task. Hence, the benefits of meditation pertain to both the mundane and spiritual realms.

The typical pattern of meditation progress is that people start doing a meditation practice, and start clinging to some quieter mental state they reach which they equate with empty mind. They're actually engaged in a habit of conceptualizing and then clinging to this quiet mental state but don't know it, and practice session after practice session they continually cling to that state of mind. That's why they never make quick progress – because they're always clinging to either the body or contents of the mind including concepts of emptiness. Sometimes they even try to suppress thoughts in order to reach a state of emptiness or quiet, and that's wrong, too.

How can you break this practice? By studying wisdom texts that tell you that you are doing this, and trying to take those realizations and incorporate them into your meditation practice. Studying helps you learn new techniques or insights that propel you out of the mental rut of clinging, and thus one cannot dismiss its importance. I am trying to give you as many pointers for studying, and introduce to the critical topics in as many different ways as possible, so that you might blossom in this regard.

TRY TO ROTATE YOUR MEDITATION PRACTICES

One of the things that you can do to help break the habit of repeatedly holding on to the same state, besides conducting *prajna* wisdom analysis to analyze your mind, is to *shake things up by trying a new meditation method every week*. Every week you can add a new meditation method to your schedule, and then change it the following week. You should try to maintain a set of basic meditation practices all the time, but introduce a new one every now and then to help keep things fresh and vibrant so you don't fall into a rut with your practice.

If you practice the several different meditation methods I've already laid out, you will find that they each attack the objective of quieting thoughts from a different working principle, and this principle of trying a new method every week, in addition to your basics, will help *rotate you through different methods that might just be what you need to provide the breakthrough you want for your practice.* You never know which meditation technique will help you reach a breakthrough, so my advice is to always practice a simple set of meditations out of the basic four (mantra, anapana, visualization and watching thoughts), and rotate a new one every week that will help you realize what is emptiness or empty mind. You want a new method that will shake up your clinging and help you to finally attain a state of no-thought.

You don't have to practice the basic four meditation practices every day or every week, for you might not have time. You might choose to focus on only one during a week, or even month, or four month period. Since mantra practice can be done at any time, I should amend that to read that you should always practice "two methods" instead of just one. The point is that you don't have to try to use every meditation method in existence, and try them all simultaneously. Stick with two or more practices as your foundational basis of meditation work, and try to work in a new method now and then as you progress, and to make more progress.

There is a very famous book from Kashmir Shaivism called the *Vijnana Bhairava*, which is readily available in print, and it lists over one hundred different meditation methods you might try as you implement this idea of a fresh method for a weekly rotation. For instance, it might say there is empty space within a jar, and that you should try to experience what your mind be like as the emptiness of that empty space. It might say to try to concentrate on following a certain sound, to try to experience a mind that is like a cloudless sky, to contemplate that the same consciousness exists in all bodies, to realize that sensations are just consciousness alone to detach from them, to contemplate on envisioning the universe as being filled with effortless silent peace, to concentrate on the space between two ideas, and so on. There are all sorts of meditation methods within this book designed to help you gain an experience of emptiness, after which you will progressively learn how to let go of thoughts and practice more correctly. You should simply try one new method per week from this ancient book while maintaining any other meditations you already practice.

By honestly following the instructions of a new method each week, you will more easily cut off the habit of clinging because you will never give yourself a chance to settle into any mental state that is not truly empty, and in this way your practice will always stay fresh and ever progressing. That will keep you from forming an attachment to a mental image of emptiness and thereby speed your practice tremendously. If you are serious about meditation, *you will shave off years of practice time if you do this.*

This is all you really need to know: (1) you should engage in a standard set of practices on a daily basis, and have an extra one that you swap out each week so that it forces you to try yet another proven means for emptying the mind, (2) you should mix the study of meditation matters with your practice, like mixing flour with water to produce bread, and (3) you should at times try to conduct a wisdom inspection of the nature of your mind using the guidance of various wisdom spiritual paths, such as Buddhism and Vedanta. Unfortunately, most people don't want to practice, but just want to think about enlightenment.

I highly recommend that people read the recent Advaita Vedanta masters of this era, such as Ramana Maharshi, Sri Nisargadatta (and Sri H. W. L. Poonja among others), so that they can clearly understand the ultimate purpose or target of meditation practice, but to especially study Mahayana Buddhism for the full details of meditation practice and the path. Then, of course, you have to practice meditation. Mahayana Buddhism is called the *wisdom path* because it teaches you how to analyze your mind and provides all the detailed understanding of cultivation practices and results you might seek. You must therefore read these special books, which take you far beyond this small one, if you want to conduct wisdom investigations of your mind's true nature.

While I encourage you to study the teachings of Vedanta to help understand the right view, the problem with most students studying Vedanta today is that while many attain the right understanding about the Self or original nature, they never move on to the stage of deep meditation practice. They remain satisfied with intellectual understanding, and never progress to prove and authenticate what they think they understand. Like bookworms, they just remain learned intellectuals that understand the path but who have no actual achievements and never move onto genuine spiritual practice to purify the mind and behavior. Of course, this is better than most practitioners who simply study religious texts that lack attainment possibilities, and better than traditions that don't present the right view to adherents at all such as the fact that one is special, destined, chosen, select or saved via belief or via membership within their group. Not only errant, such views give rise to great prejudices and evils that end up being committed because of false views. Nonetheless, having the right view is not enough because you need to mix having the right perspective with actual meditation practice, and must work to *prove* your understanding on a very deep experiential level through actual attainments. Then you and the saints, sages, holy ones, or Buddhas become one and the same, which, of course, is just a manner of speaking since you already are the same.

Intellectual understanding is not enough for anything in terms of spiritual accomplishment, and is not a spiritual accomplishment. Playing with words and concepts, definitions and logic will not bring you emancipation. You need to meditate to experience directly the nature of the mind. So while most people who study Vedanta finally attain the correct view of the spiritual path, few meditate to authenticate it and yet the proving, with the achievement of enlightenment or self-realization, is what the path is all about. In short, you cannot succeed with just study alone but must always mix study with personal meditation practice!

The situation reminds me of the story of the two brothers, Vasubandhu and Asanga, that comes to us from ancient India. One of these brothers chose the route of deep intellectual study rather than the route of meditation efforts for his spiritual practice. That was Vasubandhu, who became a great scholar, was undefeated in countless debates, and wrote many books explaining the dharma. But even with his high learning and his ability to beat anyone in debate, he made a great mistake in understanding the dharma. He realized this when he met his older brother, Asanga, who had spent twelve years rigorously practicing meditation every day and eventually achieved enlightenment through his efforts, which is the actual purpose behind all the study after all.

Realizing this, Vasubandhu regretted that he had spent all his time studying rather than working at meditation efforts. Scholarship and intellectual study may win you understanding and worldly glory, but Vasubandhu never achieved self-realization while his brother who devoted himself to meditation practice did! Another life, and another opportunity was wasted when he had all the ingredients necessary for possible success. Take heed of this example; do not waste your life on pursuing trivial things, do not lose this precious opportunity and squander your life but strive to awaken.

That is actually your situation right now if you are reading this, so pay heed. You don't need anything more than what this tiny book offers to get you started. Honestly. You have more materials available than many religious greats had when they started upon their quest, and you even have a bit of knowledge about the highest views people attain.

This idea of the inadequacy of study alone is an important lesson that has been hammered home time and again in many religious traditions, and especially in Zen Buddhism. You have countless people in the Western religions who study holy texts, memorize their words, attend religious ceremonies and worship activities, strictly follow religious rules of conduct and discipline but who never meditate and probe their own minds to discover what consciousness is, where it comes from, and who is the ultimate perceiver or experiencer of the mind. That's the important thing because everything else is what Buddhism calls "expedient means." Without that type of contemplation conjoined with meditation efforts to realize one's fundamental face, they never attain much spiritual progress.

There is another aspect to this story that most neglect to note, and yet which ties in with this topic of study and practice being matched with one another. Because of his meditation achievements, Asanga had attained many superpowers, such as clairvoyance, while his brother simply had cultivated great worldly learning. The two were both invited to a wedding feast one day, and the bride and groom asked them to divine the appearance of a calf soon to be born.

The older brother, using some degree of clairvoyance, looked inside the pregnant cow and said the calf would be born with a white spot on its forehead. How could this be wrong? The scholar brother, Vasubandhu, on hearing this said that the calf would be born with a white spot on its forehead or on its tail because he knew, from intellectual knowledge, that the tail rested on the forehead when a calf was in the womb. So he amended his brother's forecast.

When the calf was born, despite Asanga's clairvoyant abilities, it was Vasubandhu who was found to be the winner of the contest because the calf was born with a white spot on the tail. He won because he mixed worldly learning with the results that came from meditation practice. In a way, you can say he mixed study or theory with practice, understanding with practice, or wisdom/intellectual knowledge with practice results. The lesson is that the two must be mixed together, and you must always analyze the results of meditation with balanced science and logic so you don't go far astray. That is the right wisdom approach which you should do with anything in life. Meditation and its results should not be considered anything in the realm of the mystical, superstitious or mysterious.

Meditation can win you enlightenment, but enlightenment does not make you immune to mistakes. An enlightened individual can still make all sorts of mistakes. One also still needs to study to make the right decisions or be able to do great things in the world, and you must still cultivate wisdom or understanding for how to do things to create the best possible outcome. In some situations there is no such thing as a solution without a loser, and you must stand up for what is right. The ultimate wisdom is actually knowing how to solve situations in an ordinary way using the things at hand, and so you eat if you are hungry and sleep if you are tired. You are just natural in response, and this is the highest effective skillful means. What is virtuous does not conform to any set standard, but is what is right for the situation.

As to our story, the younger brother Vasubandhu had taken the results provided by someone with meditation talents, which he did not necessarily trust, and mixed it with his worldly knowledge and understanding to produce the correct result. As the story demonstrates, understanding and practice must be mixed together for the highest effectiveness, just as water and flour must be kneaded together to make dough and then baked to make bread.

Your meditation practice should be accompanied by study, and so I encourage you to read various spiritual books that explain all the aspects of meditation practice and its results, especially those that orient you to the right view. Many such sources are available from a wide variety of traditions and time periods, but if you limit yourself to Western religious sources you will surely come up lacking.

8

DIET, DISCIPLINE AND DETOXIFICATION

There are several issues that continually come up when people are just starting to meditate, and one of the big topics people ask about concerns diet.

Many people wonder if they need to become vegetarians or vegans to maximize the benefits of meditation and spiritual practice. The answer is no, but what a complicated topic this is!

To be sure, eating less meat is usually better than eating more for most people, and is usually not only healthier but a compassionate solution to much of the suffering we cause in the world. We should be eating mostly plants rather than animals, and more leaves than seeds if at all possible. Many masters have stated that being a vegetarian is the most compassionate path in life, and that being a vegetarian actually helped them with their meditation progress. Many have said they felt lighter from eating a vegetarian diet, and that their mind was clearer because meat seemed like a poison to their body.

On the other hand, many ordinary people will claim they cannot feel any mental difference whatsoever from being vegetarian or vegan, but they just don't have any energy when they try to live on a meat free diet. In fact, some people lose their health because they cannot practice these types of vegetarian-vegan diets correctly. The vegetarian or vegan diet then becomes a difficult issue because it becomes a matter of health and having sufficient energy for life.

Of course, most people are "body insensitive" in that they cannot feel much of anything in terms of either external or internal energies, so a portion of these remarks must be discounted. Most people can sense when they have a lower energy level, but few can indeed tell when their body is changing or has changed, and few can feel any energies traversing within it. As with athletes, some who are sensitive can feel an energy loss after sexual relations and others feel nothing at all, therefore there are different degrees of sensitivity for everyone. Most people are just not sensitive enough to realize anything, so the issue often comes down to health and having enough physical energy.

Many nutritionists and naturopathic doctors in the U.S., where people are prone to incorrectly practicing a vegan or vegetarian diet because of the lack of a strong cultural knowledge base, have told me that American vegetarians who come to them with sickness are often so weak or depleted from practicing vegetarianism incorrectly that no healing protocols can help them get well unless they return to eating meat for a short while. Therefore the issues of energy and illness both arise once again.

I have personally seen people whose wounds would not heal because of situations like this. Many vegetarians refuse to eat meat even when they have to recover from serious illness, and in those cases these health practitioners tell me they simply cannot help these individuals heal at all, and turn them away rather than accept their money. This deficiency scenario does not often happen in cultures where people practice vegetarianism correctly, but often occurs in cultures where people don't know how to be healthy vegetarians. If you don't know how to practice vegetarianism correctly, that wonderful desire can harm both you and your practice.

The more important issue is one of wisdom—that this type of stubborn refusal to do what is necessary to get well flies in the face of wise living. In life and on the meditation trail, compassion and wisdom must be balanced. You should never just blindly follow stringent rules that are imposed on all circumstances without flexibility. Hygienic and dietary rules, for instance, are always made by man (despite references to a higher source) and should follow circumstances, so nothing should remain inflexible.

For instance, Shakyamuni Buddha once said that if you need to eat meat as a medicine to get well, to refuse to do so is actually a violation of the discipline of the path. In Judaism, if a medical cure is non-kosher you are also violating kosher rules if you refuse to take it to get well. People think this is paradoxical, but that's because they are not using their wisdom mind and understanding but simply insisting on following artificial man-made rules for life. In life you should not live by religious rules but by the wisdom of the circumstances. Rules are only there as helpful guidelines. Men make these rules to help guide others to healthy ways, so they are not to be considered infallible injunctions by masters or from Heaven but most people are too ignorant to understand this.

Once again, the problem for unhealthy vegetarians arises from the fact that many vegetarians do not know how to eat in a healthy way (and therefore lack iron, vitamin B12, sufficient protein or fat intake in their diet), and if you get weak or become sick on the path because of your diet, then as the near death experiences of Milarepa and Shakyamuni clearly illustrate, you need to return to health and get well in order to attain enlightenment.

Enlightenment is rarely achieved by the sickly because you need your strength to succeed. Then again fasting, as these two individuals did, allows all your chi energies to be devoted towards transforming your body rather than to be diverted to digestion. Fasting can often be a great aid to meditation practice when your practice stage is high enough, and it tends to cut down on sexual desire, but no one should ever take fasting to the extreme that they die from it. Some religions incorrectly promote this as the proper route to take, but this is wrong.

In some areas of the world, a strict vegetarian diet is also simply not possible due to the general lack of food, which is why Tibetan Buddhists have traditionally eaten whatever food was available regardless of whether it was meat or not. In other areas of the world, such as the Nordic regions or the Arctic where Eskimos live, the gene pool has evolved in such a way that fish or seal blubber are absolutely essential to the diet for people to survive and feel well. How can one be a vegetarian there, or follow any religious diet when the paramount need is simply survival? You cannot.

One therefore cannot just insist upon a strict rule of vegetarianism without taking into account individual and group circumstances; it is thus best to avoid the common mistake of religions that turn everything into unbreakable rules to be followed. The dietary rules of various religions were developed for a particular time, place and culture to help people because human beings, in general, usually do not know how to manage themselves and conduct themselves in life with wisdom. Hence they are only to be considered helpful guidelines that incorporated basic understandings of hygiene and health.

In truth, it is your merit to have meat available for eating, but you are also earning merit by refraining from eating meat. Perhaps the best rule for today's world where protein and mineral intake (such as iron) is sufficient is that eating less meat is better than more, but for some people a totally vegan or vegetarian diet is impossible and not even healthy. In short, you cannot create any ironclad rules but must proceed by wisdom, which includes appropriate care for your state of health and energy needs. *The issue needs to be approached with wisdom.* For instance, many who have lived in religious ashrams have noted that few of the residents were strictly vegetarian, and the elders within them occasionally instructed the residents to eat meat for their own health. It all comes down to practical concerns. One must act with wisdom for the health and continuation of one's life.

Even if you eat meat, there is a big difference between animals raised with hormones and those who were fed natural diets in free range environments. On the scale of what meats are best, it is often said that fish is better than fowl, which is in turn better than lamb, next comes beef and then finally pork (which is worst of all). There is also a saying which aptly runs, "Eating what stands on one leg (plants) is better than eating what stands on two legs (fowl) which is better than what stands on four legs (lamb, beef, pork, etc.)."

There are a number of other helpful dietary rules encompassing food wisdom that we should try to follow and even teach to our children. For instance, organic food is always preferable to non-organic food if you can afford it. You should eat mostly plants, especially leaves. One should try to eat as many different colored vegetables as possible because those different colors represent a diversity of phytochemicals your body may need. In addition to different colors, you should also eat as many different plant species as possible, for variety is important in supplying different nutrients as well. You should only eat foods that will eventually rot, otherwise you will be ingesting preservatives or chemicals that will do who knows what to your own body. Every now and then you should eat some fermented foods such as yoghurt, kimchi, or sauerkraut. Another well known rule is to stop eating before your stomach feels full, always leaving it a bit empty. Eat slowly, chew your food, and eat less. In terms of liquids, water is certainly better than sugary drinks, and cold drinks hurt the stomach.

These guidelines are simply ideals, and must be matched by the pragmatics of money, availability, time and circumstances. There is an old maxim in the nutrition field that while you should strive to maintain a clean diet, you must not repeat the religious mistake of becoming so fervently strict with dietary rules that you cannot sit down and enjoy a beer and pizza now and then. Furthermore, there are countless health conditions impacted by the diet, and numerous illnesses that arise because of poor diets which require special diets containing or avoiding special ingredients. If your diet makes you ill, naturally this will have a negative impact on your ability to cultivate. Therefore moderation and balance, rather than inflexible extremes, are the principles you should use to guide yourself when it comes to eating. You can find many commonsense guidelines for healthy eating in Michael Pollan's book, *Food Rules*.

In addition to the topic of vegetarianism, there is also the issue of fasting that often arises. As a general rule, we are a prosperous society that tends to eat too much, and eating too much tends to increase our sexual desires, especially if our food is brimming with hormones. Fasting is beneficial because it gives your digestive processes a chance to rest and allows all your chi energies to be devoted towards transforming your body rather than be diverted to digestion.

Fasting is often a great assist to your health and meditation practice when your practice stage is high enough. It can help extend your life span and give your body time to rest and detoxify. But even for fasting, as for the diet, one must also practice it in a reasonable way and not go to extremes. Every practice on the spiritual trail needs to be balanced with wisdom, and so moderation, rather than going to the extreme in any direction, is the general principle to follow when it comes to the diet and fasting. With this in mind, the religious idea of starving oneself to death as a spiritual practice is clearly in error.

SEXUAL DISCIPLINE AND SEXUAL PRACTICE

Now the same requirement for the need of wisdom and discipline holds for sexual conduct on the spiritual path. Many people wonder whether it is necessary to be celibate in order to make progress with meditation. Is celibacy absolutely necessary and essential for spiritual progress? Is there any conflict with sexual relations and spiritual striving?

If you start to meditate, your yang chi will start to stir and then finally arise, prying open and then passing through your chi channels. All the stages of this process typically promote sexual desires. The arising of sexual desire as your chi ascends happens for everyone, men and women alike, including individuals who have taken vows of celibacy. No one is immune. This is just a natural principle for human beings: with the stirring of your yang chi comes an increase in sexual desires.

There are actually two types of sexual desires: mental desires and physical sensations. While it is easy to ignore the uncomfortable physical sensations that give rise to mental desires, if one gives in to the mental states of sexual desire then sexual activities are soon to follow. If you give in to sexual desire and then lose your chi energies through ejaculation (male), those energies won't be available to open your chakras and chi channels. Your chi is the energy that opens your chi channel orbits, so even when people practice sexual relations it is important that the man does not ejaculate too frequently and thereby lose much of his chi and semen. Since women do not lose as much chi through orgasm as men (largely because their bodies are designed to absorb energies), this injunction does not hold for them.

How to balance the body and mind when sexual desire arises is therefore one of the main hurdles to spiritual practice and progress, and the key is to either cut off the mental desires when they arise so that consequences do not go further, or balance the body energies so that the rising energies can be handled without emission or loss and thereby remain inside to help transform the body even more. If one can harmonize the body, this is the perfect solution, and one will find *exercise or pranayama techniques helpful in this effort.* One can also sometimes use sexual relations themselves to harmonize the body, too.

The principle in this type of sexual effort, called sexual cultivation, is to harmonize the energies of the body to a state of comfort by harmonizing the internal chi flow through sex, while not losing energy in the process. Once again, the principle of non-ejaculation for men therefore holds. A rudimentary understanding of sexual cultivation is that the proper practice of sexual activities can cause internal energies to flow smoothly throughout the body's chi channels, sometimes even opening chi channels or pushing the chi through channel routes just recently opened, and thereby help to harmonize both the body and mind. If you can reach a state of comfort that way, and can let go, you might have an opportunity to cultivate mental emptiness with this technique.

Your chi energies arising from meditation are meant to open up your chakras and channels, which are obstructed just as arteries and veins get obstructed by plaque and cholesterol. When those energies start working through your channels the friction initially gives rise to uncomfortable feelings, which some try to solve through the avenue of sex. These energies often feel especially uncomfortable at the earliest stages of the path because at that time the nerves, muscles and channels receiving the most attention are usually in the lower torso of the body. Your chi energies, when you begin to meditate, try to push through the obstructed channels near the bottom of the spine, root chakra and in the waist, which are all near your sexual organs. Hence, people will feel uncomfortable pressure in the genital regions (and elsewhere as well) when their energy starts to rise due to meditation, and this often leads to sexual desires.

Those energies often increase sexual desires, and so the problem and quandary always arises. To give in to sexual desire brings release from the pressure, but that release of pressure means that you lose your chi and generative energies. Therefore, there is no further progress in opening up your chi channels or in getting rid of the very desires that plague you (which tend to go away as you make more progress). Nevertheless, if one can learn how to have sex in a way that harmonizes the body's feelings without energy loss, this can then become a form of cultivation hat can be of some help.

As explained in my book, *The Little Book of Hercules*, if a woman engages in sex and experiences an orgasm she doesn't lose a fraction of the energy men lose through ejaculation, so orgasm is not as detrimental to women as semen loss is to men on the spiritual path. The vagina tends to absorb energies because of its design, so a woman has fewer problems than men when it comes to sexual orgasm. On the other hand, if men lose their rising cultivation energies through sex or masturbation, they tend to lose a lot of energy and that energy loss will definitely hinder their practice because it won't be there to open up the chi channels.

> Does it mean you absolutely cannot have sex on the spiritual path? No.
>
> Does it mean that sex is bad for you? No.
>
> Is there anything wrong, evil, dirty, immoral or shameful about sex at all, or something to feel guilty about? No.
>
> Does it mean that refraining from sex will cause you to succeed in achieving the higher goals of meditation and spiritual cultivation? No.
>
> Does it mean that refraining from sex is bad for you? No.
>
> Does it mean that engaging in sex is bad for you? The principle of wisdom once again holds in that any activity taken to an

extreme, including sexual activities and relations, can become harmful depending on the individual and the situation.

Do men lose energy through ejaculation? Yes, though not all will equally feel the energy loss, and various age groups are in general affected differently by the energy loss.

Do women lose energy through orgasm? Yes, but not to the extent that it is a problem as it is for men.

Will avoiding the loss of one's generative forces help preserve a healthy body? Yes—especially if the restraint is naturally accomplished without force. If you can retain the vital force, and not let it leak out through overindulgence in sex or by wasting energy, it can accomplish wondrous things for rejuvenating the body.

Are there times when celibacy will help with your meditation efforts? Yes, absolutely.

Does that have to be all the time? No.

Are there some situations where sex might help you with your cultivation practice? Yes, if done in the proper fashion.

If you are celibate, how will this help your meditation practice? If you try to let go and cultivate emptiness and abstinence simultaneously, then your internal energies can accumulate and finally pierce through your obstructed chi channels. Celibacy, when matched with meditation practice, helps you achieve this most quickly. Celibacy without meditation practice only accomplishes a little along these lines because you don't cultivate the necessary mental emptiness that leads to chi channel openings, so the results only appear as better health and longevity.

If you are older and have lost a large degree of your vitality, how do you regain your vitality to succeed? Meditation with abstinence will eventually restore your vitality, and some measure of youthfulness, despite advanced age.

Should you ever try to absorb the energies of your partner to supplement your own or absorb back your own energies during sex? No. This cannot be done and the effort is harmful to both yourself and your partner.

Is energy loss through masturbation worse than the energy loss from ordinary sexual intercourse? Yes.

As you can see, there are many issues one could discuss on this complicated topic, each of which could become a book in itself. These questions only introduce the tip of the iceberg of issues that must be considered.

Other factors aside (the difficulty of relationships, the possibilities of pregnancy, etc.), the main issue is essentially one of energy loss and the need to transform the energies and obstructions inside your body. To counter the problem of energy loss, many men wisely learn how to have sex without ejaculation, which is to the benefit of both parties. However, they need to learn how to do this in the *correct way*, for most teachings on non-ejaculatory sexual relations are incorrect.

Most people don't know that while there is an emphasis on non-ejaculation in these lessons, the whole purpose of sex is to bring about a balancing of the elements of the body – a harmonious body feeling because the internal chi flow has become smooth. If they are engaged in overly strenuous activities, there will be too much energy loss just as occurs from too much physical exercise or exertion. If they miss the principle of cultivating a harmonious relationship, pleasant experience and peaceful mind during the sexual relationship, they also achieve nothing through their efforts. Sexual relations should certainly embody nice, pleasurable experiences for couples, and can have a higher purpose than just being marathon sessions of jamming and poking, as portrayed in pornographic films, that simply end in excited release.

As an example of some incorrect notions on non-ejaculatory sex, men are often taught to press on their perineum right before orgasm. However, if a man tries to press on his perineum to prevent ejaculation, as is often taught, he can hurt his bladder, prostate and kidneys. This often happens to men who do this frequently. So there is a right way and wrong way to practice non-ejaculatory sexual intercourse, and the majority of ways taught are not just incorrect but actually harmful.

The correct ways for a man to avoid ejaculation during sex primarily involve that he manage his breathing and movements so that he does not rise to the brink of orgasm. In this way, he can prolong his sexual activities until both parties feel calm and comfortable, and both parties can then cultivate a peaceful comfortable state wherein they can forget their body and mind because of good chi flow. Men and women must both manage their breathing and movements so as not to arrive at orgasm too quickly, but the secret key for men is to learn how to manage their breathing to avoid ejaculation. There are some tricks such as looking upwards while curling ones toes back and forth, and silently voicing a "*sss*" sound with a slightly open smiling mouth, as the urge to ejaculate rises and one wishes to break it, but the essential method for prevention is breathing and stopping before reaching a peak.

This is a far cry from the sex we see in movies where partners are trying to reach a frenzy of excitement through all sorts of unusual positions and strenuous movements. What we see is not necessarily a nice, pleasurable experience that can possibly lead to the cultivation of one's chi and channels, or which doesn't involve much loss of energy. Oral sex, as another example, often produces release but can rarely produce an internal comfort of smooth chi flows throughout the entire whole body. To be sure, there is room for countless forms of pleasant play in sexual relations, but when we are talking about sexual cultivation, the principle is to bring about internal comfort and harmonious chi flow within the entire body along with the mental, emotional and spiritual harmony between the parties that one would naturally expect in such a relationship.

If your chi flow becomes smooth, your body feels comfortable, and your mind becomes empty and relaxed, you might be able to forgo clinging to that state (if your chi and channel cultivation has progressed far enough) and become able to recognize the bodiless clear awareness that knows the mind and body, but which is not whatever it knows. It is a clear awareness that stands behind thoughts and consciousness. If one just rests in the comfortableness of sex during and afterwards, and clings to the body and mind during sexual activities, nothing much is accomplished other than the usual results one would expect. If one can detach from the body because one has become very comfortable because of sex, and if the mind has simultaneously become empty while the channel flows have been harmonized, then one can be cultivating the channels at the same time one is cultivating open awareness. If one can enjoy the sexual relationship as the clear pure awareness witness, which is always detached, this is higher still.

All during the sexual relationship one should not become robotic or like an automaton. "Detached" does not mean divorced from normal human relationships, and it does not mean suppressing whatever emotions (or sensations) normally arise either in order to be "pure" or "clear" or "empty." These are mistaken notions about the correct route of cultivation. Natural reactions and emotions should always hold and you should never attempt to wipe them out. All the normal human emotions proper to a caring sexual relationship should still be there. One should strive to be cultivating the awareness which stands behind the mind, which you can only realize in a state of non-clinging when your chi channels are opened. Naturally, only cultivation adepts can do this, but this is the ideal.

One does not use the other party just for sex or just for cultivation either, but simply uses sex as another possible method, within the whole repertoire of methods possible within this world, to cultivate one's chi flows, channels and mind for further possible progress. No method is good or bad, it's humans which make it so. Sexual relations are therefore just another opportunity for a certain type of meditative cultivation, and if sexual opportunities do not exist (you can see that countless individuals do not have spouses in the world), one need not pursue them. In short, one does not need to be celibate to succeed in cultivation, nor does one have to be a monk or nun to succeed. There are no such restrictions, limitations or stipulations. In the old days, many laypeople attained enlightenment even though they belonged to wealthy and honored circles, including mixing with entertainers, so it is wrong to assume that the occupation of a monk or nun is best. It is all about your determination and how you practice.

Some men in Asia practice hanging weights from their penis, thinking this is sexual cultivation, but this is also an incorrect notion. Several surgeons have told me about the countless surgeries they have performed because men have torn tendons and ligaments in the sexual organs from such practices.

There is also the issue of sexual discipline, abstinence or celibacy when it is not accompanied by meditation efforts. Without meditation, sexual discipline (refraining from the loss of semen) indeed leads to a healthier constitution and helps increase longevity since your energies are retained rather than lost. However, there is very little transformation of generative force to chi. Therefore there is very little opening of the chi channels in the body as compared to celibacy combined with meditation practice. There is indeed a beneficial effect, but not as much for spiritual progress when one maintains their celibacy accompanied by meditation efforts. In light of these facts, when celibate religious officials refrain from meditation exercises it is really unfortunate. When they don't practice meditation, they incredibly limit the potential of their other spiritual practices. If the partner isn't already a cultivation practitioner with some gong-fu under their belt, they don't really have the requisite foundational basis for joint practice.

In sexual cultivation, on the other hand, the idea is that your body already has attained a smooth circulation of chi from meditation practices, which is why the partner is paramount for such practice. Sexual cultivation is really only truly possible if two individuals are themselves ardent meditation practitioners who have already cultivated their chi and channels to a high level, and then the practice can bear the best fruit. Ordinary people who do not meditate can imitate the technique, but it really only pertains to cultivation practitioners since they are the only ones who can feel and adjust their own chi and channels. However, the principles can certainly be applied within the realm of ordinary human relationships. If one goes looking for a sexual partner for cultivation practices, however, this shows the desire is for sex rather than sexual cultivation because it can only be practiced when there is a prior relationship of mutual harmony, trust, understanding and karmic relationship.

In sexual cultivation, one tries to use the thrusting (exercise or movements of sex), and attendant happiness and joy of sexual relations to not only create inner harmony, but to ignite your chi and further clean out your chi channels. That is one objective for practice, but not all. One tries not to drop into sexual desire during that time but maintain awareness and watch one's mind as one reaches a state of comfort. You can definitely set into motion a mutual circulation of comfortable chi flow when sexual relations are done in the right way. This can open up chi channels, bring a calming of the breath and relaxation wherein you forget both your body and mind, and whereupon you can realize emptiness just as with every other standard meditation technique. The comfortableness achieved through sexual relations can therefore afford an opportunity to cultivate the detachment of empty awareness that sees and knows but does not attach. Hence the entire practice avoids the principle of mental clinging, which is the antithesis of most sexual relations since they are based on the strong force of lust and longing which grab the mind.

The use of strong or gentle thrusting during sexual relations is not the issue, for both are used since it is a matter of sexual technique. Every individual is different, so what is right is what is individually required to move the chi and bring about inner harmony. The issues are the mutual circulation of chi brought about through sex to make one or both parties comfortable *without excessive energy loss*, and the possibilities of achieving a mental state free of worries and concerns that can find emptiness and relaxation at that time. This is the right approach and right way to proceed, and the most that can be discussed in a book.

Making food and making love turn out to be two of the most important things in life, yet few know how to make these activities into medicine. Practically no one in the world is meditating, but everyone is eating food and making love. Both can be used to help transform your physical body when done correctly. Both can be used to help calm your mind. But will you put the time in to learn how to do them properly?

Making love, as a physical activity, is perhaps the only practice that non-meditating people will ever encounter that can help them cultivate their chi channels a little bit, and because of the required interrelationship with the partner, sexual relations often help them to become better people, too. However, practically no one knows how to actualize the possibility of chi and channel cultivation through the medium of the sexual relationship. Such is the karma of the human being condition.

No cultivation method in the world is superior or inferior, right or wrong, but it is just that human beings misuse various techniques. There are lots of ways to misuse sexual cultivation practices, which are certainly difficult to practice correctly. Thus, celibacy is preferable for most cultivators because few are qualified with the necessary wisdom, merit and cultivation basis required for joint practice, and celibacy avoids many difficult issues which most cultivators don't want to become involved with. However, if one is already married or involved with a relationship, the option to improve one's sexual skills by applying these principles to their practices definitely becomes possible.

You need to know that the difference between celibacy, and celibacy coupled with meditation efforts to cultivate an empty mind that does not grasp, is like the difference between a pot of water that evaporates slowly, or is made to boil so that it evaporates quickly. In both cases the water evaporates but the slow method does not produce any power that can be harnessed. In the case of steam produced by a fire, there is a release of power that can be harnessed to do things if it is kept within a closed system.

In terms of meditation practice, the image of steam coming off boiling water reminds us that we can experience the opening of our chi channels and eventually a *kundalini* awakening if we refrain from losing our energies. Just as in the production of steam, the "warming" effects of meditation release internal chi energies that will open up your chakras and channels if you refuse to let them leak. On the other hand, if you practice celibacy without meditation efforts it is akin to water that evaporates very slowly to accomplish little. To be sure, the chi channels will also open a bit from a route of sexual restraint without meditation, but at a much slower pace. This slow pace is a result of celibacy unaccompanied by meditation efforts, and is a contributing factor as to why the ordinary celibate religious functionaries in many religions attain no great spiritual progress at all.

As the lives of great individuals like Moses, Abraham or even Confucius illustrate, you can still attain the Tao if you marry and lose your internal energies through sexual activities, for this is the natural path of human beings. However, the breakthrough may come at a more advanced age when you lack relevant meditation teachings and forego any concentration on meditation practice. You have all the helpful materials in this small book to practice meditation with intensity if you choose, and these examples prove you can still attain enlightenment even if you are not celibate or even if you start practicing meditation at an advanced age. You therefore do not have to avoid marriage if you want to make progress with meditation and spiritual pursuits, but can even, as explained, use marriage or cohabitation to your benefit because it affords you yet another possible way, through sexual relations, to help cultivate your body and its inner chi channels.

Often you will see monks and nuns in various traditions who have been celibate through the sheer force of will power to suppress desires and practice restraint, but who have not cultivated a realization of mental emptiness and thereby transformed their energies. In those cases, you may often see a shriveled countenance, rather than fullness in the face or a facial shine, because they never learned how to transmute the energies to end up cultivating their chi. (When someone transforms their energies and opens their chi channels, their face always appears bright and full.)

Those who purely practice celibacy or chastity like this, which the Hindus call *brahmacharya*, will always experience health benefits to the extent that they do not suppress their internal energies but let them internally flow everywhere, even though it may be uncomfortable as the channels thereby open. Whenever anyone retains their chi, this retention will help to open up internal chi channels, which is why the Asian medical schools insist that celibacy often leads to better health and longevity. The problem occurs when people maintain these energies but suppress them from arising, because of will power, in order not to experience sexual desire. That is the wrong approach to handling the situation, and causes eventual problems.

Another common consequence of monks or nuns who try to be strict with sexual abstinence by suppressing desires is that they end up trying to protect themselves by shielding themselves from people. They become afraid to face people, and therefore even shun people or start to hate them. They can become odd, isolated or lonely individuals because of this wrong approach to discipline.

For those who never solve the problem of sexual desire through the cultivation of mental emptiness (cultivating an empty mind), but who practice forceful restraint, yet another difficult problem can often arise in subsequent lives. Due to the forceful restraint they applied in this life without learning how to let go and cultivate emptiness so as to transform consciousness, they will still have sexual desires because they never purified the roots of the situation. Their solution of forcible restraint is like putting a rock on top of weeds. This may cover the problem temporarily, but the weeds will not go away because their roots are not destroyed. In fact, those weeds will often start growing up around the rock, which is why many male religious functionaries start pursuing other males since women, in their mind, are forbidden. The same goes for their pursuit of children instead of women – it is all because they have not been taught the proper principles for handling sexual energies. They have these various religious injunctions on sexual discipline and restraint that they must adhere to, but don't know how to transform their bodies and minds.

The strict discipline of sexual abstinence as a spiritual practice may lead to good fortune in subsequent lives, but after that good fortune is used up – like an arrow shot into the air which eventually falls to the ground – you have to start all over again, so who can say it ultimately produces good fortune? Unfortunately, most religions never truly face these difficult issues of sexual desire or want to discuss how to solve them.

Unfulfilled desires, held back due to forced restraints, can lead to all sorts of depravities when you finally have the opportunity to be free of those constraints and act without reserve. It is challenging for humans, having the bodies of animals with urges, to solve these difficulties concerning sexual desires and approach the problem with wisdom. In the present life, the forcible suppression of sexual desire usually breaks down after awhile, and then surges up into a bonfire of lust. In subsequent lives, sexual desires are often amplified for those who previously practiced the restraint of holding back through sheer force of will but who never solved the root of the problem by working to transform their consciousness. The individual felt unfulfilled, and so those urges within consciousness continued forward. In subsequent incarnations those individuals often tend to excessively pursue sex, in order to experience what they forcefully denied themselves, because those thoughts were always retained within consciousness and those urges will therefore manifest again. When given the right opportunities or circumstances, they then tend to go overboard.

Ask yourself, what has been accomplished if you do not learn how to dissolve the problem at its root by cultivating meditation and the transformation of your chi and consciousness? The only true cure to the problem of sexual desire is meditation that purifies consciousness and the urges within it. As you make more meditation progress and open more chi channels, the problem will become less and less over time. It will become less because consciousness purifies, or empties out, because discipline becomes easier to maintain, and because a healthier body will have smoother chi flows and less uncomfortable feelings that give rise to sexual desires.

Since the root problem lies in the mind, when it comes to the practice of celibacy that is where you should put your efforts to master the problem of retention. In cultivating your mind (consciousness) through meditation, you will also be cultivating your chi and the problem will lessen because of the subsequent transformation of your body. In time, as you start achieving a degree of mental emptiness, you will start purifying consciousness and end up tackling the problem at its root. This, of course, requires a commitment to meditation practice because without meditation it is difficult to calm your mind to the point where thoughts subside and you can realize the inherently empty nature of the mind.

As stated, one can even use sexual relations to help speed the transformation of your physical body (the opening of your chi channels) when it is pursued in the right way, but this is only possible for ardent cultivation practitioners with high wisdom. In everyday life, the effort must go into learning how to detach from thoughts and let go when sexual desire arises, but not suppressing those energies because they have work to do in opening up your chi channels. Those energies are involved with the yang chi or *kundalini* energies necessary for cleansing your chi channels, opening up chakras and harmonizing your body's five elements. Therefore you must not cling to your sexual thoughts and let them lead you elsewhere, or you will lose those energies. On the same lines, you should not stimulate sexual thoughts, such as by constantly watching internet pornography, for you will certainly end up losing your energies from this route as well. One of the benefits for going into secluded retreat to practice meditation is that you can separate yourself from these various influences that lead to sexual desires.

The correct practice, which is only initially a bit uncomfortable for those not used to it, is not to let those rising energies carry you away and pull you into sexual activities, such as masturbation. Masturbation, or other sexual activities, are the result of attaching to thoughts ("following thoughts") and letting them ensnare you and control your actions. Rather, you should let go of the energies you feel and thereby let them continually transform your body by opening up your channels, even if this is initially uncomfortable. You must learn how to detach from the body, which isn't you, and successfully disidentifying from the body involves recognizing that the body is not your self. Since the body is not you, but just a phenomenon appearing within your consciousness, you do not have to act on all its impulses but can learn how to ignore its various energies, pulls and sensations. This is difficult to do, but such independence can be learned after sufficient practice effort.

Now in certain humid climates and in certain other situations, the uncomfortable feelings of your body can often be quickly alleviated through (non-ejaculatory) sexual activities or sexual cultivation because they help move your chi when it seems stuck. There are various conditions such as this where the chi channels within your body become much easier to open, and the chi flow becomes easier to harmonize, by using the energies stimulated through sexual intercourse. The internal movement of chi brought about by sex can indeed restore a great degree of internal comfort, if sufficient time is taken to produce chi flow harmony, which is why sex is often considered medicine for the body and can become the basis of a cultivation practice.

The more one cultivates, the more one becomes able to externally feel the internal energies of one's partner inside their own body, and can thereby know how to move to help adjust the obstructed chi flow regions through massage and lovemaking activities. However, few can practice this correctly. It requires sufficient non-ejaculatory skills for the man, prior chi and channel cultivation to a high level, prior knowledge of what emptiness is, an understanding of the aim of harmony and smooth chi flow for the two bodies, an understanding of other details about the method and its objectives, and non-clinging throughout the passion. More often than not, the weather also often plays a factor in what one can achieve through these efforts. As previously stated, in muggy or humid environments (whereupon the body often feels stuck or the individual groggy from the sluggish internal circulation of chi), it is difficult to open the chi channels and transform the body, which is often helped by this remedy.

This is another reason why many masters who succeeded have often lived in dry, arid regions. In dry regions the external water element does not hamper the body and produce uncomfortable feelings of internal chi stagnation. The wind (chi) and water elements of the body are always seemingly fighting one another until all the body channels open and the body is transformed. Through cultivation you seek to create a harmonious functioning balance between the body's elements, but humid environments often dampen the internal circulation of chi. Thus the weather, and one's environment, can make it much easier or more difficult to succeed in meditation.

Certain areas in the world, especially mountains with "good cultivation chi" as their *feng-shui*, have climatic conditions that make them sought out for cultivation progress. Many countries have such auspicious regions, though some are better than others. To feel this type of chi helpful for meditation, one need only visit the four holy mountains in China (Wutai, Omei, Jiuhua, Putuo) for comparison purposes. India has certain areas with excellent cultivation chi as well, and so do various regions within the Mideast. However, just because a region is considered "holy" or "sacred," it does not mean that the chi in the area is good for cultivation regardless of what a spiritual tradition or promotional bureau may say. This is a large mistaken assumption that many often make. In short, it is truly difficult to find a good place to cultivate; many other factors must be taken into consideration other than the fact that the area has good chi.

As stated, the body at times will definitely feel uncomfortable due to the rising of chi, which might prompt thoughts of sexual desire, and as a life skill you just have to learn how to handle this problem with skillfulness. It cannot always be handled through sex, nor should it be. There are breathing practices, stretching and movement exercises, or meditation and detachment practices one can turn to. One can even alter their diet to reduce the problem in the first place. The highest method is to detach from the body and its sensations, and cultivate the root source of the mind. These efforts, because of the resultant chi flow, will return order, harmony and balance to the body and tend to purify consciousness so that the problem decreases.

If you refuse to attach to these energies and ignore the sensations of pressure that arise with sexual desire, this method, because you leave the energies alone, will allow them to open up your channels and achieve an inner harmonious circulatory flow in your meridians that is absent of obstructions or restrictions. This is the objective you are after whether you use sexual activities or not, and sometimes it is far easier and far less complicated, and the results are usually far better, if you just learn how to let go and achieve these results through meditation without sexual involvements. If sex was the cure all and end all then all past masters would have recommended it, but this paucity of discussion and actual warnings about sexual relations suggests just the opposite. In fact, there are *many* warnings as to the opposite. The correct idea is that sex is NOT the cultivation path or a form of spiritual practice. Nevertheless, in this modern world of readily available sex of all kinds, you need to know about this topic because it is a life issue. You should always strive to elevate your life skills and bring them more in line with becoming more helpful activities.

Thus, as a meditation practitioner, it is beneficial to learn how to continually release the sexual tension within your body and mind without succumbing to suppression as a means to thwart sexual energies. The pressure you feel when the chi channels start opening, which entails the chi pushing through various obstructions, is what often causes uncomfortable physical feelings or urges. You may have this strong feeling that you want to push energy through the pelvic region, and so you seek sex. This is especially true for men since most have never learned to hold their energies long enough to effect these chi channel openings. The longer you are able to do this, however, the less the problem becomes over the long run. However, there is a misguided push to encourage masturbation in today's world which relieves the pressure but doesn't solve any problems. The modern idea of teaching and actually encouraging children to masturbate is incorrect. It is not that it isn't a common tendency, but that it is not to be overly promoted or encouraged. With such a mistaken emphasis, not only will the health of males slowly deteriorate from excessive abuse, but rarely will any males develop the detachment skills that will help them improve their health and succeed in spiritual pursuits.

If you let go of sexual energies they will eventually help your body transform, and as your channels open and your chi purifies, your mind will get even quieter during your meditation practice. This is a natural process, and progress naturally builds on itself until more channels open and the problem finally no longer exists. The idea of mentally cultivating emptiness, which means knowing your thoughts but not clinging to them or trying to suppress them, means to recognize that there is sexual desire but to remain detached from it and not get swayed by it. You should avoid following it to its natural conclusions when the pressure builds. If you occupy yourself with other activities until you fall asleep, by the next day the pressure has usually shifted because the energies within can harmonize while you sleep. As with dealing with *logismos*, there are many strategies that can be employed to help someone master retention. The famous Christian monk, Saint Francis of Assisi, during wintertime would go out and lie in the snow to help cool his body in order to deal with sexual desires, but you do not have to resort to such extreme remedies when you use wisdom.

When you succeed at retaining your energies, then your channels will eventually open because you don't give into expelling those energies, and because your channels open the pressure you experience will become less and less over time as you learn to master this. This is a life skill one should definitely set out to learn; it is not just a skill meant only for meditators and spiritual cultivation. Even the skill of learning how to have sex without ejaculation will serve both partners well because it can enable them to prolong sexual relations, and that extra time might allow both parties to reach a higher state of pleasant inner comfort and a better relationship of togetherness. Sometimes there are no obstructions in the body, but it is just that the chi flow is temporarily hampered and needs a boost, and in those cases non-ejaculatory sex can often prove quite helpful, too. As often stated, you need to learn how to adjust your body yourself which extends to the topics of food, exercise, diet, and sexual activities.

If you are a celibate man and practice abstinence, you can also lose semen through wet dreams, and in that case the **Flying Bird Form** performed before bed time will help you avoid this type of leakage so that you can conserve more energies for cultivation progress. In this practice, performed three times before sleeping, you first stand straight and erect with your hands at your sides. You slowly inhale deeply, drawing the air into your lower abdomen, while lifting your hands above your head and simultaneously raising yourself on your toes. As you inhale and raise your arms above your head, you also gradually look upwards to those overhead hands where they eventually touch in the air above you. You will often feel the energy of your breath run up your spine into your brain as you inhale deeply and raise your body on your toes. After standing on your toes and looking upwards for several seconds, holding your breath deep within, you slowly descend with a slow exhalation that matches your descent while lowering your arms to your sides once again. You repeat this three times or more before sleep.

Wet dreams represent the loss of some of a man's generative force, but since this occurs naturally without our control it is nothing to be overly concerned about. It is the body's natural solution to a problem. It simply means a person's energies have become full, but have not yet become transformed, and thus they overflow rather than open up more channels beyond what they already have opened. The problem of wet dreams decreases as an individual opens their channels and gets better at meditation practice, so the solution in the long run is more meditation practice. Nonetheless, the flying bird form technique, practiced three to five times before sleeping, helps to eliminate the problem for those who become overly concerned. When one practices this form they can feel the breath rising into the head along their spine, and this tends to create a pathway to eliminate the problems of overflow.

Many of the problems with sexual desire arise because of our original topic of the diet—we're eating heavy meat diets rather than being vegetarians, and meat diets typically stimulate sexual desires and lead to more sexual activities. In today's world we are not just eating meat but ingesting high levels of stimulatory hormones at the same time. Furthermore, we are being exposed to incredible amounts of mental sexual stimulation everywhere we turn in life such as in the movies, radio songs, and on the internet. All this bombardment of sexual imagery helps to constantly promote sexual desires within society far beyond any levels known in the past. If you can avoid some of these forms of stimulation in the first place, sexual desires won't arise as frequently, and so the problem will be somewhat reduced. But in such a stimulatory environment that we now have, who can learn how to reduce their desires without the proper teachings and guidance?

When I look at world diets increasing in meat and hormone consumption, and see people surrounded by increasingly graphical stimulatory depictions of sex on the internet, radio and television, and see the pace of life increasing wherein people seek sex as a necessary outlet of relaxation to be able to handle it all, and understand that individuals don't even have time to meditate anymore, I shed a tear fearing that fewer individuals will be able to succeed at cultivation in the future. Hence, I am giving you the concentrated gist of many teachings so you can accomplish as much progress as possible given the unfortunate circumstances of our present day.

Sexual desire is one of the top reasons men fail at their cultivation, for they don't know how to handle the increasing levels of stimulation they are now exposed to. If you can throw yourself into breathing exercises, martial arts or yoga stretches, or other forms of joint and muscle exercises when sexual desire arises, this can also help alleviate the discomfort because you will be redirecting your energies elsewhere. The problem will hence dissipate. Many people throughout the ages have noted that physical exercise reduces sexual desire because those energies are diverted elsewhere – into building the muscles. Eliminating certain stimulatory foods from the diet (such as garlic and onions) also tends to reduce desire, as does becoming a vegetarian or reducing one's food intake in total. However, these are not long term solutions which can cut off the root of the problem.

If you are married or have a partner, the problem can be skillfully handled, as stated, through learning how to have sexual relations without ejaculation. This is called "sexual cultivation" when the right principles are applied, but most people do not know how to perform this correctly, as already discussed. In the final analysis, no matter what methods you employ, the solution involves some form of meditation practice. Even tantric pictures of male Buddhas with female consorts include other symbols pointing out the necessity of prior meditation practices before one can use this type of technique. The practice of mental detachment from desire leads to eventually eliminating the mind of desire, and that is the awareness practice of meditation. Like getting rich slowly, it simply takes time to master this. Desire will eventually subside through the practice of detachment rather than suppression, and this is the true long term cure to the problem.

The key in terms of cultivation is to let the body's energies transform the body, and as those transformations are worked through, the problem will become less severe. That sequence of transformations, called purification or *catharsis* in Christianity, absolutely requires meditation in some form or another. As you experience more and more of what it means to have an emptier mind, without suppressing thoughts or the energies trying to arise and without succumbing to the physical sensations and urges, you will have a much easier time with retention.

This simply means you must practice, practice, practice at learning how to detach from the pull of thoughts and physical sensations that arise within the body. This will help you avoid masturbation. As to sex itself, men should try to learn non-ejaculatory sexual techniques. If you are a man and fail at either of these avenues—and you most certainly will at first—it's no big deal and no reason for guilty feelings or dejected feelings of failure. Never give up, feel dejected or become worried that you won't be able to master this because it's all just a matter of sufficient practice. As with any worthwhile activity in life that you wish to master, you must pick yourself up after any type of failure and try again. You just have to keep working at cultivating a skill until you reach some level of mastery. It's as simple and as humanistic as that.

Like learning to ski or ride a bike, you may fall down a lot in the beginning, but with practice you will eventually gain some proficiency at non-ejaculatory sexual relations, or refraining from masturbation, and then seldom fall afterwards. It always takes practice to learn a new skill, and you have to try to develop that sort of mindset rather than succumb to the frustration of initial failures and give up trying.

Because most people don't know that the actual secret is cultivating mental emptiness through meditation, and thereby learning some degree of detachment so that you can stay independent of whatever arises in the mind without becoming entangled, the problem of celibacy and retention often becomes a psychological affair that can lead to all sorts of mood swings and neurotic behavior until the channels clear enough for mental and bodily discomforts to decrease. When your meditative stability has increased and you start to transform the roots of desire in the mind, you won't be as compulsively tossed around by the pressures of the body or sexual desires anymore. Until your channels fully open, however, some vestiges of the problem will always remain. Therefore, please remember that it takes time to develop proficiency to deal with the problem, and you must simply keep trying to learn restraint. Men should not berate themselves for failing now and then when initiating this undertaking in self-mastery.

The issue has to be solved by the transmutation or purification of your sexual energies into a more refined stage of chi and channel openings, and this is only accomplished slowly over time through meditation. Sex itself won't save you, and the movements of the lower torso won't save you or bring you to *samadhi* or enlightenment. You also cannot absorb the energies of your partner through sex in hopes it will help your physical body or empower your spiritual practice with extra energy, which is another mistaken notion many wrongly propagate. You should not try to do this either, as it leads to high blood pressure. However, you can learn how to have sex in such a way that you activate the body's chi energies so that they start to ascend, or so that the flowing energies can dissolve channel obstructions and both partners feel so comfortable that they can relax and detach from their bodies and minds. If both partners can let go at that time, they can both realize a bit of emptiness which may empower their spiritual practice and physical transformations yet further. As with vegetarianism, it is a complicated topic, so it must be approached with wisdom and caution.

DETOXIFICATION, PHYSICAL ADJUSTMENTS AND INTERNAL HEALING

Since we are talking about diet, sex and channel openings, these various issues also bring up the related issue of physical detoxification, which is purification of the outer physical body rather than the inner subtle chi body. The fact that your chi starts to open up your chi channels from meditation means that obstructions within those energy channel are being pushed out. This is a type of detoxification or purification, and because chi and your body are linked, this process will often produce external physical results such as perspiration, shaking, skin eruptions or rashes, headaches and other conditions. People will commonly experience all types of external detoxification reactions after they make very deep progress with meditation. *Tao and Longevity, How to Measure and Deepen Your Spiritual Realization* and *The Little Book of Hercules* discuss such things in detail.

At the earliest stages of the cultivation path, almost all your rising energies go into transforming your body because they must work to open up your channels. This is why many people do not initially experience as many mental signs of progress as others; it is because their energies are all being diverted into transforming their physical nature (opening up their internal chi channels and chakras). Those ascending energies will quiet your mind if they reach the head, but they must first work through your obstructed channels to get there. This is why some people who concentrate on the region of the "third eye" get quick results from their meditation practice, and others do not. It's because they've already opened up the chi channel routes from below stretching to the head, and so those energies can reach this region when they concentrate upon it.

As you open up more channels, your mind will be able to reach deeper and deeper states of quiet because more chi will reach the brain and more channels in the head will open. This opening entails discomfort during the process, and most people mistakenly try to block those feelings by suppressing the energies and transformations rather than letting them simply happen until they pass away. You must never suppress these energies but must allow let any and all the transformations to occur. Even if so much energy arises that your mind becomes disturbed and leaves a peaceful state, you must release your hold on these energies and "let a thousand flowers bloom." Soon the disturbances will die down and a new stage of quiet clarity will be attained because more chi channels have opened.

An empty mind is a mind of purity, and an empty mind also means better chi circulation (flows) or purified chi within your body. Chi becomes pure when it can flow freely because chi obstructions have been removed from the body. However, if you suppress the transformation of chi within the body in order to feel more mentally empty, you are incorrect in your practice and are adding years to the efforts required for awakening.

Many people take the slow route to meditation progress because they confuse the desire for a quiet, empty mind with the habit of suppressing energy transformations within the body since they disturb their mental peace. Just let them happen – encourage them to happen by really letting go – and they will clear out quickly and then never bother you again. The mind of clarity is the clear awareness of the mind, and what you know is content; in this case that content is a voluminous disturbance due to energy streams arising to impact consciousness, but that content will pass because it is always replaced by something new. It is the *clarity* of knowing or perceiving that there is a disturbance which is important, not the content at any particular moment. It is clear awareness or knowing that you want to cultivate. If you know you are confused or your mind is cloudy, that is correct because you are clear about your mental state. (Of course, if you want to change the content because you don't like it or need to act due to its indications, that is another issue entirely.) This understanding offers us a key for getting rid of sexual desire as well – let the desires arise and the energies transform the body fully, and after your channels are thereby opened, the problem will be reduced significantly.

If your target objective from meditation is health or longevity, you need to have your chi channels open more fully to experience those benefits. If you are seeking spiritual gains, you also need to open your chi channels to experience deeper states of empty mind. Whichever way you cut it, you need to practice meditation and let the energies that arise transform your body and mind. To enable that to happen, you cannot oppose the natural process in any way. You mustn't get disturbed by it but must simply let it happen. Such internal energy phenomena never produce any sort of deviance or error that would hurt you because they arise naturally from the simple practice of resting your mind. They always help you if you let them arise and resolve to their natural conclusion, so you should not resist or inhibit them.

However, most practitioners incorrectly try to shut down these processes once initiated because they don't understand the principles behind what is happening. Those energies create powerful sensations in the body that often disturb their mind during practice. The mind can experience confusion because of all the crazy energies felt as the channels open. People worry that something is wrong at that time when in fact they are exactly right. Desiring a cleanliness of mental emptiness (stillness), people mistakenly think they should suppress the chaotic thoughts or unclear mind that occurs within their wake, whereas *the empty mind of awareness that simply knows them* is the correct clear mind they should practice. That's your ordinary natural mind. This is what you want to cultivate, the clarity of natural knowing that just knows without attachments. Don't worry about the contents of the mind, which are destined to pass, but just stay in the clear awareness that knows those contents.

Most people do not understand this point, but if your mind is ever confused or disturbed, but you know you are confused or disturbed, that is correct! The transcending awareness, that stands behind consciousness so you can know it, is what matters. When your awareness knows that consciousness is erratic – that is correct. Of course you don't want to be confused, but sometimes confusion arises and the mind becomes groggy or unclear, such as when you are sick. However, you know that fact through your clear awareness, which itself never gets stained, so that is the correct mind at the time until sickness passes. Can you make your mind clear when you become sick, such as when you experience food poisoning or a fever? You cannot. Your knowing is clear that your mind is hazy and clouded because of the sickness and errant chi flows, and that is the correct awareness. In time that confused or groggy mental state will pass, but the important principle is to realize that the clear awareness is what one cultivates, and not to get entangled with the hazy mental states.

This transcendent clear awareness is sometimes called natural mind, or your ordinary mind. It always stands behind thoughts as what actually shines light on your mental states of consciousness. If awareness is there, that is what consciousness appears on; it is awareness that sees or experiences the totality of your mind. Naturally abiding, ever present, pristine direct awareness is the cognizer of consciousness as a whole. Mental states come and go "in your mind" or "within your consciousness" – you experience thoughts, phenomena or appearances within consciousness -- but you are not the mind. The perceivables within the mind are transient things, too, which come and go, therefore they are unreal. Hence these troubles, disturbances, problems, and confusions are not yours. That's why you should remain detached from them to cultivate the real one, the clear one that transcends them to know them. Nothing else is known to you outside your realm of personal consciousness, so to become greater you must detach from this small realm and come to know the Source.

During meditation practice, you don't have to try to enforce a purity of mental emptiness, but just cultivate a clear awareness that knows that mind is confused, cloudy, and interrupted by these energies and so on. Eventually the happenings within the mind will depart, and all that will be left is an emptier, quieter mental scenario. You don't want to attach to the happenings of the mind – for good or bad – but just know they are there. In time, confused mental states will always leave and the contents of the mind will become normal again. So the purpose is not to forcibly produce an empty mental state, but just cultivate an aware non-attachment to whatever mental states arise, and to let whatever arises come and go freely. If you need a thought it will come, and when you don't need it then it will depart, and if you need it again it will come again, so simply do not attach to mental states. At the beginning stages of meditation practice, this type of understanding is enough.

Since at the earliest stages of the cultivation path many of your chi energies get sidetracked into working to help detoxify your body, hence many confusing states will arise in the mind because of impure chi flows that reach the head. You must simply let them be experienced – because there is nothing you can do about them—and they will eventually pass as your chi purifies and your chi flow eventually becomes clear and regular. The question arises as to whether or not we can help the process of detoxification to hasten this process.

Are there things we can do that can help detoxify the physical body and rid it of poisons that build up over the years or which prevent an obstacle to cultivation, so that these chi flows become more regular in a quicker fashion? Is there something we can do in terms of body purification and detoxification just to help the body alone without regards to our objectives of meditation? Yes, of course. We will certainly benefit from such efforts for ordinary health and longevity concerns, but will this help our meditation practice and our goal of spiritual pursuits?

It is logical to assume that, with a cleaner body, not as much chi energy needs to be devoted to purifying it. However, there are still many questions for science as to how much tie-in there is between physical detoxification and the dissolution of obstructions within our chi circulatory pathways. Even though science does not know the answer to such issues, nevertheless with cancer, Alzheimer's disease, heart disease and other illnesses on the rise, physical detoxification is something we should do for health purposes anyway even if we do not understand how much it helps our inner subtle body, too.

The school of acupuncture offers some ideas on the tie-in between poor chi flow and ill organ health, but the best we can say is that more research needs to be done. It certainly is logical, however, to assume that detoxification efforts will help the body become healthier, and a healthier body that doesn't bother you will make it easier to meditate. A cleaner body will be a younger, more flexible (softer), warmer and healthier body, and certainly becomes a better, more efficient or suitable vehicle for treading the spiritual path. These are results that have been proved in the past, and which we can reasonably rely upon.

Previously we discussed pranayama exercises, which are a great antidote to sexual desires when they arise because the pranayama activities can temporarily relieve the pressure from much of these rising energies. Pranayama *kumbhaka* exercises produce definite effects on the physical body, and help open up chi channels as well. Therefore *we can classify them as detoxification techniques for the body*. The question then arises, are there other remedies we might try for other detoxification objectives?

Supplements such as **Candisol** together with **Oregacillin** will kill Candida yeast in the body, which is a problem that plagues most people by clouding their mind. Once Candida is eliminated or under better control, people usually feel as if a great fog has been lifted from their brains because the yeast is no longer giving off toxins that pollute the body and cloud the mind. Yeast reduction not only helps them in regular life, but of course the new clarity they feel helps in their meditation efforts as well. Candisol, which is a gentle supplement that kills off Candida, is something everyone should try, especially those who consume a lot of sugar and refined carbohydrates that feed the yeast.

An internal parasite cleanse, using supplements such as **Beachwood Canyon's "PC-1-2-3"** product, can also help insure that your system is free of parasites. In the old days Taoists used to kill internal bacteria with mercury formulations, but an internal immunity boosting regime, using **Purest Colloids colloidal silver** (the only true colloidal silver) to lower bacterial and viral loads, is also possible if one needs it. One can try to kill pathogens directly or try to bolster one's immune system, and I favor both approaches done simultaneously.

Some people use **colonics** and **enemas** to help clean their intestines, and when people start having regular bowel movements many will definitely say that having clean intestines also leads to a clearer head. You can often see people's cheeks immediately turn rosy after a colonic because cleaner blood flow can now reach all regions of the body, including the head and brain. That is a benefit in itself. The school of hatha yoga also offers a variety of cleansing activities to help clean the body (including the ears, stomach and sinuses), and colonics or enemas are just one of these possibilities.

Pharmaceutical grade **l-glutamine** powder and other supplements can also help heal the stomach lining and intestines so that poisons do not re-enter the bloodstream from holes in tissue linings, and it helps the bowels to become regular so that one receives those benefits as well. Many herbal formulas are available as a short term solution to battle constipation, but one needs to be careful of developing a dependency on ingredients such as *Cascara Sagrada* and *Senna.* A change in the diet can usually produce the results of regularity that one desires, and is the preferred method for eliminating constipation.

Countless herbal formulas and homeopathic supplements are also available to help both detoxify and support the liver and kidneys. Western supplement formulations contain substances like alpha lipoic acid, milk thistle extract, glutathione, N-acetyl-cysteine, etc. whereas Chinese formulas contain combinations of various herbs that have been discovered to have a therapeutic effect when used in particular proportions. The Chinese herbal formulas usually act on the principle of coarse dredging to free these organs of collected toxins and wastes, which thereby improves their functioning.

Sickness in the body most often arises from nutrient imbalances or exposure to toxins, and growingly from excessive exposure to electromagnetic radiation. Herbal formulas and nutritional supplements can help you deal with several of these problems quite effectively so you must learn how to use them.

There are all sorts of **Chinese patent formulas** readily available for a variety of health conditions. A devoted cultivation practitioner should make a concerted effort to study these formulas and use them. I ardently suggest you start learning Chinese, ayurvedic, or Western herbal medicines and nutritional supplements so that you can start to take some responsibility for better managing your body and health situation on your own. The body is not you, but akin to equipment that you use, and you must learn how to manage this equipment and keep it healthy and in balance without always running to a doctor for a prescription of exercise and pharmaceuticals. I have also seen great systemic healing results with various **green powders** that contain a number of easily absorbable nutrients, especially green and red algaes and seaweeds such as spirulina and chlorella. Various combinations of micro-algae (such as in **BioSuper Food**) that are easy to digest often provide your body valuable nutrients it can use for healing. When minerals are reduced to their smallest colloidal form, such as those supplied by **Purest Colloids**, they become the most absorbable and thus most available for rebuilding the body's structure to restore function. **Trace Mineral Tablets** by Trace Mineral Research is the mineral supplement I most often recommend. For arthritis, I often recommend people try **NeoCell collagen** for their knees and other joints.

If you want to stay healthy long term into your old age, and reduce your risk of degenerative disease and sometimes fatal conditions, you must support the elimination and detoxification of the organs of your body. Furthermore, you must go on a detoxification program to eliminate poisons and toxins that have accumulated in your body over the years. Perhaps it is because they shed the excess water weight held by the body to help dilute all the toxins we internally carry, but the fact is that many people who are struggling with weight loss finally start losing the excess pounds only after they go on a short detoxification program. If you want to lose weight, you should undertake a detoxification program as well.

As to the connective tissues of the skin and muscles, they can be slowly detoxed using **Vitalzym** or other powerful enzyme supplements. **Chlorella** (such as the Yaeyama brand) is great to help remove heavy metal accumulations, and "**Nature's Pure Body Whole Body Cleansing Program**" helps clear various toxins that have accumulated in the body's skin and connective tissues. I always use Vitalzym and Nature's Pure Body together, one bottle each per month, in order to perform maintenance cleansing once per year. However, you should use them for at least two to three months, if possible, for the best initial results when getting started. Some people say that you should devote yourself to an entire year of slow but gentle detoxification efforts if you want to get rid of many health problems that have accumulated in your physical nature and thereby help avoid degenerative disease.

We can help clean the arteries and veins of blood clots using the fabulous supplement **nattokinase** (Allergy Research/Nutricology brand), which must be taken separate from enzymes that would digest it, and we can use **Detoxamin** rectal suppositories to undergo the equivalent of intravenous chelation therapy at home. Chelation helps the blood flow throughout the body in many beneficial ways, and is especially useful to diabetics and heart patients.

As to getting rid of plaque and cholesterol from arterial walls, so many natural possibilities are possible, but kept from the public, that it almost seems as if this topic falls under the category of "suppressed information." There are the arginine and citrulline formulations of Dr. Louis Ignarro, who won a Nobel Prize with two other doctors for their natural means of reducing arterial plaque using natural combinations of these amino acids. Nobel Prize winner Linus Pauling suggested that this could be done with vitamin C and other specific amino acids, too. **Anti-homocysteine** factors can be used to prevent the cholesterol from sticking to arterial walls in the first place. These are all possible proven approaches, but doctors never tell you about them.

All these remedies seem to have been suppressed by the pharmaceutical establishment, which makes money off of people's ignorance, and yet Nobel Prize winners have worked on them and proven them! Modern nutritionists commonly use powerful combinations of vitamin E, C, D and K along with PhosChol (phosphatidyl choline) to strip cholesterol and plaque from artery walls, and so many alternative protocols are possible other than just the Nobel Prize winning solutions.

If you want to take vitamin C for such protocols or for other reasons, I always suggest a full spectrum source, such as **Rainbow Light Ultra Gram C**, and the A.C. Grace brand called "**Unique E**" is perhaps the best form of vitamin E you will ever find on this planet. The difference between a high grade brand of a nutritional supplement, and a low cost brand, is the difference between night and day; one will work and the other will barely produce the results you read about in medical studies, so I recommend this brand if you are ever told to take vitamin E for any health condition. The Jarrow **Q-Absorb** brand of CoQ10 is also the best brand I have ever found for heart health and other health problems requiring CoQ10.

As to the body itself, if it bothers you when you try to sit still, you should consider yoga for stretching or other forms of exercise, especially the energy martial arts such as *Tai Chi Chuan*, *Ba Gua Zhang*, *Hsing I Chuan* and *Akido*. I particularly like **Z-Health** stretching exercises for the joints as they eliminate old injuries and pain and expand people's range of motion after just a few sessions. It's just my own preference, but I have also found that people who learn the fifteen minute stretching routine of ***Yi Jin Jing*** improve their bodies much more than yoga enthusiasts who have practiced for years, and quickly become healthy from this simple stretching practice.

For most people, learning the martial arts will help them both understand and start to feel their internal chi, and from that basis they can go on to make great progress in their cultivation. I have never found yoga practitioners to develop this same level of understanding or expertise, even though you think this understanding would be common because many yoga practitioners typically study Vedic literature that can lead to enlightenment. This is what I have typically found even when people have had years of yoga practice, but of course this can change in time.

Chiropractic or osteopathic adjustments also can and should be used to help align your skeleton so that you feel comfortable when you sit during meditation practice, and various forms of bodywork are available to help you heal old muscular injuries. We are, in fact, inundated with various possibilities for fixing the body's structural problems that have accumulated over time. It is just that people usually do not wish to pay for such things, or do not want to search them out, or are willing to pay and search but cannot find an excellent practitioner.

Chiropractic adjustments and **massage bodyworkers** cannot be recommended enough, but the problem is always how to find a great practitioner when 80-90% of practitioners in any field are usually only average in terms of their level of competence and skillfulness. Therefore, you need a recommendation from someone who has been to many bodywork professionals, and can discriminate between the talented and untalented, the good and the bad, to identify an excellent practitioner who would rank in the top tier of the local talent pool.

This is the same rule that applies in selecting nutritional supplements, because in twenty years' time the best products I have listed will have been surpassed by new ones that have come upon the market. It is only by asking up-to-date experts that you will become able to determine what is currently best. While I cannot write down the brands or names of the best products to use in several decades, I can assure you that the need for detoxification will only grow stronger by that time. The idea that you should detox your body will hold even stronger then than it does right now, especially with debilitating neurological diseases (Alzheimers, Parkinsons, autism, ADHD, etc.) on the rise! Even before a woman wishes to get pregnant, she should undergo a routine of detoxification and then eat well to increase her nutrient stores as correctly pointed out in *Deep Nutrition: Why Your Genes Need Traditional Food.* Your genes are not your destiny, for it is what you wash over your genes through the diet that causes them to be expressed or not. Therefore more properly speaking, it is your diet and lifestyle that is your destiny.

Will these things help your meditation? Not directly, but indirectly because your body becomes healthier and thus less of a detriment or impediment to practice progress. Nevertheless you should use such detoxification supplements anyway to help manage your body in our increasingly toxic world. If your body becomes healthier, if your bones become aligned and you feel better or more comfortable, then your body won't bother you during meditation practice, and you will be able to enter a deeper level of practice. Having the bones properly aligned in your spine is especially important for quick progress in your meditation practice, and the correct positioning of the Atlas bone at the top of the spine is critical for proper spinal alignment.

No supplement or therapy will actually help your meditation, per se. But these sorts of remedies or therapies will certainly improve your health, and when the body does not represent such a troublesome burden, it becomes easier for you to meditate and make progress. You will also have more energy for life, and that energy can also be used in opening up your internal channels and transforming your body to a better state of health. Once healthy, your body will not only feel more comfortable inside and your energy more balanced and harmonious, but your body will not have to devote so much chi to fixing problems, and so, in an indirect or direct way, improving your health does help your meditation progress. With a healthier body your emotions are more easily balanced, so adjusting your body to a state of health is very important for life and cultivation.

The question always arises whether any form of supplement, drug, or any type of electro-stimulation or other therapy can help you open your chakras, and chi channels. No, not at all, despite whatever marketing claims people use to try to sell you those things. As to the objectives of *samadhi* or enlightenment, which are the two highest targets of spiritual practice, nothing can help you attain them other than the meditation practice of learning how to let go of holding onto consciousness. Psychedelic drugs, recreational drugs and alcohol cannot help you in one bit this way. One must always cultivate clear awareness and full control of one's mental faculties in meditation practice. The use of drugs and alcohol, on the other hand, negate this principle rather than increase your mental or spiritual abilities.

The fact is, to help your meditation practice you need to take care of your body, and that's exactly what you are doing with balanced approaches to sex, exercise, diet, and supplements. Just follow the rule of balance and harmony, and avoid going to extremes just as you should in nearly every area of life. The rule once again: avoid hubris and avoid extremes, but follow the golden mean. As your body gets healthier, it becomes easier to ignore its presence during meditation sessions, and as it transforms you need to learn what these transformations represent so you can ignore them as well, or so that you can pass through them quicker without any problems. Your mindset should not veer to the exotic when managing meditation affairs, but should remain balanced and concentrated on the natural humanistic way of managing things.

All these issues must be approached with wisdom, and it is through wisdom that you can eventually succeed with meditation to accomplish the objectives you want. Many people want to get rid of stress in their lives, have more pep and vigor, be healthier and live longer, but only begin to start focusing upon these objectives in a deep way when they get older. They start concentrating on their diet, exercise, supplements and also detoxification as the road to health and longevity, but almost when it is too late to reap the largest benefits that could have been possible had they started earlier. If they really want to gain those benefits in a non-superficial degree, they must certainly look to structural alignment, detoxification and diet, but please know that the only dependable pathway must include the practice of meditation in the here and now.

9

ACCUMULATING MERIT FOR YOUR PRACTICE

There is a principle behind progress in meditation practice which most people in Western countries don't even know exists. In order to make a lot of progress to reach the very deepest levels or highest stages possible in meditation, you need merit. You need to accumulate the merit of good works and good deeds, virtuous living and virtuous behavior, a clean mind and charitable ways. A clean or pure mind, which you achieve by cultivating meditation itself, is actually the highest form of merit you can cultivate and enjoy in life. It is called clear, pure fortune and extremely prized. Who doesn't want a peaceful mind that is open, free from pain while dealing with concerns, limitless and joyous? This form of merit is actually the result of meditation, and to cultivate this type of mind is actually the path of meditation as well.

The idea of personal virtue, morality and charity, civic minded philanthropy, and the cutting off of errant behaviors, is a basic teaching found at the foundational stage of all genuine religions, and it also holds as a requirement for meditation progress, too. This is another reason why people at the beginning levels of practice are always taught to watch their minds and immediately cut off errors in though and behavior to make them pure and thereby generate merit. To make more than superficial progress at meditation, you absolutely need to accumulate merit. One must act to transform their own behavior and make it better, and work to make the world a better place by helping others.

In talking about accumulating merit, I am not just talking about making charitable monetary gifts or time contributions to non-profit organizations such as Heifer International, Kiva.org, Accion International, Kick Start, HaitiWater.org, CARE, Oxfam, the Salvation Army, the American Red Cross, Doctors Without Borders and so on. Accumulating merit means cultivating a clean mind and acting from a mind of virtuous intent to help others. This idea of forgetting oneself to act on behalf of others – compassion and selflessness – is real cultivation practice. To truly accomplish this you also need meditation practice. Other forms of merit help you attain the opportunity to cultivate, such as being wealthy enough to have free time, but mental purity is once again the highest merit you can cultivate and attain in the world.

Merit comes from many things, including from such simple acts as giving hope to others, smiling, or talking to strangers in a friendly manner. It is not something only accumulated by opening a checkbook and making monetary contributions to worthwhile causes. In fact, if you financially support the wrong type of organization or an organization's efforts to pursue misguided goals, your intentions may be good but the results may be devastating, even disastrous. It is always necessary that wisdom match one's ideals of compassion. Without wisdom, which means logic, reasoning and deep understanding, one's attempts at doing the right things or compassionate things will often go astray. This is why wisdom is important for life and spiritual development. If someone lacks worldly wisdom, how can you expect them to have the higher spiritual wisdom as well?

When you give to financially support some worthwhile undertaking, you should also practice having no attachments in order that those actions actually constitute true giving. You should expect nothing in return. An example is the case of my teacher who built a railway in China from the city of Jinhua to Wenzhou. Neither he nor any other person in our group purchased any land along the railway route, even though we were given land rights whose usage would have made each of us mega-multi-millionaires. My teacher accepted the nearly impossible burden of completing such a project purely to help the people, and wanted nothing in return. He always stressed we should have no expectations of return or reward when we are working for the people, so any and all advantages that offered a profitable return to us were refused.

After its completion, my teacher turned it over to the state and was not even thanked by the provincial officials for undertaking this difficult project, which would not have been undertaken otherwise had he not been asked to sponsor it, nor did they apologize for all the obstructions they often gave him. He didn't mind his poor treatment because it was done purely as a type of offering and service on behalf of the community and nation. He spent years suffering as he finished the project, and once done, he forgot about it and moved on to other things.

The point is that if you expect recognition or reward from your charitable actions, even when they will benefit countless generations into the future, you should not consider it an offering. You do it because you know it needs to be done, and will help others. That is all. When you undertake charitable actions for a return, on the other hand, you should consider yourself as making a trade or investment. Just try to do good and bring benefit for others in the world without making yourself be known, and this will also help you break attachments to the ideas of a self. If you study the origins of the Aravind Eye hospitals documented in the book *Infinite Vision*, and the motivation of the founder Dr. Venkataswamy to relieve blindness among the poor of India, you will begin to understand the right type of attitude to cultivate

You must also rid yourself of the notion that accumulating merit always involves having a lot of power or money, otherwise you will never participate in the tiniest of actions that lead to bigger things or which themselves bring gigantic merit beyond compare. For instance, my teacher once told a group of his closest students that the reason we weren't making much progress in meditation was because we were not working to accumulate merit. He said our merit wasn't high enough because we weren't thinking of others or doing anything to help relieve the suffering of other beings, and therefore taught us a simple, inexpensive practice of making a small nightly offering of food to the hungry ghosts, saying this would help us quickly accumulate some of that necessary stock of merit. It entails taking a few grains of rice (not an extravaganza of food) with a little shot glass of water, saying a prayer of blessing and mantra over these items, and then offering them to the beings who might need them.

THE NIGHTLY HUNGRY GHOST OFFERING

Perhaps the biggest importance to the practice is that its nightly repetition teaches you to daily cultivate a boundless mind of giving and joyfulness in the practice of giving, for these are just two of the positive emotions you should cultivate at the time of making an offering. You must cultivate a mind of boundless joy, compassion, loving kindness and emptiness akin to the "four immeasurables of Buddhism." If consciousness goes on forever in endless future lives, and if the seeds or habits of consciousness are carried forward into these future lives, it makes sense to try to learn habitual mindsets, habits and motivations that will lead you to the Tao, to ending suffering, and to generating great benefit for others. This practice helps you do exactly that, which is why I recommend it for everyone.

You would want these virtues and mindsets carried over to subsequent incarnations and that is another reason you are told to cultivate these boundless minds. Even if reincarnation does not exist, or hungry ghosts do not exist, there are still great benefits to this nightly practice in terms of cultivating these mindsets. Therefore it is helpful to consider it from that angle as a training mechanism even if you do not subscribe to the idea of there being hungry ghosts.

The attitudes of compassionate generosity and offering to benefit others and relieve them of suffering are always ideas you should cultivate in life rather than the notion that you are performing an activity as a swap to attain something in return. The expectation of a payback would turn this type of practice into an investment seeking activity, or barter transaction wherein you perform activity X in order to receive a benefit, which is not the intention at all.

The development of various virtues often requires a gradual habituation through continual practice and exposure over and over again. You actually have to practice or be taught in order to learn kindness, generosity and compassion. Thus you can understand why, from this angle alone, there is a great benefit to performing the nightly task of offering food to hungry ghosts to accumulate some merit. Whereas we learn through meditation how to cut off thoughts and errors in behavior, we also need to cultivate the willingness to actively step forward (rather than remain passive) and do what must be done to make the world a better place for ourselves and others. This nightly practice teaches us that we must do this, too. We must actively work to make the world a better place by helping others and arranging situations for the better, otherwise it is not going to happen.

Our own happiness cannot be achieved independently of a society which is itself suffering, but rather, our own happiness is achieved when we live in a society where we see that others are also happy and free of suffering. Therefore, to create such a society with such conditions we all need to learn how to give, as one of many necessary virtues, because there are always some people in need suffering from some type of deficiency. If we start to create a kindness, generosity and giving mindset from this small nightly offering practice done over and over again, we can break down inner mental barriers so that the virtue of giving eventually becomes more spontaneous and natural. When virtuous types of behavior become spontaneous in expression, this type of practice then begins to produce immeasurable merit.

Shakyamuni Buddha once explained how offering flowers to Buddhas would often lead to people being reborn in subsequent lives with beautiful features, and such results become possible not because of the flowers specifically, but because those individuals cultivated a mind of joyful happiness and giving when offering beautiful things to a Buddha. This, in turn, thereby produced a karmic return in that their own features would later beautify an environment wherever they went. It was the consciousness they cultivated, through the activity of giving with a virtuous mindset of happiness and offering, that produced such great returns. To be sure, *karma follows the transformations of consciousness* as well as the results of actual physical acts. This is why the act of smiling to people, talking gently, listening to their problems, and so forth all have incredibly beneficial karmic returns. You might not think they do, but they do, and this is another reason why all spiritual and personal cultivation comes down to transforming your behavior in the end. A change in one's consciousness, habit energies and behavior produces karmic recompenses just as surely as do physical actions.

As to the practice of making a nightly offering to hungry ghosts that my teacher taught us, the idea that there is such a thing as hungry ghosts is found in several religions which simply call "hungry ghosts" by different names such as shades, wandering souls and so on. This is a stage of existence below that of the human being, but above animals, that is characterized by a constant state of suffering, lack and deprivation. For hungry ghosts, life is basically one of suffering as retribution for a greedy, acquisitive, stingy, crooked, or casual evil lifestyle. There is never enough food, or water, or shelter or anything else they need for survival, and thus the ghost state of being is considered a pitiful state of uncomfortable existence.

It is said that individuals who were excessively greedy in life and denied resources or help to others when it was in their power to be generous, are often reborn in this condition. Then they always suffer from a state of lack, sometimes because they have misshapen bodies that cannot ingest any food they find, and this deprivation is a stage of karmic retribution for being miserly, greedy, acquisitive or evil in life. Until they are born in a higher state, such beings are doom to suffer.

In Christianity, the hungry ghosts are akin to the state of beings in purgatory who are always suffering while waiting to be reborn in Heaven, and Christian doctrine maintains that our prayers can help free these beings. In the paganism of ancient Greece, this stage of the hungry ghost is represented by the fate of Tantalus who could neither drink the water in front of him nor eat the fruit that hung above him. In Hinduism, the hungry ghost existence is the stage of the *pretas*. In short, the basic idea is that not only are there human beings, heavenly beings and animals, but a ghostly state of existence as well. One becomes reborn in one of these states due to differences in the degree of good and bad in their thoughts and actions. How does this happen? I suppose that the dirtier one's chi and consciousness becomes, the easier it is to be sucked into realms wherein that stage of consciousness is natural.

This stage of spiritual beings suffering deprivation is not only recognized by Buddhism, Hinduism, Christianity, and Taoism but by many other religions ... basically anywhere the idea of ghosts and a suffering afterlife are accepted. Those with supersensible attainments often claim to be able to see such beings and confirm their existence, and we go on the word of prior sages from countless religions. The idea of sacrificing to one's ancestors is in some cases related to the idea of helping the hungry ghosts by offering them food and water to help relieve them of their suffering. If one is born into this condition, Shakyamuni Buddha said they might be able to receive the food proper to that realm, which includes the food given from offerings. But if they were not reborn in that realm, they would not, of course, receive such offerings.

The tiny ceremony for offering to the hungry ghosts can be found on the website www.MeditationExpert.com and in other places, and consists of taking a few grains of rice (or other grains) and small glass of water, saying a few prayers of blessing over them, and then pouring them outside to offer to the hungry ghosts. Through the power of the enlightened beings, the prayer in some way purifies and empowers the food to make it available for their consumption.

It is important to only offer vegetarian food to hungry ghosts, and never to offer meat. The one time I did so, my teacher, who often seemed to know whatever I did without being told, came down to my apartment the next day and scolded me, telling me not to do that again or it would make the hungry ghosts even more greedy for meat and killing. This, he explained, would make it even more difficult for them to leave their dreadful condition.

RECITING PRAYERS, MANTRAS OR CULTIVATION TEACHINGS FOR THOSE SUFFERING OR DEPARTED

The idea of making offerings for the benefit of the hungry ghosts is related to the idea of saying prayers or mantras for the deceased. The goal is to help the departed quickly leave states of suffering so that they can be reborn in Heaven or the human realm once again. In Christianity, people often recite prayers for the deceased for similar reasons. Eastern Orthodox Christian practices, for instance, encompass a series of prayers and food offerings for those who have died during the forty days after death. You'll find a variation of this forty day period in other traditions, too, such as in Chinese culture and Tibetan Buddhism, where prayers for the dead are held for forty-nine days. This is said to be the approximate maximum amount of time the experience between death and birth could last.

In Islam, Judaism and other religions, there are also specific prayers people usually recite for the benefit of the deceased. Do they help? Of course! In Buddhism, where all kinds of such things have been catalogued, people recite the mantra for the Hell Buddha, Ksitigarbha, to ask for his assistance in helping the departed transition to their next stage of development. The specific mantra has several different possibilities:

Námó Dìzàng Wáng Púsà

Namah Samantabuddhanam, Ha Ha Ha, Sutanu Svaha

Om Ksitigarbha Bodhisattva Yah

I have had quite a few individuals over the years tell me they had dreams of deceased relatives who, in the dream, asked them to recite mantras or a particular holy text for their benefit. When I asked the family member if they did so, they almost always said "No" because the requested mantra, prayer or scripture came from a different sect within their religion, or from a different religion entirely.

How foolish and ignorant! How uncompassionate not to make such a minor effort on their behalf especially when the request comes in such an exotic fashion. If a recently deceased loved one appears in a dream asking you to recite something on their behalf, they do so because they know that hearing those teachings will help them, or because it will help you, so common sense says *please do so*. After they die, the deceased are not as prone to sectarianism as the living, and are more aware of the teachings that might help them let go and achieve an empty state of mind. This, as well as your stock of merit from good deeds, is what helps you progress to a higher stage of existence. The higher your merit and stage of mental clarity of emptiness, the higher the possible Heaven you can reach, so they need those lessons to help detach from the heavy ego concepts they've developed (which weigh them down) so that they can move on.

Being free of a physical body, the etheric chi bodies of the deceased are much more amenable to instant change, as are their states of consciousness, if they simply hear the right lessons that can help them let go and reach some stage of realization. The right lesson is that everything they think is their self is not really their *true self*. What they and we take as the experience of our self or soul is something that is changing, so cannot be the homogenous true us. What they (and we) take as the assumed self is an agglomeration of parts that cannot be the true us, and so no bodily form can be the true unchanging self. Consciousness (our mind) cannot be *It* either because consciousness always changes and is an agglomeration of experiences. What is the true us, or Self, must transcend consciousness, too.

What is unchanging is an emptiness void of all substance that – just because it is so – miraculously has awareness, self-lucidity, illumination or knowingness (consciousness) as one of its functions, and we are that true nature. We think we have individual awareness but it is just that true natural awareness shining through us via the structures of individual consciousness, and that "us" (the personal "I") is a matrix of consciousness enervated by its shine through. This is what all of us actually are. We are an agglomeration of consciousness through which the real us shines, and since we are consciousness we can spin thoughts and we make the thought mistake of assuming we are independent rather than recognizing our Source. Our true Self is like bodiless awareness of pure consciousness without shape, form, substance or content, and while it is nothing substantial or material at all, yet it miraculously has the function of being able to give birth to thoughts and appearances which seem to be materially existent things, but which are not. This is all covered, for instance, in the very short and very beautiful *Diamond Sutra*.

By hearing the right lessons on emptiness and no-self, the departed can easily let go, transform and move on to a better state quickly. All the higher stages of existence involve higher experiential states of this realization, which is why they are said to be progressively more pure. Our problem in this world is that we carry around a coarse physical body and identify with it as our self. Or, we take our ego sense as being the real us when it's just a collection of thoughts. Therefore it is not easy to transform our habits or behaviors, or even to awaken to our original nature, because we cling to both our dense, coarse body and our stream of conscious thoughts. We take either of them as our true self instead of recognizing the absolute formlessness we are that has infinite possibilities. It is not speculation, but a fact that on the road of meditation you actually end up proving. Religious dogma is something you are told to just believe whereas this fact you just prove.

We can say that living beings arise in the cosmos because the right conditions came together offering the potential for life, and everything evolved from there as it always does. The unchanging pure consciousness appropriates (makes use of) those bodies and shines through them just as it shines through everything since it is All. In this case, however, life has the special capability of consciousness, and therefore the original nature becomes the functioning of consciousness within sentient beings. With the presence of consciousness comes the possibility of consciousness itself awakening to discover or understand what it actually is. That chance, or opportunity for awakening, is very rare since most forms of life do not have consciousness that is advanced enough for this self-realization. Animals, for instance, are overshadowed by biological concerns and hungry ghosts are too much involved with suffering.

Even for the sentient beings with consciousness that can awaken, most are not privy to the teachings on awakening, and others simply choose not to cultivate for self-realization so that they can free themselves from beginningless sufferings, ignorance and illusion. As I mentioned, teachings such as you find in this book are extremely rare and also precious because they can lead you to awakening, which in turn lets you jump out of all future tribulation. You can choose where to be reborn rather than having karma suck you into the next incarnation without choice, and even when suffering touches you it will never reach your true self. If you don't plant wisdom seeds from studying these teachings, however, then it is very difficult to awaken even if you practice to the edge of death, and simply by studying these materials your consciousness and channels will start to transform, which is why some feel an uncomfortable response. But that is the nature of growth and transformation until one eventually realizes joy and bliss. How can you measure the merit of awakening? It is immeasurable, just as the *Diamond Sutra* explains.

By itself, the original boundless formless awareness that we are cannot know anything, and cannot even know It exists. This is why there is required the presence of a conscious being for awakening. The absolute nature has no thoughts of consciousness and cannot know Itself. What we ultimately are just is. But by virtue of an individual body, however, consciousness can arise because of it and that consciousness can realize what it ultimately is, and thus the original nature can in this way realize Itself. There's actually no permanent person, soul, entity or self there (within the consciousness aggregate), but just consciousness recognizing its own nature. It's not a God, it's just the original nature – an essence beyond the phenomenal often called "emptiness" or "voidness" to denote the lack of anything phenomenal that we can know, but having the capacity for awareness as its nature. That's just what It is, and the whole universe is That, too.

There is no true such thing as life, selves, beings, entities or anything else like that in all existence because phenomena are all just the functionings of this original nature. Sentient forms are only special in that they have the capability of consciousness realization whereas inanimate matter does not, yet insentient matter is also the original nature, too, in the guise of something that seems to lack consciousness, but which is also consciousness of a particular form produced by the karma of the whole manifestation.

When the consciousness that knows itself as a living being does not awaken, it is basically has its back turned on recognizing what it is. It gets lost in thoughts and appearances – the world it perceives – and takes them as Real. It takes them as an "other" opposed to itself rather than recognizing that they are part of the Self. A personalized consciousness goes on and on forever entangled with these manipulations of consciousness, most of which are painful, until it finally awakens. That might take eons, but all sentient beings will finally awaken. Some simply decide to do it earlier rather than later, and thereby end the endless painful states of suffering that constantly occur to the non-enlightened consciousness. Hence, when an enlightened individual teaches consciousness how to free itself, you can see how rare this opportunity is for advancement.

When a consciousness unit or aggregate of consciousness we call a "self" does not awaken, that is because it firmly takes itself as an independent self or independent entity unit, not recognizing that it is just this original nature all along that has myriads of expressions. By getting caught up in the views of being the body or self, consciousness misses the potential for awakening and the bliss and peace this brings. Now that the ties of the coarse material body are over after someone has died, however, there is still a chance for awakening if the right teachings become available. Even as a person dies and the aggregates of the physical body and his/her consciousness begin to deteriorate, there arises an opportunity for awakening if at that time one can let go of the ties that bind and realize the underlying true awareness Self that is always there while all else disintegrates. That is what one is.

When finally free of the body it becomes much easier to reach some understanding as to what one ultimately is. If this understanding is not the actual event of Self-realization, it usually involves realizing a higher stage of mental purity or emptiness that is more pure or free of wandering thoughts. When a departed spirit can realize a higher stage of empty consciousness, which we can call a more purified state of consciousness, this always corresponds to higher realms and better states of rebirth. That is why, as humans, we always practice witnessing meditation, for the witness is always pure. By remaining in the witness that observes, rather than getting caught up with thoughts, we are not only cultivating an emptier mind, but preparing for a higher incarnation as well. If you can stay in the non-moving witness as you begin to pass away, this even becomes a meditation method for awakening called "cultivating the clear light of death" taught in Tibetan Buddhism.

By offering enlightenment teachings to the departed through sutra recitations, we can also help them make progress if they realize something from the teachings. In effect, we help them let go of the attachments to their body and mind, and if they understand and can introspect, they might awaken or at least change their behavior. That, too, will lead to a higher state of rebirth. We colloquially say they "awaken" or "attain realization," but this just means that consciousness realizes that it is consciousness and not a true self. That's the only thing that is ever happening.

Finally knowing all this after they are deceased and need not be bound or deceived by the outer garbs of religion anymore, such beings often come to relatives asking that the right teachings be spoken for them so that they might listen and make progress to quickly leave their lower state. If you mantra for them, this helps them a lot, but once again: *Choose your mantras, prayers and recitations wisely.* The most helpful do not necessarily come from your own religion.

One of my friends once wrote me an enlightening report about his experiences with mantras and recitations to help those who have passed away. While in this small book I could have emphasized the task of purifying your behavior along with giving to charitable organizations to accumulate merit, I think most people already understand those routes, so we don't have to explain them or emphasize them too much. What you need to know is how to accumulate a lot of merit quickly, and start transforming your mindset for the future as well as prepare your own self for awakening.

THE BENEFITS FROM MAKING "OFFERINGS"

I therefore often recommend making a nightly offering to the hungry ghosts, and reciting sutras or mantras for the departed, as one of the easiest ways to accumulate merit simply because it costs nothing other than time, so even the poor can do it, and it trains you to begin compassionately thinking of others and how to make the world better on everyone's behalf. My friend, in a typical example of the effectiveness of this practice, reported the following.

"I always recite mantras and the names of enlightened Buddhas and even entire sutras for people I know who have passed away. I started doing it because after doing the hungry ghost offering I started to have visions and dreams of the beings I was helping.

"Then I read *Sutra on the Past Vows of Earth Store Bodhisattva* which explains how to help people who are dead or dying by reciting the names of the Buddhas for them. It also said when you dedicate merits from your actions to others they receive $1/7^{th}$ of the merit of your action. I thought that was a pretty easy formula to follow – if I wanted someone to get the merit of reciting a mantra 10,000 times I could then recite the mantra 70,000 times and dedicate it to them."

"So I started doing this, especially when someone I know passed away. Three incidents really solidified this practice for me as very worthwhile:

- First, my cousin died very suddenly at the age of 22 from a brain tumor. Now, I didn't know him very well, he lived in another country, and we weren't close, but I decided to mantra for him. It wasn't long before I had a vision of him smiling and thanking me as he was on his way to being reborn in better circumstances.

- When my grandfather passed away I also recited the long *Usnisa Dharani* for him. He eventually appeared to me thanking me for doing this practice as he was now reborn in a minor heavenly realm.

- I even did this for our cat when he passed away. I recited the *Usnisa Dharani* for his benefit several thousand times. He appeared to me and thanked me because he was being reborn not as a cat but as human.

"I would have thought this kind of thing was crazy if I didn't have the direct experiences myself. But it turns out if you do these practices you'll start to see that they really do help people.

"And in my mind reciting a sutra, some mantras or the names of the Buddhas (previously enlightened beings) is such a small, easy thing to do but it really, really helps people. I encourage everyone I know, who is at least open to the possibility that it works, to test it out for themselves."

I myself once had a rather strange situation happen that also sounds crazy on the surface, but ties in with this story. It actually was a little show put on for my benefit, but I didn't know this at the time. One day I was reading books in my room in Hong Kong, and had several sutras strewn across the bed. Our apartment often had little tiny beetles flying around that sometimes came from the raw Chinese medicine we stored inside the house. When I turned to one of the sutras I had opened on the bed, it seemed as if one of these tiny beetles was trying to read a Chinese character from the scripture. Naturally this sounds preposterous, and I didn't know where this idea was coming from, but I was just positive this was the case for some reason.

I had previously read of stories in Buddhism and Taoism where it stated that an insect which ate just one letter from a sutra might be reborn in a Heaven, and of course I knew that this was an exaggeration of the type often used by most religions. Even so, despite this understanding, in this case I could somehow feel the chi of this tiny beetle and its intent, and I felt that something strange was definitely going on.

Feeling sorry for this tiny beetle, I wondered how I might offer it any food. I had a large bowl of birdseed in the house, and having nothing else to offer the poor little fellow, I gently nudged him into the open bowl of birdseed hoping he might find something inside that would serve as food. The very moment I performed that offering, I immediately saw a giant golden light emanate above and around the bowl and fill the room, which shocked me causing me to step back. I went back to my room, and when I came back to inspect the bowl, the tiny beetle was gone. Once again, I somehow knew that he had died, and so I went to tell the story to my teacher who lived upstairs.

As I was relating the story to my teacher in his apartment, in the corner of the room appeared a ghostlike figure of a tiny man with very large buglike eyes. He was even smaller than a midget and surrounded by four great beings whom I immediately somehow knew were Buddhas, meaning enlightened beings, sages or *jnanis*. The little being was crying with sadness, and I asked my teacher who he was and what was going on.

My teacher told me that this was the beetle which had just died, and he was crying because he had previously been a human being who had done incredibly evil deeds, had been reborn in a hell because of those deeds, and was just now slowly working his way up the incarnation ladder to become a human being once again. Because he really, really was sorry for all he had done, which he had somehow remembered or had been shown at this moment of transition, and because he really wanted to change his behavior, the Buddhas were willing to help him, watch over him and accelerate his upward climb. He still had bad karma to live through, and many debts to pay, but his progress was now going to be much, much quicker and smoother than it would have been had he not received the help.

As my teacher told me, no matter how bad a person is and how evil his deeds, the Buddhas are always extremely compassionate and willing to help people who truly and honestly want to change, regardless of what they have previously done. If a Buddha doesn't help them, who will? What do you do, kick people into the gutter? Life goes on forever, and so you must always encourage those who want to transform their behavior when the wish finally arises. Don't lose that chance to get them started on the way. Of course, the fact that you help someone to change doesn't mean that their bad karma evaporates. That's impossible. It also doesn't mean we shouldn't protect society from criminals who have done wrong, and who might do it again, or that we don't wisely try to protect ourselves when trying to help others either. If you try to save a scorpion's life, still it has a poisonous tail that might sting you when you are trying to help it. Until it transforms, that is its natural behavior, so beware.

This vision involving the beetle was just a lesson for me, and doesn't mean we should not squash mosquitos who come to bite us, ants that invade our homes, hornets' nests that threaten our families, parasites that causes illness and so on either. To survive, we kill bacteria and viruses, do we not? One can take the idea of nonviolence and the sacredness of life to absurd extremes that cause you to lose sight of the essential, practical aspects of life. As with the diet, one does what they must do to survive; it is all the original nature, and all actions have the karmic consequences of cause and effect. That's all you can say, and so our activities must be guided by a balance of wisdom and compassion.

A case illustrating these points is that my teacher once purposefully crushed a spider in front of me when I was first getting started with cultivation in order to teach me this sort of lesson. Because of a certain meditative state I had achieved wherein all the chi was fantastically coursing through my body, I was sitting on some stairs looking at it with a childish "love the whole way round" naiveté of the syrupy sort you see bandied about on cartoon TV or religious specials. It was almost as if he knew what was going through my mind.

He stopped and looked at me as he was going down the stairs, and then turned his head and looked at the spider; again, he turned his head back to look at me once more, after which he promptly stomped on the spider to kill it – all the while still looking at me, as he continued walking down the stairs with a wry smile on his face. That is an example of the Zen style of teaching, which is to immediately crush any type of strange notions or errant thinking before they can gain hold, after which such mental habits become harder to break. Cultivation is very practical, pragmatic, wisdom filled and humanistic, and it is upon that humanism that you should remain centered rather than drift off into unrealistic airy, spacey notions. If you succumb to unrealistic dreamy notions, people will end up using you for their own ends which is a problem that has commonly plagued naïve Christians for centuries.

The little lesson of the reading beetle—whether it was a fictitious visionary experience my teacher or some other being had cooked up to help teach me this lesson, or not – reminds me of another story related to this issue that concerns my teacher's retreat in seclusion on Mount Omei once again.

One day, a very distinguished looking old gentleman with white hair and beard climbed up the mountain to reach the monastery, and asked to be allowed to talk to my teacher through his door. Like many others, he had heard that an enlightened sage was living on the mountain, and had come to discuss his private issue.

It turned out that the old man had been an officer in the army and confessed that he not only killed countless people but had raped several women. Now that he was old he was both extremely sorry for what he had done and rightfully fearful of the karmic retribution that was coming, for he knew that it would be terrible. He had come to ask my teacher for his advice on what he should do.

"It's a good thing you've come to me," said my teacher. "These monks might not have enough wisdom to know what to say to you, or know how to help guide you to make amends. Before we get started, I want you to go to the temple's tower and stay there in seclusion until you read the *Diamond Sutra* one thousand times. Then we can start to talk."

The old man thanked him and ascended into the tower where he was to live until the completion of this task. Reading the *Diamond Sutra* not only brings merit, but also helps you understand the whole path of spiritual cultivation and relaxes your hold on the imaginary independent ego-self you think you are while pointing out your real self-nature. As you read it, it often leads to some stage of empty mind realization. Therefore I make a practice of reading different translations of it every now and then because I always learn something new from each translation, and reach a new realization when so doing. That makes reading sutras a type of meditation practice, too. It doesn't matter what religion it comes from if such literature is available that will help you make progress and awaken, and so I commonly read the literature from countless traditions. If such helpful literature is available, cast aside your prejudices and make it part of your own personal tradition because enlightenment is all you should seek, not doctrinal adherence.

In the case of reading the *Diamond Sutra*, it helps you realize the emptiness of the ego, or non-existence of the small self we take to be the "I" within us. As stated, understanding its non-existence as a collection of false thoughts is called an emptiness realization. The higher your stage of emptiness cultivation or realization, the easier it becomes for you to transform your karma and your ongoing behavior because you are no longer fixated on habitual ways of doing things which might be errant. This freedom from habit allows room fro your wisdom to guide your behavior rather than habitual reactions. You cannot necessarily get rid of great evil karma just by cultivating a pure mind that is free of wandering thoughts, but with wisdom and emptiness you can possibly alter how it will come to you in the future.

You can certainly transform your behavior, and thereby alter how you will accept it and deal with it when it finally arrives so that it becomes far more palatable.

The very next morning the man returned to my teacher's door crying, and holding a crumbling copy of the sutra in his hands. He explained that its pages had been torn to pieces during the night while he slept. He was crying bitterly, lamenting that his karma must be so bad that even the Buddhas were unwilling to help him, for look what they had done to the sutra. They had torn it up so that he could not read it and start to change his karmic retribution.

My teacher then called some of the senior monks together and asked them if there were any rats in the building that would do this. "No," said one of the senior monks, "there is only a single holy rat that lives in the building. His hair is totally white because he's so old, and in fact has been there over one hundred years. When any other rats try to come in to make the temple their home or try to eat the books, he chases them all away to protect the sutras."

My teacher immediately knew it was this rat which had destroyed the sutra because it didn't like the man, and didn't want him to be able to change his hellish karma. He immediately got angry and raised his voice, shouting out, "Where's the Protector God of this temple? What type of poor job is the Protector God doing that he let someone interfere with a man's sincere desire to change? The Buddhas always show compassion to anyone who truly and sincerely wishes to change their behavior, no matter what they've done! This Protector God isn't doing his job!"

A little later, as the monks were performing their daily prayer ceremony, they all heard a large sound like a crack of thunder, and rushed out to see what had happened on the monastery grounds. Some, who had been outside, reported that they saw what looked like a Protector God dressed in shining armor, standing in the empty sky, send forth a bolt of lightning from his palm that hit the ground somewhere. When the monks searched the temple for damage, they could find nothing at all until they went into the library. There they found that the hundred year old white rat was now dead, lying on its back.

My teacher was extremely sorry that the Protector God had misinterpreted his anger to the extent that he killed the rat. One should always try to educate and reform, rather than simply kill people to punish them. Feeling partly responsible for the death, although it was not his intention, he recited the same one thousand *Diamond Sutras* for the rat because of its demise. Perhaps it was time for the rat to go, and this was the only way it could happen, but in any case, I always remember this story because it once again emphasized the usefulness of *Diamond Sutra* recitation for the living and deceased, and the fact that the Buddhas are willing to help anyone who sincerely desires to change their behavior.

Spiritual masters always take on students of different calibers, including some who have done great evil. After all, if the wicked come to a teacher, they thereby demonstrate that they have a desire to transform themselves which should be met with encouragement. How else, other than by associating with the evil, ignorant and errant, can the enlightened help human beings? How else, other than by receiving genuine spiritual teachings and associating with those who are pure, will we ourselves personally become able to transform our minds and behavior? If we learn to watch our thoughts through mindful vipassana practice, perhaps we can prevent bad behavior and bad karma in the first place, just as Liao Fan demonstrated, and this is why I hope cessation-observation practice becomes more prevalent within society.

But how do you help beings who have become hungry ghosts, or beings suffering in realms of extremely bad karma such as the Hells? You mantra for them, offer to them, or read texts that will help them realize emptiness and thereby become able to break free of lower states. You can also warn the living not to commit terrible deeds, or try to stop them in the midst of bad tendencies and thereby save them from such a fate in the first place. Usually this is accomplished by the fact that one has good parents who teach you well, and by the fact that religious ideas of virtue, ethics and morality are embedded within the culture and impressed upon you. You must expose people to the right teachings and also teach them how to meditate so they can know their own minds, for people who watch their thoughts tend not to commit the types of evil deeds that would land them in unfortunate rebirths.

The best type of cure is in the preventive measure of teaching mindfulness meditation of watching one's mind, as I have stressed over and over again. You reduce the occurrences of a problem by preventing it, so work on disseminating the methods of prevention, and disseminate them in the culture. To empty the Hells, reduce the number of beings who head for the hells, and then those within the Hells will eventually depart over time, without being replaced, to eventually reduce its numbers.

The *Diamond Sutra* is one such book that can be read for the departed regardless of one's tradition. The *Diamond Sutra* is wisdom literature that is short, well translated, tells a story to hold the interest, reveals the nature of reality and how to cultivate, and is easy to comprehend. While sections in books such as the *Ribhu Gita* are quite suitable, if someone cannot understand the terminology within the literature then the effort is virtually useless. Most every religion which recognizes the possibility of enlightenment has such materials, as the *Ribhu Gita* demonstrates, but to help beings who have become ghosts or who are in the Hells, the recitation should be something that helps them spiritually advance by helping them immediately realize/achieve a stage of emptiness (empty mind) or which motivates them to change their ways.

When people hear the right teachings, it becomes easy to let go of thoughts and then spiritually advance. That's why we say a realization is quick or instantaneous – you hear something, realize the meaning, and then instantly let go. To my mind, mantra and sutra recitation are the best practices to help the departed. For the beings in the Hells, reciting mantras is one of the most helpful services you can possibly offer. Only a very high stage enlightened being, past what is called the eighth stage "Bodhisattva *bhumi*," understands why this helps, so I can only say that this practice has been recommended by countless enlightened individuals.

The importance of generating merit for the path of spiritual cultivation through activities like this, which are done purely for the benefit of others without any return to yourself, cannot be underestimated. In fact, the importance of generating merit for the path can be summed up in the phrase, "No merit, no enlightenment." This is why Buddhism relates that only the cultivators who choose to compassionately enter this lower world of ours to help liberate others end up realizing complete and perfect enlightenment. The cultivators who choose not to help liberate others or free them from sufferings, but just enjoy their good fortune in the Heavens, reach an inferior stage of attainment and are said to eventually fall back into the mental clingings involved with cyclical existence.

Chinese Taoism even gives us a "formula" that states you need to accumulate at least three thousand good deeds in order to have the merit to achieve enlightenment, though of course this is just a large figurative number meant to stress the importance of virtuous living and the need for compassionate action to help others. It basically means you need to do a lot of merit-making and cultivate pure behavior. You can do this by transforming your behavior from bad to good so that you are always doing good, and by working to help others with compassion. What is a "good deed"? In Taoism, saving one life counts as just one good deed.

If three thousand good deeds then sounds like a daunting task, you can appreciate why reciting sutras and mantras for beings which have just died, or who are in the lower realms, is so powerful in terms of both helping them and in terms of merit-making, because you are, in effect, saving a life. It's your chance to help save other beings with no cost and very little effort. In performing such a recitation you also tend to understand the meaning of the text a bit deeper yourself, and hence end up helping yourself, too.

People fall into the lower realms because they commit evil deeds, and they commit evil deeds because they don't watch their thoughts and police their actions and behavior in the first place. So in the end, one must help prevent people from falling into terrible fates of their own making, and also save them when they fall into unfortunate states due to error, for they are our brothers and sisters. Actually, they are our self, and in helping them we help ourselves. That's why we study the sutras now, and why we should make enlightenment teachings or meditation teachings available to others.

After enlightenment one is still presented with the task of purifying one's behavior. Before enlightenment you must strive to purify your behavior, and after enlightenment you are still working on this task as well because habit energies still arise within consciousness, and they can still lead you astray at times. If you want to help people, thus it all comes down to the task of teaching them how to meditate and how to change their behavior for all the reasons mentioned.

People never stop to think that after enlightenment, sages still have impulses to be purified and natural behavioral responses to be transformed. They think their job is done, but they forget that the flow of consciousness goes on seemingly forever. The stream of consciousness which "flows through the false self" still has unpurified energies or tendencies that continue until you work on them to transform them, and they must be purified to become totally virtuous.

The universe goes on forever, and so when living in this universe it all comes down to transforming your behavior during this eternality so that it becomes pure and virtuous through and through. By watching your behavior, you gradually eliminate the bonds and compulsions that bind you to the production of unfortunate outcomes, and by observing your mind until your conduct becomes pure, *samadhi* is naturally attained. By getting rid of incorrect notions and feelings, you are in reality governing your mind. Accumulating merit therefore means correcting personal faults as well as doing good deeds on behalf of others. It also means perfecting skillful virtuous ways so that you can help others on a vast scale, as exemplified by the Bodhisattvas mentioned in Buddhism.

It may seem strange that one of the chapters within a book on meditation is all about accumulating merit, but that's what the spiritual path is all about in the end: behavior and merit. This is what behavior should become like – virtuous through and through so that it is always generating merit for oneself and others. After your enlightenment there is still the issue of functioning, or behavior, because it will always exist and always be necessary. You are never annihilated but will always exist in some form and have need of *skillful* effort that solves problems and helps, rather than hurts others who are, in effect, also *you*. Therefore, it all comes down to cultivating wise, skillful and purified or virtuous behavior in the end.

This, then, is actually the task of self-perfection. People never stop to think that they are, in essence, only the functioning of consciousness. Since that is the case, what does selfishness or greediness actually accomplish in life? One must perfect the functioning of consciousness since it will be there forever, and how it turns into thoughts, activities and behavior therefore becomes important. Karma and the habits of consciousness are carried with you from life to life. Money and possessions are not carried forward. In fact, any merit you use up through enjoyments is merit gone forever, so people squander their chances to create a better world for others, and better future for themselves, because of a selfish lack of generosity along with errant actions and bad emotional behaviors they should be striving to purify. But who does this? Who devotes themselves to self-perfection?

Consciousness cannot hold on to anything or claim anything as its own. It can only experience itself, consciousness (which is always changing and which is a false reality itself), and that experience can be pleasant or painful. No one likes suffering, and others are essentially us – the same one consciousness. Therefore, one must learn how to help relieve others of their suffering without causing them to suffer much in the process, for sometimes suffering is unavoidable in the helping. This is why we all need to learn how to act not just with compassion, but with wisdom so that our efforts are skillfully effective and accepted. To learn how to act with a balance of compassion and wisdom is the task of self-perfection.

One strives to realize enlightenment, and then works to transform one's mind and behavior into a continual functioning of skillful helpfulness. How can you help in a world of difficulties and obstructions if you don't learn to be skillful, using insightful strategies such as roundabout means to accomplish helpful ends? The ignorant usually do not understand the necessities for skillful actions required within this world, which my teacher encapsulated by joking about the need to also be a mafia don and thief. They often believe that saint-like behavior will always produce beneficial results whereas it will often immediately get crushed or simply pushed aside to accomplish nothing at all. In many political or religious regimes, such individuals are the first to get killed. Such efforts might have a pure motivation, but their ineffectiveness means they lack skillfulness and wisdom.

How little the ignorant truly understand the world and what goes on behind the scenes of the popular news, and how little they will be able to become big Buddhas without understanding the need for skillful, adaptive actions that need to change shape and form according to the circumstances. In any case, you must learn to compassionately think of others when it comes to your behavior, and should strive to make the world a much better place rather than simply consume and collect more experiences that you will quickly forget next week, and which you cannot take with you. When your heart warms because you do a good deed, that is due to the opening of chi channels within you. What other activities do you know can help you cultivate your chi and mind in that way?

In essence, all living beings are you, but few people reach a high enough stage to realize this or take this teaching seriously. They put most of their focus on their relationships or jobs and on putting money in their pockets. Therefore, their lives are all about themselves and their personal experiences and consumption. They revolve through endless indulgences seeking to fulfill their urges for new experiences, but the truth is, to succeed in meditation, you have to abandon the idea of the self we call the ego – which results in true charity, humility and selflessness – and you thereby start accumulating merit.

If you truly wish to succeed in spiritual pursuits, not only must you practice meditation and study the spiritual path, but you must also work to become more virtuous in your deeds and behavior. You want to cultivate so that your behavior becomes virtuous with each thought and action. You must definitely work at accumulating merit by accomplishing small and great deeds for others and stopping evil things when they arise or preventing them from arising in the first place. But those are just some examples as to how to accumulate merit. The highest merit is to cultivate a pure mind that is virtuous through and through. This is both the result of meditation practice and the path of meditation practice itself.

10

CONCLUSION

This has been just a short book, in the sense that tons more could be written, to help you get initially started with meditation practice and to answer some of the most common questions that usually arise. I am constantly disappointed with the quality of the information you find on meditation since it usually does not touch any of these important topics at all. Teachers simply tell you to sit cross-legged, close your eyes and meditate. That is not enough guidance, for as you can see, meditation practice involves a variety of deep issues.

Every single topic we have discussed has more detailed explanations available in books such as *Tao and Longevity*, *The Little Book of Hercules*, *How to Measure and Deepen Your Spiritual* Realization (also known as "*Measuring Meditation*"), *Twenty-Five Doors to Meditation*, and *Internal Martial Arts Nei-gong.* They were all written to emphasize different aspects of the spiritual quest and discuss deep issues rarely discussed in the fields of religion, spirituality, philosophy, psychology, sociology, ontology, soteriology, morality, science and more. We had to avoid the deeper issues in a beginner's text like this, so please look to these other publications if you want to delve further.

I don't like to plug my own books, but most of the information you have just read is simply not found elsewhere or is extremely difficult to find, which is why I took the time to write this and these other books in the first place. Frankly, due to the lack of correct information and the prevalence of wrong views, people usually have strange or deficient ideas as to what personal cultivation really entails, and waste years of their life pursuing the wrong things and adopting all sorts of wrong habits. People all over the world are continually making mistakes regarding their religious and spiritual practices. They waste incredible sums of money, time and effort on false trails and outside paths that look for spiritual answers outside their own mind. You absolutely must cultivate your mind in order to reach the highest levels of self-improvement, personal cultivation, and religious or spiritual practice. Without a doubt, this requires meditation practice. Actually, you can summarize much of cultivation in two little formulas:

Meditation (Method) + Health (Gong-fu) + Morality (Virtue and Good Works) = Cultivation.

Cultivation Practice + Consistent Effort + Patience = Result.

This small book therefore contains everything you need to know to get started at meditation practice, and I've simplified many important issues so that you could become familiar with their introduction. You could say this book was written to help answer four questions: 1) "What would I like to have known, and what would I have liked to have been stressed to me, if I was just getting started at meditation practice all over again? 2) What would I have liked to have known about how and why meditation works so I could have saved lots of time and effort in accelerating my own progress? 3) What questions are people always asking about these topics that need to be answered, and what assumptions are they usually making that are wrong? 4) What is the highest achievement one can attain through meditation in terms of awakening, and how does that work?"

Here's a short list of points to summarily address those very issues. I leave you with these conclusions:

1. **You should take up mantra practice even if you don't know how or why it works.** You should mantra as much as possible using whatever spare time you have because this is the easiest practice available to you and makes use of wasted time. Mantra moves the results of meditation practice closer to you. However, pick your mantra wisely and use one that countless others have also used to succeed rather than some strange mantra few have ever used. It is incredible the number of people who pick some exotic mantra that hardly anyone has ever heard of as compared to mantras that countless others

have used for attaining success. *Remember that most masters who succeeded at spiritual cultivation said they did millions of mantra recitations.* This shows they were committed to a final result, were always practicing and also that mantra recitation works. It costs nothing to recite a mantra and it can be done at any time without anyone knowing you are even doing your practice, so make use of your unproductive time in life and make mantra recitation a new daily habit. As your mantra practice grows, so will your meditation progress.

2. **You need to begin to develop the lifelong practice of always watching your thoughts and behavior, and thereby "knowing your mind" so that you can cut off errant thoughts and actions at the very moment that you first notice them going astray.** This is a life skill well worth learning, for in preventing large errors by immediately cutting them off, you will be able to bring peace into your life rather than create giant circumstances that lead to pain, suffering and disturbance. Most people never notice what they are really thinking and doing but instead get carried away by their thoughts and emotions, and in becoming entangled with them they lose perspective and make giant mistakes in their life that they always live to regret … if they are honest enough to admit them. The capability of knowing your thoughts—with a type of third person clear awareness—comes from meditation practice. Learning this skill will bear fruit in many ways for yourself and others. If everyone learned how to witness the contents of their minds, rather than just impulsively act on every thought that came up, there would be less crime and other large problems in the world due to more people immediately correcting themselves when they noticed errant behaviors. *The ability to always introspect and police our mind, through mindfulness practice, is something everyone should learn and is also something we should teach our children.* It is the basis of creating a better life for ourselves, creating a better society, and even for changing our fortunes. Changing your life comes down to changing your thoughts and behavior, and meditation is the technology that allows you to do this. People think that going

to the Church, temple, synagogue or mosque to attend religious ceremonies is spiritual practice but this is the *real* spiritual practice that brings results in behavioral change and mental purity. I have a dream that in the far future people can greet each other with the words, "How is your cultivation going?" or "I hope your cultivation is going well," and can say upon departing, "I hope your cultivation goes well." I don't care about your religion, *I just care that you are cultivating because that's what matters.* Cultivation means a pursuit to realize your true nature, and also entails your daily work on the task of self-perfection – changing your habits and behavior so they become more virtuous – which requires mindfulness. Life goes on forever, so we are all tasked with the challenge of purifying or perfecting our accumulated behavioral tendencies, which includes all our bad habits. What better greeting, or farewell, could there then be?

3. **You need to learn sitting meditation, the practice of quietly watching your mind as you sit in a cross-legged lotus posture, so that you can stop holding on to your thoughts and your busy mind can settle.** The problem is that no one knows how to let go of their mind; everyone keeps holding onto thoughts and people often play the same mental scenarios over and over again within their minds. Most people don't even know they are holding on to their mental states in the first place because the habit of mental clinging is so ingrained that it has become nearly invisible, and so they are always following and getting lost in streams of consciousness. Therefore they are in a rut of continuously repeating the same patterns of mental clinging even during their meditation practice sessions. This is why people feel that they never seem to make any progress in purifying their mind and finding internal peace. I've seen people meditate for years who continually cling to thought streams and have fallen into a rut of also clinging to mental states, but who think they are meditating correctly with freshness. Therefore, *you must always try to shake things up to break your habit of attaching to consciousness.* You must shake things up to prevent from falling into a rut of

mental clinging. One such way is to try to analyze your mind using the five skandhas or Abhidharma methods of Buddhism (especially within the school of Yogacara) so that you can identify specific contents of consciousness, and try to let go of clinging to their functioning. I particularly recommend this form of wisdom, insight or inquiry analysis, which is analyzing this thing of ours called consciousness during meditation practice. *With wisdom inquiry analysis you actually start directly examining consciousness-stuff itself rather than continue focusing on thoughts and objects, which are the appearances that arise within consciousness.* During meditation, you should sit there and examine your mind and ask yourself about it. You can try the meditation methods of Zen and Vedanta, such as trying to answer "Who am I?" when directly looking at your consciousness. **Inquiry analysis is the quickest way to detach from the mind stream and penetrate through to the root nature of the mind.** You can look at the appearances within consciousness, but you actually want to look at the stuff of consciousness itself which becomes appearances, and analyze *that.* To stay fresh and try to cultivate a more empty mind, you can also try a new meditation each week from the *Vijnana Bhairava* to help shake up your tendency to hold on to mental events, for these exercises are all aimed at helping you attain some experience of emptiness from some different angle. Whatever you do, keep it new and keep it fresh by continually trying new ways to always let go of clinging to the realm of consciousness, and try to read spiritual texts that might teach you where you are clinging. That will help prevent you from getting into a rut, and as soon as you start cultivating real states of emptiness your chi will start to change and you'll feel the movements instantly.

4. **Understand that when you finally start letting go of the flow of consciousness, your yang chi will arise and it will produce various phenomena in your physical body**. This is just a natural reaction that will happen when you let go of thoughts and your true chi circulation can start to reassert itself. That yang chi will start to open up your chi channels and

chakras, and various phenomena will resultantly occur. Those responses are all natural phenomena that arise due to the increasing flow of your chi, so there is nothing to worry about because you are simply resting your mind, and *as your mind rests, the body will, in turn, start going through a process of detoxification and healing that produces these phenomena. It is supposed to happen that way. The energies you feel due to meditation are just a natural process of physical cleansing and detoxification at the level of subtle energy which eventually produces external physical results*, and it is just that the initial consequences of these responses can be startling due to their novelty. If you aren't getting any such experiences then it's because you're still not sufficiently letting go, or not working long enough and hard enough at your meditation practices; a lack of results is not because those results are fictional. *The habit of holding onto your thoughts is so strong that the majority of people don't even recognize how they are clinging to the flow of consciousness and impeding its natural purification*, hence they rarely feel anything due to meditation because they are always still clinging to consciousness. You must always be working on new ways of mentally letting go of clinging to thoughts, desires and sensations, and especially try to learn to let go of your body. You must learn how to stop identifying with your body's energies which you are always feeling each and every moment, and which you thus tend to mistakenly take as part of your true self. Your body consciousness is always busying the mind with a tremendous amount of input, so it's almost impossible for people to realize that the body is not their true self unless they engage in meditation and learn how to detach from thoughts and the sensations of the body. Then they can start realizing the principles of spiritual cultivation from direct personal experience. The sensations you always feel are just the energies of the body, but from wrong habits you've learned to take them as part of your ideas of self. You have to break this wrong habit of identification.

5. Another related mistake from meditation practice is that people tend to try to suppress the energies of physical transformation that start arising because they want quiet in

both their body and mind. When the energies of the body start arising, those energies disturb people who then mistakenly try to stamp them out through suppression. People don't know how to ignore the distractions they cause, which is affecting what Buddhism calls the "body consciousness" of physical feelings and sensations, and thus they try to suppress them rather than let them arise in full and finish their task of internal cleansing of the chi channels. If you try to suppress the movements of the chi energies within your body by shifting consciousness in any way, you will inhibit your meditation progress. **You need to just detach from the energies that arise, and if that letting go causes even more energies to arise that create even greater disturbance, just let it happen. They will in time die down and clear.** Let a thousand flowers bloom without restraint—that's correct practice! After your chi channels finally clear out because you did not inhibit those transformative chi energies, those disturbances will all calm down and you will begin to experience a mental state of emptiness and clarity (your mind will become quiet and clear), but if you keep suppressing the energetic transformations, thinking this is correct because you are therefore more empty, you will delay your meditation progress for years. Let it all arise, and pay it no mind because mind and body both are not you, so just let them go to do whatever they please.

6. **Practice anapana**. Either practice anapana by itself, or at the very end of some other form of meditation practice session you should practice ten to fifteen minutes or so of anapana. If you practice the white skeleton visualization, end the practice session with anapana. If you are prone to strong sexual desires, focus on anapana practice rather than visualizations. If you have a tendency to overthinking or playing with thoughts, practice following your breath—anapana. If sexual desire is not a problem then you should still learn anapana, and should try to practice anapana and the white skeleton visualization together. Imagine the presence of the white bones within your body, and then notice the internal energy sensations of the

body without clinging to your physical nature. You can switch back and forth between the two – light then energy, energy then light, bones without flesh, internal space without bones. This dual practice will help open up all the channels in the body (or in a specific region) as long as you do not push or cling to the body, the energy, or its sensations. Remember that if you put your attention where you feel no energy, your chi will run there and try to open up the channels in that region. Maintain effortless awareness (concentration or fixated focus on an area without pressure or pushing) on some region of your body and the channels will eventually open in that region. Anapana is how adepts improve the chi flow within their body after all the major meridians have been opened and they are presented with the task of transforming their entire body even more, including places where the tiniest channels have not yet opened completely. Anapana practice accomplishes this because you are focused on the body as an entire independent sack or container of chi, and maintain detachment from it because of the focus on the entire body's form and breathing. When you are an advanced practitioner and have already opened up all your major meridians, practicing anapana in various yoga positions might also help your practice. **You might also start practicing the horse stance of marital arts which, like the famous cross-legged lotus posture of meditation, helps you open up the chi channels in the legs**, which are very difficult to open, and can help prepare you for anapana or other meditative progress. You want to eventually feel the entire body as one containerized wholeness (until you can forget it completely) while remaining detached from the body and *not viewing it as yourself in any way*. After all your channels have opened, which represents a state of physical perfection, thoughts will drop out (such as the view of being your body) to such an extent that the underlying empty clear awareness (our original nature that is emptiness with awareness) that always exists, but which has been intercepted through the vehicle of the body and mind just as a filter intercepts light to change its color, can be realized. You are this pure awareness (pure self-existing consciousness that has always been so) which merely witnesses whatever is going on as presented to you by the body or thoughts of consciousness, and what "goes on" are the manifestations, doings, forms, appearances or phenomena of consciousness. Why do you just sit and watch the breath? For no reason other than to just sit and watch. Get rid of any expectations. You sit just to sit. Don't hold to any expectations when you do anapana practice because if you are waiting for something to happen, or something in particular, you are always holding on to subtle thoughts that interfere with the process. Therefore, just sit to watch the breathing for no reason at all other than to sit and watch. As stated, just practice sitting and watching the breathing and knowing the movements of your internal chi. This is a principle you should apply when sitting to watch your thoughts with vipassana, too. Just sit to watch without holding any expectations whatsoever. **This is the easiest and fastest way to cultivate the high stages of *samadhi* or *dhyana*.**

7. **Try to learn a visualization technique so that you train yourself to master concentrate and become able to hold a steady mind**. The younger you are when you first try to learn how to visualize an image with stability, the better. Visualization is a mental skill that can be learnt and then used for achieving exceptional life accomplishments. In terms of spiritual practices, don't fall into the trap of thinking that the complicated tantric visualizations and empowerments from India and Tibet are the secret, most profound and most efficient methods ever invented that will bring you high stage meditation progress. The simple white skeleton visualization method is enough along these lines, although these other methods are always available. But don't think that the skeleton visualization practice is in any way deficient as compared to other tantric visualization techniques that involve chakras and channels. You need not prefer a method referencing internal esoteric anatomy when you want to practice meditation. In fact, everything has a reason or cause behind it, so seek the simple, logical explanations of events rather than fall for

anything mystical or superstitious when it comes to meditation methods. *The simplest practices, performed over and over again, also typically produce the best results of mental calming*, which in turn produces physical body transformations of the chi and channels. Few like to hear the sagely advice to learn the basics well, but that's what meditation practice comes down to. With the skeleton visualization, your practice first involves something to focus on – your internal white skeleton. Then after you reach mental stability, practice involves nothing to focus on – you let go to experience emptiness. Your body will accordingly fill with chi, your channels will open and you will become able to forget the view of the body because of skeleton visualization practice. You cultivate a mental image and by focusing on that image alone, while ignoring the body, you become able to detach from the body and then, in later releasing the image, detach from the mind as well to experience an empty mental scenario. If your practice proceeds far enough in realizing some stage of emptiness, the next stage of progress involves having no self involved during the functioning of mental witnessing (awareness). The many conceptions and ideas bundled up together that produce the sense of a self just naturally die away in time to become extinguished since they are just thoughts rather than anything real. There is even further progress possible past this particular attainment, but this is just a beginner's book that explains the basics of meditation practice. The important point to this meditation method is to develop a quiet mind of concentration, and to afterwards discard all mental images to try and experience a scenario of mental emptiness. This is actually a way to open up all your chi channels to make the body healthy. This is why Australian research has found that cancer patients can sometimes experience "spontaneous remission" if they truly practiced image free meditation. Because of an empty mind, free of mental clinging to thoughts and bodily chi flows, your real chi can arise, go through your channels, and accomplish physical healing.

8. **Know that sexual desires will often stir when your yang chi starts arising due to meditation practice, and recognize that this is a sign of progress; it is a natural result for everyone.** For women this is not as big an issue as for men, who usually succumb to sexual desire and end up losing their transformative energies through intercourse or masturbation. If you can avoid this and retain your energies, those energies will exist long enough within your body to start working on opening your chakras and chi channels. This is a bit uncomfortable at first because chi channels are never truly open when you first start meditating; nevertheless, the force for opening them is supplied through sexual discipline and restraint. That is why you shouldn't lose your energies too readily; if you let go of sexual urges and uncomfortable feelings rather than give in to them, they can be "transmuted" because they'll get around to opening up your chi channel obstructions. After that happens, the problem of sexual desire decreases dramatically. Men can also learn the safe methods of sexual intercourse without ejaculation to handle these energies, and thereby make progress by using sex to help open their channels, which is good for both partners. In any case, men should definitely learn how to forego masturbation regardless of what the experts claim is "normal" and "healthy." Experts simply poll people to find out that many engage in masturbation and feel better afterwards – duh! For this topic, you must listen to thousands of years of Indian and Asian medical tradition based on careful observation, as well as the consistent words from the masters of all of the great world traditions: **preserve your generative energies and you'll be able to stay healthy as well as achieve higher states of empty mind and open your chi channels more quickly**. Achieving a *kundalini* awakening is due to this. In other words, for men, you must stop carelessly losing your semen and chi. You will have fewer health problems and will live longer as a result.

9. **If at all possible, practice several different meditation methods simultaneously, but use a set of meditation**

methods that work on entirely different principles for helping you reach states of mental emptiness, or calming. The method you practice at any point in time should depend on your body and circumstances, and you should adjust your methodology or technique whenever appropriate. I favor the four basics of mantra, vipassana, the white skeleton visualization and anapana. If there is a method you absolutely hate, you might want to include that one in the mix, especially if after some wisdom consideration you can confirm that it's helping you truly change for the better. *The difficult meditation practices or ones you dislike are the very ones that often tend to help you grow the most*, and that's often why the strongest reactions often arise from meditation practices you find difficult or distasteful. Who ever said that you will make progress when exercises are easy to practice? If you want progress, what you don't like is what often challenges you, and challenges will often force you to grow. This is not an unbreakable rule, but something to think about in regards to your own practice situation.

10. **You need to develop an understanding of the nature your mind and you need to accumulate merit if you want to succeed on the cultivation path**. You should work to purify your behavior to become more virtuous, and act to do good deeds that help others because this is what life is all about anyway – helping others and making various situations better. You must do things for the welfare and benefit of other people who are, in the absolute sense, also you. From a materialistic or philanthropic aspect, the ideas of Andrew Carnegie in *The Gospel of Wealth* provide some excellent notions on this. Nevertheless, accumulating merit is not limited to the single idea of just philanthropy. Furthermore, you don't have to try to help everything and everyone, but should choose your contributions *wisely* as you only have so much time, energy, expertise and money available. One of the easiest and simplest ways to accumulate merit is to perform an offering to hungry ghosts every evening, and to mantra for other people including the deceased. To generate merit there are things you should actively/energetically/vigorously do or support, things

you should avoid doing, and things you should stop doing. The central self-policing effort required for merit-making, as for the task of changing one's behavior, is centered around the mindful witnessing practice of knowing your own mind. This is why Confucian mental watching practice, which is simply the mindfulness of mental witnessing as you go about your daily activities, is so essential to our world. You should always be checking whether your thoughts are clean or not, or whether they are good or bad. You should always be watching your thoughts and behavior in order not to hurt people or bring them harm. In truth, every moment you should be cultivating because every moment your mental state is here, right now. At every moment you should be practicing mindfulness as the right usage of consciousness. To be able to practice all the time, the effort should require no energy or effort at all, and witnessing (awareness) is automatic so it fulfills these requirements. You must therefore learn how to remain attentive to watch, observe, or witness your mind with awareness. Meditation is often called mindfulness practice, meaning you should always be mindful of the contents of your mind and your actions. Meditation is nothing exotic or extraordinary other than the humanistic practice of every moment knowing your behavior and mind, and correcting them when errant. The result of such practice is that every moment your mind becomes clear. Of course, you also start to derive all the traditional benefits we have discussed such as mental peace, more energy, and a transformed body that becomes healthier.

11. **You should set up a daily practice schedule if you want to get better at meditation and succeed in your spiritual practice.** I don't care what the ultimate design of this schedule is, or what your targets are, but a written schedule will help you make the most progress, especially when you are the type of person whose motivation waxes and wanes. That schedule will remind you what to do, and must always be created in such a way that you must record your results. *You can even combine the schedule as a monitoring system with some type of goal*

> *setting method for the following day.* At the end of each day, you can make your recording of the day's progress as a type of report to Heaven, mimicking what Liao Fan did in his attempt to change his fortune and behavior. You can find free downloads of Liao Fan's story and Benjamin Franklin's efforts at self-improvement on the internet to study these techniques. Both these men recorded their daily results. *A practice log will sometimes make all the difference between achieving great results in meditation, mediocre results, or hardly any results at all.* I particularly like the fact that you can combine a meditation schedule with a daily "to do" list and a weekly or monthly goals schedule. This is a powerful combination for life.

The earlier in life you start the practice of meditation, the better it is for the ability to accomplish quick progress because you'll have more vitality available for opening up your chi channels. Older people who get started usually have to spend some initial time just renewing their lost vitality, which returns after they practice celibacy along with meditation practice for a while. My advice is to just get started and make meditation a daily activity, like brushing your teeth, even if it's only for fifteen minutes a day. In time, the results of practice will accumulate, almost imperceptibly like compound interest, until those positive effects start growing exponentially. Because meditation tends to transform your chi channels and consciousness, progress in meditation is one of the few things you can take with you from life to life.

No one said that you could attain big results from meditation immediately, so you should not be impatient with your practice results. After all, who learns how to play tennis, the violin, or even surf in a single day? It's impossible! No one can do so because it takes time to develop any skill, and so it similarly takes time to start reaping the benefits of meditation practice. Nevertheless, meditation is one of the premier skills to learn in life for all the benefits it provides. But to achieve those benefits you have to practice, and practice doesn't mean anything unusual. It just means applying yourself over and over again to the basics of sitting down, crossing your legs, forgetting your body, and resting your mind. You practice the basics over and over again, and the results appear in time.

If we realize that we should be using this rare human life to reach the difficult target of enlightenment, then we should also absolutely say that meditation is the premier skill to master while we are alive rather than just "one of" the things we need to learn among hundreds we want to be doing. In addition to studying the nature of our mind, and really looking at it, meditation prepares us to be able to realize our original source nature. This small book can help you learn this one critical skill for life. It's not Buddhist, Taoist, Confucian, Christian, Hindu, Shintoist, Muslim, Jewish, Jain, Sikh, Zoroastrian or anything else. It just explains the basics of meditation using all sorts of helpful teachings pulled from many different schools, including modern science, to make things clear such as the phenomena which will usually arise from your practice.

There is no theology to this. There is no belief, ritual, ceremony, politics, sociology or any artificial construction to it. It is all a matter of cause and effect. You meditate, the mind quiets, and with insight probing you can eventually penetrate through the quiet structure of consciousness to the root source of the mind and being. With an insight you will finally understand after your mind clears enough to have the recognition. That recognition is built upon a base of wisdom and physical/mental gong-fu, and so meditation and study are the two preparations for attainment.

People continually talk about the brotherhood of world religions, but world religions will always disagree with one another. They will always remain separated by dogmas because this is how they differentiate themselves, so you will never win any arguments along those lines. However, the aspect by which to find commonality among religions includes the shared meditational methods of spiritual practice and the common stages of practice people thereby reach. Those world leaders who wish to promote world unity should take up the mantle and stress this harmonious channel of commonality. The approach destined for failure is the one that has always been tried, which is to try to bring about an appreciation of different dogmas. No matter how much groups with different beliefs talk to one another, each group will still think of themselves and their beliefs as supreme because they have been brought up to think that way, and would not remain in that group if they thought otherwise. This is why I hope that the greeting or farewell of the future might be along the lines of, "I hope your cultivation goes well." This is what personally matters, for the actual experiential results of personal practice subsequently prove or disprove all other dogmatic claims and beliefs. These results are non-denominational. Personal meditation or cultivation practice is a path that leads to a transcendent mode of being, without suffering, in harmony with the universe, and capable of accomplishing vast goodness.

There is an activity called "benchmarking" where you pull the best practices from a variety of different sources and assemble them all together into one single system to optimally accomplish a task. In this book I have applied benchmarking to pull the best explanations from a variety of meditation traditions to discuss various matters, which explains why Eastern teachings might seem to be overly represented. Yet this is not a book of Eastern teachings, but a humanistic and scientific book on what needs to be done to accomplish the quieting of the mind, and the laying of a strong foundation for deeper searching if you so desire. A true product of world citizenship, it pulls knowledge from all sources, without prejudice, if they can be helpful in explaining to you how to find peace, health, energy, clarity and spiritual gains for your life. There are a lot of teachings from the East simply because when it comes to meditation practice and its results, that's where most of them are to be found.

If you ever wanted to give a small book to friends to help them learn how to meditate, *that* book was my objective when I assembled all these teachings in one place. This book contains the basics they need to know to get started at mastering deep meditation as well as other crucial information that is not available elsewhere. I know hundreds of meditation techniques, but I have reduced so many different methods to just four major meditation techniques that you can consistently practice to get whatever results you want.

I can look back and truthfully say that if I had this collection of condensed information available when I started meditating years ago, it would have shaved years off my efforts to get profound results from my meditation practice. I didn't know what I was doing during my practice, what was supposed to happen, or what was the ultimate target or result I was seeking. This information would have helped me to know what it was all about, what to expect, and how to meditate correctly and efficiently to get the highest results possible in the shortest time possible. Naturally, I have sometimes introduced but left out detailed discussions of more complicated topics beyond a beginner's text so that it is simple to get started. The major focus has been to teach the basics of meditation practice, how to improve that practice, and the various outcomes likely to occur at the initial stages of that pursuit. In just four weeks, with devoted practice of about thirty to forty-five minutes per day, you can surely start getting into the swing of things and start obtaining the benefits of meditation practice. I hope you start to lay that foundation, and start to receive all the benefits meditation can offer.

People who cultivate meditation should avoid using the name of religion in their practice, which limits them, and then they will be truly free to achieve and prove something substantial in their efforts. Personal cultivation, achieved through the practice of meditation, is a kind of science – **the science of human beings** – that has nothing to do with the outer uniform of religion which often does not match with the realities of science and the needs of the world. You sit down, cross your legs, and arrange your body so that it's in a comfortable position, and then start watching your mind while foregoing an attachment to the doings of consciousness. You just practice being an observer, because an observer is what you truly already are. That's it – it takes all of just two minutes to learn any of the techniques discussed, but the results can be so profound if you truly, truly practice. What do you want? Health results, mental results, spiritual results? They are all achievable if you just practice.

Hence, you now have two levels of practice in front of you. At the first level of practice, if you just pursue the path of meditation for no other reason than to calm your mind, you have all the teachings necessary to learn how to abolish high degrees of stress, truly learn relaxation, and improve your health in the process. These are all accomplished through the simple process of mental calming, and the resulting harmonious flow of chi it produces. As your chi channels open, your health will definitely improve, internal latent illnesses will go away (as chi channels to those diseased regions open), and you will even increase your longevity. Meditation is simply resting the mind, so learning to let go of thoughts is like going on a vacation that can refresh you, rejuvenate you and empower you with new health, life, energy and vigor.

The second level of practice extends to those who use this basis to go further. If you meditate with a great degree of commitment, you can eventually start to open up all the chi channels of the body to such an extent that you forget the view of the body. At the highest achievement along these lines, the body almost seems non-existent because of the perfection of chi flows and channel openings. When your internal chi channels all fully open, this, rather than the sculpted results of bodybuilding or the expertise of skillful athletics, is the real perfection of the physical body. This is what people seeking health, longevity or physical perfection should go after. This achievement allows you to extinguish the view of the body being the self. Later, due to further meditation progress, the view of an existent self eventually dissolves, too, because that view is just a bunch of thoughts that simply purify, meaning they drop out because they were false to begin with. If those thoughts were true and/or necessary they could not go away, so there is nothing to worry about with their departure since nothing changes with their absence except that ignorance is abolished.

You simply let go of mental holding, and ignorance will disappear all on its own. What you discover is a vast, endless awareness without substance that is everything and all, and actually is the "you" shining through this one vehicle of your human body. It is all other sentient being bodies and matter as well. Everything is It. Your real nature is not an experience that happens to you, but rather, you discover that the "you-experience" of the "I" you take yourself to be is just one of all the universal experiences happening within *This One*. Everything is It. You are It. You discover that It is you, you are It, and it has always been this way; there is no true personal self – those are just thoughts. The existence of personal consciousness has simply let you finally know what consciousness is and that you are what stands behind consciousness able to know anything. That knowledge of what you truly, actually are always remained absent when there was no vehicle for consciousness to arise within it and know itself. As an infinity without a limited body, purest consciousness cannot know itself because it has no vehicle by which it can know anything since it is stationary and pure. Consciousness needs a limited vehicle or body so that it can awaken to understand its nature, including the fact that it is infinite. With personalized consciousness you always imagined yourself to be a false self rather than the workings, expression, functioning or existence of the True Self that you actually are. We are all *That, It*, the original nature, the absolute nature, the One-Without-A-Second. It is not that you have consciousness, but rather that consciousness has all these various forms that mistakenly take themselves as independent selves until these smaller consciousness aggregates awaken to the fact they are all that one underlying pure consciousness, and that consciousness is itself a functioning of the one absolute nature. That's what you are.

This realization, or enlightenment, is not an awakening that happens immediately. It is hard to get to this stage of realization which finally frees you from the manifested realm of all consciousness. People spend their whole lives practicing to realize their identity as the Source. It requires deep and consistent meditation practice to let go of ignorance so that it dissolves away, and one naturally experiences a sequence of spiritual progress until they can directly experience their true nature without the intercession of the assumed ego self or personality, which are like ripples in consciousness instead of its pure nature.

After the view of being the body and self die out, the view of phenomena as being "self-so externally real" also vanishes, and one can realize a real union of self and phenomena. You don't feel separate from anything, and can have the perception of anything you want as if from within it, as being it. Hence, you realize you are All. There is an intimacy with all things. We don't say "you *become* All" because you always were everything from the start, and always will be because you are the underlying awareness of the universe, cosmos or "Triple Realm (a term from Buddhism)." You are the mind of the universe that thinks itself an assumed self. One can, through meditation, eventually realize they are actually the immaculate true body of reality, behind all matter and life of which all matter, life and the cosmos are as if a tiny speck within its limitlessness. This is your true self, and the universe of continual transformations is its manifestation.

This idea of being an ego, "I" or small self in the human world – the existence of self-awareness—has arisen because this pure fundamental awareness has intercepted the vehicle of a body through which was produced the personal consciousness and the idea of self-awareness. From beginningless time, this view has contaminated, obscured, or prevented a realization of the Source, your True Self. Those wrong views, and the incorrect usages of the mind in attaching to consciousness that keep the errant views alive, are progressively extinguished on the road of meditation practice.

This higher road of realization, achieved through the practice of wisdom analysis and meditation, is the road to spiritual enlightenment and is available to all who choose it. If you try to achieve this highest of universal targets you always get the lower achievements of health, longevity, mental clarity, energy, etc., as a natural by-product or bonus. If you only target the lower achievements and stop there, however, you will never rise to this ultimate attainment. It therefore makes sense to target the highest attainment, for even if you fail to achieve it, you will tend to progress further in obtaining everything else you might seek.

You are the one original fundamental awareness functioning, and discovering this fact in a direct experiential fashion brings spiritual liberation, freedom from suffering, and the ability to end suffering for others because of the capabilities which awakening brings. The fundamental body of awareness, empty of content, is always shining and becomes intercepted through the filter of the physical body to become the manifested "you" or person. Those ideas of being an "I" held by this aggregate of consciousness are false, but they arise nonetheless. That sense of internal "I" we all have, experiencing things as a witness, is actually our original self-nature awareness itself being reflected in the I-sense as a sort of echo, shadow or shining. Self-awareness is the reflection of that original fundamental awareness when a living body vehicle arises that supports consciousness. The apparatus of a body vehicle comes upon our original essence, which shines through it as consciousness, but you are not this apparatus, nor the consciousness either. You are the transcendent one, the original nature itself.

For the culture of human beings, which is a level of sentient beings within the cosmos created due to beginningless karma, that infinite awareness has become obscured by mental attachments to a body and by a self-identification with the stream of consciousness that arises when there is a body. This internal sense of being an "I" works, just as it functions during dreams, and is operational for the world of consciousness perceived by it, so you take it to be real and your true self. But it is not real, and it is not your true self. It is just a bunch of false thoughts you developed within your consciousness aggregate and started to hold onto because of the habit of clinging. It is an afflicted, polluted or obscured view. As to the cleaner or higher view of beings in the Heavens, one has to be reborn there to know their particular mental states and barriers to self-realization. Every level of beings in the cosmos have their own barriers to Self-awakening.

We are therefore not what we take ourselves to be. We have imagined independent selves and "a world out there" because of mental obscurations and the wrong use of our minds. Everything is appearing within one whole undivided realm of consciousness that, because of clinging, we cannot experience in full glory. The consciousness of all beings together is one single realm called consciousness, and supporting that consciousness is an illuminating empty awareness (totally pure consciousness) powering all that which is, in itself, empty of essence or substance because it transcends the phenomenal. The source of phenomena is not within phenomena.

When you cultivate meditation you can start abandoning all the incorrect mental habits that you have inherited in your thought stream from countless past lives and this present life's environmental influences, which is why meditation is the best practice for finding your true self and altering your behavior for the better. Through study and cultivation you can reach the stage where you realize that the body is not you, and you can realize that the mind you have is not you either. They are all just creations known by the internal witness which is your true self, that fundamental nature.

The I-presence we all sense inside us is a bundle of thoughts, and thus it is part of this entire set of constructions of consciousness manifesting within pure consciousness. The sense of being this individual independent self in a body is due to a set of thoughts rather than being something that is really so. When that opaqueness of obscuring thoughts (that assume this independent self/soul) vanishes, you can finally realize that the *real you* is the ever functioning underlying pure consciousness, and that pure consciousness or absolutely pure awareness is actually everything because *all of constructed consciousness* appears within it. You become that, but not in the sense of becoming something new or different since you are already *That.* You simply awaken to realize without any possibility of error that this is what you are, and you realize this after ignorance drops away. The ideas of being a small self dissolve away, but an identity as the real self remains. That identity encompasses all of creation rather than that you are specifically a this or that.

This is not an intellectual realization. You can fully let go of the thoughts that have divided you from this realization, and when they depart, what is real remains. So you are not making up anything to experience this sort of realization – you are simply letting go, and then errors and ignorance depart on their own. You are already the absolute original nature in being, and are only and ever that, so nothing in terms of a true becoming ever really happens.

What happens is that consciousness is ever turning and transforming, but the purest base consciousness never itself changes but always remains pure, stationary, unmoving, unstained. You can eventually discover and realize that base nature of yourself—which can reflect all phenomena in the cosmos including all past and future--by letting go of false thoughts, and in that unity attained by abandoning useless pollution you will find peace, bliss and freedom from suffering. That purity, peace, and infinity is what you are.

Since nothing ever really happens from the level of the absolute because you only awaken to discover what you were anyway, this idea of the enlightenment journey is only a conventional way of speaking. Nothing fundamentally changes because you are only discovering what is really so and has always been true even though you never previously recognized it. It might take millions of lives to recognize this, your consciousness going through endless transformations all the while, until you hear these teachings and start to meditate so that your mind can clear enough that consciousness can awaken. Due to meditation practice, false thoughts drop out that were part of consciousness but their eventual absence is just another transformation of the false consciousness that is always turning and which, in its essence, is that underlying clear awareness of "pure consciousness." So there is only a transformation that is ever occurring in the realm of false consciousness, which is in essence always pure consciousness, and that's the pure one you must discover. The original pristine awareness is always clean, pure and bright throughout the individually imagined mind-streams of clarity and confusion within sentient beings. Nothing is ever really happening in these seemingly individual mind streams because nothing ever changes in the original nature. What changes is an apparent change of empty appearance rather than essence. All the while the substance of consciousness, even when confused, dark or unclear, is still that unchanging clear awareness nature.

Right now you don't know what you really are in a fundamental sense. You suffer because you think you are something else, and self-identify with the constructions of consciousness, or consciousness itself rather than its nature. You get entangled and enmeshed with thoughts, and thereby experience all sorts of pain and suffering. You imagine all sorts of independent selves and others that are only various forms of the same one consciousness—the clear essence of consciousness. When thoughts finally dissolve through the purifying effects of meditation, which is simply letting go of the mind so that clinging rests, all these types of ignorance will slowly dissolve and you can discover that you are *That*, and everything experienced is also that underlying fundamental face. That's what you ultimately are in essence, function, and appearance. You don't create anything in this abandonment of mental clinging, which is why this method is ontologically sound. You let go and discover the Truth that has always been.

Sages or prophets of all religions continually arise by discovering this underlying original true nature. They do not arise from any other method other than by self-realization. They thereby find peace at the end of their searching and then teach these truths out of compassion, but these priceless teachings become distorted over time and difficult to find in this particular world characterized by bad karma. Enlightenment teachings are incredibly difficult to encounter in this world of lower karma, and enlightened individuals are truly rare. People therefore end up substituting religion for the true way to find liberation and spiritual salvation, and this actually prolongs their spiritual longings when it does not lead to awakening.

By exercising their functioning abilities, which extends to all matter and all beings, the enlightened sages compassionately teach and help save other beings by liberating them from the unnecessary, self-imposed suffering that all comes about as a result of an afflicted view of consciousness. The wisdom available is common, but teachings through a body and mind are individualistic, so what each sage teaches and how they help will vary according to the time and circumstances. This is why spiritual paths always seem to differ. They are individualistic explanations of the one true Way.

That is the spiritual path of higher attainments in a nutshell. Countless details have been left out, but you can actually experientially prove the Truth of the self-nature by following the road of meditation. By their words and teachings you can know which spiritual greats have attained *This*. It is not some belief or faith you must blindly swallow, but something you can actually prove as being so when you find your true self. You only need to start practicing meditation and start reaping the results until there is the knowing, or realization, of discovering what you ultimately are.

That awakening is called liberation. You sit in meditation, your chi changes, your chakras and channels open, your mind pacifies, consciousness purifies or empties out, and when the right moment or circumstances arise you can suddenly — with insight — realize the True One, the True You. You can realize what your underlying essential nature is, and thus we call this "seeing Truth" or awakening. This is the apex of spiritual possibilities of attainment for then "you and the Father are one." Meditation is the only road that can take you to this Self-realization.

Let us forget about the grand view for a second, and return to more modest objectives. I remember that I once read a quote which said, "From the Emperor down to the common people, all must regard cultivation of their personal life as their root or foundation. There is never a case where the root is in disorder and yet the branches are in order."

I agree with this, and therefore recommend the method of *witnessing meditation,* or mindfulness of mental introspection, as a daily life practice for all people. At the highest it will lead you to understand your true nature, which is all that matters, and failing that it will still help you with mundane benefits. It will still help you with the task of improving the world and ending your own sufferings and miseries caused by wrong actions. The educational system of our schools today should not confine its role to helping us solely acquire knowledge, but should also give us the skills to inspect ourselves and change our personalities and behaviors. They, too, need to be teaching us how to meditate by watching our minds rather than simply the tools for making money. If people are not taught how to watch their minds so that they can take a stand in what is wholesome, virtuous and moral, society is doomed to decline.

Whether or not you decide to strive for the highest reaches of perfection in body and mind, you are always left with your behavior in the world which you need to cultivate to a state of virtue. To do so, the task starts with the ability to become directly aware of your own personality, thoughts, actions and behavior, and to learn how to monitor these things with mindful alertness. This is why I so often stress the stories of Liao Fan and Benjamin Franklin who showed us how to change our habits and personalities through mindfulness. This is how you change your life, fate, karma or fortune – however you wish to word it. Whether you are the Emperor or a common man, there are two goals that you must always be working on in life regardless as to whether they are fully accomplished: you must strive to achieve self-realization and purify your inherited karmic habits and behaviors. Even if you do not pledge yourself to the grand objective of spiritual enlightenment, you still need to learn the practice of meditation to learn how to change your karmic habits and personal behaviors.

You can, through meditation, learn how to know your individual thoughts, and can even learn how to cut them off to find silence and peace. Nevertheless, the flowing aspect of consciousness means they will always return. You might, for instance, say you don't hate someone anymore, so you've stopped the specific phenomenon of hate, but not the underlying flowing force. Under specific conditions, the flowing force for hating will come back, and it will rise again.

This is the case for all our faults and bad behaviors, and good ones, too. It is cultivation that attempts to purify that underlying karmic flowing force of consciousness which is extremely deep and subtle. You cannot cut off the endless flowing of the force of consciousness, but can only transform it by trying to make what arises more pure, namely, more virtuous, moral generous, patient, skillful, compassionate and wisdom oriented. It will always be there in the future, and so you must strive to start transforming it now, in the present, while you have the knowledge, teachings, presence of mind and chance to do so. You want to learn how to purify it, and replace bad responses with virtuous responses. You want to change yourself by purifying deep-rooted wrong tendencies and habit energies. You want to learn how to avoid evil, do good, and purify your mind. Stopping evil, stopping so as not to go too far, putting an end to the laziness of effort to do good, and stopping at the highest pollution-free realization of the mind's true nature itself, are all critical to this success.

This is how you can create a better future for yourself and the world. This is the only thing that does so, for the entire future is composed of the karma of human beings and originates from the doings of their deeds spawned by consciousness. The karma or course and destiny of the world evolves in line with the morality of the beings within it. Do not lose your chance, while you have these teachings in hand, to therefore raise the motivation to start purifying your thoughts and behavior. Life after life, the stream of consciousness and your karma are the things you take with you.

Meditation, which is the methodology of self-cultivation, is the only true technology that can lead to the purification of consciousness necessary for enlightenment, the creation of a better future and self-perfection. It is the only trustworthy methodology you can rely upon for self-improvement, self-perfection or self-actualization. Meditation not only transforms consciousness but the body as well whose chi and constituent elements have an impact on the workings of consciousness. Our body is the result of karmic forces, and because the body also transforms due to meditation, meditation gives us the capability to liberate ourselves from the normal karmic forces and impulses of the body.

As the body transforms during the course of meditation, it becomes less of an impediment to the goal of attaining a perfect clarity of mind. The tendencies to errant habitual reactions and chi flow induced behaviors, which form part of the personality, also lessen greatly. The view of being the body and other false notions also drop out as you properly cultivate the body and mind. So you can see, whether you are talking about a journey for health and longevity, mental clarity, personality change, self-improvement or spiritual progress (self-realization), it all comes down to meditation in the end!

There are countless meditation methods you can practice. We have gone over mantra, prayer, the white skeleton visualization, anapana, vipassana, seeing the light, sexual cultivation, wisdom contemplation, pranayama and other techniques. Many more techniques are possible. The two basic principles involved with all these meditation techniques, which you now understand, are the principles of cessation and witnessing (observation). You meditate to reach a point where thoughts stop, or cease, and then you must witness, observe or "contemplate" the mind. You learn how to stop the mind and then *stay* until enough purifying transformations of body and mind both occur for you to reach attainment. Progress in stopping and staying, or cessation and observation, and the various mental-physical purifications of this path of perfection are achieved in gradual step-by-step stages, or transformations.

By first creating a contrived, provisional mental object to connect with and focus upon, you can quiet your wandering thoughts and gradually enter into a direct experience of the nature of the mind after it quiets. You basically train yourself, through meditation practice, to eventually stop and stay in pure awareness until its penetrating power extends infinitely and can behold all of existence naturally, and without effort. If you reach a state of concentration on the mind itself then there is no self and other as long as you stay concentrated, and so you thereby gradually burn up the habit of ego-consciousness until it dies out and you find yourself united in one selfless unity of eternal illumination that transcends consciousness. Enlightenment and awakening entail the great penetration of realizing the substance of the entire spiritual and material universe.

Paramount to meditation success is that you apply yourself to a meditation technique with mindfulness. You focus all your attention on a single thing and become empty of everything else. This quiets the mind. This in time helps you discover pure consciousness. It also ends up creating conditions that transform your body so you can "empty the view of the body." How? By activating internal energy that opens up its energy channels and allows chi life-force energy to freely flow through them. That higher state of physical perfection then creates a foundational support for attaining great mental quiescence.

It is essential to tie all your attention to something to fix upon and thereby *collect all thinking and perception onto a single point* for this activity is what can then lead to mental calming and eventually the knowing of true reality. You don't hold your mind on a thought to achieve enlightenment, however, for the method of holding your mind in one-pointed concentration is simply to collect all thinking processes in order to quiet thoughts. You have to let go of all thoughts and not dwell on any mental states to achieve self-realization. The highest method of abiding is to mentally abide nowhere, and to develop a pure mind you should not dwell on anything but rest in emptiness without support, and that unsupported emptiness with awareness is the true nature of the mind. You cannot "see the Truth," you cannot see the real as long as you remain looking at the constructs of consciousness.

That's the secret—there is no secret. That's the basic technique and its explanation, and so meditation has many different forms that make use of these simple principles. You must practice and in time your meditation accomplishments will gradually grow in depth, intensity and stability. You will eventually be able to achieve undisturbed calm and clarity, free from distractions and hindrances, which is something everyone desires. All the human virtues we prize will then start to become more natural, too. As your mind purifies you are basically dissolving all the factors that make you unenlightened, which include false thoughts, incorrect views, errant perspectives, and wrong ways of thinking.

We started this book with the simple promise that it would teach you the basics of meditation and introduce you to other related topics as well, and those goals have been accomplished. You now know how to practice mantra, vipassana, visualizations, anapana and other meditations, too. You have also learned how to investigate this thing called consciousness or mind that we carry with us our entire lives, and yet we never bother to investigate what it truly is or how to master it and perfect it. We investigate what appears within consciousness, but we never investigate the very thing that consciousness is itself – "consciousness-stuff" – but you now have a way of discovering the real, pure consciousness essence behind the human being, and all other sentient beings as well. While these instructions are simple, the chance to hear them presented this way is actually quite rare.

By no means should you consider this information definitive or all-inclusive, for much more can be said and many discussions have been abridged and simplified for your benefit. There might even be errors of expression within this simplification, but I have given you the best guidance I know at this particular time. Despite this possibility of errors, you now actually have more helpful information than what was available to many spiritual greats when they first began their own devoted efforts at self-cultivation, and I hope you use this information well. You now know enough to get yourself firmly started on that journey, and I hope it will bring more health, energy, mental peace, clarity of mind, wellbeing and longevity, spiritual strength, and awakening to your life.

OTHER BOOKS OF INTEREST

If you enjoyed this work, you may find some of these other books helpful. Most are available in paperback while some are only available at the site www.MeditationExpert.com:

- *Spiritual Paths and their Meditation Techniques*, William Bodri and Nan Huai-chin (Top Shape Publishing, Nevada, 2010).

- *Twenty-Five Doors to Meditation: A Handbook for Entering Samadhi*, William Bodri and Lee Shu Mei (Red Wheel/Weiser, Maine, 1998).

- *Tao and Longevity: Mind-Body Transformation*, Nan Huai-chin and Wen-Kuang Chu (Weiser Books, Maine, 1984).

- *Working Toward Enlightenment: The Cultivation of Practice*, Nan Huai-chin (Red Wheel/Weiser, Maine, 1993).

- *To Realize Enlightenment: Practice of the Cultivation Path*, Nan Huai-chin (Weiser Books, Maine, 1994).

- *How to Measure and Deepen Your Spiritual Realization*, William Bodri and Nan Huai-chin (Top Shape Publishing, Nevada, 2002).

- *The Little Book of Hercules*, William Bodri (Top Shape Publishing, Nevada, 2011).

- *Internal Martial Arts Nei-gong*, Bill Bodri and John Newtson (Top Shape Publishing, Nevada, 2011).

- *Your Destiny is in Your Own Hands*, William Bodri (Top Shape Publishing, Nevada, 2012).

Mantra Practice pg 16

Namo saptanam samyaksambuddha Kotinum Tadyā
Om Cale Cule Cundhi Svaha pg 26,

Namo Amitofo pg. 27

Witnessing Practice pg 33 (Vipassana)

Watching your thoughts pg 40

Visualization Practice pg 69

The White Skeleton Practice pg 77

Pranayama (holding ones breath) & Anapana (pg 107)

Nine Bottled Wind Pranayama Practice pg 109

Natural Kumbhaka Respiratory Cessation pg 114

Anapana Practice (Watching Ones Breath) pg. 119

pg. 144 examples of when to use different types of meditation

Made in the USA
Lexington, KY
09 October 2012